A HISTORY OF No.6 SQUADRON ROYAL NAVAL AIR SERVICE IN WORLD WAR I

Also by Mike Westrop
A History of No.10 Squadron Royal Naval Air Service in World War I

A HISTORY OF No.6 SQUADRON ROYAL NAVAL AIR SERVICE

IN WORLD WAR I

Mike Westrop

Schiffer Military History
Atglen, PA

Acknowledgements

This book would not have been possible without the support and encouragement of my wife and children and the enthusiasm and assistance of many friends and contacts around the world. I would particularly like to mention the following who have provided help and research materials and spurred me on: Les Rogers, Frank Cheesman, Stuart Leslie, Colin Huston, Stewart Taylor, Justin Young, Rick Duiven, Greg VanWyngarden, Tony Mellor-Ellis, Norman Franks, Johan Ryheul, Errol Martin, Nick Forder, Hal Giblin, Trevor Henshaw, Frank Olynyk, Andrew and Donna Smith, Pete Wood, Ernie Jupe, Mr & Mrs William Rothera, Tony Tiarks, the many members of the forum at www.theaerodrome.com, Jan Keohane at the Fleet Air Arm Museum, The RAeC Trust, the RAF Museum, the New Zealand Air Force Museum, The New Zealand Navy Museum, The Royal Netherlands Air Force History Unit, The John Oxley Library, Corpus Christi College - Oxford, Nottingham High School, and most especially the three "M"s, Mark Miller for his superb colour artwork, Mike O'Connor for his aerodrome layouts, and Mick Davis for his scale drawings.

On the front cover

On the 29th April 1917 three Nieuports from No.6 Squadron's C Flight were jumped by twelve Albatros DIIIs of *Jasta* 26. Flight Commander EW Norton finding himself unable to escape, turned and flew through the Albatros formation. At close range Norton fired at the DIII of *Ltn* Hermann Göring, shooting away the machine's rudder controls. Norton was credited with an "out of control" claim and whilst Göring may not have crashed he was placed in serious difficulty having to put his machine down rapidly without lateral control. *Cover Artwork by Mark Miller*

On the rear cover

No.6 Squadron's longest serving officer, Colin Temple MacLaren. MacLaren was a Flight Commander with the squadron from January to August 1917 and after a period as Commanding Officer of the Walmer Defence Flight he returned to command the newly reformed No.6 Squadron in January 1918. When the squadron became No.206 Squadron RAF on the 1st April 1918, MacLaren continued to command the squadron with the rank of Major until May 1919.

Book design by Robert Biondi.

Library of Congress Catalog Number: 2006923827.

Printed in China.
ISBN: 0-7643-2425-X

We are always looking for people to write books on new and related subjects. If you have an idea for a book, please contact us at the address below.

Published by Schiffer Publishing Ltd.
4880 Lower Valley Road
Atglen, PA 19310
Phone: (610) 593-1777
FAX: (610) 593-2002
E-mail: Info@schifferbooks.com.
Visit our web site at: www.schifferbooks.com
Please write for a free catalog.
This book may be purchased from the publisher.
Please include $3.95 postage.
Try your bookstore first.

In Europe, Schiffer books are distributed by:
Bushwood Books
6 Marksbury Ave.
Kew Gardens, Surrey TW9 4JF
England
Phone: 44 (0)20 8392-8585
FAX: 44 (0)20 8392-9876
E-mail: info@bushwoodbooks.co.uk
www.bushwoodbooks.co.uk
Free postage in the UK. Europe: air mail at cost.
Try your bookstore first.

CONTENTS

INTRODUCTION

This work, the second volume in the author's series of histories of Royal Naval Air Service squadrons, deals with No.6 Squadron. Until recently, a relatively obscure squadron that briefly served on the Western Front in the scout role until disbanded in August 1917 and was then reformed as a day bomber squadron in 1918.

The Naval presence at Dunkerque during the early years of World War I has a somewhat confusing history, not made any easier to comprehend by the ambiguous Flight and Squadron naming conventions employed by the Royal Naval Air Service at different times. Fortunately, for the reader and the author, the history of No.6 Squadron Royal Naval Air Service, or "Naval 6", corresponds to the period when the RNAS adopted the more conventional squadron-naming regimen used by the Royal Flying Corps.

No.6 Squadron briefly came to prominence as a scout squadron during the spring and summer months of 1917, at a time of furious expansion for the Royal Naval Air Service. Equipped with the first production twin gun scout to see British front line service, the squadron's pilots served on the Western Front under RFC control. Due to a lack of trained pilots and slow supply of aircraft, the squadron was pulled out of the intense air fighting encountered during the battle of Arras in April 1917 and relocated to a quieter front. Encumbered by aircraft that did not perform to expectations and two Flight Commanders who were not pulling their weight, the squadron struggled to make its presence felt.

The poor performance of their twin-gun fighter, the Nieuport 17Bis, prompted a rapid re-equipping with the newly introduced Sopwith Camel in June 1917. The squadron's performance started to pick up but the heavy losses experienced by the RNAS squadrons that were on loan to the R.F.C. on the Western Front were unsustainable and the decision was taken to reduce the number of scout squadrons. Together with No.11 Squadron, No.6 Squadron was disbanded at the end of August 1917, with its aircraft and pilots being used to reinforce other squadrons.

RNAS requirements for 1918 included new day bombing squadrons flying the D.H.9, the first of these new units was No.6 Squadron, reformed at Dover on the 1st January 1918 around a small core of experienced personnel. New officers and new aircraft were formed into a cohesive unit during January and February, with operations over Belgium commencing in March. The dreadful reliability and poor performance of the Siddeley Puma engine fitted to the D.H.9 seriously affected the squadron's early effectiveness, mirroring the problems experienced by the squadron in the spring of 1917.

The squadron became No.206 Squadron on 1st April 1918 when the Royal Naval Air Service and the Royal Flying Corps were amalgamated to form the Royal Air Force. No.206 Squadron RAF was still in existence at the beginning of the 21st Century, flying the Nimrod maritime reconnaissance aircraft. Sadly, the squadron was disbanded in April 2005.

My aim in this work has been to detail the history of No.6 Squadron RNAS, starting with a discussion of why the RNAS had to expand its scout capability at the end of 1916 and working through to incorporation into the RAF on 1st April 1918. The book deals with the people, the machines, the places, the incidents and the day-to-day victories and losses.

Readers should be aware that the author takes a sceptical view of combat claims, especially where the original documentation does not support them. The more outrageous claims made at a later date by, or on behalf of, certain pilots, have been discounted. The reference to original documentation is significant, the content of this work being based upon original squadron documents, RNAS Wing documents and RFC Wing and Brigade documents, backed up by pilot's log books and letters written by the Senior RNAS Officer at Dunkerque HQ. The author does not wish to be dragged into disputes over how many victories a certain pilot did or did not score. For this reason the following notes may clarify the criteria used in the presentation of this aspect of the work.

Combat claims were generally regarded as either "decisive" or "indecisive". A decision that was initially made by the Squadron's Commanding Officer after reviewing the combat and associated reports. The ultimate decision of whether a claim was granted would not be made until the claim and all associated evidence had been considered by Wing HQ and RNAS HQ, or in the situation where a Naval squadron was working for the RFC, by Wing, Brigade and then RFC HQ. Evidence might well be obtained from sources such as balloon observers, infantry and artillery units, intelligence agencies and other flying units.

Decisive

A decisive claim generally fell into one of two camps:

> "Destroyed": where an enemy machine was seen to break up in the air, fell in flames, or was seen to crash.
>
> "Out Of Control": where an opponent's machine was considered to fall in an uncontrolled manner with little chance of recovery.

Of course, the "out of control" category was open to significant personal interpretation and abuse. It must be remembered however, that whether an opponent left the battle zone in an inverted spin and after a fright recovered at a much lower altitude or simply stalled his machine and spun away to fight another day, he ceded the battle zone to the victor. An important objective of a scout machine was to make the sky safe to enable the observation, spotting and bombing machines to go about their normal business. An "Out Of Control" achieved this objective.

Indecisive

An indecisive claim generally fell into the following categories:

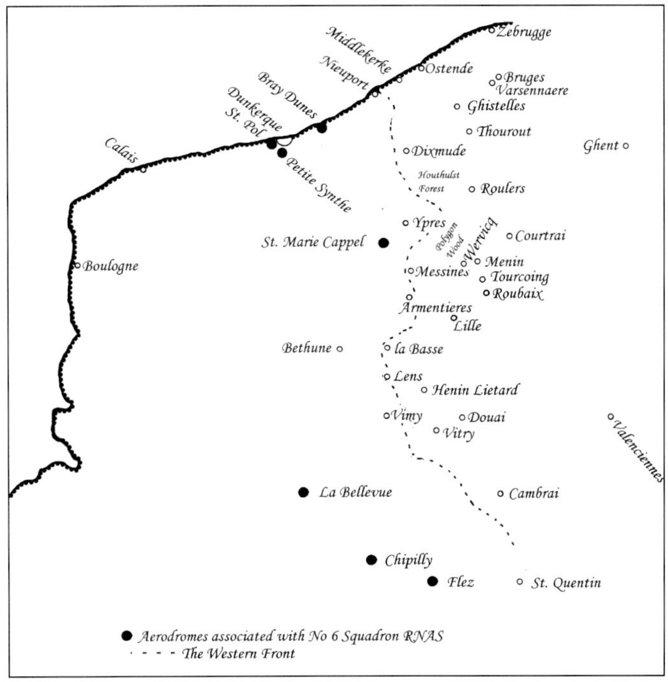

Sketch map showing the area of operation of No.6 Squadron during 1916, 1917 and 1918

> "Apparently Out of Control": where an opponent's machine was considered to fall in an uncontrolled manner with little chance of recovery but there was no evidence to support the claim.
>
> "Driven Down": Where an opponent declined combat and dived away.
>
> "Driven Down and FTL": Where an opponent declined combat, escaped and blatantly landed to wait for the opponent to go away.

When discussing victory claims, it helps to remember a few truths:

- Most encounters took place over enemy territory making verification difficult, if not impossible.
- We now know that gross over-claiming on the part of the Allies was a regular occurrence.
- When trying to match Allied claims with German losses, unless the German machine was destroyed completely, or the German pilot was unable to return to his unit, no loss was recorded in the German records.

In the heat of battle, even the most experienced pilot sometimes made mistakes in observation.

The claims presented in this book are pilots' declarations, *not* necessarily corroborated victories. The claims are all supported by primary documentation sources, squadron record books and Combat In The Air Reports (CITARS). This work does not place a strong emphasis on RNAS and RFC Communiqués which were basically morale boosting summaries produced by clerical staff and were often unreliable. It does not place any emphasis at all upon secondary published sources, many of which have fed off their predecessors.

GLOSSARY

AA Anti-Aircraft
AAP Aircraft Acceptance Park
AD Aeroplane Depot
ADD Aircraft Depot Dunkerque (situated at St. Pol)
AFC Air Force Cross
AM Air Mechanic
AP Aeroplane Park
ASD Aeroplane Supply Depot

Bde Brigade

Capt Captain
CBE Commander of the British Empire
Cdr Commander
CFS Central Flying School
COL Crashed on landing
CPO Chief Petty Officer
Cpl Corporal
CSD Central Supply Depot

DD Driven Down
DFC Distinguished Flying Cross
DFM Distinguished Flying Medal
DFW *Deutsche Flugzeug-Werke*
DSC Distinguished Service Cross
DSM Distinguished Service Medal
DSO Distinguished Service Order

EA Enemy Aircraft
Eng Lt Engineering Lieutenant

F.A.U. Friends Ambulance Unit
FCdr Flight Commander
FlgObm *Flugmaat* (Flying Mate)
FIS Flying Instructors School
FLt Flight Lieutenant
FSgt Flight Sergeant
FSL Flight Sub-Lieutenant
FTL Forced to Land
Fw *Feldwebel* (Sergeant)
FwLt *FeldwebelLeutnant* (Master Sergeant)

GHQ General Headquarters

HA Hostile Aircraft
Haupt *Hauptmann* (Captain)
HOP High Offensive Patrol
Hp Horsepower
HQ Headquarters
Hrs Hours

Jasta *Jagdstaffel* (scout unit)

KB Kite Balloon

LAM Leading Air Mechanic
LFG *Luftfahrzeug Gesellschaft*
LM Leading Mechanic
Lt Lieutenant
2Lt Second Lieutenant
Ltn *Leutnant* (2nd Lieutenant)
LVG *Luft-Verkehrs Gesellschaft*

MBE Member Of the British Empire
MC Military Cross
MFJ *Marinefeldjasta*
MM Military Medal

NAD Naval Aeroplane Depot
NADD Naval Aeroplane Depot Dunkerque
NAP Naval Aeroplane Park

OBE Order Of The British Empire
Oblt *Oberleutnant* (1st Lieutenant)
Offstlvtr *OffizierStellvertreter* (Warrant Officer)
OOC Out Of Control
OP Offensive Patrol

PFO Probationary Flying Officer
PFSL Probationary Flight Sub-Lieutenant
PO Petty officer
POW Prisoner of war
PRO Public Records Office (National Archive)

RAE Royal Aircraft Establishment
RAF Royal Air Force
RFA Royal Fleet Auxiliary
RFC Royal Flying Corps (Military Wing)
Rittm *Rittmeister* (Cavalry Captain)
RN Royal Navy
RNAS Royal Naval Air Service/Royal Naval Air Station
RNR Royal Naval Reserve
RNVR Royal Naval Volunteer Reserve
R/T Radio Telephony

SCdr Squadron Commander
SD Stores Depot
SDF Seaplane Defence Flight

TDS Training Depot Station
TPFO Temporary Probationary Flying Officer
TPFSL Temporary Probationary Flight Sub-Lieutenant
TS Training Squadron

Uffz *Unteroffizier* (Corporal)
USAS United States Air Service

Vzfm *Vizeflugmeister*
Vzfw *Vizefeldwebel* (Acting Sergeant)

WCapt Wing Captain
WCdr Wing Commander

W/T Wireless Telegraphy

CHAPTER ONE

EXPANSION OF THE RNAS AT DUNKERQUE

The history of the Royal Naval Air Service's presence at Dunkerque is beyond the scope of this book, however, in order to understand why new scout squadrons were introduced during 1916 and 1917, we need to briefly look at the policies and re-organisation of the Dover – Dunkerque command.

By the late summer of 1915, Wing Captain CL Lambe was in charge of two reconnaissance squadrons at Dover and six squadrons at Dunkerque. The Dunkerque squadrons comprised two spotting and reconnaissance squadrons, two bombing squadrons and two fighter squadrons. Lambe had ambitious plans for his command and by December 1915 had obtained Admiralty approval to form two more Wings. Each Wing was comprised of four squadrons to concentrate on offensive operations. It is important to realise that at this stage an RNAS Squadron was the equivalent of a more conventional Flight and was comprised of six aircraft.

During 1916 the Dover – Dunkerque command expanded rapidly under Lambe's direction. Its three main objectives being:

- To protect the cross-channel supply routes of the British Expeditionary Force.
- To harass enemy submarines using Belgian ports.
- To take offensive action against the channel end of the German lines.

By mid 1916, Wing Captain Lambe had established 1 Wing at Dunkerque, 4 Wing at Petite Synthe and 5 Wing at Coudekerke. The Wings were structured as shown:

1 Wing	A Squadron	No.1 Flight
		No.2 Flight
	B Squadron	No.3 Flight
		No.4 Flight
	C Squadron	No.14 Flight

Responsibilities included photoreconnaissance, artillery spotting (by day and night) and fighter patrols over front and fleet.

4 Wing	A Squadron	No. 9 Flight
		No. 10 Flight
	B Squadron	No. 11 Flight
		No. 12 Flight

Responsibilities included bombing and fighter patrols.

5 Wing	A Squadron	No.5 Flight
		No.6 Flight
	B Squadron	No.7 Flight
		No.8 Flight

Responsibilities were primarily bombing but included some fighter patrols and reconnaissance.

In June 1916, the two flights of A Squadron 1 Wing moved nearer to the front at Furnes aerodrome in Belgium, the squadron quickly becoming known as the "Detached Squadron". The Detached Squadron was equipped solely with Nieuport single seat scouts and was the first uniformly equipped squadron in the RNAS. Due to the closer proximity to the front, the Detached Squadron took on new duties of providing French reconnaissance and artillery spotters with fighter escort.

By the autumn of 1916, the RFC was experiencing difficulties on the Somme. In October, Wing Captain Lambe agreed to provide a squadron to assist the RFC. In order to achieve this, each of the Dunkerque Wings contributed a Flight of pilots and aircraft, Sopwith Pups from 1 Wing, Nieuport Scouts from 4 Wing and Sopwith 1 1/2 Strutters from 5 Wing. The newly formed "detached" squadron was activated on the 25th October 1916 and was eventually designated No.8 Squadron RNAS or more familiarly "Naval 8". This designation did not come into effect, however, until February 1917.

Also in the autumn, possibly prompted by Major-General Trenchard's request to borrow a scout squadron, Lambe embarked upon another session of "rationalisation", rearranging his existing squadrons into specialist units and re-labelling them with sequential unique numbers:

A Squadron 1 Wing	became No.1 Squadron	Scouts
B Squadron 1 Wing	became No.2 Squadron	Spotting/Reconnaissance
C Squadron 1 Wing	became No.3 Squadron	Scouts
A Squadron 5 Wing	became No.4 Squadron	Scouts
B Squadron 5 Wing	became No.5 Squadron	Bombers
A Squadron 4 Wing	became No.6 Squadron	Scouts
B Squadron 4 Wing	became No.7 Squadron	Bombers
Squadron on loan to RFC	became No.8 Squadron	Scouts

These re-designations took place from the week commencing 20th November 1916, although in most cases, no change was seen at Squadron level for a number of weeks.

By the autumn of 1916, the Germans had introduced the Albatros DI and DII twin gun scouts, precipitating a crisis for the RFC. Major-General Trenchard requested a substantial strengthening of the fighter squadrons attached to each British army. Nothing was done until December 1916, when it rapidly became obvious that any realistic action would be too late. The Detached Squadron had proved its value to the RFC and Trenchard informally approached Lambe to discuss the possibility of borrowing four more scout squadrons, he required a Triplane squadron, a Nieuport scout squadron, plus two more scout squadrons. In December. the War Office made a formal request to the Admiralty for the loan of four additional fighter squadrons to assist the RFC and material help in the form of engines and aircraft.[1] The Admiralty was not in any real position to refuse, being in the "overkill" situation of having Lambe's newly restructured squadrons attached to Dunkerque, exacerbated by the political embarrassment of having been recently "caught-out" circumventing the agreed protocols for obtaining funding for aircraft.

At the end of 1916, the RNAS Dunkerque "Order of Battle" for landplane scout/fighting squadrons was as shown below:

No.1 Squadron: Equipped with a mix of Nieuports and Sopwith Triplanes at Furnes. In the process of re-equipping with Sopwith Triplanes. Carrying out coastal protection.

No.3 Squadron: Initially equipped with Sopwith 1 1/2 Strutters, to be re-equipped with Sopwith Pups.

No.4 Squadron: Initially equipped with Sopwith 1 1/2 Strutters, to be re-equipped with Sopwith Pups.

No.6 Squadron: Equipped with a variety of Nieuport 2-seaters and scouts. To be re-equipped with Nieuport 17bis scouts.

Detached Squadron: On secondment to the RFC at Vert Galant. Equipped with Sopwith Pups. To be renamed No.8 Squadron and re-equipped with Sopwith Triplanes.

From the Naval point of view, five fighter squadrons, even when fully equipped would not be adequate to meet the commitment to the RFC and to provide coastal and fleet protection. Lambe therefore embarked upon another round of expansion in 1917:

No.9 Squadron: No.9 Squadron was formed at St. Pol on 1st February 1917. Initially equipped with Sopwith Pups and Nieuports. No.9 Squadron performed coastal defence duties until seconded to the RFC in June.

No.10 Squadron: No.10 Squadron was formed at St. Pol on 12th February 1917. Core personnel were taken from Cranwell and Eastchurch but later heavily reinforced with experienced personnel from the disbanding No.3 Wing. Initially equipped with Sopwith Triplanes. Performed coastal defence duties from Furnes until seconded to the RFC at Droglandt on 15th May 1917.

No.11 Squadron: Formed at Petite Synthe on 8th March 1917 and equipped with Nieuport scouts, Sopwith Pups and Triplanes. Evidence indicates that No.11 Squadron was intended to be a scout Squadron but due to shortage of pilots and aircraft effectively became an Operational Training Unit and Pilots Pool for the other scout Squadrons. The Squadron was eventually activated in July and called upon to provide fleet and port protection duties.

Further expansion of scout squadrons took place in June 1917 to strengthen the coastal defence and training provision:

No.12 Squadron: Formed at Hondschoot on 8th June 1917, served primarily as an Operational Training Unit and Pilots Pool, with some port defence duties.

No.13 Squadron: Formed at St. Pol on 30th June 1917 as the Seaplane Defence Flight with coastal and fleet protection duties. Became the Seaplane Defence Squadron on 23rd September 1917 and No.13 Squadron on 15th January 1918. Initially equipped with Sopwith Pups.

As stated above, a Detached Squadron had been seconded to the RFC since the end of October 1916. The squadron was withdrawn back to Dunkerque control early in February 1917 for re-equipping and reallocation of some officers and ratings to new squadrons. On the same day, No.3 Squadron came under RFC control and took responsibility for both the Detached Squadron's duties and their aircraft. Secondment of Naval scout squadrons to the RFC during 1917 took place as shown below:

Senior Officer at Dunkerque and architect of the RNAS expansion at Dunkerque, Wing Captain CL Lambe. This photograph was taken during 1918, Lambe is wearing RAF uniform and has the rank of Brigadier General. *Courtesy John Oxley Library*

No.1 Squadron: Seconded to the RFC on 15th February 1917, initially based at Chipilly. Returned to RNAS control on 2nd November 1917.

No.3 Squadron: Seconded to the RFC and took over No.8 Squadron's Sopwith Pup aircraft at Vert Galant on 3rd February 1917, returned to RNAS control on 18th June 1917.

No.6 Squadron: Seconded to the RFC on 11th March 1917, based at La Bellevue. Disbanded on the 27th August 1917 with the pilots dispersed to other squadrons and the aircraft transferred to No.10 Squadron. No.6 Squadron would be revived in 1918 but as a bombing squadron.

No.8 Squadron: Brought back under RNAS control and returned to Dunkerque on 3rd February 1917 for rest and re-equipping with Sopwith Triplanes. Seconded to RFC on the 29th March 1917, initially based at Auchel. Returned to RNAS control on 1st March 1918.

No.9 Squadron: Seconded to RFC on 15th June 1917, initially based at Flez. Returned to RNAS control on 28th September 1917.

No.10 Squadron: Seconded to RFC on 15th May 1917, initially based at Droglandt. Returned to RNAS control on 27th November 1917.

When the new RNAS scout squadrons started to form in late 1916, Lambe's intention was to maintain a squadron strength of 20 pilots. However, losses sustained by the squadrons serving on the Western Front were considerably higher than the RNAS had previously experienced. With a much lower recruiting intake than the RFC, the RNAS found it impossible to keep their squadrons staffed at their optimum level. On numerous occasions new recruits were thrown into the fray with no time allowed for adjustment, the inevitable outcome depleting numbers even further. For much of 1917, squadron strength hovered around a core of 15 pilots, sometimes dropping as low as 10 or 11.

By August 1917, it had become apparent that the RNAS could not support five scout squadrons on the Western Front and on 27th August 1917, No.6 Squadron and No.11 Squadron were disbanded, their pilots and Sopwith Camel aircraft dispersed to reinforce other squadrons.

NOTE

[1] Discussions between Trenchard and Lambe, later formally raised at the 30th meeting of the Air Board, on 11th December 1916. ref ADM1/8449.

CHAPTER TWO

FORMATION

No.4 Wing was formed during the week ending 11th October 1915 from the Eastchurch based No.4 Squadron as part of Wing Captain Lambe's initial expansion of the RNAS presence at Dunkerque. The new Wing set up its headquarters at Petite Synthe in April 1916 under the command of Squadron Commander CL Courtney. Additional pilots and aircraft were drafted in and by mid June 1916 the Wing comprised No.1 Squadron and No.2 Squadron These names were changed to A Squadron and B Squadron during July.

Both A and B Squadrons were, in effect, multi-role squadrons. A Squadron comprised No.9 and No.10 Flights equipped with scout and bombing machines respectively and B Squadron comprised No.11 and No.12 Flights which were similarly equipped. To add to the confusion, there were also A and B Squadrons attached to both No.1 Wing and No.5 Wing at the same time. As discussed in Chapter 1, towards the end of 1916 Wing Captain Lambe instigated a final rationalisation of the squadrons in the Dunkerque Command, aimed at enabling each squadron to function independently, tailoring each squadron to a specific function and employing the structure of uniquely numbered squadrons used by the Royal Flying Corps. Whilst the changeover date for most of the squadrons can be determined with a fair degree of confidence, the activation date for No.6 Squadron is more difficult to determine.

It is known that the squadron name officially changed from A Squadron to No.6 Squadron during the week preceding the 27th November 1916, the weekly publication "Disposition of Officers of the Royal Naval Air Service" records the change in the issue dated 27th November 1916. There was no immediate change to the squadron structure however, during December 1916 and most of January 1917, the squadron still officially comprised a flight of scout pilots and a flight of bomber pilots. New pilots and administrative officers were drafted in to the squadron towards the end of January 1917 but it was not until the 5th February 1917 issue of the Disposition List that the squadron structure was officially reported as being composed of two flights of scout pilots.

The date of the 5th/6th February 1917 is significant as the 6th is the first day that a Daily Operations Report was

Petite Synthe Aerodrome, situated on the eastern outskirts of Dunkerque, the headquarters and base of No.4 Wing RNAS. *Courtesy JMB/GSL Collection*

released in the name of No.6 Squadron and signed by the squadron's new commanding officer, SCdr JJ Petre. All Operations Reports prior to the 6th February were released by No.4 Wing and signed by Wing Captain Courtney.

For the purposes of this work, it has been decided to regard the 27th November 1916 as the date that A Squadron was renamed No.6 Squadron and the 6th February 1917 as the date that No.6 Squadron was activated as a functional and independent scout squadron. The interim period between these dates was mostly devoted to practice flying and pilot evaluation, although very occasional solo fighting patrols were carried out. Wing Commander Courtney exchanged pilots between No.6 and No.7 Squadrons on a weekly basis during December 1916 and January 1917, this occurred so often that it's probably better to say that certain pilots were attached to No.4 Wing rather than trying to pin them down to any particular squadron.

The structure of No.4 Wing's two squadrons on the 27th November 1916 was as follows:

No.6 Squadron

A Flight

FLt ADW Allen, Flight Commander)
FSL C Perrett)
FSL CL Bailey) – scout pilots
FSL WHR Brown)

C Flight

FLt FT Digby, Flight Commander)
FSL RE Darnton)
FSL AHV Fletcher) – bomber pilots
FSL VE Sieveking)
FSL LW Ormerod)

No.7 Squadron

A Flight

FLt CT MacLaren, Flight Commander)
FSL GL Hartgill)
FSL JA Shaw) – scout pilots
FSL GCW Dingwall)

C Flight

FLt HG Brackley, Flight Commander)
FSL CH Darley)
FSL AL Thorne) – bomber pilots
FSL GP Powles)
FSL A Frauenfelder)

This balance of official allocation of pilots did not change significantly throughout December 1916 and January 1917 although many of the pilots were swapped about between the two squadrons from week to week. Several new pilots were transferred to No.4 Wing at the end of January such that on 5th February No.6 Squadron had the following composition:

SCdr JJ Petre, Commanding Officer
SL (RNVR) W Todd, Armaments Officer

A Flight

FCdr CT MacLaren, Flight Commander
FLt BHP De Roeper
FLt LC Keeble
FSL GL Hartgill
FSL JdeC Paynter
FSL GP Powles

B Flight

FCdr ADW Allen, Flight Commander
FLt CL Bailey
FSL GCW Dingwall
FSL RR Winter
FSL RK Slater
FSL VR Gibbs

It is the author's impression that during December and January, Wing Commander Courtney did not regard his pilots as belonging specifically to No.6 or to No.7 Squadrons but to the No.4 Wing scout pilot resource and bomber pilot resource. The sudden formal rationalisation of scout pilots into No.6 Squadron and bomber pilots into No.7 Squadron at the beginning of February 1917 gives added weight to the suggestion that No.6 Squadron was activated on the 6th February 1917.

The Squadron's initial scout provision comprised four Nieuport 12s, two Nieuport 10s and a Nieuport 11 single-seat scout. Several of the Nieuport 10 and Nieuport 12 machines were single-seat conversions. A further five Nieuport 11 scouts slowly filtered in from the depot at Dunkerque during January and the early part of February 1917.

Whilst No.6 Squadron was in its formative stage during December 1916 and January 1917 several Caudron G.IV 2-seaters were attached to the squadron.

It was intended that when No.6 Squadron was operational it would be equipped with the Nieuport 17Bis, powered by a Clerget 130hp engine and armament consisting of a synchronised Vickers gun firing through the propeller arc, combined with a Lewis gun mounted on the top wing. The first 17Bis was delivered on the 1st February 1917 and whilst one more was delivered on the 24th February, it was not until March that the new model began to arrive in significant numbers.

November 1916

As related above, the assumption has been made that the training and staffing of No.6 Squadron commenced on the 27th November 1916. By this date, both A and B Squadrons had almost completely ceased carrying out war flights and started to concentrate upon practice and test flights.

27th November

FLt Allen with FSL Hartgill as passenger flew Nieuport 12 2-seater 8741 to No.5 Wing at Coudekerke and returned with two single-seater Nieuport 12s, 9205 and 8712.

Unfavourable weather conditions prevented any other flying during the day.

28th November

FLt Allen carried out a fighting patrol to Zeebrugge at 13.15 in Nieuport 11 serial 8746. Allen patrolled around Zeebrugge for 40 minutes but no enemy aircraft were encountered. He reported that a train was observed entering Ostende at 13.40.

Three Nieuport 12s were collected from the Depot at Dunkerque, Hartgill collected 8726, Perret collected 8512 and Shaw collected 9206.

The rest of the day was given over to test and practice flights:

FSL WHR Brown	Nieuport 10 serial 3185 63 minute practice flight
FLt ADW Allen	Nieuport 12 serial 8712 15 minute test flight
FLt ADW Allen	Nieuport 12 serial 8734 20 minute test flight with LM Webb
FLt CT MacLaren	Nieuport 10 serial 3185 30 minute practice flight
FSL JA Shaw	Nieuport 10 serial 3965 15 minute practice flight
FSL WHR Brown	Nieuport 10 serial 3185 20 minute practice flight
FSL LW Omerod	Caudron serial 9119 30 minute practice flight
FSL RE Darnton	Caudron serial 9119 15 minute practice flight
FSL AHV Fletcher	Caudron serial 9120 36 minute test flight with AM Morgan

29th November

Unfavourable weather conditions prevented any flying during the day.

BELOW: Nieuport 10 serial 3185 was on the squadron strength from the 27th November 1916 to the 3rd February 1917 on which date it was crashed and written off by FSL VR Gibbs. This machine was converted to single seat configuration by sheeting over the forward cockpit. There does not appear to have been a standardised method of carrying out the conversion, 3185 being somewhat unusual in having the cladding taper up from the firewall to the pilot's cockpit. Author's collection

30th November
Unfavourable weather conditions prevented any flying during the day.

• • •

December 1916

Bad weather during December seriously interfered with Courtney's training and pilot assessment programme.

1st to 3rd December
Unfavourable weather conditions prevented any flying activity.

4th December
Twelve test and practice flights were carried out:

FSL JA Shaw	Nieuport 10 serial 3965 11 minute practice flight
FSL GL Hartgill	Nieuport 10 serial 3962 15 minute practice flight
FSL CL Bailey	Nieuport 12 serial 8712 15 minute practice flight
FSL GCW Dingwall	Nieuport 12 serial 8712 20 minute practice flight
FLt CT MacLaren	Nieuport 10 serial 3185 25 minute practice flight
FSL WHR Brown	Nieuport 10 serial 3185 20 minute practice flight
FSL C Perrett	Nieuport 12 serial 8512 12 minute test flight
FLt ADW Allen	Nieuport 11 serial 8746 20 minute test flight
FLt ADW Allen	Nieuport 10 serial 3962 13 minute test flight
FLt ADW Allen	Nieuport 12 serial 8712 15 minute test flight
FSL CL Bailey	Nieuport 10 serial 3962 15 minute test flight
FSL LW Omerod	Caudron serial 9119 10 minute practice flight

5th December
Unfavourable weather conditions prevented any flying during the day.

6th December
FLt Allen carried out a fighting patrol at 10.00 in Nieuport 11 8746. He patrolled to Ostende in search of a hostile kite balloon, which was reported to have broken loose but failed to find it.

Later in the day, Allen travelled to the Depot where he carried out a 35 minute test flight in a SPAD VII serial 9611 on behalf of No.4 Wing.

Four test and practice flights were carried out during the day:

FSL C Perrett	Nieuport 12 serial 8512 20 minute test flight
FSL WHR Brown	Nieuport 10 serial 3185 35 minute practice flight
FLt CT MacLaren	Nieuport 10 serial 3185 20 minute practice flight
FLt ADW Allen	Nieuport 11 serial 8746 10 minute practice flight

BELOW: The Caudron G IV bomber. Six of these aircraft were inherited from A Squadron and remained on No.6 Squadron's charge until January 1917. This particular machine was photographed with No.5 Wing at Coudekerke. *Courtesy JMB/GSL Collection*

7th December

Five test and practice flights were carried out:

FLt CT MacLaren	Nieuport 10 serial 3185 15 minute test flight
FSL GL Hartgill	Nieuport 10 serial 3962 15 minute test flight
FSL CL Bailey	Nieuport 10 serial 3962 35 minute practice flight
FSL JA Shaw	Nieuport 10 serial 3965 5 minute practice flight
FLt CT MacLaren	Nieuport 10 serial 3185 15 minute test flight

8th to 10th December

Unfavourable weather conditions prevented all flying.

11th December

Four pilots carried out a 30 minute formation practice:

FSL GL Hartgill	Nieuport 12 serial 9206
FSL GCW Dingwall	Nieuport 12 serial 8712
FSL JA Shaw	Nieuport 10 serial 3185
FSL CL Bailey	Nieuport 10 serial 3962

Eleven test and practice flights were carried out:

FLt Allen	Nieuport 12 serial 8734 15 minute practice flight and CPO Gott
FSL GCW Dingwall	Nieuport 10 serial 3962 35 minute practice flight
FSL JA Shaw	Nieuport 10 serial 3185 40 minute practice flight
FLt CT MacLaren	Nieuport 12 serial 8726 35 minute test flight
FSL CL Bailey	Nieuport 12 serial 8712 40 minute test flight
FSL C Perrett	Nieuport 12 serial 8512 36 minute test flight
FSL C Perrett	Nieuport 12 serial 8726 10 minute practice flight
FSL RE Darlton	Caudron serial 9130 42 minute practice flight with PO Clarke
FSL VE Sieveking	Caudron serial 9113 30 minute practice flight
FSL LW Ormerod	Caudron serial 9119 25 minute practice flight
FLt FT Digby	Caudron serial 9121 35 minute test flight

12th December

Unfavourable weather conditions prevented all flying.

13th December

Eight test and practice flights were carried out during the day:

FSL C Perrett	Nieuport 12 serial 8726 6 minute practice flight
FLt ADW Allen	Nieuport 12 serial 8734 20 minute test flight and FLt CT MacLaren
FSL GL Hartgill	Nieuport 12 serial 8712 15 minute practice flight
FLt CT MacLaren	Nieuport 10 serial 3185 20 minute test flight
FSL CL Bailey	Nieuport 12 serial 9206 50 minute test flight
FSL GCW Dingwall	Nieuport 10 serial 3962 15 minute practice flight
FLt ADW Allen	Nieuport 11 serial 8746 40 minute test flight
FSL JA Shaw	Nieuport 10 serial 3185 25 minute practice flight

14th December

Four test flights were carried out:

FLt ADW Allen	Nieuport 12 serial 8726 20 minute test flight
FLt ADW Allen	Nieuport 11 serial 8746 35 minute speed test
FSL GL Hartgill	Nieuport 12 serial 8712 35 minute speed test
FLt ADW Allen	Nieuport 11 serial 8746 15 minute test flight

15th December

Unfavourable weather conditions prevented all flying.

16th December

Three test and practice flights were carried out:

FSL GL Hartgill	Nieuport 10 serial 3962 15 minute practice flight
FLt ADW Allen	Nieuport 10 serial 3965 15 minute test flight
FLt ADW Allen	Nieuport 12 serial 8734 35 minute test flight with AM Bentley

17th December

At 13.35, Shaw carried out a fighting patrol between Dunkerque and Nieuport in Nieuport 10 3965. The patrol was uneventful and Shaw had nothing to report.

Two test and practice flights were carried out:

FLt CT MacLaren	Nieuport 11 serial 8746 20 minute practice flight
FLt ADW Allen	SPAD VII serial 9611 25 minute test flight

18th December

Six test and practice flights were carried out:

FLt ADW Allen	Sopwith serial 9343[1] 20 minute practice flight
FLt CT MacLaren	Nieuport 11 serial 8746 35 minute practice flight
FSL GL Hartgill	Nieuport 10 serial 3962 25 minute practice flight
FSL JA Shaw	Nieuport 10 serial 3965 30 minute practice flight
FLt ADW Allen	Nieuport 11 serial 8746 30 minute practice flight
FLt ADW Allen	SPAD VII serial 9611 25 minute test flight

19th December

Two test and practice flights were carried out:

FLt ADW Allen	SPAD VII serial 9611 55 minute test flight
FSL VE Sieveking	Caudron serial 9113 15 minute practice flight

20th December

Fourteen test and practice flights were carried out:

FLt CT MacLaren	Nieuport 11 serial 8746 50 minute total practice
FLt CT MacLaren	Nieuport 11 serial 8746

BELOW: SPAD S7, serial 9611 underwent Type Trials with No.4 Wing during December 1917 and whilst at Petite Synthe was flown exclusively by FLt ADW Allen. For reasons unknown, the SPAD was supplied to the RNAS with the incorrect serial N3399 as depicted here, this was changed at the St. Pol depot to the correct serial. FLt Allen flew 9611 to Eastchurch on the 24th December 1916 where it underwent further evaluation by the Design Flight under the supervision of Squadron Commander Harry Busteed. *Courtesy C&CI Archive*

FSL JA Shaw	Nieuport 10 serial 3185 14 minute practice flight
FLt ADW Allen	Nieuport 11 serial 8746 20 minute practice flight
FSL JA Shaw	Nieuport 10 serial 3965 25 minute practice flight
FLt ADW Allen	SPAD VII serial 9611 160 minute total test flights
FLt ADW Allen	SPAD VII serial 9611
FSL RE Darnton	Caudron serial 9130 35 minute practice flight with FSL JE Ruthven
FSL LW Omerod	Caudron serial 9119 55 minute total practice flights
FSL LW Omerod	Caudron serial 9119
FSL RE Darnton	Caudron serial 9130 40 minute practice flight with LM Scotcher
FSL VE Sieveking	Caudron serial 9113 75 minute practice flight with AM Walker
FSL JE Ruthven	Caudron serial 9120 120 minute total test flights
FSL JE Ruthven	Caudron serial 9120

21st December

Unfavourable weather conditions prevented all flying activity.

22nd December

Two practice flights were carried out:

FLt CT MacLaren	Nieuport 11 serial 8746 30 minute practice flight
FSL GL Hartgill	Nieuport 10 serial 3965 10 minutes practice flight

23rd December

Unfavourable weather conditions prevented all flying activity.

24th December

FLt Allen delivered the SPAD VII to Eastchurch at 10.50.

FSL Bailey was performing duties at the Depot and ferried Sopwith Triplane N5425 from Sopwith's facility at Brooklands back to Dover.

Seven practice flights were carried out:

FSL GL Hartgill	Nieuport 10 serial 3962 15 minute practice flight
FSL JA Shaw	Nieuport 10 serial 3965 20 minute practice flight
FSL JE Ruthven	Caudron serial 9120 64 minute total practice flights
FSL JE Ruthven	Caudron serial 9120
FSL RE Darnton	Caudron serial 9130 38 minute practice flight with FSL RB Frame
FSL LW Omerod	Caudron serial 9119 20 minute practice flight

25th December

Unfavourable weather conditions prevented all flying activity.

26th December

Five practice flights were carried out:

FSL CL Bailey	Nieuport 10 serial 3962 40 minute practice flight
FSL JE Ruthven	Caudron serial 9120 42 minute practice flight
FSL VE Sieveking	Caudron serial 9123 40 minute practice flight
FSL RE Darnton	Caudron serial 9130 80 minute practice flight
FSL LW Omerod	Caudron serial 9119 35 minute practice flight

27th December

Six conventional test and practice flights were carried out:

FLt CT MacLaren	Nieuport 11 serial 8746 35 minute practice flight
FSL GCW Dingwall	Nieuport 12 serial 8726 30 minute practice flight
FSL GCW Dingwall	Nieuport 12 serial 9206 45 minute practice flight
FSL RE Darnton	Caudron serial 9130 35 minute practice flight with LM Blanksby

FSL VE Sieveking	Caudron serial 9123 35 minute practice flight
with LM Dell	
FSL RE Darnton	Caudron serial 9130 15 minute test flight after repair with AM Marshall

Two formation practice flights were carried out:

30 minute formation practice

FSL CL Bailey	Nieuport 10 serial 3962
FSL C Perrett	Nieuport 10 serial 3185
FSL JA Shaw	Nieuport 10 serial 3965
FSL GL Hartgill	Nieuport 12 serial 8734 with LM Stonebridge

40 minute formation practice

FSL GL Hartgill	Nieuport 10 serial 3962
FSL JA Shaw	Nieuport 10 serial 3965
FSL CL Bailey	Nieuport 12 serial 8734
FSL C Perrett	Nieuport 10 serial 3185

FSL Bailey led the first formation and Hartgill led the second. Hartgill reported that as a leader he flew too fast.

28th December
Two test and practice flights were carried out:

FLt CT MacLaren and	Nieuport 12 serial 8734 25 minute test flight
FSL CL Bailey	
FSL RE Darnton	Caudron serial 9130 25 minute practice flight

29th to 31st December
Unfavourable weather conditions prevented all flying activity.

• • •

January 1917

There are no surviving daily records from January 1917 for No.4 Wing/No.6 Squadron, however, it is surmised that they followed a similar pattern to that seen during December 1916 and indeed the pattern followed by other new scout squadrons whilst working up to readiness. This would involve the less experienced pilots making local practice flights, initially carried out in the Nieuport 10 and Nieuport 12 machines, building up to flights in the Nieuport 11 scouts. This surmise is supported by the logbook of New Zealand pilot FSL GL Hartgill. Much of George Hartgill's previous experience was gained in Caudron bombers and the Nieuport types 10 and 12. His continuing progress with the smaller scout type of machine can be followed below.

2nd January
Local practice flight at 13.45 in Nieuport 10 serial 3962. Airborne for 30 minutes at 3000 feet.

5th January
Local practice flight in Nieuport 10 serial 3962. Airborne for 20 minutes at 2000 feet.

7th January
Local practice flight in Nieuport 10 serial 3962. Airborne for 45 minutes at 4000 feet.

11th January
Local practice flight in Nieuport 11 serial 8746. Airborne for 20 minutes at 3000 feet. Hartgill recorded that this was his first time in a Bébé and that he thought it was a "fine bus".

14th January
Local practice flight in Nieuport 11 serial 3991. Airborne for 35 minutes at 5000 feet.

Squadron formation practice carried out at 3000 feet for 20 minutes. Hartgill again flew Nieuport 11 serial 3991.

29th January
Local practice flight in Nieuport 11 serial 3988. Airborne for 65 minutes at 6000 feet. Hartgill recorded that he made two bad landings, bending the axle the first time and hitting the road on his second landing.

Towards the end of January, AFCdr JJ Petre, a highly experienced officer from 1 Wing was transferred to 4 Wing to take command of No.6 Squadron.

• • •

February 1917

February saw the pace of activity accelerating, activation of No.6 Squadron, new pilots brought on strength and expansion to three flights, contact with enemy aircraft, the commence-

ment of re-equipping with new aircraft and the squadron's first losses.

The flight structure at the beginning of February is shown below:

A Flight
AFCdr CT MacLaren, Flight Commander
FLt BHP De Roeper
FLt LC Keeble
FSL GL Hartgill
FSL J deC Paynter
FSL GP Powles
FSL CL Thorne

B Flight
FLt ADW Allen, Flight Commander
FLt CL Bailey
FSL GCW Dingwall
FSL RR Winter
FSL RK Slater
FSL VR Gibbs

1st February

The squadron's first Nieuport 17Bis, serial number N3184, arrived on the 1st, together with a couple of old Nieuport 11 machines. Nieuport 11 serial number 3991 was returned to the depot for repair.

A fighting patrol was carried out by MacLaren and Winter, both pilots flying Nieuport 11 scouts. The route flown was from Nieuport to Dixmude and Ypres. Heavy anti-aircraft fire was experienced over Ypres and two enemy aircraft were encountered. These retreated in the direction of Roulers when approached.

Allen collected Nieuport 11 serial 3987 from the depot, whilst there he carried out a number of test flights on Sopwith Pups and Triplanes.

Three practice flights were carried out:

FSL VR Gibbs	Nieuport 10 serial 3962 95 minute practice flight
FSL CL Thorne	Nieuport 10 serial 3185 11 minute practice flight
ASCdr JJ Petre	Nieuport 11 serial 3689

55 minute practice flight, shooting at fire balloons. He destroyed two balloons and collided with a third.

2nd February

FLt Allen led Dingwall, Paynter and Bailey on an offensive patrol at 10.40. The patrol was flown from Poperinghe to Ypres, east to Roulers, then Thourout and returning to the north of Dixmude. Paynter observed several hostile machines in the vicinity of Moorslede.

ASCdr Petre carried out a height test and fighting patrol to Dixmude and Pervyse in Nieuport 17Bis N3184. When returning he observed antiaircraft fire over Nieuport, before he could investigate, N3184 ran out of fuel and Petre made a forced landing on the beach at La Panne. The Nieuport was refuelled by No.1 Squadron.

Petre recorded the following test results:

Climb	1000 feet in 45 seconds 4000 feet in 3 minutes 10000 feet in 8 minutes 15000 feet in 15 minutes 20000 feet in 50 minutes
Ceiling	23000 feet

FCdr MacLaren delivered Nieuport 10 3965 to the newly formed No.9 Squadron at St.Pol.

Seven practice and test flights were carried out during the day:

FSL AL Thorne	Nieuport 11 serial 3988 20 minute practice flight
FSL AL Thorne	Nieuport 11 serial 3988 25 minute practice flight
FSL AL Thorne	Nieuport 10 serial 3962 30 minute practice flight
FSL AL Thorne	Nieuport 12 serial 9206 10 minute practice flight
FSL LW Ormerod	Nieuport 12 serial 9205 15 minute practice flight
FSL VR Gibbs	Nieuport 10 serial 3962 25 minute practice flight
FSL VR Gibbs	Nieuport 10 serial 3962 30 minute practice flight

3rd February

Bailey carried out a patrol at 07.20 to search for missing aircraft. He was able to locate a Sopwith 5 miles west of Dunkerque, 10 yards out from the shore, a Caudron on the sands at Malo and an unattended Sopwith floating in the sea between Malo and La Panne. The Caudron belonged to Sieveking of No.7 Squadron who had participated in a bombing raid to Bruges on the night of the 2nd/3rd February but had made a forced landing on the beach at Malo upon his return.

Dingwall and Paynter carried out a fighting patrol at 10.10 in response to reports of an enemy machine over Hondschoote. Heavy shelling was observed but the pilots were unable to find the hostile machine. The patrol was continued over Alveringhem, Nieuport, Ostende, Zeebrugge, Bruges and Dixmude. No enemy aircraft were encountered but observations of train movements and shipping were carried out.

FLt Norton carried out a fighting patrol at 11.00 and reported that the coast was clear of shipping as far as Ostende.

FCdr Petre carried out a fighting patrol at 14500 ft in the Nieuport 17Bis during the morning. No enemy aircraft or shipping were observed. On his return, Petre carried out a speed test along the beach.

Six practice and test flights were carried out:

FSL AL Thorne	Nieuport 11 serial 8746 40 minute practice flight
FSL CL Bailey	Nieuport 11 serial 3981 40 minute practice flight
FSL RR Winter	Nieuport 11 serial 8746 65 minute practice flight
FSL RR Winter	Nieuport 11 serial 3987 30 minute practice flight, firing at fire balloons
FSL VR Gibbs	Nieuport 10 serial 3185 30 minute practice flight
FSL VR Gibbs	Nieuport 10 serial 3185 30 minute practice flight, crashed.

Gibbs crashed and wrecked Nieuport 10 serial 3185. He was subsequently "washed out" on scouts and transferred to No.7 Squadron.

4th February

Dingwall and Bailey carried out a fighting patrol at 15.30 in response to an enemy machine reported to be over Calais. Dingwall climbed to 10,500 ft and patrolled between Dunkerque and Gravelines, visibility was very bad and no hostile machines were observed. Bailey found that mist rolling in from the sea obscured the ground and he was forced to cut his patrol short.

No.6 Squadron's Commanding Officer, Acting Squadron Commander John Joseph Petre. Jack Petre was a very experienced and capable officer, brought in from No.1 Wing to lead No.6 Squadron. *Courtesy Les Rogers*

A practice formation patrol was carried out:

20 minute formation	
FCdr CT MacLaren	Nieuport 11 serial 3989
FCdr EW Norton	Nieuport 11 serial 3994
FSL RR Winter	Nieuport 11 serial 3987

5th February

Unfavourable weather conditions restricted activity to test and practice flights:

FCdr ADW Allen	Nieuport 17Bis serial N3184 40 minute test flight
FCdr ADW Allen	Nieuport 11 serial 3989 15 minute test flight
FCdr ADW Allen	Nieuport 11 serial 3989
FSL JdeC Paynter	Nieuport 11 serial 3981

20 minute formation practice

FSL GP Powles	Nieuport 11 serial 3987
FSL RR Winter	Nieuport 11 serial 3994
FSL AL Thorne	Nieuport 11 serial 8746

6th February

ASCdr Petre filed No.6 Squadron's first Daily Operations Report on the 6th and it is assumed that Wing Commander Courtney finally regarded the squadron as being activated.

Nieuport 11 serial 3994 arrived from the depot.

In the afternoon, FLt Norton led Thorne, Winter and Slater, all flying Nieuport 11s, on a fighting patrol between Ypres, Dixmude and Nieuport. The patrol reported a train leaving Ostende at 14.50, another train leaving Ghistelles at 14.57 and the coast to be clear of enemy shipping as far as Blankenberghe.

FLt Allen travelled to the depot at St. Pol where he carried out test flights on two Sopwith Pups and two Nieuport 12 2-seater machines.

SCdr Petre flew the Nieuport 17Bis to No.1 Squadron at Furnes for a series of comparative tests with Sopwith Triplane N5426. He initially found that the Nieuport had a significantly better climb, reaching 10,000 feet by the time that the triplane had ascended to 8,200 feet. Unfortunately, the test conditions were not recorded, so we do not know whether the aircraft were armed.

7th February

At the request of No.1 Squadron, offensive patrols between Nieuport, Dixmude and Ghistelles were continuously maintained during the morning:

FCdr JJ Petre	Nieuport 17Bis serial 3184
FLt BHP De Roeper	Nieuport 11 serial 3989
FSL GP Powles	Nieuport 11 serial 3987
FSL AL Thorne	Nieuport 11 serial 8746
FSL CL Bailey	Nieuport 11 serial 3981
FSL GCW Dingwall	Nieuport 11 serial 3981
FSL RK Slater	Nieuport 11 serial 8746
FSL JdeC Paynter	Nieuport 11 serial 3981

The patrols were relatively uneventful and reported a train in Essen station, two trains in Ostende harbour station, a train approaching Beerst and one enemy aeroplane landing at Ghistelles.

Petre and De Roeper carried out a hostile aircraft patrol at 11.40 when enemy aircraft were reported to be in the vicinity of Dunkerque. Allied anti-aircraft fire was observed but the enemy machines were not encountered.

Petre and Bailey carried out another hostile aircraft patrol at 12.45 upon reports of hostile aircraft at Calais and Gravelines. The two Nieuports patrolled in the vicinity of Dunkerque but failed to see any enemy machines.

Petre carried out further tests with the Nieuport 17Bis at Furnes when he reported that the Triplane, flown by FLt Allen and the Nieuport were found to have an identical climb rate to 15,000 feet but the triplane was 4 knots faster in level flight at that altitude. In a dive, the Nieuport was found to be significantly better than the triplane but in manoeuvrability, neither machine showed any advantage.

8th February

Six fighting patrols were flown in the Ypres, Dixmude and Nieuport area:

FLt EW Norton	Nieuport 17Bis serial N3184
FLt BHP De Roeper	Nieuport 11 serial 8747
FLt LC Keeble	Nieuport 11 serial 3989
FSL GCW Dingwall	Nieuport 11 serial 8746
FSL RK Slater	Nieuport 12 serial 9205
FSL RR Winter	Nieuport 11 serial 3994

FLt EW Norton, whilst patrolling over Houthulst Forest at 18000 feet, encountered an Aviatic 2-seater flying 4000 feet below his patrol height. Norton dived on the 2-seater and fired a dozen rounds at very close range, he then made a right turn and came up underneath the enemy machine and fired a burst of 25 rounds from 50 yards. Tracers were seen to hit the enemy machine, which fell away out of control emitting clouds of black smoke from the front of the fuselage. Norton followed the Aviatic down to 10,000 feet whereupon the anti-aircraft fire became intense. When last seen the machine was falling erratically and emitting smoke. Norton reported that at no stage in the encounter did the enemy pilot attempt to manoeuvre, or the observer return fire. The gun-sight fitted to Norton's Nieuport 17Bis was a Collimateur Chretien single point telescope and Norton was very enthusiastic regarding its ease of use when compared to a standard double point telescope.

At 12.20, a report was received of a hostile machine heading northeast from Calais, Paynter was dispatched in a Nieuport 11 3981 to intercept the intruder but was unable to locate it.

Two local test flights were carried out:

FLt ADW Allen — Nieuport 11 serial 8747
FLt ADW Allen — Nieuport 11 serial 8746

9th February

At 07.40, hostile aircraft were reported over Dunkerque, Petre and Bailey attempted to intercept the intruders. The engines proved difficult to start due to the intense cold and the resulting delay prevented the defenders from catching the enemy aircraft.

Eight fighting patrols were flown along the Nieuport-Dixmude line during the course of the day:

FCdr JJ Petre	Nieuport 17Bis N3184
FLt LC Keeble	Nieuport 11 serial 3989
FSL CL Bailey	Nieuport 11 serial 8746
FSL GCW Dingwall	Nieuport 11 serial 3981
FSL RR Winter	Nieuport 11 serial 8746 and 8747

No enemy aircraft were observed but the patrols reported a number of train movements and two enemy ships to the north of Ostende Pier.

De Roeper and Bailey were both given the opportunity to made short practice flights in the Nieuport 17Bis.

10th February

At 06.40 Bailey and Thorne were "scrambled" to intercept a reported incursion over Dunkerque. Bailey flying the 17Bis climbed rapidly to 3000 feet and sighted the enemy aircraft heading seawards and gave chase, he was catching the intruder when his engine stopped and he was forced to glide back. The Nieuport's engine picked up again and Bailey resumed the pursuit, he chased the enemy machine to Westende whereupon it dived away towards Middlekerke. Both pilots reported being heavily shelled by the Allied anti-aircraft defences in the vicinity of Nieuport.

The squadron flew nine fighting patrols from Furnes to Nieuport, keeping two scouts in the air continuously between 11.00 and 15.00:

FCdr JJ Petre	Nieuport 17Bis serial N3184 65 minutes total
FLt BHP De Roeper	Nieuport 11 serial 3981 120 minutes total
FSL AL Thorne	Nieuport 11 serial 3989 180 minutes total
FSL CL Bailey	Nieuport 17Bis serial N3184 180 minutes total
FSL RR Winter	Nieuport 11 serial 3994 90 minutes total
FSL RK Slater	Nieuport 11 serial 3987 75 minutes total

FCdr EW Norton, one of only three pilots to become an "ace" whilst a member of No.6 Squadron (although a fair number of the squadron's pilots went on to become aces with other squadrons). Norton, another pilot recruited from No.1 Wing, was easily No.6 Squadron's most aggressive and accomplished Nieuport pilot. *Courtesy John Oxley Library*

The patrols proved uneventful, the only report being a smoke screen observed at Langemarck.

11th February

Visibility was poor for most of the day, the heavy overcast not clearing until late afternoon.

New pilots FSL H Lawson and FSL FC Walker arrived at the squadron.

FLt De Roeper led Bailey, Paynter, Slater and Thorne on a practice formation patrol, all of the pilots flying Nieuport 11 scouts:

50 minute formation practice

FLt BHP De Roeper	Nieuport 11 serial 3989
FSL CL Bailey	Nieuport 11 serial 8746
FSL JdeC Paynter	Nieuport 11 serial 3981
FSL RK Slater	Nieuport 11 serial 3987
FSL AL Thorne	Nieuport 11 serial 8747

Slater dropped out after 15 minutes, Paynter after 30 minutes and Bailey after 35 minutes.

12th February

Heavy overcast throughout the day and rain in the afternoon again prevented any war flying.

Nine practice and test flights were carried out, including first flights by Lawson, Plaistowe and Walker:

FCdr JJ Petre	Nieuport 12 serial 8734 20 minute flight
FSL JdeC Paynter	Nieuport 11 serial 3981 15 minute flight
FSL RR Winter	Nieuport 11 serial 3994 20 minute flight
FSL AL Thorne	Nieuport 11 serial 8735 15 minute flight
FSL GP Powles	Nieuport 11 serial 3987 15 minute flight
FSL D Plaistowe	Nieuport 12 serial 8712 15 minute flight
FSL HA Lawson	Nieuport 10 serial 3962 40 minute flight
FSL FC Walker	Nieuport 10 serial 3962 20 minute flight

13th February

The weather was initially cloudy but cleared by 10.30. Five uneventful fighting patrols were flown between Ypres, Houthulst and Slype:

SCdr JJ Petre	Nieuport 17Bis serial N3184
FLt LC Keeble	Nieuport 11 serial 3981
FSL GP Powles	Nieuport 11 serial 8747
FSL RR Winter	Nieuport 11 serial 3987
FSL RK Slater	Nieuport 11 serial 3994

Eight practice and familiarisation flights were carried out:

FSL H Lawson	Nieuport 10 serial 3962
FSL H Lawson	Nieuport 12 serial 9206
FSL D Plaistowe	Nieuport 10 serial 3962
FSL D Plaistowe	Nieuport 12 serial 9206
FSL FC Walker	Nieuport 10 serial 3962
FSL FC Walker	Nieuport 12 serial 8712
FSL FC Walker	Nieuport 12 serial 9206
FSL JdeC Paynter	Nieuport 11 serial 3981

14th February

Activity was more intense on the 14th February.

Thorne and Dingwall took off at daybreak and patrolled in the vicinity of Dunkerque, no enemy aircraft were encountered.

BELOW: Nieuport 12 serial 8734, depicted here after suffering an accident with No.11 Squadron on the 9th May 1917. FCdr ADW Allen was flying this machine on the 26th November 1916 when he lost a wheel at take off, he landed safely and was commended for his flying skills. The Nieuport 12s were generally used for practice flights but were occasionally pressed into service to carry out line patrols. *Courtesy JMB/GSL Collection*

No.1 Squadron again requested that fighting patrols be carried out, Thorne patrolled along the Nieuport Dixmude line and Bailey covered the area between Ypres, Ghistelles and Ostende.

From 11.00 to 15.00, the squadron maintained continuous double patrols between Dunkerque and Furnes:

FLt BHP De Roeper	Nieuport 11 serial 8747
FLt LC Keeble	Nieuport 11 serial 3989
FSL GP Powles	Nieuport 11 serial 8746
FSL RK Slater	Nieuport 11 serial 8747
FSL JdeC Paynter	Nieuport 11 serial 8746
FSL AL Thorne	Nieuport 12 serial 8712, Nieuport 11 serial 3987 and Nieuport 11 serial 8747

At 11.30, Paynter encountered four hostile machines near Houthulst at 15000 feet, he gave chase but was unable to catch them.

At 17.20 three enemy aircraft appeared over Dunkerque, Petre, Keeble, Powles, Bailey, Thorne and Winter took off immediately to give chase but lost the intruders in the haze.

Four test and familiarisation flights were carried out during the day:

FSL GCW Dingwall	Nieuport 11 serial 3981
FSL H Lawson	Nieuport 10 serial 3962
FSL H Plaistowe	Nieuport 12 serial 9206
FSL FC Walker	Nieuport 12 serial 8712

15th February

The squadron maintained continuous three machine patrols from daybreak until dusk to protect Dunkerque:

SCdr JJ Petre	Nieuport 17Bis serial N3184
FLt BHP De Roeper	Nieuport 11 serial 3982
FLt ADW Allen	Nieuport 12 serial 8734
FSL GP Powles	Nieuport 11 serial 3987
FSL AL Thorne	Nieuport 11 serial 8747
FSL CL Bailey	Nieuport 17Bis serial N3184 and Nieuport 11 serial 8746
FSL RK Slater.	Nieuport 11 serial 3989

Petre, De Roeper and Powles left at daybreak on the first patrol. Thick fog blew in from the east whilst the patrol was in the air, two of the pilots were unable to find the aerodrome and eventually landed on the beach near Gravelines.

Allen and Norton had previously been sent to the Nieuport factory at Paris and they returned on the 15th with two new Nieuport 17Bis machines, serials N3186 and N3187 respectively. Both of these aircraft were delivered to the depot at Dunkerque.

Four practice flights were carried out:

FSL H Lawson	Nieuport 11 serial 3987
FSL D Plaistowe	Nieuport 12 serial 8726
FSL D Plaistowe	Nieuport 11 serial 3987
FSL FC Walker	Nieuport 10 serial 3962

16th February

Nine fighting patrols were carried out during the day:

FLt BHP De Roeper	Nieuport 11 serial 3981
FLt ADW Allen	Nieuport 17Bis serial N3184
FSL AL Thorne	Nieuport 11 serial 8747
FSL GCW Dingwall	Nieuport 11 serial 3989
FSL RR Winter	Nieuport 11 serial 3981
FSL GP Powles	Nieuport 11 serial 3989
FSL RK Slater	Nieuport 11 serial 8746
FSL H Lawson	Nieuport 11 serial 8747

The enemy activity, which had been intermittent, increased considerably on the 16th. At 06.25, Powles observed an LVG 2-seater 3 miles out to sea from Dunkerque and heading eastwards. Powles pursued and overhauled the enemy aircraft off Coxyde and opened fire at the rather optimistic range of 150 yards, he reported that tracers hit the enemy aircraft, which dived away towards Westende, Powles followed, changed his ammunition tray and fired again. The enemy 2-seater was last seen to flatten out at 2000 feet near Westende, at which point Powles came under heavy fire from Allied anti-aircraft defences.

Allen carried out a patrol at 16000 feet to Ghistelles at 06.40, no enemy aircraft were encountered but Allen came under heavy defensive anti-aircraft fire in the vicinity of Ghistelles.

Thorne was patrolling near Dunkerque at 17.10 when an Aviatic descended through the clouds above him. Thorne closed to 100 yards and fired a whole drum, tracers being seen to hit the enemy machine which climbed steeply and was lost in the clouds.

Several other enemy aircraft were encountered by patrols during the day but could not be brought to action.

Six test and practice flights were carried out:

FLt ADW Allen	Nieuport 11 serial 8746
FSL JdeC Paynter	Nieuport 11 serial 3981
FSL H Lawson	Nieuport 11 serial 3987
FSL D Plaistowe	Nieuport 11 serial 8747
FSL FC Walker	Nieuport 11 serial 3962
FSL FC Walker	Nieuport 11 serial 8747

17th to 23rd February

A period of bad weather set in from the 17th to the 23rd of February, curtailing all flying activities.

24th February

Nieuport 17Bis serial N3187 was collected from the depot.

The weather cleared enough on the 24th to allow twenty local test and practice flights to be carried out:

SCdr JJ Petre	Nieuport 17Bis serial N3187 70 minutes total
FCdr CT MacLaren	Nieuport 17Bis serial N3184 35 minutes total
FCdr CT MacLaren	Nieuport 11 serial 3989
FLt EW Norton	Nieuport 17Bis serial N3187 15 minutes total
FLt BHP De Roeper	Nieuport 11 serial 3989 35 minutes total
FSL JdeC Paynter	Nieuport 11 serial 3981
FSL JdeC Paynter	Nieuport 11 serial 3987
FSL JdeC Paynter	Nieuport 17Bis N3184
FSL GP Powles	Nieuport 17Bis serial N3184 10 minutes
FSL RK Slater	Nieuport 10 serial 3962 35 minutes total
FSL RK Slater	Nieuport 11 serial 3994
FSL FC Walker	Nieuport 11 serial 8747 30 minutes
FSL H Lawson	Nieuport 11 serial 3981 60 minutes total
FSL H Lawson	Nieuport 11 serial 3994

Thorne ferried Nieuport 12, serial 9205, across to No.10 Squadron at St. Pol.

Two pilots practiced firing at a ground target using Le Prieur incendiary rockets, they reported that successful results were obtained:

FSL AL Thorne	Nieuport 11 serial 8746
FSL JdeC Paynter	Nieuport 11 serial 8746

New pilot FSL OJ Gagnier arrived at the squadron.

25th February

The weather was overcast on the 25th but Thorne and Paynter were able get more practice with Le Prieur rockets:

FSL AL Thorne	Nieuport 11 serial 8746
FSL JdeC Paynter	Nieuport 11 serial 8746

Several local practice flights were carried out:

FSL OJ Gagnier	Nieuport 10 serial 3962 30 minutes total
FSL OJ Gagnier	Nieuport 11 serial 3994
FLt CT MacLaren	Nieuport 12 serial 8734 30 minutes
FSL RK Slater	Nieuport 11 serial 3994 8 minutes
FSL GCW Dingwall	Nieuport 12 serial 9206 crashed and injured his back.

26th February

Six fighting patrols were flown between Ypres, Nieuport and Ostende:

FLt EW Norton	Nieuport 17Bis serial N3187
FSL JdeC Paynter	Nieuport 11 serial 3981
FSL RK Slater	Nieuport 11 serial 3989
FSL GP Powles	Nieuport 11 serial 3987
FSL H Lawson	Nieuport 11 serial 3994
FSL OJ Gagnier	Nieuport 11 serial 8747

Slater, flying at 13000 feet near Houthulst, observed a hostile machine at his own height. He pursued the enemy aircraft down to 9000 feet and 7 miles behind the enemy lines, 50 rounds were fired at long range without effect. Paynter reported observing heavy anti-aircraft fire over Ostende at 09.40 and what appeared to be a machine falling in flames. Norton reported observing an enemy machine at low altitude over Ostende at 10.50.

At 11.45, Keeble, Thorne and Powles were despatched to No.1 Wing to provide an escort to a photoreconnaissance mission to Zeebrugge. Thorne observed two enemy seaplanes "shadowing" the patrol but he was unable to climb up to their altitude. Powles flying Nieuport 11, serial 3981, became the squadron's first loss in action after his fuel tank was damaged by ground fire and he made a forced landing at Cadzand,

ABOVE: Nieuport 11 serial 3981, depicted here with an optimistic twin gun armament whilst serving with No.1 Wing. FSL GP Powles was flying 3981 with a single gun on an escort mission on the 26th February 1917, anti-aircraft fire damaged the machine's fuel tank and Powles made a forced landing in Holland. Both pilot and machine were interned, the Netherlands authorities purchased the Nieuport and used it as a pattern machine for a batch of Nieuport 11s built under licence by Trompenburg. *Courtesy JMB/GSL Collection*

Zeeland. Powles was interned in Holland.[2] Thorne reported three enemy destroyers seen between Ostende and Zeebrugge and seven enemy seaplanes parked on the Zebrugge Mole with several more in the water.

When Powles failed to return, SCdr Petre in N3187 flew along the coast and surrounding country to try to locate the missing machine.

27th February

No war flying took place on the 27th February due to overcast conditions and mist. Several local practice and test flights were carried out by Norton, Thorn and Fletcher.

SCdr Petre travelled to the depot at Dunkerque to test the Sopwith Camel prototype N517. The Camel was referred to as "F2" at this time and Petre recorded the following performance figures:

Climb to 10,000 feet	8 1/2 minutes
Speed at ground level	103 knots
Speed at 5,000 feet	95 knots

28th February

The bad weather persisted through to the 28th of the month, closing down all war flying activities.

Petre, Norton and Plaistowe carried out test flights and Norton led Thorne, Fletcher, Paynter and Lawson on a 30 minute practice formation patrol, the first occasion that the members of C Flight flew together.

• • •

March 1917

The squadron was transferred to RFC control on the 17th March, re-equipping with the Nieuport 17Bis scout was noticeably accelerated as the transfer date approached. With more emphasis on practice of formation flying when weather permitted, the Squadron's Flight composition becomes easy to discern.

At this juncture the squadron structure was as follows:

A Flight, AFCdr CT MacLaren
AFCdr BHP De Roeper
FLt LC Keeble

FSL GL Hartgill
FSL J deC Paynter
FSL OJ Gagnier

B Flight, AFCdr ADW Allen
FLt CL Bailey
FSL D Plaistowe
FSL FC Walker
FSL RK Slater

C Flight, AFCdr EW Norton
FSL RR Winter
FSL H Lawson
FSL AL Thorne
FSL AHV Fletcher

1st March

The squadron mounted eight fighting patrols to Ostende, Ghistelles and Dixmude and several patrols to Dunkerque in response to reports of enemy incursions. SCdr Petre, Keeble, Thorne, Paynter, Fletcher, Slater and Gagnier were involved in these operations. Five hostile aircraft were pursued, two of which were driven down by Paynter. When in the vicinity of Ostende, Paynter, flying Nieuport 17Bis N3184, fired at a hostile seaplane which dived away before he could close with it. Paynter then observed three enemy machines over Ghistelles and dived to attack. Two of the machines dived towards the aerodrome and the third, a scout, climbed away and wasn't seen again. Paynter attacked the nearest enemy machine, a 2-seater, at very close range and followed it down to 7,000 feet firing all the time. Tracers were seen to hit the aircraft which was still diving vertically when Paynter broke off the attack. Paynter was subjected to heavy anti-aircraft fire as he returned to the lines.

At 12.30, Slater observed a hostile machine low over Ostende.

SCdr Petre performed some tests on N3187, the squadron's second Nieuport 17Bis machine, Petre was trying to determine the "performance hit" incurred by using two machine guns:

Armament	Climb to 12,000 feet
Fixed Vickers + Lewis + double tray	16 minutes
Fixed Vickers only	14 minutes

Speed at 12,000 feet was reduced by 2 knots carrying both guns.

2nd March

The day was misty and overcast with rain in the afternoon, the conditions restricted flying to just one practice flight and a delivery flight when Thorne collected Nieuport 17Bis serial N3186 from the depot.

3rd March

The bad weather continued, with all war flying activities abandoned.

4th March

Fletcher, Slater and Gagnier carried out a sweep of the lines between Dixmude and Nieuport, an enemy machine was observed but the old Nieuport scouts were unable to overhaul it.

Thorne and Paynter flew the Nieuport 17Bis machines on fighting patrols between Ypres, Bruges and Nieuport, one enemy machine was seen over Houthulst at 14.45.

Petre and De Roeper ferried two new Nieuports, N3193 and N3194, from Paris, later taking them on to the depot.

Hartgill, newly returned from a period of sick leave carried out a practice flight in one of the Nieuport 11s. Obviously conscious of his last landing at the end of January he reported that he made a good landing. A second flight in another "Baby" Nieuport rated a "fair landing".

FCdr Allen had previously travelled to England and returned with Sopwith Triplane N5459. He later delivered the triplane to the Depot and whilst there was able to make a test flight in the prototype Sopwith Camel, F2.

5th March

It was overcast and foggy on the 5th, however, Hartgill carried out a short practice flight to Bergues and back in Nieuport 11 3991.

6th March

The weather was overcast throughout most of the day, restricting the squadron to test and practice flights:

FCdr CT MacLaren	Sopwith Camel serial F2
FSL GL Hartgill	Nieuport 11 serial 3991
FSL AHV Fletcher	Nieuport 17Bis serial N3184
FSL RK Slater	Nieuport 17Bis serial N3184
FSL FC Walker	Nieuport 17Bis serial N3184
FSL FC Walker	Nieuport 11 serial 8747
FSL OJ Gagnier	Nieuport 17Bis serial N3184

35 minute formation practice

FCdr CT MacLaren	Nieuport 11 serial 3989
FLt BHP De Roeper	Nieuport 11 serial 8746
FLt LC Keeble	Nieuport 11 serial 8747
FSL GL Hartgill	Nieuport 11 serial 3991
FSL OJ Gagnier	Nieuport 11 serial 3994

At the end of MacLaren's A Flight formation practice, Hartgill flying Nieuport 11 serial 3991 made another bad landing coming down on his wing tip.

FCdr Allen flew Nieuport 17Bis N3186 to No.1 AD at St. Omer.

7th March

No flying due to unsuitable weather conditions.

8th March

No war flying was carried out due to unsuitable weather conditions.

New pilot FSL AE Hall arrived at the squadron.

Nieuport 17Bis N3189 was collected from the depot at St.Pol.

9th March

FCdr Allen returned from St. Omer on the 9th. Later in the day he led B Flight on a practice formation patrol:

FCdr ADW Allen	Nieuport 11 serial 8747
FSL RK Slater	Nieuport 11 serial 3991
FSL CL Bailey	Nieuport 11 serial 8746
FSL FC Walker	Nieuport 11 serial 3989
FSL D Plaistowe	Nieuport 17Bis serial N3184

The re-equipping of the squadron started to gather momentum when three new Nieuports, N3190, N3195 and N3198 were collected from the depot by De Roeper, Paynter and Winter respectively.

A number of test and practice flights were carried out:

FSL GL Hartgill	Nieuport 17Bis serial N3184
FSL AHV Fletcher	Nieuport 17Bis serial N3184
FSL RK Slater	Nieuport 17Bis serial N3184
FSL JdeC Paynter	Nieuport 11 serial 3991
FSL CL Bailey	Nieuport 11 serial 8747
FSL H Lawson	Nieuport 11 serial 3994
FSL D Plaistowe	Nieuport 11 serial 3989
FSL AE Hall	Nieuport 10 serial 3962

Hartgill recorded his first flight in a Nieuport 17Bis, noting that he was having trouble understanding the Clerget engine.

10th March

Low cloud and mist prevented all war flying on the 10th, however SCdr Petre was able to carry out a five minute test flight.

BELOW: Nieuport 17Bis, N3195, collected from the depot at St Pol on the 9th March 1917 by FSL JdeC Paynter. N3195 later became FSL RR Winter's regular machine and carried the C Flight identification number "16". A new pilot, FSL RW Berridge, was killed when he stalled N3195 at take off from Citadel Aerodrome on the 3rd May 1917. *Courtesy EF Cheesman*

Allen, Paynter, Winter and Fletcher made the short trip to the depot, to collect another four new Nieuports, N3196, N3194, N3192 and N3201.

New pilot FSL P Wood arrived at the squadron.

11th March

A further five Nieuports were collected from the depot, N3202, N3191, N3197, N3189 and N3200 by De Roeper, Keeble, Fletcher, Paynter and Gagnier respectively.

The re-equipping was marred by an incident at 12.00 when Bailey was despatched in N3186 in response to a report of an enemy machine at Gravelines, Bailey choked the engine at take-off and crashed in a nearby field. Hartgill took off immediately after the accident in N3184 but failed to make contact with the intruder.

A number of test flights were carried out during the day, checking out the New Nieuports:

SCdr JJ Petre	Nieuport 17Bis serial N3195
SCdr JJ Petre	Nieuport 17Bis serial N3196
FCdr ADW Allen	Nieuport 17Bis serial N3186
FCdr ADW Allen	Nieuport 17Bis serial N3196
FCdr ADW Allen	Nieuport 17Bis serial N3200
FCdr ADW Allen	Nieuport 17Bis serial N3201
FSL AHV Fletcher	Nieuport 17Bis serial N3184
FSL GL Hartgill	Nieuport 17Bis serial N3190
FSL JdeC Paynter	Nieuport 17Bis serial N3189
FSL RK Slater	Nieuport 17Bis serial N3190
FSL D Plaistowe	Nieuport 17Bis serial N3189
FSL H Lawson	Nieuport 17Bis serial N3184
FSL H Lawson	Nieuport 17Bis serial N 3191
FSL P Wood	Nieuport 17Bis serial N3191

Practice flights were also carried out by several pilots:

FSL FC Walker	Nieuport 11 serial 8747
FSL AE Hall	Nieuport 10 serial 3962
FSL P Wood	Nieuport 10 serial 3962

FSL Wood's first flight with the squadron followed the normal pattern of a practice flight in a Nieuport 10, he was obviously considered competent as he was later trusted to take one of the new Nieuport 17Bis machines up for a test flight.

New Pilot FLt FP Reeves arrived at the squadron.

12th March

The weather proved difficult, being overcast with occasional rain. Just four local practice flights were carried out

FLt Reeves	Nieuport 17Bis serial N3193
FSL P Wood	Nieuport 17Bis serial N3184
FSL AE Hall	Nieuport 11 serial 3991
FSL AE Hall	Nieuport 10 serial 3962

SCdr Petre collected Nieuport 17Bis N3193 from the depot.

13th March

The weather was overcast for the greater part of the day.

Fletcher collected Nieuport 17Bis N3202 from the depot but crashed and damaged the aircraft when landing. The machine was returned to the depot for repair.

Two local test flights were carried out:

FSL AE Hall	Nieuport 17Bis serial N3184
FSL AE Hall	Nieuport 11 serial 3991

14th March

Reeves and Paynter collected Nieuports N3204 and 3206 from the depot.

As previously mentioned, the Admiralty had agreed to assist the Royal Flying Corps on the Western Front and No.6 Squadron would shortly follow No.1 Squadron and No.3 Squadron to the south. To this end, the squadron's personnel, stores and motor transport left Petite Synthe on the 14th for the new Aerodrome at La Bellevue on the Arras Front.

15th March

FSL Thorne collected Nieuport N3205 from the depot.

Two local test flights were carried out:

FCdr EW Norton	Nieuport 17Bis serial N3184
FSL AL Thorne	Nieuport 17Bis serial N3205

SCdr Petre flew N3184 several miles to the south of St. Omer to check weather conditions which proved cloudy.

16th March

With the weather still proving difficult just two local test flights were carried out:

SCdr JJ Petre	Nieuport 17Bis serial N3195
FSL AL Thorne	Nieuport 17Bis serial N3184

ABOVE: An unidentified Nieuport 17Bis is refuelled. The photograph shows that refuelling was not an elegant process, one rating to hold a funnel, another to pour the gasoline into the funnel and others on hand to pass new tins of fuel up as necessary. *Courtesy SK Taylor*

BELOW: No.6 Squadron's Nieuports lined up at Petite Synthe just prior to departure for La Bellevue and service with the RFC. *Courtesy Fleet Air Arm Museum*

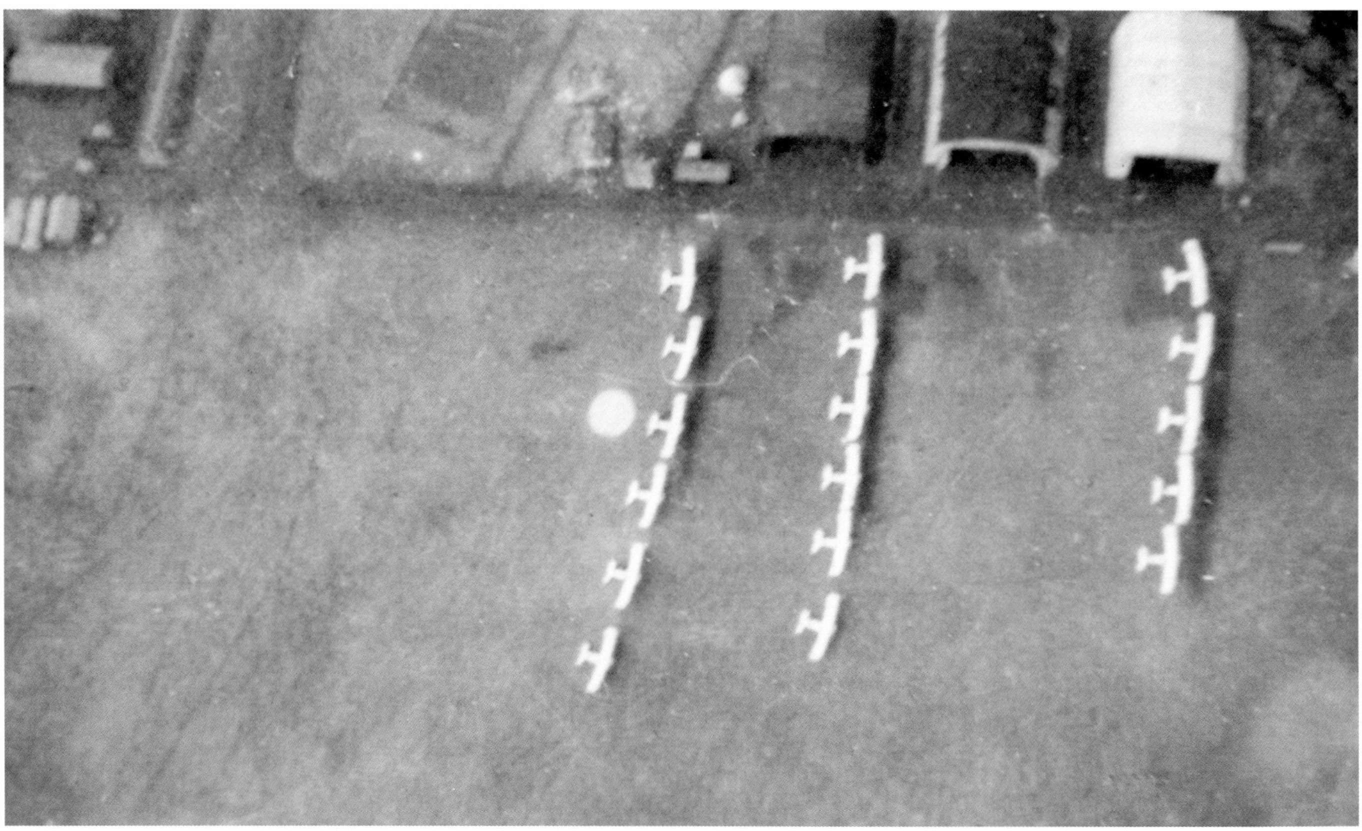

17th March

At 08.30, the pilots flew their aircraft south to La Bellevue. Control of the squadron was transferred from 4 Wing RNAS to 13 Wing 3 Brigade Royal Flying Corps in support of the 3rd Army. Hartgill flew N3191 from Petite Synthe to La Bellevue, having to land at Vert Gallant to get directions. He reported that the aircraft's pressure system was faulty.

FSL FC Walker had the dubious distinction of becoming the squadron's first fatality. Walker was killed at Savy when he stalled N3201 at 400 feet and crashed.

Wing Captain Lambe was able to report No.6 Squadron's move to the Vice Admiral, Dover Patrol:

Headquarters, R.N.A.S
Dunkerque
17th March 1917

Sir,

In accordance with Admiralty letter M.010977/16 of the 20th December 1916 and as agreed with Major General Trenchard, commanding R.F.C, I have the honour to report that the Personnel, Stores and Motor Transport of No.6 Squadron left to join the R.F.C. on Wednesday March 14th, arriving at their new destination on the same day.

This squadron is commanded by Acting Squadron Commander JJ Petre, DSC and is composed of 130h.p. Clerget Single Seater Nieuport machines.

Owing to unfavourable weather conditions the machines and pilots were unable to proceed until this morning.

This makes the third Squadron now attached to the R.F.C.[3] *and the date of departure coincides with the original programme drawn up in accordance with Major General Trenchard's wishes.*

I have the honour to be,
Sir,
Your obedient servant

Signed CL Lambe
Wing Captain

Vice Admiral

NOTES

[1] It is not known which machine Allen flew, the serial 9343 does not relate to any know Sopwith serial number and must be assumed to have been incorrectly transcribed.

[2] The Netherlands authorities salvaged Nieuport 11 serial 3981 and eventually repaired and flew it. It was subsequently given the Netherlands registration LA40 and sent to the Trompenburg factory at Amsterdam to be used as a pattern for a batch of licence built Nieuport 11s. In September 1917 it was purchased for £1700 and given the Dutch serial number N213.

[3] No.1 Squadron and No.3 Squadron were already attached to the RFC. No.8 Squadron had been recalled to RNAS control for rest and re-equipping.

CHAPTER THREE

WORKING FOR THE RFC - 13 WING, 3 BRIGADE

Although the control of No.6 Squadron had been handed over to the RFC, the squadron was still unprepared for the hardship that it would face on a more active section of the front. When the weather permitted, training proceeded with more intensity and every effort was being made to ensure the new Nieuport 17Bis aircraft were in first class condition.

The weather proved difficult at first and little could be done other than brief test flights to check out new machines. It soon became apparent that the Nieuport 17Bis, of which much was expected, was not going to produce the performance that the authorities had hoped for.

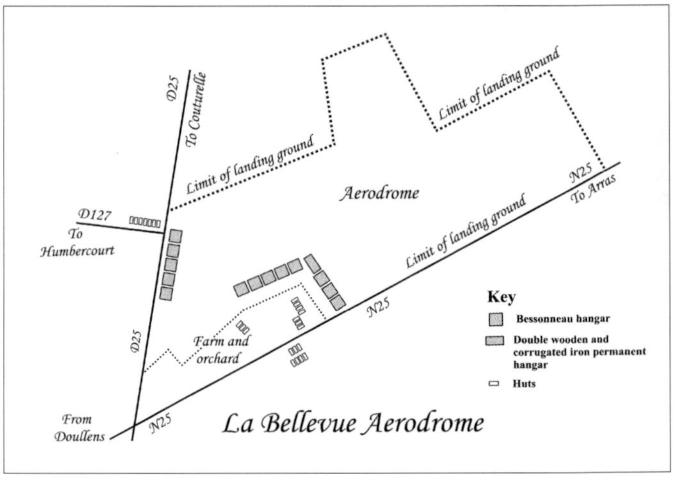

18th March

Flying was not possible until after 17.00 when four test and practice flights were carried out:

FSL AL Thorne	N3187	at 17.00
	40 minute practice flight	
FCdr EW Norton	N3195	at 17.00 – local test
FCdr EW Norton	N3187	at 18.50 – local test
FSL RK Slater	N3198	
	machine crashed and wrecked	

19th March

Weather unfavourable, no flying possible.

20th March

Weather unfavourable, no flying possible.

21st March

Weather unfavourable, no flying until 16.05:

SCdr Petre	N3195	at 16.05

test flight, the engine was bad and the machine flew with its left wing down.

22nd March

SCdr Petre carried out a climbing test in N3187 at 13.55, he regarded 5000 feet in 5 minutes and 20 seconds as unsatisfactory. He also reported that the engine was not giving its full revs and that the rudder was very stiff.

At 16.00, AFCdr Allen flew Nieuport 17Bis N3190 in a test against a 110hp Nieuport and a Bristol F2A. He reported that the 17Bis out-climbed both.

The accommodation huts at La Bellevue Aerodrome were situated within an orchard belonging to the local farm. This shot taken after a light fall of snow gives the camp a picturesque appearance. *Courtesy Fleet Air Arm Museum*

A less photogenic shot of the accommodation at La Bellevue. *Courtesy Justin Young*

23rd March

Three test flights were carried out:

FCdr CT MacLaren N3204 at 09.20
weather test, the cloud cover started at 1000 feet.
FSL AL Thorne N3197 at 14.25
engine test, satisfactory
AFCdr Allen N3200 at 14.30
machine test, ok

The weather improved sufficiently in the evening to allow FCdr Norton to lead most of C flight on a 30 minute formation practice at 19.15, Winter missing the practice.

The Flight structure at this juncture was as follows:

A Flight

FCdr CT MacLaren, Flight Commander
FLt BHP De Roeper
FLt LC Keeble
FSL JdeC Paynter
FSL GL Hartgill
FSL OJ Gagnier

B Flight

FCdr ADW Allen, Flight Commander
FSL P Wood
FSL RK Slater
FSL D Plaistowe
FSL CL Bailey
FLt FP Reeves

C Flight

FCdr EW Norton, Flight Commander
FSL RR Winter
FSL AL Thorne
FSL AHV Fletcher
FSL AE Hall
FSL H Lawson

24th March

MacLaren and Allen had their flights practising formation flying during the day, A Flight at 07.10, B Flight at 10.00 and A Flight again at 15.20. All of the pilots were reporting the status of their aircraft in a very critical manner:

FCdr CT MacLaren N3204 at 07.10
formation practice
FSL JdeC Paynter N3190 - formation practice
FLt LC Keeble N3203 - formation practice
FSL GL Hartgill N3191 - formation practice
FSL OJ Gagnier N3189 - formation practice
FSL AHV Fletcher N3192 - formation practice,
engine trouble (slight)
FCdr ADW Allen N3206 at 10.00
formation practice
FSL OJ Gagnier N3189 - formation practice
FSL D Plaistowe N3200 - formation practice
FSL CL Bailey N3199 - formation practice,
engine satisfactory, rev counter out of action

FCdr MacLaren N3196 at 15.20
formation practice

ABOVE: N3196 and N3203 are identifiable in this line of immaculate Nieuports. N3203 was delivered from Dunkerque on the 22nd March 1917 and later carried the A Flight identification number "3". N3203 was FLt LC Keeble's normal mount until 22nd April 1917, thereafter being flown by FSL AMcB Walton who crashed it on the 20th May 1917. N3196 was normally flown by FLt BHP De Roeper and later carried the A Flight identification number "2". *Courtesy JMB/GSL Collection*

FSL GL Hartgill	N3191 - formation practice, engine now satisfactory
FSL OJ Gagnier	N3189 - formation practice, timing to be checked
FLt LC Keeble	N3203 - formation practice, engine vibrating
FSL JdeC Paynter	N3190 - formation practice, engine satisfactory

MacLaren reported that A Flight kept better formation during their morning practice. As a counterpoint to MacLaren's report, Hartgill felt that his first formation practice was not very satisfactory and he reported yet another bad landing. During his second practice he recorded that he was able keep better formation but was not yet acceptable.

De Roeper collected N3206 from the depot at 07.50.

Several test and practice flights were also carried out:

FCdr EW Norton	N3187 at 07.10 machine and engine satisfactory
FSL JdeC Paynter	N3190 at 10.00 - practice, machine and engine satisfactory
FSL GL Hartgill	N3191 at 10.38 engine test, unsatisfactory

25th March

Fighting practice was introduced, pilots pairing up to attack and defend. Keeble and Paynter, Hartgill and Gagnier and Allen and Bailey teamed up for the exercises. Most of the pilots reported problems with their machines.

Mock fights were also carried out with the Bristol F2As of No.48 Squadron RFC which shared the aerodrome at La Bellevue.[1]

A number of test and practice flights were also carried out:

FSL AL Thorne N3197 at 09.27
test, eng. revs 1200, quite true, best climbing speed 40 knots
FCdr CT MacLaren N3204 at 11.15
engine revs 1150 climbing, compass out of order

FCdr ADW Allen	N3199 at 12.00 pressure from engine not working
FLt LC Keeble	N3202 at 15.00 engine unsatisfactory
FSL D Plaistowe	N3200 at 15.00 – practice

FCdr ADW Allen N3203 at 15.00 – everything OK
FCdr ADW Allen N3206 at 16.00 – everything OK
FCdr ADW Allen N3204 at 17.00 – engine 1200 revs

26th March

Bad weather again interrupted the squadron's preparations.

27th March

FCdr Norton led C Flight on a formation practice at 09.40.

BELOW: No.48 Squadron RFC shared La Bellevue Aerodrome, and No.6 Squadron's pilots occasionally practiced attacking 48 Squadron's Bristol Fighters. Bristol F2a serial A3322 flown by 2Lt H Davies and 2Lt RSL Worsley was shot down on the 13th April 1917. *Courtesy EF Cheesman* BOTTOM: Another example of a No.48 Squadron RFC Bristol F2a. *Courtesy EF Cheesman*

FLt Reeves had been sent to Dunkerque several days earlier to pick up a new Nieuport. The depot finally released the repaired N3202 and Reeves ferried it back to Bellevue at 12.55.

28th March

B and C Flights both carried out formation practice flights in the morning, Hall flying N3197 damaged his machine slightly when he had to make a forced landing at Sus-St.-Leger. Many of the pilots were still reporting numerous problems with their machines:

FCdr ADW Allen N3206 at 09.30
formation practice, engine revs bad and pressure bad
FLt FP Reeves N3207 at 09.30 - formation practice, safety belt defective
FSL D Plaistowe N3200 at 09.30 formation practice, machine ok
FSL AE Hall N3197 at 09.30
formation practice, forced landing at Sus St.-Leger, damaged machine slightly.
FCdr EW Norton N3187 at 09.30 formation practice
FSL AL Thorne N3205 at 09.25 - formation practice, right wing down
FSL AHV Fletcher N3192 at 09.26 formation practice
FSL RR Winter N3195 at 09.25 formation practice
FSL H Lawson N3194 at 09.28 formation practice

SCdr Petre carried out a test flight in N3206 at 15.10 to evaluate the effectiveness of a new carburettor adjustment. He reported the machine to be much more satisfactory.

29th March

The weather closed down all flying on the 29th.

30th March

The weather continued to interfere with flying, however FCdr Allen was able to make a 25 minute test flight in N3206 at 17.00. He reported that the machine climbed to 8700 feet in 10 minutes.

Canadian pilot FSL Oliver Joseph Gagnier from Montreal. Gagnier served with No.6 Squadron until the 11th May 1917, when he was shot down at Villers Outreaux. He was seriously injured with gunshot wounds to arm and chest and had to have his left arm amputated. OJ Gagnier claimed one victory with No.6 Squadron, an Albatros scout shot down to the northwest of Fresnoy le Grande on the 10th May 1917. *Courtesy Justin Young*

31st March

The weather continued to make flying difficult. Allen was able to make a 17 minute test flight on the last day of the month, reporting that Nieuport N3202 managed to climb to 7000 feet in 7 1/2 minutes.

Hartgill was admitted to hospital for treatment to a hernia and whilst remaining on the squadron's books for several weeks, would not return to the squadron.

• • •

April 1917

This was "Bloody April", a period of crisis for the RFC when losses of men and machines reached disastrous proportions. From the perspective of No.6 Squadron RNAS, the air offensive for the Battle Of Arras commenced on the 4th April and the British Front ran from Givenchy-en-Gohelle to Croiselles. The key objective was the capture of Vimy Ridge, a task given to the First Army, with the Third Army attacking elsewhere along the front.

No.6 Squadron, along with No.29 Squadron RFC and No.60 Squadron RFC, all flying Nieuport scouts, were attached to 13 Wing 3 Brigade in support of the Third Army. The duties of the RFC Nieuport scout squadrons were offensive patrols and attacks on kite balloons, No.6 Squadron was assigned offensive patrols.

Losses amongst the Nieuport squadrons of 13 Wing 3 Brigade were heavy, No.6 Squadron suffered six crashes between the 4th April and the start of the infantry attack on the 9th, four of these resulted in total loss of the aircraft. The squadron was also plagued with engine, fuel and gun problems.

By the 16th April the British offensive had ended and General Nivelle launched the French attack in the south, this collapsed disastrously after a promising start and the British army was forced to keep up a pointless attack along their front to relieve pressure on the collapsing French armies.

1st April

The bad weather experienced at the end of March continued into April, restricting flying on the 1st to a couple of test flights:

FSL RK Slater	N3202	at 10.20 – test, engine ok
FSL AL Thorne	N3205	at 13.35 – test, engine ok, truing up correct

2nd April

The bad weather closed down all flying.

3rd April

The weather cleared sufficiently for Allen, Slater, Plaistowe and Thorne to make a total of eleven flights to Le Hammeau in order to practice firing at a ground target.

Five test flights were carried out during the afternoon and evening:

FCdr EW Norton	N3197	at 15.05 – rigging bad, engine very good
FSL JdeC Paynter	N3194	at 15.30 – ok
FCdr EW Norton	N3197	at 18.00 – ok
SCdr JJ Petre	N3197	at 18.30 – ok
FSL AE Hall	N3197	at 19.00 - ok

New pilot FSL MR Kingsford arrived at the squadron.

4th April

The weather closed in again on the 4th April, the planned start of the air offensive of the Battle Of Arras.

FCdr Allen was able to carry out a test flight in N3206 at 17.50, reporting that the machine was OK.

FCdr Norton led a C Flight patrol off at 18.50 but reported that the weather was too thick over Arras to continue.

5th April

The squadron was able to fly five patrols on the 5th, however many of the pilots reported problems with the synchronised Vickers gun.

Allen led B Flight on a patrol at 09.30, Bailey fired at an enemy machine from the extreme range of 300 to 400 yards, the enemy aircraft dived away unscathed. Allen reported that N3206's engine revs were very bad and the gun would not fire at height, Slater's machine, N3202 suffered from a failed rev counter.

Norton led C Flight on a patrol at 11.20, the patrol being "shadowed" by a hostile machine which kept out of range.

MacLaren led A Flight on a 30 minute practice formation patrol at 13.00. Paynter damaged the elevator and plane of N3190 on landing.

A Flight carried out a full patrol at 14.05. Gagnier in N3189 became separated from the flight over Arras and eventually landed at Bus. MacLaren in N3207 had the engine cut out and then suffered from petrol flooding out of the release valve. Paynter and De Roeper were unsure of their position and dropped below the cloud cover between Douai and Arras and subsequently came under heavy anti-aircraft and ground fire. Kingsford flying N3191, suffered from an engine failure and crashed from 200 feet, Kingsford was injured and hospitalised.

Norton led C Flight out again at 15.08. At 17.00 when to the west of Douai, Norton attacked hostile machines from 20 yards range and claimed one Albatros scout shot down in flames and another spinning rapidly out of control. Thorne engaged an enemy machine at 50 yards range which fell away out of control. After the combat, Norton flying N3187 made a forced landing at Bouque Maison at 17.15, damaging the lower plane. Winter landed beside his Flight Commander and Norton used Winter's Nieuport to return to La Bellevue, leaving Winter to return by road.

Allen led B Flight on a patrol at 16.50. Wood had to abandon the patrol with gun stoppages and Gagnier also experienced problems with his Vickers gun. At 18.45 near Arras, Allen was attacked by an enemy scout, during the engagement his gun suffered a stoppage but the enemy scout transferred its attentions to Slater. Slater, flying N3202, was shot down and made a prisoner of war.

New pilots FLt GD Kirkpatrick and FSL AMcB Walton arrived at the squadron.

A number of test flights were carried out during the day:

FCdr CT MacLaren N3204 at 09.30
test, engine not satisfactory, Aldis Sight vibrating
FSL AE Hall N3197 at 10.10
test, tail skid broke on landing.
FLt OJ Gagnier N3189 at 10.10 – test, ok
FSL JdeC Paynter N3190 at 11.55
gun test, Vickers not firing above 9000 ft
FSL Kirkpatrick N3192 at 18.30
practice, tail heavy

6th April

At 08.40, FCdr MacLaren led A Flight on an offensive patrol. MacLaren's machine, N3204, suffered from failure of both its mechanical and hand pressurisation systems, Paynter's Vickers gun failed and Gagnier suffered a gun stoppage and damaged N3189 upon landing.

Reeves and Wood flew a line patrol at 09.40, the patrol had to be abandoned when Reeves discovered a defective wire on his gun control.

Allen and Plaistowe flew an uneventful line patrol at 10.35.

Three test and practice flights were carried out:

FCdr ADW Allen N3194 at 09.00 – test, ok
FSL AMcB Walton N3207 at 11.40 - practice, left wing heavy
FSL AMcB Walton N3207 at 15.00 - test, ok

7th April

FCdr Norton led C Flight on a patrol at 12.15 to the district around Douai. Two hostile aircraft were seen but the patrol reported that visibility was poor due to the cloud cover. Lawson flying N3194 ran low on fuel and landed at Aux le Chateau at 14.30.

The A Flight Commander, Colin Temple MacLaren, sitting in front of his troublesome Nieuport 17Bis, N3204. Not really suited to scout operations and an ineffective flight leader, MacLaren was posted to the Walmer Defence Flight in August 1917. He was promoted to Squadron Commander and became the Commanding Officer of No.6 Squadron when it was reformed as a day bomber squadron on the 1st January 1918. *Courtesy Justin Young*

A Flight carried out a patrol at 14.00. MacLaren's machine, N3204, had previously exhibited problems with fuel pressurisation and he reported that the pressure system failed again during the patrol.

Uneventful line patrols were carried out by Wood and Reeves at 15.10 and by Allen and Plaistowe at 15.30.

Thorne collected the repaired N3187 from Bouque Maison and returned at 15.25.

De Roeper and Paynter carried out an offensive patrol over Lens - Douai - Arras at 17.25. They reported seeing an aerial battle but were too far away to offer assistance.

FCdr Norton led an offensive patrol over Lens – Douai – Arras at 18.10. Norton was involved in an indecisive engagement with an enemy machine.

Lawson returned from Aux le Chateau at 19.15.

Two test and practice flights were carried out during the day:

FSL AMcB Walton N3199 at 15.15 – practice, ok
SCdr JJ Petre N3206 at 19.15 – engine and gun test, satisfactory

8th April

Three patrols were flown on the morning of the 8th.

FCdr Allen led B Flight on a line patrol at 06.00, several of the pilots again reporting trouble with their guns. Plaistow flying N3200 suffered damage to his propeller and Reeves in N3207 suffered a gun stoppage.

C Flight carried out an offensive patrol at 06.20. Norton observed anti-aircraft fire and upon investigation discovered two hostile machines but was unable to overtake them.

A Flight carried out an offensive patrol at 11.30, the pilots were again beset by gun problems. MacLaren's machine, N3204, again suffered from complete failure of its fuel pressurisation system.

9th April

The infantry attack at Arras was initiated on the 9th April but the weather presented difficult conditions for flying. Rain and snow flurries combined with a gale at altitude caused most offensive patrols to be abandoned, however, C Flight managed to perform a distant patrol when FCdr Norton led De Roeper, Thorne and Paynter to Cambrai. Norton shot down a scout at Cambrai at 11.45, supported by FSL Thorne, Norton dived on the enemy machine at 9000 feet and followed it down to 6000 feet at which point it was seen to fall out of control and was observed to crash. Fifteen minutes later, Norton and Thorne were attacked by 4 scouts, Norton rolled and got underneath the tail of one of his attackers and fired both guns hitting the fuselage whereupon the enemy machine fell away completely out of control. Norton then turned his attention to the remaining enemy machines but they dived away and escaped. The two successes were tempered by death and injury caused by the storm. Thorne was killed when he crashed N3205. Paynter was injured and hospitalised when he crashed N3190 at Hinges and Norton was injured when he crashed N3187 at Maricourt.

10th April

The 10th was described as "a day of wild weather" in HA Jones' "The War in the Air", contemporary reports described the weather as a gale of wind with frequent snow and hail storms. The weather effectively grounded all aircraft on the 10th.

11th April

RNAS Headquarters had come to the conclusion that No.6 Squadron was not performing to expectations and not ready for battle. A combination of too few pilots, high aircraft losses and the slow delivery and poor performance of replacement aircraft led to a decision to transfer the squadron to a quieter front at St. Quentin and replace them with a more capable battle hardened squadron. Thus, on the 11th, No.6 Squadron moved to Chipilly Aerodrome with command transferring to 14 Wing 4 Brigade. Their role in 13 Wing 3 Brigade was taken by the Sopwith Triplane equipped No.1 Squadron RNAS.

NOTES

[1] In his logbook, FSL Hartgill described this as a, "huffing match with RFC Bristols".

CHAPTER FOUR

WORKING FOR THE RFC - 14 WING, 4 BRIGADE

RNAS Headquarters was less than impressed by No.6 Squadron's performance and state of readiness. On the 15th April Wing Captain Lambe wrote to the RNAS Liaison Officer with the RFC, Wing Commander Chambers, informing him that to get the squadron back up to strength he would be sending a complete flight from No.11 Squadron under acting Squadron Commander Draper. FCdr Allen who was suffering from nervous exhaustion would be removed, as would FLt LC Keeble, another pilot not standing up well to scout operations.

The reinforcements from No.11 Squadron were all, with one exception, experienced pilots that had previously served with No.3 Wing, the strategic bombing group based at Luxieul and Ochey.

11th April

The squadron moved to Chipilly aerodrome and came under the control of 14 Wing 4 Brigade on the 11th. After the recent losses, only thirteen aircraft were available, eleven of these completed the transfer from Bellevue to Chipilly without trouble. De Roeper in N3196 made a forced landing at Bailleul, the aerodrome of No.52 Squadron RFC and Reeves in N3207 landed at Meoul and damaged a wheel which delayed his arrival at Chipilly by several hours.

12th April

The weather was initially bright with high winds, turning to snow and rain in the afternoon.

One test flight was carried out:

FCdr Allen	N3206 at 11.00 propeller unsatisfactory.[1]

There was considerable concern that the squadron was short of both pilots and aircraft. To remedy this problem Wing Captain Lambe wrote to Wing Commander SDA Grey of No.5 Wing:

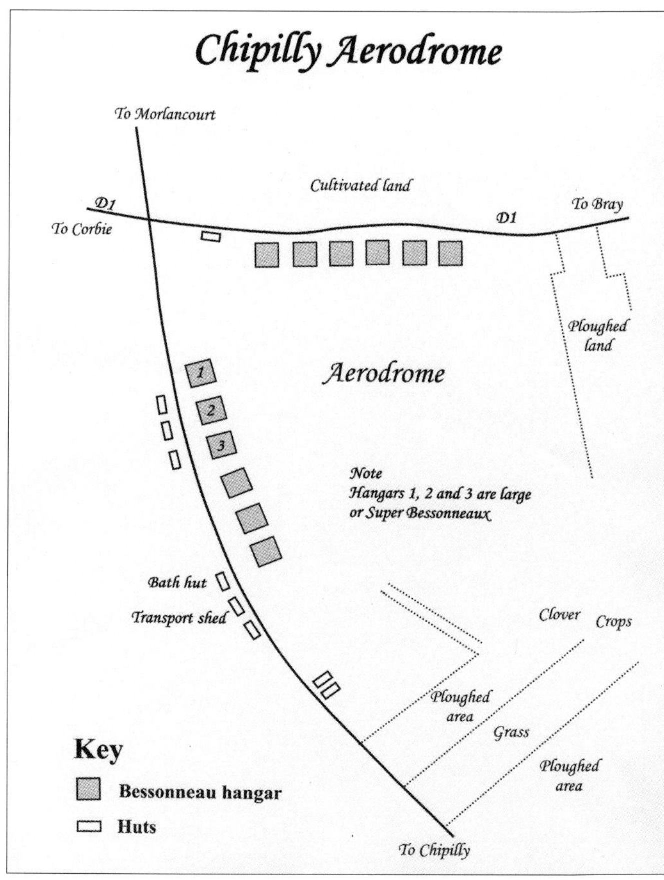

From: Senior Officer
R.N.A.S. Dunkerque
12th April 1917
for C.O. No.11 Squadron

To: Commanding Officer
No.5 Wing

Confidential
Owing to casualties, one complete Flight of pilots and one spare pilot, making a total of seven in all, will be required to join Naval Squadron No.6. I propose that Flight Lieutenant MacLennan's Flight should be sent and made up to strength.

Also, three 130h.p. Clerget Nieuports will be required from No.11 Squadron to bring No.6 up to strength.

Although I realise this will seriously interfere the training and completion of No.11 Squadron yet this course is absolutely necessary in the best interest of the country and the Squadron will eventually have preference over the other Squadrons here, after No.10 Squadron has been completed.

The names of the seven pilots to be transferred to Naval Squadron No.6 are to be forwarded to me as soon as possible.

Wing Captain

The Officers Mess at Chipilly. *Courtesy Fleet Air Arm Museum*

A shot that proves decking and a pergola are not new concepts. Another very poor quality photograph shows this structure at the end of the Mess being constructed by the squadron's officers. *Courtesy Justin Young*

13th April

This was Friday the 13th, an unlucky day for the Squadron Commander, JJ Petre who was killed at 11.55 when his Nieuport, N3206, broke up whilst diving at a practice ground target at Dernacourt.

One of the squadron officers described the event:

"The accident occurred at 11.50 a.m. yesterday; April 13th, when he went up to practise firing at a target on the ground. He did one dive from about 1500 feet to about 200 and appeared to flatten out rather quickly. He then climbed up again, did a very steep bank and then started to dive again. After diving two or three hundred feet the machine broke in the air and the result was fatal. I do not think there was ever a C.O. who was admired and liked more".

SCdr Jack Petre was buried at Dernacourt but later re-interred in the French Cemetery at Cerisy Gailly.

Earlier in the morning, at 08.15, FCdr Allen led B Flight on the squadron's first patrol from Chipilly. The patrol was completely uneventful.

At 10.09, De Roeper returned from his forced landing at Bailleul having turned the journey into a line patrol. He reported heavy anti-aircraft fire with a piece of shrapnel passing through his machine.

At 12.20, Keeble collected N3209 from No.2 AD at Candas.

14th April

No flights were carried out on the 14th.

15th April

SCdr CD Breese arrived at Chipilly to take command of the squadron. Up until the 13th April, Breese had been in command of No.10 Squadron which was in the process of "working up" to combat readiness at Furnes in Belgium.

Bailey took the recently delivered N3209 back to No.2 AD. He complained that fuel pressure trouble and mist had caused him to land several times.

Wing Commander Grey replied to Wing Captain Lambe with a list of pilots to be transferred and this enabled Lambe to write to Wing Commander Chambers, the RNAS liaison at RFC Head Quarters:

From: Senior Officer, R.N.A.S. Dunkerque
To: Wing Commander Chambers RN, H.Q. R.F.C.
Date: 15th April 1917, HQ ref 543

With a view to completing Naval Squadron No.6, I intend to send a complete Flight from No.11 Squadron under Acting Squadron Commander Draper who will undertake the duties of Flight Commander of the Flight.

The remaining officers will be:

Flight Lieutenant MacLennan
Flight Sub Lieutenant Redpath
Flight Sub Lieutenant Masson[2]
Flight Sub Lieutenant Edwards
Flight Sub Lieutenant Beasley
Flight Sub Lieutenant Macgregor

With Flight Sub Lieutenant Macgregor and one of the existing pilots as spare pilots. For Naval Squadron No.6.

This being so, Flight Lieutenant Allen will be withdrawn[3]*, leaving Flight Commanders MacLaren and Norton as the other two. Flight Lieutenant Keeble*[4] *is also to be returned to Dunkerque on being replaced.*

Three, or possibly four of these pilots will fly down machines and the remainder will proceed by road.

Wing Captain

SCdr JJ Petre was killed on the 13th April 1917 whilst practicing diving at a ground target at Dernacourt, his machine broke up in the air, probably due to failure of the lower wing (see Appendix K). This photograph shows the remains of the Clerget engine after it was recovered from the wreck of N3206. *Courtesy Justin Young*

16th April

Eight test and practice flights were carried out:

SCdr Breese N3193 at 09.35 – test

FLt Keeble N3203 at 11.45 – gun test, both guns fired well but Vickers gun put a bullet through the propeller.

FCdr MacLaren N3204 at 11.40
Lewis gun satisfactory

FSL Plaistowe N3200 at 13.50 – engine satisfactory, gun jammed with cross feed after considerable amount of firing.

FSL Wood N3193 at 13.55
gun test, satisfactory

FSL Lawson N3194 at 14.45
practice, satisfactory

FSL Winter N3195 at 15.10 – target practice, Vickers fired well, Lewis jammed.

Another view of the engine recovered from Petre's fatal crash. The Clerget's crankshaft can be seen to be bent. *Courtesy Fleet Air Arm Museum*

FCdr Allen	N3207 at15.45 gun test, gun irregular

SCdr CD Breese was a very tall man, he must have found the cramped cockpit of the Nieuport 17Bis quite restrictive and uncomfortable.

The first replacement pilot from No.11 Squadron, FSL PE Beasley, arrived at Chipilly.

17th April

No flying due to unsuitable weather.

18th April

No war flying due to unsuitable weather.

19th April

Bailey carried out a solo line patrol at 06.30, he reported that mist and clouds forced him to fly at 800 feet. He returned at 07.45 as conditions were too difficult to continue the patrol.

Keeble carried out a solo line patrol at 09.20, he reported light anti-aircraft and machine gun fire near St. Quentin.

During the course of the morning, one practice and three test flights were carried out:

FSL Bailey	N3199 at 08.55 – engine test, satisfactory
FSL Fletcher	N3192 at 09.23 – practice
FLt De Roeper	N3196 at 11.15 – machine and engine test, satisfactory
AFCdr Allen	N3207 at 11.17 – gun bad, engine good

Gagnier took off at 08.15 in N3189 to deliver despatches. The machine developed engine trouble after 30 minutes and Gagnier was forced to land at Matigny where the problem was diagnosed as faulty high tension leads.

FSL ST Edwards, another of the promised 3 Wing/No.11 Squadron pilots, arrived at the Chipilly. Five of his colleagues, ASCdr C Draper, FSL RF Redpath, FSL NM Macgregor, FLt GG MacLennan and FSL GLE Stevens, carried out test flights of N3101, N5861, N3100, N5860 and N3186 at the St. Pol depot. N5860 and N5861 were manufactured by the British Nieuport Company at Cricklewood and differed in small details from the French built machines then in use by No.6 Squadron. The British built machines were readily identifiable by being finished in PC10 brown dope instead of the French built machines' aluminium doped finish.

Squadron Commander Charles Dempster Breese was transferred from No.10 Squadron, which was in the process of "working up", to take over No.6 Squadron after the death of Squadron Commander JJ Petre. Breese held a Naval Engineering rank and had transferred to the RNAS in 1915. After the squadron was disbanded on the 27th August 1917, Breese held a number of administrative jobs and was granted a permanent commission in the RAF. Breese achieved the rank of Air Vice Marshal in the RAF and died in 1941 in a Coastal Command Lockheed Hudson that crashed on Wick Aerodrome. *Courtesy Justin Young*

20th April

Draper, Redpath, Macgregor, MacLennan and Stevens, who were still attached to No.11 Squadron, ferried their new Nieuport machines to Petite Synthe.

Back at Chipilly, four solo line patrols were carried out as follows:

FLt Keeble at 06.30, the patrol was completely uneventful.

FLt De Roeper at 09.30, the patrol was abandoned after an hour due to engine trouble.

FLt Reeves at 11.30, the visibility had deteriorated and the patrol was uneventful.

ABOVE: The much photographed Nieuport 17Bis N3195. This photograph presents a puzzle, being apparently marked with the A Flight Identification number "1". Records show that this machine was not flown by A Flight, is it possible that N3195 was photographed before its more familiar number "16" had been finished? *Courtesy SK Taylor*

BELOW: Another photograph of N3195 in its more familiar state marked as "16" of C Flight with a red cowl and red wheel covers. Flown regularly by FSL Rupert Randolph Winter between 27th March and 29th April 1917. Winter claimed an Albatros scout as out of control at Guise on the 29th April 1917, but was badly shot up by ground fire. *Author's collection*

FSL Kirkpatrick at 17.00, the visibility was still bad and no enemy aircraft were seen.

Gagnier returned from his forced landing at Matigny at 15.20.

The squadron's pilots spent the day carrying out test and practice flights, whilst SCdr Breese and his senior Flight Commander, EW Norton paid a visit to the aerodrome at Flez which would shortly become the Squadron's new base:

FLt Reeves	N3207 at 09.25 gun test, satisfactory
FCdr MacLaren	N3204 at 09.25 gun test, Vickers gun satisfactory
SCdr Breese	N3194 at 09.30 practice, engine running well
FSL Walton	N3200 at 09.45 gun test, satisfactory
FCdr Norton	N3208 at 10.00 test, satisfactory
AFCdr Allen	N3200 at 10.10 practice, satisfactory
FSL Lawson	N3194 at 10.10 practice, satisfactory
FSL Kirkpatrick	N3197 at 10.40 practice, satisfactory
AFCdr Allen	N3199 at 11.00 - gun test, gear went out of commission
FSL Fletcher	N3192 at 15.10 - practice
FSL Wood	N3193 at 15.45 - test, engine and machine satisfactory
AFCdr Allen	N3195 at 16.00 test, satisfactory

SCdr Breese and FCdr Norton flew from Chipilly to Flez at 14.00 and returned at 15.25.

21st April

The visibility was very bad on the 21st, Winter attempted to carry out a line patrol at 06.05 but was forced to return after 25 minutes.

22nd April

The remaining new pilots from No.11 Squadron, Draper, MacLennan, Stevens, Macgregor and Redpath arrived at Chipilly having flown down from Petite Synthe in their new

Posing for the camera at Chipilly in Navy Blue, FLt BHP De Roeper, FCdr CT MacLaren, SCdr CD Breese and FLt LC Keeble. *Courtesy Fleet Air Arm Museum*

Nieuports which had been collected from the depot on the 19th April.

Keeble carried out an uneventful solo line patrol at 06.35.

Allen carried out a brief weather test at 09.25.

At 08.15, Gagnier ferried dispatches to the French aerodrome at Ham, returning at 11.30.

FCdr Norton led C Flight on a line patrol at 08.00. Visibility was poor and the Flight became dispersed, Winter being the only pilot able to keep station with Norton. Bailey abandoned the patrol after 8 minutes due to overfilling of his fuel tank. Kirkpatrick patrolled alone but damaged the starboard lower plane of N3197 upon landing. Fletcher and Lawson both patrolled on their own, Lawson being forced to land at La Lovie to refuel. Norton and Winter landed at Mesmil.

Walton carried out a solo line patrol at 09.40 and landed at Bellevue.

FCdr MacLaren led A Flight on a line patrol between Savy and Bertincourt at midday. The visibility had improved but no hostile aircraft were seen, however, an observation balloon was seen to fall in flames near Bertincourt.

Kirkpatrick carried out an uneventful solo line patrol at 13.40 and another at 17.00. The visibility had deteriorated and was described as very poor.

At 17.45, A Flight carried out a line patrol covering Bapaume, Roisel and St. Quentin. The cloud base was at 1000 feet and the visibility poor. No enemy aircraft were seen.

Several of the squadron's Nieuports were supplied from Paris with French cockades on the wings. These aircraft were used with these markings until such time as the national markings could be corrected. In this photograph, Nieuport 17Bis number "2" is clearly marked with French Cockades. This 17Bis, N3196, was FLt BHP De Roeper's regular machine from the 7th April to 13th May 1917. *Courtesy EF Cheesman*

On the 13th April 1917, N3196 was damaged by anti-aircraft fire during a line patrol. A new port top plane was provided from the RFC depot's stock of standard Nieuport 17 spares, this gave N3196 a somewhat bizarre appearance with an overall aluminium dope finish but with the port top plane finished in brown PC10. The new wing carried British cockades and in this photograph it can be seen that the starboard wing's French cockade is in the process of being over-painted with the correct British colours. This view shows that the Flight identification number was repeated on the top decking of this particular machine. *Courtesy EF Cheesman*

A Morane Saulnier type AC from Escadrille N.49 visiting No.6 Squadron at Chipilly. The Escadrille's emblem of a golden pennant outlined in red can be seen on the Morane's fuselage. *Courtesy EF Cheesman*

Another visitor from Escadrille N.49, a SPAD S7. It was not uncommon for neighbouring squadrons to visit for aircraft type recognition and familiarisation purposes. *Courtesy Justin Young*

23rd April

Bailey carried out a line patrol at 09.30 and landed at Flez with pressure trouble. He observed an enemy machine at 10000 feet when he was flying at 4000 feet.

Edwards carried out a line patrol in N3200 at 10.25, the gun suffered a stoppage and the pressure system was faulty. Edwards crashed and overturned N3200 on landing.

Fletcher carried out an uneventful line patrol at 13.35.

SCdr Breese flew despatches to Guizancourt at 13.35 and returned at 16.25.

At 14.30, FCdr Norton led Bailey and Winter on a patrol to protect the kite balloon line between Germaine and Villevaque.

ASCdr Draper led Stevens, Macgregor, Redpath and MacLennan on a line patrol at 18.30 to gain familiarisation with the local landmarks. Many aircraft were observed but were too far away to identify.

Four test flights were carried out:

FSL Macgregor	N3100 at 11.10 practice, machine left wing down
FSL Redpath	N5861 at 11.25 gun test, Vickers jammed
FSL Stevens	N3184 at 13.40 gun test, top gun out of position
FSL Wood	N3193 at 19.20 engine test, satisfactory

24th April

Macgregor carried out an uneventful solo line patrol at 05.30.

FCdr Norton led C Flight on a two hour line patrol at 08.00. Redpath accompanied the patrol in N5861 but again experienced gun problems.

Walton carried out a solo line patrol at 10.00, five enemy aircraft were observed flying 4000 feet higher than the Nieuport.

Stevens carried out an uneventful line patrol at 13.35.

At 15.30, Edwards collected N3102 from No.2 AD at Candas.. During the short flight to Chipilly, the Nieuport's engine failed and Edwards made a forced landing on an RFC aerodrome near Doullens. A faulty magneto was diagnosed as the source of the problem.

Nieuport 17Bis N3101 was tested at the St. Pol depot by ASCdr Draper on 19th April 1917. N3101 was Draper's regular B Flight machine and is seen here prior to being painted with the two red bands around the fuselage that denoted the B Flight Commander's machine. Draper claimed one scout crashed and another out of control at midday on the 6th June 1917. *Courtesy EF Cheesman*

OPPOSITE: A well known group photograph of the pilots drafted in from No.11 Squadron to bring No.6 Squadron back up to strength: Back Row, L to R: FSL ST Edwards, FSL NM Macgregor, FSL PE Beasley, FSL GLE Stevens, ASCdr C Draper. Middle Row, L to R: FSL RF Redpath, FLt GG MacLennan. Front Row: "Joey" (Draper's dog) Draper, MacLennan, Edwards, Macgregor, Beasley and Redpath were all veterans from the Royal Naval Air Service's strategic bombing group, No.3 Wing. *Courtesy JMB/GSL Collection*

ABOVE: Draper's B Flight, from left to right, N3101 marked with two red stripes on the fuselage, unknown, N3186 marked "12" plus a diagonal red stripe, N3200 marked "9" and N3199 marked "8". *Courtesy EF Cheesman*

ABOVE: A general view across the aerodrome at Chipilly showing three machines from C Flight in the foreground and two from B Flight in the background. The red bands on Draper's aircraft N3101 can be clearly seen. At this stage, the C Flight machines do not have red cowls and wheel covers. *Courtesy Les Rogers*

BELOW: FLt ST Edwards, one of the new pilots sourced from No.11 Squadron, made his first flight from Chipilly in Nieuport 17Bis N3200 on the 23rd April 1917. The aircraft's fuel pressure system was faulty resulting in erratic engine control. Edwards overturned the machine when landing. *Courtesy Les Rogers*

MacLennan carried out a line patrol at 18.30. No enemy aircraft were observed.

Four test flights were carried out:

FCdr MacLaren	N3204 at 17.30
	gun test, satisfactory
FLt Reeves	N3203 at 18.20
	gun test, jammed in No.3 position
FSL Walton	N3196 at 18.10

test, engine missing, exhaust valve stuck

FSL Redpath	N5861
	gun test following remedial work

25th April

Kirkpatrick carried out a line patrol at 06.10, no enemy aircraft were encountered.

Five test flights were carried out during the day:

FSL Wood	N3193 at 08.52

test, engine unsatisfactory, gun satisfactory.

FSL Walton	N3196 at 09.30

test, engine satisfactory, gun jammed

FSL Stevens	N3186 at 11.50
	test, engine unsatisfactory
FSL Stevens	N3186 at 14.45
	gun test, gun jammed
FSL Redpath	N5861 - test

The squadron was in the process of moving further south and nearer the lines to a new aerodrome at Flez. Flez was located approximately 3 1/2 miles due west of St. Quentin and was, in reality, an aerodrome complex with several flying fields. Situated close to the ruins of the village of Guizancourt, it was a common occurrence for period documents to make reference to the unofficial name of Guizancourt Aerodrome. Somewhat

ABOVE: N3102 was collected from the RFC's No.2AD at Candas on the 24th April 1917. Cockades were painted on the fuselage, and appear to have remained whilst the machine was in service. There is no evidence that N3102 was ever marked with a red Flight identification number. FSL ST Edwards flew N3102 from 24th April to 13th June 1917, during this time he experienced more than his fair share of unreliability. *Courtesy JMB/GSL Collection*

BELOW: Nieuport 17Bis N3203 was marked with the A Flight identification number "3", delivered on the 22nd March 1917, it was regularly used by FLt LC Keeble from the 24th March to the 22nd April 1917. FSL AMcB Walton took over N3203 on the 30th April and flew it until the 20th May 1917 when he crashed and wrote it off at Flez. An unidentified British built Nieuport 17Bis can be seen behind N3203. *Author's collection*

unusually, the squadron moved its aircraft over a period of several days.

SCdr Breese flew to Flez at 13.30 and returned to Chipilly at 15.10.

C Flight transferred to Flez at 19.30.

26th April

Reeves flew despatches from Chipilly to Flez at 09.30, returning to Chipilly at 10.30.

Edwards carried out two test flights:

FSL Edwards — N3102 at 09.00
gun unsatisfactory
FSL Edwards — N3102 at 09.15
gun unsatisfactory

B Flight transferred from Chipilly to Flez at 15.40.

The reformed B Flight carried out their first full patrol from Flez, this proved to be uneventful, with the exception that Edwards experienced a gun stoppage.

An escort mission set off at 18.30. The mission was a washout, Redpath reported that the pilots had been called too late to make contact.

27th April

Edwards carried out two further unsatisfactory gun tests in N3102, recording the tests as "NBG" usually taken to mean "*No Bloody Good*".

28th April

Two test and practice flights were carried out:

FSL Edwards — N3102 - gun test, satisfactory
FSL Redpath — N5861 at 07.30 - practice

Bailey carried out a duty flight to Chipilly at 17.00, returning at 19.15.

FCdr Norton led Fletcher, Winter and Lawson on a patrol at 17.10. Lawson crashed and damaged N3194 at Flez. No enemy aircraft were encountered.

ASCdr Draper led B Flight on an uneventful offensive patrol at 17.30. Conditions were reported as being very cloudy on both sides of the lines.

FCdr Norton, Fletcher and Winter carried out another relatively short patrol at 19.40, no enemy aircraft were encountered.

29th April

Draper led B Flight on an offensive patrol at 07.40, British aircraft were observed over St. Quentin but no hostile machines were encountered.

Bailey was again assigned the duty flight and flew to Chipilly at 09.05 returning to Flez at 11.00.

Winter collected a new machine, N3209, from No.2 AD at 12.15 and returned via Bellevue at 14.35.

B Flight carried out an offensive patrol at 07.20, Edwards suffered engine failure and was forced to drop out after ten minutes.

OPPOSITE
TOP: An excellent view of No.6 Squadron's corner of the aerodrome complex at Flez, thought to have been taken by FSL NM Macgregor whilst flying one of the squadron's Nieuports. *Courtesy EF Cheesman*

BOTTOM: A second aerial view of Flez taken a few seconds later, one of the Squadron's Nieuports can be seen to be in the process of taking off. *Courtesy EF Cheesman*

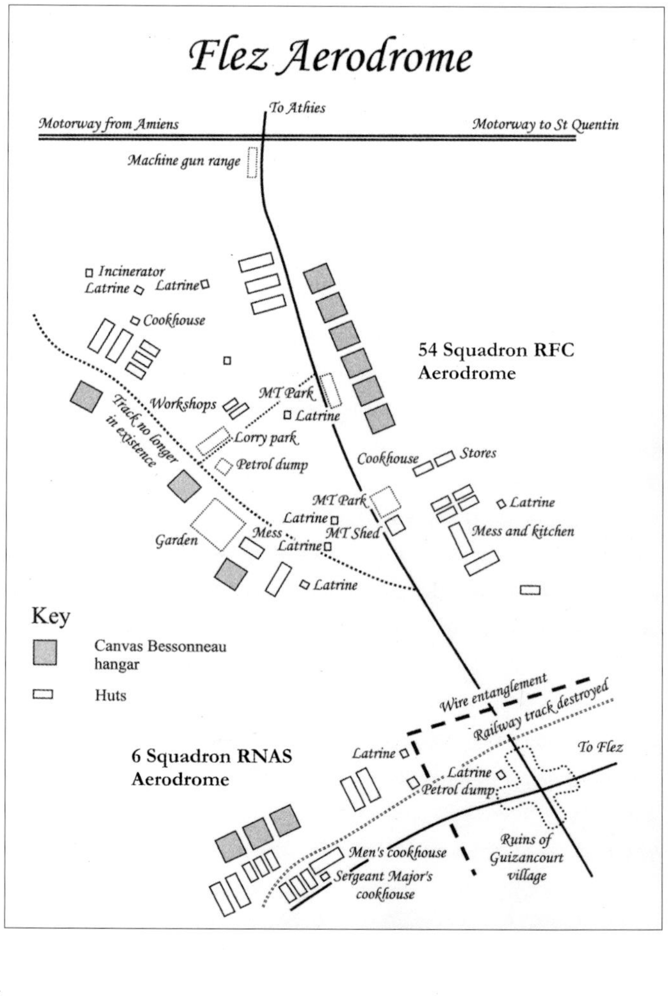

At 11.00, B Flight carried out an exhibition patrol over the aerodrome during an inspection by General Rawlinson.

FCdr Norton led C Flight on an offensive patrol at 12.20. FSL Beasley was forced to abandon the patrol when his machine's rev counter failed. At 13.15, Norton observed a lone Albatros scout at Beheries, seven miles east of Honnecourt. He watched the enemy machine for five minutes before attacking and then led Fletcher down in a dive, both Nieuports firing at very close range. Tracers were seen entering the Albatros fuselage and the enemy machine side-slipped, nose-dived and went down out of control.

Three of C Flight's members were in action again when Norton led Winter and Fletcher on an offensive patrol 17.45. At 18.55 over Guise, the patrol was attacked by a formation of 12 Albatros scouts. Norton dived and rolled to get out of the way but found that his Nieuport was being overtaken. He turned and met his attacker head-on, firing at close range, whereupon the enemy scout fell in flames. Winter was attacked from behind by three scouts which took turns to shoot at him. Winter and the attackers were flying in a vertical bank, with Winter trying to get into a position to be able to turn the table on his opponents. When Winter was able to fire, his Nieuport stalled and both the Nieuport and the Albatros spun down. Winter recovered at 1000 feet and thought he saw the enemy machine crashed on the ground, this proved optimistic as it turned out to be an anti-aircraft gun that started to fire at him. Winter flew back at 800 feet under heavy ground fire and eventually landed four miles southeast of Albert. He then flew back to the aerodrome, however, his machine, N3199, was badly shot-up. FCdr Norton had seen Winter and his opponent spinning down and believed the Albatros to be Out of Control. Norton then came under attack from several more enemy machines. After endeavouring to get away, Norton turned and went through their formation, firing at one machine which went down completely out of control with the pilot thought to be seriously wounded. Norton then tried to disengage but was still being followed, he landed in enemy territory and as the enemy machines shot past he took off again and was pursued all the way to the lines at a height of 100 feet. Fletcher failed to return from the patrol, being wounded and taken prisoner.

An interesting view of the 18.55 combat can be gained from the combat logs of *Ltn* Hermann Göring of *Jasta* 26.[5] Göring flew three missions on the 29th April:

10.05 – 11.30 Albatros D.III 2049/16
one indecisive combat with a biplane.

14.45 – 16.10 Albatros D.III 2049/16
no details

1850 – 20.00Albatros D.III 2049/16
Result: successful combat at 19.45 over Renicourt. At 20.00, an unsuccessful combat was broken off because the rudder cable was shot through.

Combat report:
Mission: Jagdflug
Weather Good visibility

About 7.45pm aerial fight over Ramicourt with a Nieuport single-seater. I shot it down. He tried to land SW of Ramicourt. Turned over on landing. The pilot, 2nd Lt Fletscher (sic) was severely wounded with a ricochet shot to his lower calf.

When I flew at 100m height to Bohain a second enemy single-seater came from above, chased by an Albatros. The Britisher attacked me shortly and hit my lateral control. He himself was then pursued by an Albatros and forced to land. I could not observe any further developments since I had to fly without a lateral control which demanded my whole attention.

The Nieuport had the No.3192 Fabr. No.2756 (17Bis) Motor No.2813 Type 9B

Number of shots: 120 rounds

(Signed) Göring
Leutnant

Göring's combat report corresponds remarkably well with Norton's report[6], with the exception that Norton escaped by taking off again. According to Göring's statement, it would seem likely that Norton was flying the Nieuport that shot his controls away.

ASCdr Draper led B Flight on an offensive patrol at 18.00, no enemy aircraft were observed but some anti-aircraft fire was encountered near St. Quentin.

30th April

The squadron's move to Flez was completed on the 30th when A Flight transferred from Chipilly at 11.30. No.6 Squadron shared the complex with No.22 Squadron RFC flying FE2bs and No.54 Squadron RFC flying Sopwith Pups.

FSL Fletcher's C Flight Nieuport 17Bis N3192 in German hands after Fletcher was wounded by Ltn Hermann Göring and forced to land on the 29th April 1917. Earlier in the day, Fletcher had submitted his first claim which he shared with FCdr EW Norton, an Albatros scout out of control to the east of Harcourt. *Courtesy EF Cheesman*

Carrying three red bands to denote the C Flight Commander's machine, N3208 was flown by FCdr EW Norton between the 22nd and 29th April 1917. Norton submitted three claims on the 29th April, an Albatros scout out of control to the east of Harcourt, an Albatros scout in flames at Guise and an Albatros scout out of control at Guise. The last claim was against Herman Göring of Jasta 26 who was forced to land with his rudder controls severed. N3208 was also flown by SCdr CD Breese, who claimed a 2-seater "apparently out of control" on the 1st June, and by FSL RR Winter. *Courtesy Justin Young*

ABOVE: On the 29th April 1917, an element of Jasta 26 was in combat with No.6 Squadron's C Flight. FSL Fletcher was wounded in the calf and forced to land, his opponent, Ltn Hermann Göring, was flying this interestingly marked Albatros DIII 2049/16. Göring was subsequently attacked by FCdr EW Norton, the DIII's rudder controls were severed and Göring was forced to land. *Courtesy Greg VanWyngarden*

ASCdr Draper led B Flight on an offensive patrol at 07.30. Macgregor abandoned the patrol when the pipe to his machine's pressure gauge broke. Redpath recorded that the patrol observed the circus but that an engagement did not take place, Edwards was more succinct, reporting that the odds were 16 against 4. Draper reported 14 hostile machines that were too far away to engage

SCdr Breese flew to Chipilly at 08.55, returning to Flez at 10.00.

B Flight were scheduled to carry out a balloon strafe at 15.20, the mission proved to be a failure as no balloons were in the air and Draper led the Flight back at 16.10.

FCdr MacLaren led A Flight on a second Balloon patrol at 17.30. The Flight patrolled the line between St. Quentin and Cambrai but no balloons were encountered. FEs were observed working near Le Catelet and coming under anti-aircraft fire. Gagnier and Wood lost formation and both landed at Gurny.

One test flight was carried out:

FLt MacLennan N5860 at 11.10 – engine test, 1235 revs at 2000 feet.

• • •

May 1917

Hostile activity in the 4 Brigade area during May was reported as being normal. May proved to be something of a buffer between the Arras offensive of April and the Messines offensive of June.

No.6 Squadron's offensive capability suffered a setback in May when the squadron's most aggressive and effective pilot, FCdr EW Norton, was promoted and left to become Commanding Officer of No.12 Squadron.

1st May

The Squadron structure at the beginning of May was as shown:

A Flight

AFCdr CT MacLaren — Flight Commander
FLt BHP De Roeper
FLt FP Reeves
FSL OJ Gagnier
FSL A McB Walton
FSL P Wood

B Flight

ASCdr C Draper	Flight Commander
FLt GG MacLennan	
FSL RF Redpath	
FSL ST Edwards	
FSL PE Beasley	
FSL NM Macgregor	

C Flight

AFCdr EW Norton	Flight Commander
FSL H Lawson	
FSL RR Winter	
FSL RW Berridge	
FSL GD Kirkpatrick	
FSL CL Bailey	

Spare Pilot	FSL GLE Stevens

At 06.05, Wood and Gagnier returned to Flez from their unscheduled lading at Gurny on the 30th April. Walton returned from Montdidier at 15.00.

MacLaren led A Flight on an offensive patrol at 09.40. The Flight attempted to engage an enemy machine about 3 miles east of Cambrai but were unable to get within range. Reeves and Walton were forced to abandon the patrol with a gun stoppage and engine trouble respectively. At 11.15, the weakened patrol encountered nine enemy aircraft attacking a flight of FEs. The enemy aircraft broke off and headed east when the Nieuports approached.

Draper led B Flight on an escort patrol at 13.30 to protect FEs of No.22 squadron RFC. The patrol combined with the Sopwith Pups of No.54 squadron RFC and ranged as far as Cambrai. Four enemy aircraft were observed to the east but were too far away to be brought to action. On re-crossing the lines an enemy machine was encountered, Draper turned and gave chase but it rapidly pulled away out of range.

Four test and practice flights were carried out in the evening:

FCdr MacLaren	N3204 at 18.00 target practice on aerodrome

BELOW: No.6 Squadron was occasionally required to provide an escort for the FE2bs of No.22 Squadron RFC. An unidentified FE2b believed to be from No.22 Squadron RFC is shown here, apparently with Australian connections. Note that the code "B1" is repeated in a red or black circle under each lower wing. *Courtesy EF Cheesman*

No.6 Squadron often joined forces with Sopwith Pups belonging to their 14 Wing neighbours, No.54 Squadron RFC. This photograph of Sopwith Pup A7344 shows the 54 Squadron RFC markings of a white horizontal line running below the top longeron between the cockpit and the fin. *Courtesy EF Cheesman*

Another 54 Squadron RFC Sopwith Pup, A648. *Courtesy EF Cheesman*

FSL Walton	N3203 at 18.00 target practice on aerodrome
FLT Reeves	N3207 at 18.00 target practice on aerodrome
SCdr Breese	N3204 at 18.35 test, satisfactory

2nd May

B Flight carried out an offensive patrol at 06.10 intending to link up with the Sopwith Pups of No.54 Squadron RFC. Visibility was described as "very thick and hazy" and the patrol failed to find the Pups. A flight of eight French Paul Schmitt bombers and a solitary SPAD were observed. A hostile machine was encountered near St. Quentin but could not be brought to action. Macgregor suffered a gun stoppage at 06.50 and was forced to land in order to get it cleared. At 07.00 he attempted to rejoin the patrol but mistook a flight of enemy aircraft for the Nieuports, he was attacked by two of the enemy aircraft, suffered another gun stoppage and was forced to descend and land.

BELOW: Nieuport 17Bis N3204 displaying the single red stripe of the A Flight Commander's aeroplane. FCdr MacLaren flew this machine from the 14th March to the 25th May 1917, it was then taken over by FLt FP Reeves from the 25th May to the 6th June 1917. Reeves was killed on the 6th June when N3204 broke up in the air during a general engagement to the northwest of Cambrai. *Courtesy JMB/GSL Collection*

SCdr Breese carried out a gun test at 13.40 prior to leading an offensive patrol at 16.00. The patrol was a complete shambles with FCdr MacLaren dropping out with a badly vibrating engine and the other pilots loosing formation. Breese patrolled at 15000 feet and reported anti-aircraft batteries active near Havincourt Wood. Gagnier carried out a line patrol at 15000 feet, he crossed the Lines at St. Quentin and joined up with a formation of Pups from No.54 Squadron RFC. Walton patrolled at 16000 feet, no enemy aircraft were observed. Wood patrolled alone and was attacked from behind whilst he was observing three other enemy machines. Reeves patrolled at 16000 feet without encountering any enemy machines.

Six practice and test flights were carried out:

FSL Berridge	N3197	at 09.35 – practice
FSL Berridge	N3197	at 10.45 – practice
SCdr Breese	N3195	at 13.40 – gun test, satisfactory
FSL Beasley	N3186	at 16.35 – practice
FSL Beasley	N3186	at 17.45 – practice
SCdr Breese	N3195	at 18.35 – gun satisfactory

3rd May

Reeves flew N3207 to Albert at 08.45.

ABOVE: A front view of N3204. A Flight aircraft, had blue painted cowls and wheel covers. *Courtesy JMB/GSL Collection*

Bailey collected N5862 from the Depot at 09.30 but suffered a broken push rod and was forced to land at Villers Bertonneux. After repairs he returned to Flez at 20.25.

Seven test and practice flights were carried out during the course of the day:

FSL Macgregor	N3100 at 09.35 - local practice
FSL Berridge	N3195 at 10.10 diving and gun practice
FSL Macgregor	N3100 at 10.40 - gun test, tension on recoil too great
FSL Berridge	N3197 at 14.10 - practice
FSL Macgregor	N3100 at 14.15 machine satisfactory
FSL Berridge	N3195 at 15.15 gun test, gun satisfactory
FSL Wood	N3193 at 18.10 engine exceptionally good

B Flight carried out a hostile aircraft patrol along the Somme at 16.00 in search of an enemy aircraft reported to be over Aberville. Beasley in N3186 suffered engine trouble and made a forced landing at Bellevue. After failing to find the enemy machine, Draper led the flight from St. Quentin to Cambrai on an uneventful offensive patrol.

Breese led Kirkpatrick, Lawson and Berridge on an offensive patrol at 18.00. Berridge landed at Citadel Aerodrome, Marieux. He was killed at 19.15 when he stalled N3195 immediately after taking off to return to Flez

4th May

Draper led Redpath and Edwards on a hostile aircraft patrol at 09.40 to search for an enemy machine reported from Peronne. The intruder was observed at 10000 feet heading southeast towards St. Quentin but the Nieuports were unable to get close enough to attack. Redpath noted in his log book that his machine, N5861, climbed to 10000 feet in 14 minutes and that the aircraft was armed with both guns. Whilst diving, the Nieuport's starboard bottom plane twisted but Redpath was able to get down safely.

A Flight carried out an offensive patrol at 11.30, no enemy aircraft were observed. Stevens dropped out of the patrol with a gun stoppage.

Breese collected N3207 from Albert at 11.45.

Beasley collected N3196 from Bellevue at 13.25.

SCdr Breese led Kirkpatrick, Lawson and Bailey on an offensive patrol at 15.20. Breese was forced to drop out when

N3196's pressure system failed. No enemy aircraft were observed.

B Flight carried out an uneventful offensive patrol at 19.05.

A number of test and practice flights were carried out:

FCdr Norton N3201 at 09.30 – machine unsatisfactory
FSL Lawson N5862 at 10.05 – satisfactory
FSL Lawson N5862 at 11.25 – satisfactory
FSL Lawson N5862 at 11.45 – gun test, unsatisfactory
FSL Lawson N5286 at 13.45 – gun test, satisfactory
FSL Stevens N3196 at 14.10 – gun test, satisfactory
FSL Stevens N3196 at 18.15 - unsatisfactory

The remains of an unidentified Nieuport 17Bis crash. *Courtesy Fleet Air Arm Museum*

Another view of the unidentified crash. The unusual double telegraph poles may eventually lead to the crash site being identified. *Courtesy Fleet Air Arm Museum*

5th May

C Flight carried out an offensive patrol at 08.30, no enemy aircraft were observed. Lawson attempted to attack an enemy kite balloon to the north of Hombilières but was driven off by heavy anti-aircraft fire.

Reeves collected N5865 from the depot at 12.00.

MacLennan led B Flight on an escort patrol for the FEs of No.22 Squadron RFC at 15.00. MacLennan was forced to return with a broken valve spring and defective magneto. Redpath, Macgregor and Edwards continued the mission which proved uneventful.

Several test and practice flights were carried out:

FLt De Roeper N3196 at 09.00
machine, engine and gun satisfactory
FSL Lawson N5862 at 17.55
practice, satisfactory
SCdr Breese N3202 at 17.15
machine, engine and gun satisfactory
ASCdr Draper N3101 at 16.45
testing engine and gun
ASCdr Draper N3101 at 18.45
testing engine and gun, satisfactory
FSL Edwards N3102 at 18.50
five minutes into the flight the throttle fell off and the engine stopped, resulting in a forced landing.
FSL Edwards N3102 at 19.10 - satisfactory

A Flight carried out an offensive patrol over St. Quentin at 18.00, thick clouds were encountered up to 15000 feet. MacLaren took the patrol down to 7000 feet where the visibility was found to be worse.

6th May

Three test flights were carried out:

FSL Walton N3203 at 08.00
weather test, cloud from 8000 feet
FSL Macgregor N3100 at 10.00
weather test, thick cloud from 8000 feet
ASCdr Draper N3186 at 15.05 - satisfactory

B Flight carried out an offensive patrol at 18.00, Macgregor reported observing one enemy aeroplane.

7th May

SCdr Breese led De Roeper, Bailey, Kirkpatrick and Lawson on an offensive patrol at 05.55, De Roeper and Lawson dropped

Believed to be N3189 of A Flight and flown by FSL OJ Gagnier, number "6" has not had its cowl or wheel covers painted when this photograph was taken. Gagnier claimed an Albatros scout crashed northwest of Fresnoy le Grand on the 10th May 1917, but was seriously wounded when he was shot down at Villers Outreax on the following day. *Courtesy EF Cheesman*

A line-up of A Flight aircraft, number "6" (third machine from right) now sports a painted cowl and wheel covers. *Courtesy Justin Young*

out with a gun stoppage and engine trouble respectively. An enemy kite balloon was observed near Framont and other ground based observations were reported.

Gagnier and Wood took off at 09.35 in pursuit of an enemy machine reported to be over St.Quentin. Neither pilot encountered the hostile aircraft.

B Flight carried out an offensive patrol at 10.00. Redpath engaged an enemy machine two miles south of Cambrai but suffered a gun stoppage. Draper reported an enemy kite balloon at Crevecoeur.

A Flight carried out a line patrol at 18.00, between St. Quentin and Havrincourt Wood. The visibility was very poor and no enemy aircraft were observed.

8th May

No flying due to bad weather.

9th May

A number of test flights were carried out during the day:

FSL Edwards	N3102	at 09.25 engine satisfactory
ASCdr Draper	N3101	at 10.00 gun and machine satisfactory
FCdr MacLaren	N3204	at 10.00

engine satisfactory, machine flying left wing heavy.

SCdr Breese	N3209	at 13.45 - gun satisfactory
FSL Walton	N3203	at 14.35 engine slightly harsh
FLt Reeves	N3207	at 14.35 - satisfactory

MacLaren led A Flight on an offensive patrol to Cambrai, St. Quentin and eastwards for 10 miles at 18.00. The visibility was poor and the patrol came down from 15000 feet to 10000 feet and followed the lines. No enemy aircraft were encountered.

SCdr Breese led Bailey and Lawson on a 25 minute formation practice at 18.30.

10th May

SCdr Breese carried out a solo offensive patrol at 04.50. Breese flew at 12000 feet and reported that the visibility was bad.

MacLaren led A Flight on an offensive patrol from north of Le Catelet, east of Bohain to the river Oise at 13.55. The patrol dived on three enemy aircraft which fled away towards Le Catelet before they could be engaged. At 15.15, an Albatros scout was observed heading for St. Quentin, MacLaren and De Roeper dived on the Albatros which dived and pulled away from them. Gagnier, however, dived at an angle and caught the Albatros at 7000 feet, he fired two bursts and saw tracers enter the wings and fuselage around the pilot. He got to within 100 feet and fired another burst into the fuselage, the combat was at 5000 feet by this time and the enemy machine was last seen going down in a spinning nose dive northwest of Fresnoy le Grand.

Draper, Macgregor, Redpath and Lawson carried out a balloon offensive at 14.45:

> ASCdr Draper: N3101 - Crossed the lines at 800 feet but failed to find the balloon in his sector, he returned towards St. Quentin but no balloons were encountered.
>
> FSL Macgregor: N3100 - Crossed the lines at 800 feet and attacked the balloon in his sector, firing at it until within 150 yards at which point his gun jammed.
>
> FSL Redpath: N5861 - Crossed the lines at 1000 feet towards Fresnoy, however, his allocated balloon was not aloft. After firing 100 rounds into the trenches Redpath turned west and observed two kite balloons to the south of Fresnoy, he re-crossed the lines at 250 feet but was unable to locate the balloons believing that they had been winched down during Macgregor's attack.
>
> FSL Lawson: N5862 - Lawson crossed the lines at 2000 feet near Hombilières and attacked his balloon from the south but his gun jammed after just 20 rounds. Lawson re-crossed the lines and cleared the stoppage then attacked the balloon from the northwest. His gun suffered another stoppage after firing 100 rounds.

Breese led Kirkpatrick and Bailey on an offensive patrol at 18.00 but was forced to return to the aerodrome after 15 minutes due to rain and an approaching storm.

Three test and practice flights were carried out:

FSL Kirkpatrick	N5865	at 09.55
FSL Bailey	N3199	at 09.55 gun working well
FSL Bailey	N3199	at 15.00 - satisfactory

11th May

Breese led Bailey, Kirkpatrick and Lawson on an offensive patrol at 05.00. Thick cloud was encountered at 6000 feet and no enemy aircraft were seen, the patrol was aborted and returned to the aerodrome at 05.45.

Breese was intent upon completing the offensive patrol as he had the same pilots up again at 06.40. Lawson flying N5862 was forced to return at 07.00 with engine and propeller trouble. The patrol failed to encounter any enemy aircraft but returned with a detailed list of train movements on the Cambrai – St. Quentin line.

B Flight carried out an offensive patrol at 09.10. Macgregor observed an enemy machine at 12000 feet and dived upon it from 14000 feet, the hostile machine was faster and Macgregor was unable to get within firing range. No other hostile machines were encountered.

At 12.50 a hostile machine was reported to be in the vicinity of Merville. Breese, MacLaren, De Roeper, Gagnier, Reeves, Wood and Walton all took off in an attempt to intercept the intruder. De Roeper patrolled between Peronne and St. Quentin in a large circle. At 13.20 he observed aircraft to the south of St. Quentin, these turned out to be a formation of fourteen Albatros scouts. De Roeper manoeuvred and got behind the formation with the intention of overtaking one of the scouts. This proved impossible and after following the formation as far as Cambrai, De Roeper gave up and patrolled between St. Quentin and Havrincourt at 18000 feet. At 13.55 he observed an enemy aircraft cross the lines at 16000 feet between Vendhuick and Epehy. The intruder turned on a wide radius towards Poisel but then spotted the Nieuport and immediately dived for his own lines. De Roeper dived after the enemy machine and fired 2 bursts of 70 rounds from a range of about 300 yards. Tracers from the second burst were seen to enter the planes and fuselage, The enemy machine went down in a very steep dive but appeared to be under control. De Roeper gave up the chase due to heavy anti-aircraft fire and his goggles misting up. None of the other patrolling pilots observed any hostile machines. Reeves suffered engine trouble in N3207 and was forced to return for adjustments before resuming his patrol.

Five test flights were carried out during the day:

FSL Wood	N3193	at 10.00 - satisfactory
FSL Walton	N3203	at 10.05 - satisfactory
FSL Stevens	N3186	at 10.30 – valve sticking
FSL Stevens	N3186	at 10.50 – valve sticking
FSL Stevens	N3186	at 15.40 - satisfactory

A Flight carried out an offensive patrol 17.55. MacLaren was forced to return to the aerodrome with engine trouble and excessive vibration leaving De Roeper to take over as patrol leader. When at 17000 feet, De Roeper observed an enemy machine at 10000 feet, he dived to attack but lost the hostile machine in the haze. Reeves attacked an enemy machine, firing 100 rounds before he lost it in the haze. At 19.30, Gagnier observed 4 enemy machines 4000 feet over Villers Outreaux. He climbed above them and tried to attract the attention of his Flight. Unable to attract his colleagues' attention, he followed the enemy machines. Two aircraft detached themselves from the formation and moved northwards. Gagnier circled twice and then dived on to one of the hostile aircraft when it came very close to him. He pulled the trigger control lever but the gun failed to fire, a collision was narrowly avoided and Gagnier was able to later relate that the pilot was wearing a sweater and black flying helmet. The other enemy machines immediately attacked Gagnier's Nieuport and a machine gun round shattered his left arm. Gagnier attempted to get down and away, losing consciousness on the way down. He saw the ground approaching and knocked the stick back, Nieuport N3189 hit the ground and turned over. Gagnier scrambled through intense machinegun fire and took refuge in a shell hole, he later made his way to the British lines where he again lost consciousness.

12th May

SCdr Breese carried out a solo patrol at 05.45. No enemy aircraft were seen and Breese returned with detailed observations of railway and road traffic.

B Flight carried out an uneventful offensive patrol at 07.00.

Breese made a local flight to Hargicourt and back at 09.00.

A Flight carried out an offensive patrol at 11.00. After 45 minutes MacLaren's engine started to misfire and the revs dropped to 1020, he persevered for another 15 minutes then returned to the aerodrome. Reeves also suffered with mechanical problems and was unable to keep up with the formation. De Roeper led the remaining pilots to St. Quentin, Cambrai and Bohain at 17000 feet. No enemy aircraft were encountered.

B Flight provided an escort for the FEs of No.22 Squadron RFC at 14.00. Redpath reported that enemy aircraft were active but the patrol was not attacked.

Four practice and test flights were carried out:

FSL Beasley N3186 at 09.25
abandoned practice after 20 minutes when a high tension wire broke.

FLt Reeves	N3207	at 17.00 - satisfactory
FSL Walton	N3203	at 17.40 - satisfactory
ASCdr Draper	N3101	at 19.45 - satisfactory

13th May

Two test flights were carried out:

FCdr MacLaren N3204 at 05.20. – weather test, unsuitable for either offensive or line patrol.
ASCdr Draper N3101 at 11.20 – test, gun satisfactory

Despite MacLaren's findings at 05.20, he led A Flight on a line patrol at 05.55. Visibility was poor at the start of the patrol but improved later. No enemy aircraft were encountered, the patrol reported three fires burning at St. Quentin.

FCdr EW Norton and FSL RR Winter pose for the camera in front of Norton's Nieuport N3208. *Courtesy Justin Young*

FSL RR Winter and the A Flight Commander, CT MacLaren, pose in front of Norton's Nieuport. *Courtesy Justin Young*

B Flight carried out an offensive patrol at 18.00. The patrol was abandoned after 90 minutes due to low cloud and hazy conditions.

14th May

SCdr Breese led Wood, Kirkpatrick, Reeves and Lawson on an offensive patrol at 07.00. Lawson's Nieuport, N5862 suffered engine trouble and he briefly returned to the aerodrome for adjustments to be made. The patrol did not encounter any enemy aircraft but returned with detailed railway observations.

B Flight carried out an offensive patrol at 11.00. Edwards in N3102 suffered problems with the aircraft's pressure system and the front tank[7] reading empty. The wind was reported to be very strong at 14000 feet. No enemy machines were encountered.

A Flight attempted to carry out an offensive patrol at 14.00 but was forced to return after 50 minutes due to the weather conditions. De Roeper in N3209 had to return after just 20 minutes with engine trouble.

Seven test flights were carried out during the day:

FSL Walton	N3203	at 11.15 suffered gun stoppage
FSL Walton	N3203	at 11.45 suffered gun stoppage
FLt Reeves	N3199	at 11.55 suffered gun stoppage
FSL Walton	N3203	at 12.15 - gun satisfactory
FSL Edwards	N3102	at 18.00 pressure system satisfactory
FSL Walton	N3203	at 18.30 suffered gun stoppage
SCdr Breese	N3203	at 18.35

machine out of true, engine vibrating.

15th May

B Flight attempted to carry out an offensive patrol at 05.00 but bad weather caused it to be abandoned after 20 minutes.

Three test flights were carried out:

FSL Walton — N3203 at 08.50
weather test, clouds at 400 feet.
FSL Walton — N3203 at 11.30
suffered gun stoppage
FSL Wood — N3193 at 13.30
engine unsatisfactory.

16th May

No war flying due to unsuitable weather, however, Redpath carried out a brief test flight at 14.00.

17th May

Low cloud and rain prevented all war flying.

ASCdr Draper carried out a brief test flight in N3101 at 16.00.

18th May

Redpath carried out a 20 minute practice flight in N5861 at 06.00. The flight was not a success as the starboard lower wing twisted during a dive and the high tension leads on 4 cylinders broke. A new wing was fitted to N5861 and Redpath carried out a brief test flight at 21.30.

FLt De Roeper led C Flight on an offensive patrol at 07.00. The visibility was reported as fair but no enemy aircraft or ground activity was observed.

A Flight attempted to carry out an offensive patrol at 11.00, the wind at 10000 feet held the aircraft stationary and thick cloud was present at 11000 feet. The wind increased and MacLaren reported that the machines were only controlled with difficulty.

19th May

A number of test flights were carried out throughout the day:

FLt Reeves — N3297 at 04.50
weather test, unsuitable for offensive patrol
FSL Walton — N3203 at 06.00
weather test, cloud at 3000 feet
FCdr MacLaren — N3204 at 06.05
weather test, cloud at 3000 feet
FLt Reeves — N3207 at 10.20
engine and gun satisfactory

A group photograph of five of No.6 Squadron's pilots, back, L to R: FSL NM Macgregor, FSL GD Kirkpatrick, FSL FP Reeves, FSL P Wood. In front is FSL ST Edwards. *Courtesy SK Taylor*

FSL Walton — N3203 at 10.25 - engine better, gun good
ASCdr Draper — N3101 at 14.30 - gun satisfactory
FSL Macgregor — N3100 at 15.00 - satisfactory
FSL Redpath — N5861 at 21.10 - satisfactory

20th May

B Flight carried out an offensive patrol at 07.00 but abandoned it after 75 minutes due to low cloud. No enemy aircraft were encountered. Edwards was forced to abandon the patrol after 20 minutes with engine trouble.

FLt De Roeper led Bailey, Winter, Kirkpatrick and Lawson on an offensive patrol at 11.00. Lawson was forced to abandon the patrol with engine trouble. At 11.40 the patrol encountered an enemy 2-seater and a scout heading southwest over Elincourt. De Roeper manoeuvred and got his patrol between the 2-seater and the sun and then attacked the machine. The 2-seater was 500 feet below the patrol, De Roeper put the Nieuport's nose down and got into a favourable position for attack. When about to open fire, the enemy machine turned slowly to east, apparently not seeing the formation of Nieuports. De Roeper manoeuvred again and got on the inside of the curve and opened fire at 30 yards, tracers were observed to enter the fuselage and the enemy machine went down in a steep nose-dive. After a few seconds a thick trail of black smoke was observed to be coming from the 2-seater which had turned partly over on to its back and continued in an inverted dive. Winter also attacked the enemy 2-seater. De Roeper noted that the escorting Albatros scout had dived away as soon as the combat commenced.

The patrol then encountered a formation of Albatros scouts to the northeast of St. Quentin at 11.50. Bailey attacked a scout which was 500 feet below him, following it down for 2000 feet until it flattened out. Bailey fired 60 rounds and believed that he observed tracers entered the scout's fuselage before he lost sight of the machine which was going down in a nose dive. Bailey was then in turn attacked by two more scouts, his gun jammed but he had enough speed to climb above his attackers. The two enemy scouts chased Bailey back to St. Quentin but did not fire again.

At 14.30, MacLaren led Walton, Reeves, Beasley, Wood and Edwards on an escort patrol for three FE2s of No.22 Squadron RFC. Walton crashed N3203 just after take-off and MacLaren was forced to return after 20 minutes due to excessive vibration of his machine.

Four test flights were carried out during the course of the day:

FLt ST Edwards	N3102 at 08.30 test, unsatisfactory
FLt ST Edwards	N3102 at 09.00 test, unsatisfactory
FLt ST Edwards	N3102 at 12.00 test, satisfactory
ASCdr C Draper	N3204 at 15.35 test, unsatisfactory

21st May

Low cloud and bad visibility resulted in greatly reduced enemy aerial activity. No combats were reported by any of the squadrons attached to the 4th Brigade.

Stevens delivered despatches to Bornouil Chateau at 12.00, returning at 13.00.

Four test flights were carried out in the evening:

FLt FP Reeves N3207 at 18.00
weather test, unsuitable for patrol
FCdr CT MacLaren N3204 at 18.20
test, machine and engine satisfactory
FSL P Wood N3193 at 18.45
engine test, unsatisfactory, revs poor
FSL AMcB Walton N3196 at 19.05
test, satisfactory

22nd May

Unfavourable weather prevented all war flying.

FSL AMcB Walton from Toronto crashed N3203 just after taking off on a 14.30 escort mission on the 20th May 1917. Although the damage to N3203 looks to be superficial, the machine was written off and deleted. *Courtesy Justin Young*

23rd May

De Roeper led Kirkpatrick and Stevens on an offensive patrol at 11.00. The patrol was quickly abandoned due to bad visibility but not before De Roeper's engine gave trouble and Kirkpatrick's synchronisation gear failed and he shot through his Nieuport's propeller.

MacLaren led Beasley, Reeves, Edwards, Macgregor and Walton on a combined offensive patrol and escort for the FE2s or No.22 Squadron RFC. The FEs abandoned their photographic shoot due to poor visibility over the lines and the patrol returned after just 30 minutes.

Six test and practice flights were carried out:

FLt FP Reeves N3207 at 11.45
test, satisfactory, machine true
ASCdr C Draper N3101 at 11.40
test, engine unsatisfactory
FSL RF Redpath N5861 at 11.40
test, engine satisfactory
FSL NM Macgregor N3100 at 11.00
practise, satisfactory
FLt GG MacLennan N5860 at 17.45
gun and engine test, satisfactory
FLt FP Reeves N3207 at 17.20
gun test, fired 700 rounds, one unclearable stoppage in the no.3 position

24th May

De Roeper and Edwards carried out a hostile aircraft patrol an 09.10. Both pilots failed to locate the enemy machine.

B Flight carried out an uneventful offensive patrol at 06.35.

Six test and practice flights were carried out:

ASCdr C Draper N3101 at 05.35
weather test, very thick
FSL P Wood N3193 at 10.30
engine test, satisfactory
FLT FP Reeves N3204 at 17.20 - weather test
FSL H Lawson N5862 at 18.00
practice, satisfactory
FLt ST Edwards N3102 at 18.00
test, local flight to No.3 Squadron at Marieux
FSL RF Redpath N5861 at 19.10
practice, satisfactory

25th May

FCdr MacLaren led an eight machine offensive patrol along the lines between Havrincourt Wood and St. Quentin at 06.00. The formation became fragmented due to poor visibility and only two machines remained with MacLaren. The patrol was certainly eventful and considerable enemy activity was encountered by some pilots. FCdr MacLaren's engine was unsatisfactory over 13000 feet. Beasley was forced to return due to a faulty engine. Walton made no report. Reeves lost formation at the start of patrol and continued alone. Wood crashed N3193 when landing at the end of the patrol. Kirkpatrick in N5865 encountered an Albatros scout over Fresnoy at 06.45. The enemy machine was heading south and 500 feet below Kirkpatrick. When above and behind the enemy machine, Kirkpatrick dived and fired 200 rounds from a range of 100 yards observing tracers passing between the enemy machine's wings and in front of its engine. The Albatros was apparently undamaged and Kirkpatrick was forced to break off the attack when he suffered a gun stoppage in the No.3 position. Lawson encountered an enemy machine at 17000 feet over St. Quentin, the enemy machine used dive and zoom tactics to attack him twice before breaking off the engagement. Lawson suffered two gun stoppages during the encounter. Stevens suffered gun problems and returned to change his machine, the rest of his patrol was uneventful. De Roeper attacked a single seater at 07.00, he dived and fired 30 rounds whereupon his gun jammed and he was forced to disengage to clear the stoppage. He then encountered a 2-seater reconnaissance machine to the south of St. Quentin at 07.45. De Roeper dived and opened fire at 60 yards range observing tracers entering the enemy machine's fuselage. The observer returned the fire, De Roeper was hit in the lower jaw and also had his gun's Bowden cable severed. With no gun and blood over his goggles De Roeper broke off the engagement and returned to the aerodrome. Winter had nothing to report.

FLt Reeves, led Wood, Beasley and Walton on an offensive patrol to the north of St. Quentin at 08.00. Reeves and Wood reported an enemy kite balloon observed 3 miles northeast of St. Quentin, Beasley saw one enemy machine near St. Quentin and Walton observed an enemy machine flying 2000 feet above the patrol.

B Flight carried out a relatively uneventful offensive patrol at 10.00, Redpath reported chasing an enemy machine but was unable to bring it to action.

Just one test flight was carried out:

FCdr GG MacLennan N5860 at 17.45
engine and gun test, shot through propeller four times.

26th May

B Flight carried out an uneventful line patrol at 08.00, visibility was reported as very bad with thick mist up to 11000 feet.

FLt MacLennan led Stevens, Kirkpatrick, Lawson and Winter on an offensive patrol at 10.00. Steven's Nieuport suffered engine trouble and he was forced to return after an hour. Visibility was bad and no hostile machines were encountered.

At 13.45, FLt Reeves led Walton and Wood on an escort mission in conjunction with the FEs of No.22 Squadron RFC and Pups of No.54 squadron RFC. Wood was unable to keep formation but the patrol was otherwise uneventful.

One test flight was carried out in the morning:

FSL P Wood N3207 at 09.20 – test,
engine satisfactory

27th May

FCdr MacLennan led Kirkpatrick, Macgregor, Winter and Stevens on an offensive patrol at 07.30, the patrol encountered considerable enemy activity. Stevens suffered from engine trouble and returned after 20 minutes. MacLennan made an ineffective attack on a pair of 2-seaters over Cambrai at 08.50 and dived on another 2-seater to the east of St. Quentin at 09.15, again without result. He reported that many enemy aircraft were active on their own side of the lines. Kirkpatrick reported the two 2-seaters over Cambrai, plus two hostile machines to the south of St. Quentin, one of which appeared to fall out of control. Macgregor dived on a hostile machine to the east of St. Quentin at 09.15 but suffered a gun stoppage, he left the flight above him and then encountered a patrol of six to eight enemy aircraft over St. Quentin. These enemy machines dived away. Winter dived on a 2-seater to the southeast of St. Quentin but his attack was ineffective. He later attacked another 2-seater over St. Quentin, again without result.

ASCdr Draper led a nine machine escort for a flight of D.H.4s at 11.20. Draper, Macgregor and Redpath circled around Bellenglise from 12.00 to 12.45 at 15000 feet. They failed to make contact with the 2-seaters and returned. Reeves, Beasley, Edwards, Walton, Stevens and Wood also failed to find the D.H.4s over Bellenglise, they headed for Bohain without locating the 2-seaters. Upon returning to the Grand Prix Road at 12.50 they observed six machines flying towards Bellenglise, the Nieuports followed in the direction of Bohain but could not distinguish the type of machine they were following. Another five aircraft joined the original six over Bohain but were then lost to sight in the mist.

ASCdr Draper led B Flight on an offensive patrol and escort for the FEs of No.22 Squadron RFC at 16.30. The mission was reported as being uneventful.

Two test flights were carried out during the day:

FLt GLE Stevens — N3186 at 08.30
engine test, unsatisfactory
FSL Winter — N3208 at 12.10
test, satisfactory

28th May

FLt Reeves led A Flight on an offensive patrol at 07.30. Wood experienced engine trouble and was unable to maintain formation. No enemy aircraft were observed.

B Flight carried out an offensive patrol at 14.00. Edwards suffered a burst oil pipe in N3102 and was forced to return to the aerodrome. No enemy aircraft were observed but hostile anti-aircraft fire was encountered over Bateaux and St. Quentin.

MacLennan led C Flight on an escort mission at 16.30, heavy cloud was encountered up to 15000 feet and it proved impossible to locate the bombing aircraft.

Two test flights were carried out in the afternoon:

FLt MacLennan — N3209 at 14.20
engine and machine test, engine ok but left wing low.
FLt Reeves — N3197 at 17.45
test, engine and machine satisfactory, gun jammed in No.3 position

FLt BHP De Roeper, one of No.6 Squadron's three aces, and a man that several of the squadron's Canadian pilots were convinced was a German spy! De Roeper was wounded in the lower jaw during combat on the 25th May 1917 and was discharged from the squadron for hospital treatment. He returned to No.6 in July to lead C Flight, he rapidly adjusted to the Sopwith Camel, scoring four of his five victories on the type. De Roeper remained in the RAF after the war, eventually rising to the rank of Group Captain.

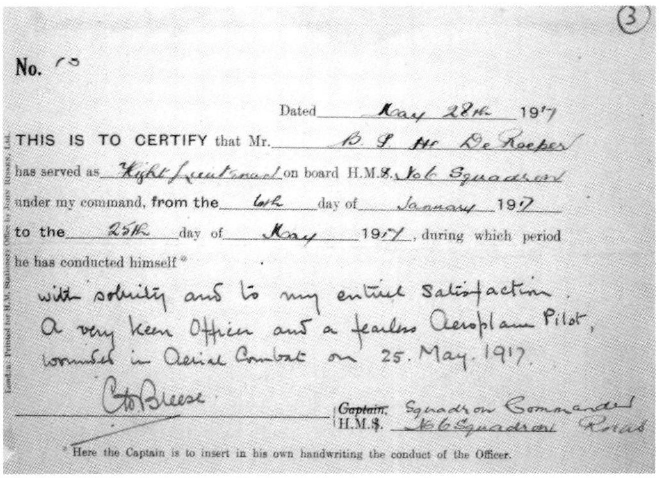

(3)

No. 10

Dated May 28th 1917

THIS IS TO CERTIFY that Mr. B. P. H. De Roeper
has served as Flight Lieutenant on board H.M.S. No 6 Squadron
under my command, from the 6th day of January 1917
to the 25th day of May 1917, during which period
he has conducted himself*
with sobriety and to my entire Satisfaction. A very keen Officer and a fearless Aeroplane Pilot, wounded in Aerial Combat on 25. May. 1917.

C.D. Breese
~~Captain~~ Squadron Commander
H.M.S. No 6 Squadron RNAS

* Here the Captain is to insert in his own handwriting the conduct of the Officer.

When an RNAS pilot left a squadron, he was issued with a "flimsy" (part of his discharge paperwork) which was effectively a report that recorded his Commanding Officer's impressions. It can be seen from De Roeper's flimsy that SCdr CD Breese though very highly of him. *Courtesy Fleet Air Arm Museum*

29th May

A low cloud base throughout the day prevented all war flying until 18.20 when Beasley, Reeves, Wood and Walton attempted to carry out an offensive patrol. Beasley was forced to return with a badly vibrating engine and Walton also experienced engine trouble and was unable to keep formation. Reeves and Wood continued the patrol but no hostile machines or kite balloons were observed.

A number of test flights were carried out in the evening:

FLt Beasley — N3196 at 18.00
engine and gun satisfactory
FSL Winter — N3208 at 18.10 - satisfactory
FSL Kirkpatrick — N5865 at 18.15
engine and machine satisfactory
ASCdr Draper — N3101 at 18.50
engine test after overhaul, satisfactory
FSL Redpath — N5861 at 18.50 - satisfactory
FSL Macgregor — N3100 at 19.00
machine and engine satisfactory
FSL Holyman — N3188 at 19.20
engine test after overhaul, unsatisfactory
FLt MacLennan — N3186 at 19.30
machine and engine test, satisfactory

30th May

Eight test flights were carried out during the course of the morning:

ASCdr Draper — N3201 at 07.25
weather test, unsuitable for offensive patrol
FSL Macgregor — N3100 at 07.25
engine satisfactory
FSL Redpath — N5861 at 07.25
engine satisfactory
FSL Holyman — N3186 at 09.40
machine satisfactory
FLt Reeves — N3204 at 10.30
engine and gun good
FSL Wood — N3197 at 10.30
engine and gun good
FLt MacLennan — N5860 at 10.50
engine missing, ignition
FLt MacLennan — N5860 at 12.50
engine and machine now satisfactory

MacLennan led C Flight on an offensive patrol at 14.20. Visibility was still poor due to heavy cloud and no hostile aircraft were encountered.

Reeves led Beasley, Walton, Wood and Redpath on an offensive patrol at 18.00. The patrol was abandoned after 75 minutes due to bad weather which was deteriorating as the patrol progressed.

31st May

C Flight carried out an offensive patrol at 07.30, heavy haze affected visibility and MacLennan led the patrol back to the aerodrome after 80 minutes.

Four test flights were carried out:

ASCdr Draper — N3101 at 10.30 – satisfactory
SCdr Breese — N3209 at 10.10 – gun test, suffered stoppage, able to clear
FLt Reeves — N3204 at 13.50 – weather test, unsuitable for offensive patrol
FLt Beasley — N3207 at 13.50 – engine satisfactory

Redpath flew N5861 to Bertangles at 14.35 in order to give a demonstration to Army officers. Redpath left Bertangles at 16.35 to return to Flez.

B Flight carried out an offensive patrol at 18.00, thick cloud resulted in the patrol being abandoned after 50 minutes.

• • •

June 1917

Hostile machines were active during the first part of the month decreasing considerably thereafter. In the early part of the month determined attacks were made against 14 Wing's reconnaissance patrols culminating in two large general engagements

Towards the end of the month the 4th Brigade and its constituent parts moved to the coast where the 4th Army would be taking over the northern part of the lines from early July.

German units were also moving north to oppose the Flanders Offensive.

1st June

Squadron structure at the beginning of June was as shown:

ABOVE: N5860 was one of the squadron's four Nieuport 17Bis machines built by the British Nieuport Company at Cricklewood. Readily identifiable by the brown PC10 finish, N5860 unusually carried a cockade on the fuselage. FLt GG MacLennan flew this aircraft from the 24th April to the 5th June 1917 and claimed an Albatros scout shot down to the east of Templeux le Guerard on the 1st June. *Courtesy SK Taylor*

A Flight
FSL FP Reeves, Acting Flight Commander
FLt PE Beasley
FSL H Lawson
FSL AMcB Walton
FSL P Wood

B Flight
ASCdr C Draper, Flight Commander
FLt ST Edwards
FLt GLE Stevens
FSL NM Macgregor
FSL RF Redpath

C Flight
FLt GG MacLennan, Flight Commander
FLt RR Winter
FSL H Lawson
FSL GD Kirkpatrick
FSL VC Holyman

SCdr Breese led Beasley, Reeves, Walton and Wood on an offensive patrol at 07.30. Beasley suffered a gun jam when testing and turned back to clear it, after leaving the formation he was unable to find it again. Reeves also suffered a cross feed and returned to get it cleared. Unable to rejoin the patrol he encountered Beasley and they patrolled the lines together. Reeves encountered one enemy machine flying 2000 feet above him which made off to the south. Breese and Walton encountered an enemy 2-seater at 08.35 flying at 14000 feet over St. Quentin. SCdr Breese got beneath its tail and FSL Walton attacked from above. Walton fired 150 rounds and saw tracers entering the fuselage, the enemy machine finally went up on one wing, side-slipped and nose-dived and Walton believed it to be out of control. SCdr Breese opened fire from a range of 50 yards and fired 100 to 150 rounds but was hit by the observer's fire and driven down in a spin. Breese landed with a graze on his cheek and his Nieuport, N3209, very badly shot about. The tailplane was buckled on the left side so that the machine was just stalling with full elevator control and full left rudder. Breese was not sure of the fate of the 2-seater but felt sure that it was damaged. The 4th Brigade War Diary credited Breeze and Walton with an indecisive "apparently out of control". FSL Wood saw one enemy machine at St. Quentin and indecisively attacked it from above.

B Flight carried out an offensive patrol at 14.00, low clouds interfered with the effectiveness of the patrol which was cut short after 90 minutes.

FCdr MacLennan led C Flight on an offensive patrol at 18.00, visibility was poor with thick cloud and mist. At 18.55, when at 14000 feet and to the east of Catelot, MacLennan observed a British RE8 crossing the lines under heavy anti-aircraft fire. Shortly afterwards, an Albatros scout appeared from enemy territory, whereupon the RE8 turned about and made back for the lines. MacLennan led the patrol into a dive towards the Albatros, which turned away and dived for home. MacLennan was able to fire 150 rounds at the scout from a range of 150 yards. The Scout turned and then "cart-wheeled" to both left and right before being lost in the mist. MacLennan was closely followed during the combat by Winter. An anti-aircraft battery reported that MacLennan's victim fell to the east of Templeux Le Guerard. Holyman flying N3186, was hit by anti-aircraft fire when over Catelot, shrapnel damaged the propeller which resulted in bad engine vibration. Holyman left the formation to return to the aerodrome but the engine stopped over Athies leaving him no option but to land there. The lower plane was damaged and the propeller smashed during the forced landing.

Three test flights were carried out during the day:

FSL Holyman N3185 at 14.15
very unsatisfactory, vibration and low revs
FLt Beasley N5186 at 15.35
engine and gun satisfactory
ASCdr Draper N3101 at 19.25

2nd June

B Flight carried out an offensive patrol at 07.30, Stevens and Macgregor were forced to drop out with pressure trouble and a gun stoppage respectively. Draper, Edwards and Redpath did not encounter any enemy machines.

Redpath reported in his log book that his engine had accumulated 39 hours and 40 minutes running time and that it was put in for overhaul.[8]

Two test flights were carried out:

FLt Reeves N3204 at 09.10 - gun satisfactory
FLt MacLennan N5860 at 14.00
weather test, patrol cancelled due to heavy cloud

3rd June

Kirkpatrick carried out a hostile aircraft patrol at 07.05 in pursuit of an enemy machine sighted from the aerodrome.

C Flight carried out an offensive patrol at 07.30. At 09.15 MacLennan observed an Albatros scout at 13500 feet and to the southwest of St.Quentin. MacLennan manoeuvred for position in the sun, dived on the enemy machine and fired 150 rounds from close range. Winter and Kirkpatrick also fired at the scout but from longer range. The Albatros went down in a dive, spinning and twisting but finally stabilised into a steep nose-dive and rapidly pulled away from the pursuing Nieuports. Winter reported that four pieces of fabric flew off of the enemy machine whilst MacLennan was firing at it. The Albatros was last seen going down over the German lines, apparently under control.

A Flight carried out an offensive patrol at 14.00. Beasley missed the patrol and elected to carry out a solo line patrol. Walton suffered engine trouble and returned early. The depleted patrol headed north of St. Quentin in the direction of Bohain and along the lines. No enemy aircraft were sighted.

B Flight carried out an offensive patrol at 17.45, no enemy machines were encountered but the patrol came under anti-aircraft fire over St. Quentin at 18.30.

Reeves and Wood carried out a hostile aircraft patrol at 19.30 in an attempt to intercept a reported intruder. The pilots patrolled the lines at 12000 but failed to find the enemy machine.

Three test flights were carried out during the day:

FSL Redpath N5861 at 10.00
post overhaul test, satisfactory
FLt Reeves N3204 at 18.45
engine and gun satisfactory
FSL Walton N3199 at 18.45
engine satisfactory

4th June

FLt Reeves led A Flight on an offensive patrol at 07.30. Lawson's aircraft, N3208, suffered from a fault in the pressure system and Lawson was forced to return to the aerodrome. At 09.00 Walton observed Allied anti-aircraft fire over St. Quentin, he went down to investigate but was unable to locate any aircraft.

Stevens, Lawson and Edwards carried out a hostile aircraft patrol at 09.30 after receiving a wireless report of a hostile incursion. Stevens observed anti-aircraft fire but could not find the enemy machine. Lawson found an aircraft in the reported area and followed it round to St. Quentin and back to Ham, finally identifying it as a French 2-seater. Edwards observed a machine being shelled and followed it until it went down to land at Mairieux Aerodrome. Edwards tentatively identified the machine as a Sopwith Pup.

MacLennan, Redpath and Lawson carried out a hostile aircraft patrol at 11.40. MacLennan and Redpath failed to find the enemy machine but Lawson observed Allied anti-aircraft fire near St. Quentin. Lawson investigated but was unable to find any enemy aircraft.

Breese, Edwards and Macgregor carried out a hostile aircraft patrol at 11.35 when Allied anti-aircraft fire was observed from the aerodrome. Breese failed to find any hostile machines but when to the north of Morecourt observed an untethered balloon at 5000 to 6000 feet. Macgregor observed a flight of enemy aircraft heading east away from the lines. Edwards saw an enemy machine pass over the aerodrome and set off in pursuit, following it north to Arras where it re-crossed the lines. On his return, Edwards saw another enemy machine being shelled just north of Havrincourt Wood. Edwards got beneath the 2-seater, 200 feet below it as the Nieuport would not climb any higher and attempted to use the Lewis gun on the top plane. The Lewis gun jammed without firing a single shot. Edwards then got in a burst from the Vickers gun by stalling the Nieuport. The enemy machine promptly turned for the lines and climbed out of range.

B Flight carried out an offensive patrol at 14.00. An unescorted Flight of FEs was discovered over Cambrai and Draper kept the patrol in contact with them. Four hostile machines later attacked the FEs but made off to the east when they saw the Nieuports.

MacLennan led C Flight on an offensive patrol at 18.00. No enemy aircraft were encountered but a blazing fire was observed in St. Quentin.

Two test flights were carried out during the day:

FLt MacLennan	N3902	at 09.50 - satisfactory
FLt Stevens	N3188	at 18.40 - satisfactory

5th June

At 06.00, in conjunction with sixteen Sopwith Pups of No.54 Squadron RFC, ASCdr Draper led ten Nieuports on an escort patrol for two FE's of No.22 Squadron RFC. The patrol comprised all ten available pilots from No.6 Squadron and sixteen pilots from No.54 squadron RFC. Approximately thirty to forty hostile machines were encountered and a general engagement took place. No.54 squadron RFC claimed three enemy aircraft as out of control with one of them later seen to be wrecked on the ground. A Pup from No.54 Squadron and an FE2 from No.22 Squadron were lost during the engagement. Although No.6 Squadron was involved in the dog fight, no claims were made or CITARs[9] submitted. The pilots' individual reports are reproduced below:

SCdr Draper: N3101 - Several H.A.[10] observed near Cambrai, dived to attack but could not get a shot in owing to too many machines.

FLt MacLennan: N5869 - Went over with another Nieuport Flight and Pups escorting two FEs. Encountered Albatros east of Sohain and dived on him, H.A. immediately dived out of range. Four Albatros encountered over Cambrai. Dived on one with a Pup but he dived out of range. H.A. kept much below us.

FLt Beasley: N3196 - Observed several H.A. below formation. Developed a miss-fire in engine at 07.45 and returned.

FSL Walton: N3199 - Saw H.A. about ten in number over Cambrai. Could not get close enough for accurate shooting.

FSL Redpath: N5861 - Special escort to FEs at 14000 feet. Saw a number of H.A. saw the FEs attacked twice. Dived on H.A. twice with other pilots but could observe no other result but that H.A. were driven off.

FLt Edwards: N3102 - Saw eight or ten Huns over Cambrai and engaged. Dived on four but Aldis sight was oiled and fired blindly, probably not getting any. Saw H.A. firing into Nieuport from behind. Dived on it and it turned away.

FLt Stevens: N5865 - No H.A. observed. Nothing to report.

FLt Winter: N3208 - Saw H.A. east of Bohain. Was not near enough to attack. Six Albatros encountered over Cambrai at about 9000 feet. Dived and fired on one but he dived away out of range.

FSL Wood: N3197 - Saw 2 H.A. south of Cambrai, dived on one and fired short bursts with no visible effect. Left him being attacked by the others from above.

FSL Macgregor: N3100 - Saw 4 H.A. 2000 to 5000 feet below over Cambrai. Dived on two of them but without apparent effect.

Lieutenant Colonel R Lorraine of the 14th Wing, attached a great deal of importance to the engagement and wrote the following confidential memo to the 4th Brigade GOC:

> *Confidential*
> *Headquarters*
> *14th Wing*
>
> *GOC*
> *4th Brigade*
> *Royal Flying Corps*
>
> *Sir,*
> *I have the honour to report that the general action which was fought this morning between 7.0 and 8.0 a.m. east and southeast of Cambrai, which resulted in the complete routing of the enemy, was not a spontaneous offensive of the enemy but was a natural outcome of the daily reconnaissance for railway movement.*
>
> *Until recently I carried out this reconnaissance with six F.E.s escorted by six Sopwith Scouts but on considering reports of pilots and observers and in view of the increasingly determined attempts of the enemy to interfere with this reconnaissance, I decided to double the number of the escorting Sopwith Scouts and on June 1st, as a result of the character of the fighting reported, I reduced the number of the F.E.s to two, the remaining four F.E.s being an encumbrance to the escort as soon as the fighting became severe.*
>
> *I found this formation of two F.E.s and twelve Sopwith Scouts strong enough for the duty until June 4th, when they were attacked by about thirty hostile machines; and although the enemy did not entirely succeed in preventing the reconnaissance being done, he interfered badly with the work and finally drove my machines back over their own lines, one of the two reconnaissance F.E.s being shot through the petrol tank and just able to glide to our side and one of the escorting Sopwith scouts being shot down in enemy country.*
>
> *As a result of his successful action on the morning of June 4th, the enemy was active and aggressive all that day, several times crossing our lines and one machine coming straight over my headquarters and proceeding in a northwest direction.*
>
> *I came to the conclusion that he would be waiting to attack my reconnaissance with a strong force before dawn this morning.*
>
> *I therefore sent the reconnaissance one hour later than the day before so that his force would have been some time in the air before coming into action; and I sent an escort in two groups, one of eleven Nieuport Scouts and one of sixteen Sopwith Scouts, one group to stay with the reconnaissance machines and the other to be as high as possible ready to dive into the fight as soon as action was joined.*
>
> *As was foreseen, a strong force of enemy machines were in the air when my reconnaissance and escort crossed the line and a running fight commenced in the course of which one of my reconnaissance machines was forced to land in enemy country near Lesdain and, later, one of my escorting machines was also forced to land near Crevecoeur and the pilot (Lieut Chalmers) was seen to promptly set fire to his machine.*
>
> *Notwithstanding these casualties, the reconnaissance was thoroughly and completely done by the other F.E., while the escorting machines fought a general engagement which lasted continuously for fifty minutes.*
>
> *The attacking force was reinforced by fighting machines which rose from the aerodromes between Cambrai and Le Cateau and while it is difficult to estimate accurately the number of the enemy, from the pilot's accounts it would appear that between thirty and forty hostile aircraft were engaged.*
>
> *There is great difficulty also in assigning justly the destruction of enemy machines to individual pilots, owing to the heat of the mêlée but all the enemy machines were driven down so that after nearly one hour's fighting our machines patrolled between Cambrai and Le Cateau over the aerodromes of Carnieres, Rousieres, Quievy and Neuvilly and could not find a single German machine to fight.*
>
> *The enemy has not yet recovered from this defeat as my photographic reconnaissance later this morning experienced no interference whatever and my offensive patrols have been unable to find a single fighting machine, only having seen two 2-seater Albatrosses attempting to do a wireless shoot both of whom ran away directly they were approached.*
>
> *In addition, the 3rd Wing and 4th Balloon Wing inform me that their machines have worked all day without interference, so that it would appear that the encounter of this morning was all that was needed to keep the enemy on the floor for the day.*

I submit that this principle of seeking and if necessary provoking a decisive engagement daily is more profitable an employment of the forces of an Army Wing than attempting to guard the Army front with feeble patrols all day long.

While everyone concerned did well, the following officers' work was especially good:

1. *Capt. J.C. Russell, leading Sopwith Scouts*
2. *Actg.Sqn.Comdr Draper, leading the Nieuport Scouts.*
3. *Lieut. O.M. Sutton*
4. *Lieut. Chalmers (for so promptly lighting his machine)*

I have the honour to be,
Sir,
Your obedient servant,

R. Lorraine. Lieut. Colonel
In the field.
5th June, 1917

In the afternoon of the 5th June, FLt ST Edwards ferried Nieuport 17Bis N5182 back to the depot at St. Pol. To Edward's embarrassment the last stage of the flight did not go as smoothly as he'd perhaps hoped. *Courtesy EF Cheesman*

Later in the day, N3196 and N5862 were flown back to the depot at Dunkerque. Edwards crashed N5862 at Dunkerque, photographs of the crash would indicate that he ran a wheel into a ditch after landing.

Edwards, MacLennan, Winter, Kirkpatrick and Holyman reported to the depot to collect No.6 Squadron's first Sopwith Camels.

From this angle it seems clear that Edwards ran a wheel into a ditch. *Courtesy SK Taylor*

6th June

Draper was again called upon to lead an escort patrol of Nieuports for the FE's of No.22 Squadron RFC. As on the previous day, the mission was carried out in conjunction with the Sopwith Pups of No.54 Squadron RFC. Eight Nieuports left at 10.30 and at midday, to the northwest of Cambrai, a general engagement took place with a large number of enemy machines. No.6 Squadron was heavily involved in the fighting and a number of Combat Reports were submitted:

ASCdr Draper: N3101 - Draper dived on an enemy scout and opened fire at close range, the enemy machine fell away completely out of control. Draper then immediately

RIGHT: FSL GLE Stevens posing for a photograph in the unfortunate N5182. *Courtesy EF Cheesman*

dived on to another scout but suffered a gun stoppage after opening fire, he turned away to clear the stoppage and observed the scout going down in a dive to crash on the ground. Draper then broke off towards the lines, climbed and cleared the stoppage. He returned to the engagement and dived on a third enemy scout but the gun immediately jammed again.

FSL Macgregor: N3100 - Macgregor dived and fired on one enemy machine at very close range and attacked another when his gun jammed due to the tail of the crank handle getting over the stud on the cocking handle. The first machine that Macgregor fired at spun away but he did not believe it to be out of control. Macgregor returned to the lines to rectify the gun but was unable to make enough height to rejoin the patrol.

FLt Stevens: N5865 - Stevens dived on to an Albatros scout which was 1200 feet below him. After firing 200 rounds, Stevens reported that his opponent slowly stalled, side slipped and fell in a spin, apparently out of control. Stevens was unable to observe the machine any further as he came under attack from four more scouts.

FSL Redpath: N5861 - Redpath reported combats with three enemy aircraft and long range encounters with two more. Redpath first attacked an Albatros scout from behind while its pilot was preoccupied with attacking a Sopwith Pup. Redpath fired 75 to 100 rounds at close range. The enemy machine turned over on its back and carried on down in a spin. Redpath engaged the second machine head-on whilst it was trying to get behind the formation, it fell away in a nose-dive. The third scout was engaged from behind and was driven down towards Cambrai, Redpath reporting that his Nieuport was not fast enough to keep up with it. Redpath was unable to state if any of the encounters were decisive. Reeves was attacked by an Albatros and Redpath saw Reeves' Nieuport, N3204, break up in the air.

FSL Walton: N3199 - Walton saw numerous enemy aircraft but could not get to close quarters.

FSL Beasley: N5860 - Beasley observed numerous hostile aircraft and dived on one without success.

FSL Wood: N3097 - Wood fired a few shots at long range with no success.

FLt Reeves: N3204 - Failed to return, killed when his machine broke up in the air.

Franks, Bailey & Duiven[11] attribute Reeves demise to *Ltn* Werner Voss of *Jasta* 5 who claimed a Nieuport to the west of Graincourt at 13.10. Voss was reported as wounded in action during the engagement, however, despite various claims by other authorities, it is not possible to attribute this pyrrhic victory to any particular pilot from No.6 Squadron or for that matter to No.54 Squadron RFC. Following the engagement, No.54 Squadron RFC submitted five claims for enemy aircraft destroyed, for the loss of two Pups. German records admit no losses during this engagement.

Redpath carried out two engine tests in the evening, one in his usual Nieuport N5861 and the second in N3101.

7th June

FLt GA Gooderham arrived at the squadron.

B Flight carried out an uneventful offensive patrol at 07.30.

Thunder storms prevented any war flying after midday, however, two test flights were carried out:

FSL Macgregor	N3100 at 17.10 machine flying right wing down
FSL Walton	N3199 at 18.15 engine satisfactory

8th June

B Flight carried out an offensive patrol at 07.30. Redpath flying his usual machine, N5861, suffered fuel pressurisation trouble and was forced to return to the aerodrome. Wood, in N3197 also suffered engine trouble and had to return. Draper, Beasley and Macgregor encountered hostile machines being shelled to the north of St. Quentin. The Flight could not get to them in time to engage.

Five new 130hp Clerget Sopwith Camels were delivered from the depot at 12.00:

FLt Edwards	N6356
FLt MacLennan	N5360
FSL Winter	N6358
FSL Kirkpatrick	N6357
FSL Holyman	N6359

The pilots had made a number of acclimatisation test flights in the squadron's first Camels whilst at the depot.

Redpath flew Nieuport N5861 in trials against Camel N6359 flown by Holyman at 14.05, unfortunately the pilots' impressions were not recorded.

9th June

Macgregor carried out a weather test in Nieuport N3100 at 06.45, visibility was reported as very bad with cloud between 6000 and 9000 feet.

A number of test and practice flights were carried out during the day:

FSL Kirkpatrick	Camel N6357 at 11.25 - satisfactory
FSL Winter	Camel N6358 at 14.00 - satisfactory
SCdr Breese	Camel N6358 at 14.40 - satisfactory
FSL Wood	Nieuport N3197 at 15.00 - satisfactory

10th June

The weather was again cloudy and no enemy aerial activity was reported. The day was spent carrying out test and practice flights:

FSL Holyman	Camel N5359 at 11.10 - satisfactory
FSL Macgregor	Nieuport N3100 at 11.25 - satisfactory
FSL Holyman	Camel N5359 at 11.50 testing guns, both jammed in No.3 position
SCdr Draper	Camel N6358 at 11.35 - practice
FSL Holyman	Camel N6359 at 15.30 - practice
FSL Winter	Camel N6358 at 15.50 - practice
FSL Kirkpatrick	Camel N6357 at 15.50 testing guns, right gun jammed
FSL Kirkpatrick	Camel N6357 at 16.05 testing guns, right gun jammed

11th June

SCdr Breese had been dissatisfied with ASCdr Draper's performance as a Flight Commander for some time. As the result of an official complaint to Dunkerque Headquarters, Draper was recalled to Home Establishment on the 11th.

Low cloud during the day made flying difficult, just one test flight was carried out:

FSL Holyman	Camel N 6369 at 08.55 engine and machine satisfactory.

A major relocation of the 4th Brigade to the coast was imminent and to this end, Operation Order No.88 was issued by Brigadier General JHW Becke DSO, Commander of the 4th Brigade. The order gave advance warning of squadron movements, in No.6 Squadron's case, a move from the Fourth Army to XV Corps was provisionally scheduled for the 16th June.

12th June

Eight test flights were carried out:

FSL Winter	Camel N6358 at 09.30 - satisfactory
FLt Gooderham	Nieuport N3208 at 10.35 - satisfactory
FLt MacLennan	Camel N6360 at 10.20 - testing windscreen
FSL Holyman	Camel N6359 at 15.00 - satisfactory
FSL Winter	Camel N6358 at 15.55 - satisfactory
FSL Holyman	Camel N6359 at 17.40 machine satisfactory
FSL Kirkpatrick	Camel N6357 at 17.40 machine satisfactory
FLt MacLennan	Camel N6360 at 17.45 both guns jammed, burst both tyres

FLt Beasley led Wood, Macgregor, Redpath and Walton on an offensive patrol at 07.30. The patrol, flown with Nieuports, was uneventful, no enemy aircraft being seen due to poor visibility caused by haze and cloud.

13th June

Six of the pilots left Flez at 08.55 to deliver the squadron's serviceable Nieuports to the depot at Dunkerque but were forced to return by bad weather. They made another attempt in the afternoon at 15.45:

FLt Edwards	N3102
FLt Gooderham	N3208
FSL Redpath	N5861
FSL Wood	N3197
FSL Walton	N3199
FSL Macgregor	N3100

Redpath suffered engine trouble and made a forced landing in N5861 at Marieux, breaking a strut. The machine was dismantled on site and returned to the depot by road.

The other pilots continued to carry out practice and test flights in the Sopwith Camels:

FSL Holyman N6359 at 08.55
weather test, clouds at 1000 feet, visibility of ground very bad.
FSL Winter N6358 at 09.20 - satisfactory
FSL Kirkpatrick N6357 at 09.25 - satisfactory
FSL Holyman N6359 at 14.40
engine test, satisfactory
FLt MacLennan N6360 at 16.05
Both guns jammed, separated case in port gun, loose cartridge in starboard gun. Forced to land as unable to clear stoppages whilst airborne.
FLt MacLennan N6360 at 18.00
port gun suffered a broken plunger spring, starboard gun satisfactory.
FSL Holyman N6359 at 18.00
Port gun jammed due to separated cartridge case, starboard gun jammed with a cross feed.
FLt Beasley N6356 at 18.10 - satisfactory

14th June
Camel test and practice flights continued to be carried out. Problems with the guns started to be of concern:

FSL Kirkpatrick N5356 at 09.00 - satisfactory
FSL Winter N6358 at 09.15
starboard gun jammed in 3rd position
FLt Beasley N6356 at 09.25 - satisfactory
FSL Holyman N6359 at 09.25
testing guns, starboard gun jammed twice in 3rd position, port gun jammed in third position, propeller shot through.
FLt Beasley N6356 at 17.35 - gun satisfactory
SCdr Breese N6360 at 17.50
one clearable stoppage
FLt MacLennan N6360 at 18.20
Left gun ran away, overcome by jamming, right gun satisfactory.

The date for the squadron's move was amended by 4th Brigade Operation Order No.91 which is reproduced below:

SECRET
4th Brigade, RFC
Operation Order No.91
By
Brigadier General JHW Becke, DSO
Commanding 4th Brigade, Royal Flying Corps.

In The Field
14th June 1917

1. Naval Squadron No.6 will move from Flez to Bray Dunes on the 18/19th instant.

2. Heavy transport will move on the 18th. via Villers Carbonnel, Bray, Albert, Doulens, St. Pol, Pernes; on the 19th. St. Venant, Hazebrouck, Cassel, Bergues and Dunkerque to Bray Dunes.

Billets for the night 18/19th will be allotted by the Town Major, Pernes.

3. Machines will fly on the 19th but will not start to do so, until ordered by 4th Brigade.

4. Light transport which it is necessary to retain at Flez until the machines start will move on the 19th by the same route as heavy transport.

5. Departure of machines will be reported by telephone to 4th Brigade.

6. On arrival at Bray Dunes, the squadron will come under the orders of 3rd Wing.

Signed Major Godman
Brigade Major
4th Brigade, Royal Flying Corps

15th June
In addition to test and practice flights in the Sopwith Camels, the Squadron's last three Nieuport 17Bis machines were test flown preparatory to returning them to the depot at Dunkerque.

Nieuport 17Bis:

SCdr Breese N5860 at 14.45 - satisfactory
FLt Gooderham N5865 at 18.10
engine and machine satisfactory
FLt Gooderham N3101 crashed and wrecked near aerodrome

Sopwith Camel:

FLt Beasley	N6356	at 08.45 - gun satisfactory
FSL Kirkpatrick	N6357	at 08.45 - satisfactory
FSL Winter	N6358	at 09.05 - satisfactory
FLt MacLennan	N6360	at 18.00 testing new propeller, unsuitable

The Sopwith Triplanes of No.9 Squadron RNAS arrived at Flez, initially under the command of 14 Wing, 4 Brigade but transferring to 13 Wing 3 Brigade on the 1st July when 4 Brigade Headquarters relocated to Bray Dunes..

16th June

Test and practice flights included a formation practice by C Flight:

Formation practice		
FLt MacLennan	N6360	at 09.00
FSL Holyman	N6359	at 09.05
FSL Winter	N6358	at 09.05
FSL Kirkpatrick	N6357	at 09.00
FSL Holyman	N6359	at 18.45 - satisfactory

No.6 Squadron continued to re-equip, three more Sopwith Camels, N6334, N6350 and N6351 being collected from the depot. These machines were not flown to Flez but were taken to what would shortly become No.6 Squadron's temporary residence at Middle Aerodrome, Bray Dunes.

17th June

A solitary practice flight was carried out on the 17th:

FLt Beasley	N6356	at 08.40 - satisfactory

Sopwith Camel N6342 was collected from the depot, again being taken directly to Middle Aerodrome.

18th June

The squadron's heavy equipment left on the two-day journey to Middle Aerodrome at Bray Dunes by road transport.

FLt Edwards had remained at the depot testing new Camels, on the 18th he carried out a comparison test against a Sopwith Dolphin using Camel N6331.

19th June

The squadron's pilots flew their collection of old Nieuports and new Sopwith Camels back to the coast. The Nieuports were handed back to the depot at Dunkerque and the Camels were flown to Middle Aerodrome, Bray Dunes, where the squadron would briefly come under the control of No.3 Wing 4 Brigade, pending the relocation of both 14 Wing Headquarters and 4 Brigade Headquarters to the coast.

FLt Edwards who was still residing at Dunkerque made a visit to No.3 Squadron at Furnes in Camel N6331.

NOTES

[1] A number of Nieuport 17Bis machines were delivered from Paris with standard Nieuport 17 propellers. The 17Bis should have been supplied with Helice Levasseur type "130h.p. Clerget Nieuport series 502" propellers.

[2] FSL Masson failed to join the squadron, having been killed in a flying accident on the 20th April. FSL GLE Stevens was substituted for Masson.

[3] AFCdr Allen was suffering from nervous exhaustion.

[4] FLt Keeble was also unfit and had made very few flights in the previous month.

[5] Courtesy Frank Olynyk, "The Combat Reports of Herman Göring", *Over The Front* journal, Volume 10 No.3.

[6] It must be remembered that German time was one hour ahead of British time.

[7] The Nieuport's oil tank.

[8] The official recommendation was for rotary engines to be stripped after 40 hours of accumulated war flying.

[9] CITAR – Combats In The Air Report.

[10] H.A. – Hostile Aircraft.

[11] *The Jasta War Chronology*, Grub Street, 1998.

CHAPTER FIVE

A DEMORALISING INFLUENCE

When the squadron was reinforced with the seven pilots from No.11 Squadron, Draper, MacLennan, Macgregor, Beasley, Edwards, Stevens and Redpath, the expected improvement in Squadron performance did not materialise. In fact, the new B Flight led a very quiet life throughout May 1917 making practically no contact with enemy aircraft.

SCdr Breese had arrived at the squadron to take control a matter of days before the arrival of the new B Flight. There was obviously a developing personality conflict between the reserved Breese and the extrovert Draper, not helped by Draper's continuing lack-lustre performance as a Flight Commander. Draper's lack of aggression was not just in Breese's mind alone, the squadron's daily operations reports show that B Flight rarely made contact with the enemy. Surviving B Flight members RF Redpath and PE Beasley were very critical of Draper's leadership when interviewed by respected Canadian aviation historian SK Taylor.

On the 29th May 1917 Breese visited Wing Captain Lambe at Dunkerque Head Quarters with a view to having Draper replaced. Lambe requested that Breese's objections to his B Flight Commander be put in writing and the following letter was written on the 4th June:

Naval Squadron No.6
In the Field
4th June 1917

To S.O. H.Q.
R.N.A.S.
Dunkerque

Submitted,
With reference to your conversation with me at Headquarters on 29th May, I make the following report with reference to acting Squadron Commander Draper.

I request that this officer be removed from this squadron and another pilot sent in lieu. A Flight Commander is not necessarily required, as I have an officer who is quite capable of running the Flight.

My reason for making this request is:

> *Acting Squadron Commander Draper although an exceptionally fine pilot and very "full out" as regards flying at an Aerodrome for the edification of onlookers, making a great noise in the Mess at nights and leading conviviality generally; yet after six weeks in this squadron he has produced no results.*
>
> *Both in his talk and in his actions, he exerts a depressing influence on the other pilots, - frequently asserting the weakness and inferiority of our machines, declaring that it is madness to attack a two-seater and so on. As regards actions, there has been a considerable and frequent increase in drinking since his advent, on nearly all occasions he is the leader.*

This officer has a bad influence on this squadron and I shall be glad if he may be sent elsewhere. As a substitute, may I suggest that an instructor at Cranwell – Acting Flight Lieutenant Alfred HM Gilligan may be relieved and sent in lieu. He is a very good pilot, exceptionally keen and would be of great use in this squadron.

I have the honour to be,
Sir,
Your humble and obedient servant

Signed. CD Breese
Squadron Commander

Breese, although evidently not approving of Draper's Mess entertainment and flying exhibitions over the aerodrome, certainly had grounds for complaint relating to B Flight's work rate. A study of the squadron's patrols carried out from the end of April to the first few days of June shows that even the under-achieving A Flight led by the plodding FCdr MacLaren was more aggressive and had more contact with enemy aircraft than Draper's B Flight. It is not uncharitable to state that B Flight gave the impression that enemy aircraft were only engaged when circumstances forced the event, such as during escort missions.

Wing Captain Lambe appeared to lean towards Breese's opinion of Draper and on the same day forwarded Breese's letter to the Director of Air Services together with the following Memo:

Director of Air Services
Hotel Cecil

Submitted,
Forwarded.
Adverse report on this officer from Sq.Cdr Breese.

What I have seen of Acting Squadron Commander Draper confirms the opinion expressed of him by Squadron Commander Breese. I am afraid I cannot recommend him for any position of responsibility but should be much obliged if he could be removed from this squadron to another Command, in order to obtain an independent opinion.

I hesitate to place him in one of the other Squadrons here in case he has a demoralising effect.

4th June 1917
Wing Captain

Wing Captain Lambe's comments were also recorded in Draper's official record, adding to a long line of disapproving comments such as:

Christopher Draper, shown here in 1916 with the Eastchurch War Flight. *Courtesy EF Cheesman*

Very little idea of discipline but a brilliant pilot.
Good command when he cares to exercise it but is too inclined to be boisterous.
A very bad example to young pilots.

To be fair to Draper, his record also contains many positive comments but in life it generally takes many positives to outweigh one negative. Chris Draper had joined the RNAS before the war started in 1914 and whilst a remarkably accomplished pilot, his superiors often had problems with his attitude, which was not considered to be particularly "war like". They felt that he endangered discipline within the lower ranks.

In his autobiography, "The Mad Major", published in 1962 by Air Review Ltd, Draper tends to skirt around this period of his career. He does not mention No.11 Squadron at all, implying that he moved straight from the disbanding No.3 Wing to No.6 Squadron. The account of his altercation with SCdr

Breese is covered, however, and provides an interesting contrast to Breese's complaint to Wing Captain Lambe.

In Draper's account, Breese informed him that he had arranged for a joint patrol between No.6 Squadron and the Sopwith Pups of No.54 Squadron RFC which would "finish off the circus once and for all". As senior officer, Draper was to lead the combined patrol and the time, height and point of crossing the Lines had been predetermined. Draper stated that he argued that it should be up to the Flight Leader's discretion to determine where and when to cross the Lines but Breese was adamant that it had to be exactly as he had ordered. At this point Draper lost his temper, told Breese to "do the bloody job himself" and then stormed out.

If we accept Draper's account, it seems reasonable to deduce that the joint patrol referred to above was the first mass escort for the two FE2s of No.22 Squadron to be carried out at Squadron strength by the Pups of No.54 Squadron RFC and the Nieuports of No.6 Squadron on the 5th June 1917. This mission, of course, had been devised by Lieutenant Colonel R Lorraine of No.14 Wing, Breese would have not been at liberty to make any changes to Wing Orders as the crossing point and time would have had to have been synchronised between the FEs, Pups and Nieuports.

Breese, however, had initially complained to Wing Captain Lambe on the 29th May, almost certainly too early for Breese to have briefed Draper about a mission scheduled for the 5th June. The author's conclusion is that Breese had already decided to have Draper removed from the squadron and that relations between the two officers had deteriorated before Draper told Breese what to do with his mission.

It is unusual to be presented with both sides of the story and does offer the reader the opportunity to make his or her own mind up as to what actually was behind Draper's recall from the Western Front.

Whilst Breese had his request granted and Draper had been removed from the Squadron by the 11th June 1917, somewhat ironically he was thrust into close contact with enemy aircraft several days earlier on the 5th and 6th June. As mentioned above, No.14 Wing RFC required the squadron to mount a large patrol on the 5th June to escort two FE2b photographic machines of No.22 Squadron RFC. This was part of a Wing master plan whereby No.6 Squadron's Nieuports and the Pups of No.54 Squadron RFC would hopefully catch a large number of German defenders in the air, just as they were getting low on fuel. Draper led the patrol on the 5th June and was singled out for praise in an official 14 Wing report, he also led a similar patrol on the 6th June claiming one enemy machine destroyed and another out of control.

The epitome of fashion, Draper in casual attire at No.6 Squadron. *Courtesy Justin Young*

Despite Draper's performance, Lambe had already set the wheels in motion and Draper was recalled and posted to Home Establishment on the 11th June 1917 where he was kept under independent observation by Captain Steel at Eastchurch. Draper obviously impressed Steel enough to be given another chance and he was posted back to France and No.8 Squadron RNAS by the end of July, taking command of the squadron by the end of October.

Probably more comfortable performing on stage than when commanding men, Christopher Draper led a fascinating life and the author would urge any reader interested in learning more about Draper to obtain a copy of his autobiography "The Mad Major".

CHAPTER SIX

THE COAST AND CAMELS

As related in Chapter 4, the 4th Brigade and 14 Wing relocated to the coast at the end of June in support of the 4th Army. No.6 Squadron was withdrawn from the front at St. Quentin and transferred to Middle Aerodrome, Bray Dunes, to the east of Dunkerque. Control was briefly transferred to No.3 Wing 4 Brigade pending the move of 14 Wing and 4 Brigade Headquarters.

Bray Dunes was not just an aerodrome, it was a complex of three distinct aerodromes, The French Aerodrome, the RNAS Aerodrome (Frontier) and Middle Aerodrome. No.6 Squadron was initially housed at the Middle Aerodrome, moving to Frontier after a few days. At this time, Middle Aerodrome was under construction, a process severely handicapped by the necessity to wait for local farmers to finish growing their crops before access roads could be built. It must be assumed that the facilities available at the Middle Aerodrome at this time were very basic.

The squadron had already returned their Nieuport 17bis aircraft to the depot at Dunkerque and started to replace them with Sopwith Camels. Over the following days the squadron finished their re-equipping.

20th June

FLt Edwards rejoined No.6 Squadron at Middle Aerodrome in Camel N6331 after staying the night at Furnes with No.3 Squadron.

FLt Redpath collected Camel N6342 from the depot and later carried out a 45 minute practice flight.

21st June

No return for the 21st.

22nd June

Low cloud and showers prevented all war flying.

FLt Edwards made a practice flight in Camel N6331. The Camel's cowl came off at 3000 feet damaging the engine, centre section, upper plane and propeller. The cowl finally caught in a landing wire and lodged there until Edwards landed.

23rd June

No return for the 23rd.

24th June

New pilot FSL WA Curtis arrived at the squadron

25th June

In the afternoon, Sopwith Camels N6339, N6371, N6373 and N6379 were collected from the depot by Findlay, MacLaren, Gooderham and Breese.

FSL WA Curtis carried out his first flight with the squadron, a familiarisation flight in Camel N6342. He reported that he choked the engine at take off and touched the fence with an aileron on landing.

26th June

At this point, the squadron reported 14 pilots and 15 Sopwith Camel aircraft on strength.

Eight test and practice flights were carried out:

FLt Beasley	N6356 at 08.40 gun test, satisfactory
FLt Edwards	N6331 at 09.00 practice, exhaust valve stuck

THE
SOPWITH
AVIATION

OPPOSITE
TOP: An oblique view of the Bray Dunes area. It is believed that Frontier Aerodrome comprised the dark hangers backing on to the town of Bray Dunes and the landing ground to the west of these hangers, the lower light coloured hangers and the landing ground facing south were used by the French. In 1917 Middle Aerodrome was constructed just to the west of Frontier Aerodrome. Whilst No.6 Squadron was resident, there was very little present in the way of infrastructure, the RNAS having to wait until the farmers' crops were gathered before building roads and erecting buildings. *Courtesy Mike O'Connor*

BOTTOM: This Sopwith Camel photograph, taken at Brooklands, includes the statement "2nd Machine" on its official caption. The Camel is quite clearly not a prototype and so must therefore be the second production machine from the first batch produced for the Royal Naval Air Service. The photograph could depict N6330 which was the second production Camel to be delivered, or N6331 which was the second production Camel by serial number. Whatever the actual serial number of the aircraft in this photograph, both N6330 and N6331 were used by No.6 Squadron. The photograph shows the typical Sopwith factory finish to good effect. This would have been PC12 upper surfaces, clear doped linen under surfaces, fin and wheel covers, copal varnish on the plywood panels, and unpainted aluminium panels. The metal side cladding and the cowl display the "swirl" effect typical of an engine turned finish. *Courtesy JMB/GSL Collection*

RIGHT: FSL Wilfred Austin Curtis from Ontario. Curtis went on to become an ace with No.10 Squadron claiming a total of thirteen victories. After World War II, Curtis became Chief of Air Staff in Canada from 1947 to 1953. *Courtesy EF Cheesman*

FSL Curtis — N6342 at 09.00
formation practice with Edwards

FSL Walton — N6350 at 09.10
gun test, port gun would not cease firing

FSL Wood — N6334 at 09.25
practice, satisfactory

FSL Holyman — N6359 at 09.45
gun test, two slight cross feeds, cleared in the air, otherwise satisfactory

FSL Holyman — N6359 at 15.30
machine and engine test, satisfactory

FCdr MacLennan — N6360 at 16.10
test, satisfactory

Camel N6355 was collected from the depot.

27th June

More test and practice flights were carried out:

FSL Findlay — N6339 at 08.40
practice, engine satisfactory

FLt Edwards — N6331 at 08.55
test, guns satisfactory

FSL Walton — N6350 at 09.00 - practice

FSL Curtis — N6342 at 09.00
test, satisfactory

FLt Gooderham — N6373 at 09.20
test, engine vibrating

FSL Winter — N6358 at 09.30
practice, satisfactory

FCdr MacLennan — N6360 at 10.25
test, satisfactory

FSL Holyman — N6359 at 11.35
test, satisfactory

FSL Findlay — N6339 at 16.30 - practice

FSL Lawson — N6355 at 16.30
practice, both guns in order

FCdr MacLaren — N6371 at 18.00
test, guns and engine satisfactory

FSL Holyman — N6359 at 18.40
test, satisfactory

FLt Edwards — N6331 at 18.46
test, satisfactory

The first patrols were carried out from Middle Aerodrome out on the 27th:

FCdr MacLennan led Winter and Kirkpatrick to Ostend at 11.15. No enemy aircraft were sighted, MacLennan reported that a large fire was burning at Ostend.

FLt Edwards led Macgregor, Walton and Curtis to Ostend at 12.30 and along the lines from Nieuport to Dixmude. No enemy aircraft were encountered. Edwards experienced trouble with the engine in N6331 and was forced to return after half an hour. Curtis reported firing into trenches.

FCdr MacLaren led Gooderham and Wood on a line patrol at 16.30. MacLaren experienced problems when N6371's pressure valve fell off and dropped down inside the cockpit, forcing an early return to the aerodrome. Gooderham and Wood continued the patrol and observed an Allied kite balloon go down in flames behind Dixmude. They saw the attacking aircraft but were unable to intercept it.

28th June

Two test flights were carried out:

A variation of the Nissen hut was the Nissen Hospital hut, these were 60 feet long, 20 feet wide and 10 feet high. Windows were added to the hut sides. In this photograph, No.6 Squadron officers are relaxing outside a Nissen Hospital hut. FSL RR Winter, the middle officer, is easily identified.

An unusual view of the ubiquitous Nissen Hut under construction. The ends were fabricated from plywood sections that were rapidly assembled. The deck comprised wooden panels resting upon a framework of 2"x4" timber, whilst the roof and sides were made of corrugated steel. The whole structure was supported on curved I-beam steel ribs. The interior was lined with timber. Each hut had a few small windows and doors and was lit by paraffin lamps. Heating was provided by a small coke and coal stove. The Nissen hut was 27 feet long, 16 feet wide, and 8 feet high. *Courtesy EF Cheesman*

Also intended for rapid assembly was the canvas covered Bessoneau hanger. Constructed from braced girder assemblies these structures were nothing more than giant tents. *Courtesy Justin Young*

Although these photographs of a Bessoneau under construction are of poor resolution, it is interesting to see one of these familiar structures in a state of undress! *Courtesy Justin Young*

FCdr MacLennan	N6369 at 09.30 testing a new windscreen
FSL Winter	N6358 at 13.55 test, satisfactory

FCdr MacLennan led Findlay, Lawson and Wood on a line patrol at 14.00. The patrol ran into two rainstorms and unable to find any gaps in the cloud cover, MacLennan abandoned the patrol and returned to the aerodrome after 25 minutes.

Edwards led Macgregor, Walton and Curtis on a line patrol at 17.45. The weather was still bad and the patrol was abandoned after 20 minutes.

The 17.45 patrol was FLt Edward's last flight with No.6 Squadron. He left for a period in hospital followed by sick leave, before being posted to No.9 Squadron on the 10th August 1917.

29th June

At 09.20, the squadron changed aerodromes, moving from Middle Aerodrome to Frontier Aerodrome[1], a journey of less than 5 minutes, with control reverting back to 14 Wing 4 Brigade.

At 12.45 an enemy aircraft was observed over the aerodrome, MacLennan, Beasley, Lawson and Holyman took off in an attempt to intercept the enemy machine. Holyman was the only pilot to find the intruder but soon lost it in the clouds.

Three line patrols between Nieuport and Dixmude were flown on the 29th, the weather getting progressively worse during the day:

> FLt Gooderham led Wood and Findlay on the first patrol at 14.00. The patrol was uneventful and no enemy aircraft were encountered.
>
> FSL Walton led Carroll and Curtis on the second patrol at 16.30. The patrol was uneventful, however, the weather had started to deteriorate.
>
> FCdr MacLennan led Beasley and Holyman on the last patrol at 19.00. MacLennan encountered a heavy mist at 400 feet and immediately abandoned the patrol.

30th June

No flying due to unfavourable weather.

• • •

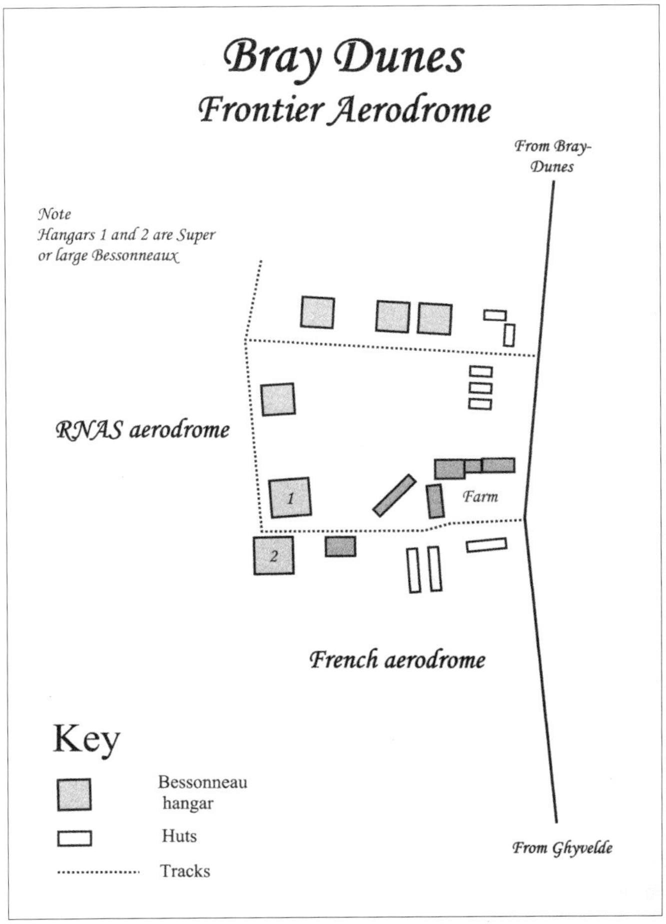

July 1917

The RFC's 4th Brigade completed its move to the Zuydcoote area on the 1st July. The Brigade War Diary reported enemy activity as slightly below normal throughout the month, no large enemy formations were encountered and few 2-seaters crossed the lines. The work done by No.6 Squadron and the Brigade's other scout squadrons was said to be successful in keeping hostile machines well behind their own lines with the result that the Corps machines were able to go about their work with little interference.

Regardless of the Brigade's official report, it was evident that No.6 Squadron's work rate had picked up dramatically, especially towards the end of the month.

1st July

The Flight structure at the beginning of July was as follows:

A Flight

FCdr CT MacLaren, Flight Commander
FLt PE Beasley

FSL AMcB Walton
FSL Wood
FSL Findlay
FSL WA Curtis

B Flight
AFCdr GG MacLennan, Flight Commander
FLt GA Gooderham
FLt GLE Stevens
FLt RF Redpath
FSL NM Macgregor

C Flight
FLt RR Winter, Acting Flight Commander
FLt GD Kirkpatrick
FSL H Lawson
FSL VC Holyman
FSL RE Carroll

The weather on the 1st was unsuitable for flying.

2nd July
Four test flights were carried out on the 2nd, two of these proved to be more eventful than anticipated:

FSL P Wood N6334 at 08.45
test, satisfactory
FLt GA Gooderham N6373 at 08.50
test, satisfactory
FCdr CT MacLaren N6371 at 08.50 – test. went over on to its nose after landing, damaging the bearer plates, propeller and both top planes.
FSL H Lawson N6355 at 08.50 – test, encountered an enemy aircraft during the test flight but was unable to catch it, he then encountered a second machine at which he fired a few rounds at long range. Lawson then emulated MacLaren by turning N6355 over upon landing.

OPPOSITE
TOP: An overhead view of Bray Dunes/Frontier Aerodromes. The French landing ground can be seen at the bottom of the photograph, the RNAS landing ground at the top left. *Courtesy JMB/GSL Collection*

BOTTOM: An oblique view of Frontier and Bray Dunes Aerodromes. Caudrons and Nieuports can be seen parked on the landing grounds. *Courtesy Mike O'Connor*

Walton led Carroll and Curtis on a line patrol at 09.00, the patrol saw several enemy machines but was unable to bring any to action.

Beasley carried out an uneventful enemy aircraft patrol at 11.10.

FCdr MacLennan led Holyman and Beasley on a line patrol at 18.00. The patrol reported heavy cloud cover at 7000 feet.

3rd July
At 06.30 FCdr MacLaren led Gooderham, Wood and Findlay on a line patrol from Pervyse to Nieuport and 2 miles out to sea. An enemy machine was discouraged from crossing the lines, MacLaren was unable to pursue it as his engine was down on power, giving only 975 rpm. FLt Gooderham chased the enemy machine as far as Ostende where it dived down beneath the port's anti-aircraft fire.

FCdr MacLennan led Holyman, Winter, Beasley and Kirkpatrick on a line patrol at 10.30. MacLennan engaged an enemy 2-seater to the northwest of Nieuport at 11.30, he dived on the enemy machine, came up under its tail and fired 25 rounds from each gun at very close range. He was forced to zoom up over the 2-seater in order to avoid a collision, allowing the enemy observer to shoot away the Camel's landing wires and put holes through the lower main spar, axle and propeller. To add insult to injury, one of MacLennan's guns jammed when a round shook loose from the belt. Holyman escorted MacLennan's shot-up Camel back to the aerodrome and then resumed the patrol. He spotted Allied anti-aircraft shells bursting over Nieuport and an enemy 2-seater escaping across the lines. Holyman waited and the enemy machine eventually came back and was working a zigzag pattern over a battery. Holyman followed the enemy machine for 2 miles out to sea, dived and opened fire from 50 yards range, after 50 rounds both guns jammed and the enemy aircraft was last seen heading towards Ostende.

Four practice flights were carried out in the morning:

FSL VC Holyman N6359 at 09.00
practice, satisfactory
FLt RR Winter N6358 at 09.05
practice, satisfactory
FCdr GG MacLennan N6360 at 09.10
practice, satisfactory
FLt GD Kirkpatrick N6357 at 09.10
practice, satisfactory

4th July

FCdr MacLennan led an early line patrol at 04.30 on the 4th but gun stoppages prevented the patrol from effectively engaging the enemy aircraft they encountered.

FCdr MacLaren led a five machine line patrol at 08.30, a single enemy machine was observed off Westende.

FSL Curtis flew a solo line patrol at 11.30 after reports were received of a hostile machine attacking trenches. No enemy aircraft were seen.

The continuing gun problem was obviously causing concern, as SCdr Breese made a rare flight in a Camel to test the armament.

New pilot FSL Kendall arrived at the squadron.

5th July

FSL Curtis was sent up to check the weather at 06.30, he reported thick cloud at 2500 feet and very bumpy conditions.

Despite the earlier findings, FLt Winter led a five machine line patrol at 07.25 but was forced to abort the mission after 30 minutes.

FCdr MacLaren carried out a test flight at 10.20 and found the cloud base to be even lower.

Gooderham, Wood and Findlay took off at 15.45 to carry out a line patrol to provide air cover for a visit by King George V.

6th July

Five engine and machine tests were carried out during the day:

FLt GA Gooderham	N6373 at 09.25 test, machine satisfactory
FLt RR Winter	N6379 at 11.40 engine test, satisfactory
FSL RE Carroll	N6351 at 11.45 engine test, satisfactory
FSL EH Kendall	N6331 at 12.00 engine test, satisfactory
FCdr GG MacLennan	N6360 at 13.20 machine test, satisfactory

FCdr MacLennan led Beasley, Kirkpatrick and Holyman on a line patrol at 15.00 but the flight soon suffered from gun problems again. MacLennan suffered from a stoppage in his port gun, whilst Beasley's machine suffered from synchroniser gear trouble which caused him to damage his propeller.

FLt Winter led Kendall, Carroll and Curtis on a line patrol between Nieuport and Dixmude at 19.00. The anti-aircraft fire was reported as very heavy and accurate over Ostende.

7th July

FCdr MacLaren led a patrol at 04.30, however, the engine in his Camel wouldn't give more than 1000rpm so he left the patrol to return to the aerodrome. He observed Allied anti-aircraft fire out to sea from Furnes and intercepted the machine which turned out to be a Sopwith Pup. MacLaren then observed two aircraft to the east of Dixmude, he eventually discovered that these were Belgian.

FCdr MacLennan led a line patrol at 06.30. A few enemy machines were observed on the enemy side of the lines and a number of kite balloons were mapped.

FCdr MacLennan led seven Camels off at 10.45 to intercept a formation of Gotha bombers returning from the second daylight raid on London. The Camels patrolled from Dunkerque to Zeebrugge, up to 25 miles out to sea but saw no enemy aircraft.

FSL Wood took off at 15.50 to chase an enemy machine but was unable to locate it.

8th and 9th July

Bad weather prevented all flying activity.

10th July

FCdr MacLennan led a four machine offensive patrol at 14.35 on the 10th. The patrol chased an enemy machine back over the lines to the south of Nieuport. They also reported seeing an ammunition train explode near Furnes, it being presumed that a German shell had destroyed the train.

FLt Winter led a line patrol at 20.00. No enemy aircraft were encountered.

11th July

Heavy overcast developed during the day and affected flying. FLt Winter led a line patrol at 05.55. No enemy aircraft were encountered but the positions of four kite balloons were mapped. Curtis reported that several RE8s were being heavily shelled.

FCdr MacLaren led an offensive patrol at 08.00, thick cloud over the lines made conditions difficult.

FCdr MacLennan attempted to lead a line patrol at 15.00 but was soon forced to abandon it due to the cloud. Another patrol was attempted at 16.05 during which MacLennan ob-

TOP LEFT: No.6 Squadron pilots relaxing. RR Winter and H Lawson swimming in what is believed to be the Dunkerque-Nieuport Canal. Winter is the one making the rude gesture to the camera. *Courtesy Justin Young* TOP RIGHT: Winter and Lawson. Lawson appears to be sitting upon a makeshift diving board. *Courtesy EF Cheesman*

served two enemy machines. At the end of the patrol Beasley turned N6351 over on its nose and Kendall repeated the same feat with N6331, wrecking the machine.

FLt Winter led an offensive patrol at 17.00, two enemy machines were observed off Ostende. Anti-aircraft fire over Westende was described as accurate, with the patrol's height gauged to within 10 feet.

12th July

Lawson and Findlay carried out an enemy aircraft patrol at 09.05. Three enemy machines were observed heading east between Nieuport and Ostende.

Winter and Kendall carried out a similar patrol at 10.20. At 10.50 near Slype, a lone enemy scout got behind Kendall and shot him down in flames from 13,000 feet. Winter described the incident in his combat report:

Slype, 13000 feet, 10.50
offensive patrol for reported wireless machine

On looking round I observed an enemy machine directly behind FSL Kendall.

FSL Kendall dived, closely followed by the enemy aircraft and I turned and dived also but was unable to fire at once as I was afraid of hitting our own machine. When I was able to I fired 200 rounds at the enemy aircraft, which left Kendall and continued to dive. I observed a trail of smoke and discovered that Kendall's machine had been set on fire.

The enemy machine was not seen again but I do not believe that it was out of control.

FCdr MacLennan and FLt Winter led their flights on an offensive patrol at 12.45, very few enemy aircraft were seen. Gooderham in N6375 had to return after 10 minutes with engine trouble.

SCdr Breese flew Camel N6371 to a French Aerodrome on the Dunkerque – Berques road to a demonstration in the afternoon.

13th July

FLt Winter led an offensive patrol at 05.40. Three hostile machines attacked the patrol from out of the sun, Winter was attacked by one and the other two attacked Curtis who was forced to dive away.

Winter and Curtis carried out a hostile aircraft patrol at 11.35. Two enemy aircraft had been reported from Nieuport but could not be found.

FCdr MacLennan led an offensive patrol at 12.45. The patrol reported seeing a few enemy machines behind their lines at 13.30.

14th July

SCdr Breese carried out a weather test at 07.45, thick cloud made conditions unsuitable for patrols.

FCdr MacLennan and FLt Winter led their flights on an offensive patrol at 13.45 but found the cloud cover to be too thick to continue the patrol. The Camels remained over Nieuport from 14.30 to 15.50 to protect an RE8. At 15.50, the patrol came down and patrolled the lines at 5000 feet, numerous Allied machines were seen but no enemy aircraft were observed.

FSL NM Macgregor made a couple of practice flights in the evening.

15th July

At 09.45, FCdr MacLaren led his flight on an offensive patrol to St. Pierre Capelle between Westende and Middlekerke. The patrol observed one enemy machine near St. Pierre Capelle heading in an easterly direction at 10.15 and an unidentified machine which eventually turned out to be a SPAD. Wood flying N6334 had to make a forced landing just after taking off when his engine seized.

FCdr MacLennan and FLt Winter led offensive patrols at 15.45. Kirkpatrick's machine suffered from broken ignition leads and he had to return to exchange his Camel. MacLennan and Kirkpatrick saw no enemy aircraft, however, Winter's flight encountered three groups of enemy aircraft stacked at different heights. Winter declined to attack, as it was an obvious trap.

16th July

The weather was bad on the 16th. FCdr MacLaren carried out a weather test at 05.45 and reported that the conditions were unsatisfactory.

Despite MacLaren's report, FCdr MacLennan led a patrol at 06.00 but was forced to abandon it after 20 minutes. He tried again at 06.30 but the visibility was very poor and he led the Flight down to 7000 feet and carried out a defensive patrol. No enemy aircraft were seen and little activity along the lines.

FLt Winter led an offensive patrol in the vicinity of Nieuport and Dixmude at 13.40. A lone enemy machine was encountered off Westende but it turned and dived into the clouds when approached.

SCdr Breese led an offensive patrol at 18.45. His patrol comprised Winter, MacLennan, Kirkpatrick and Macgregor. The patrol encountered three large enemy machines coming in from the sea at 19.40, these dived away when approached. The patrol also saw black smoke on the sand dunes at Westende Plage at 19.20 and thought it might be issuing from a burning aircraft.

17th July

FLt Winter led a defensive patrol at 05.10. The patrol encountered two enemy machines flying low near Dixmude being chased by a SPAD. Three kite balloons were located at Wilkerske, Zevecote and Leffinge.

FCdr MacLaren led a defensive patrol at 08.15. Two of the kite balloons were still up at Wilkerske and at Leffinge. At 10.00, Lawson observed a large enemy aeroplane over Nieuport at 14000 feet. As Lawson climbed, the enemy machine matched his rate of climb and effectively prevented him from getting within attack range. Findlay observed an enemy machine gliding down towards Ostende after being shelled.

FCdr MacLaren led an offensive patrol at 11.15. The patrol observed six enemy aircraft heading towards Ostende at 12.00.

FCdr MacLennan and FLt Winter led Offensive patrols at 15.40. They encountered two enemy aircraft near Ostende and another flying low over Slype. The patrol also reported a British machine on the beach to the east of Nieuport Piers.

FCdr MacLaren attempted to carry out an offensive patrol at 19.15 but due to the thick clouds changed to a defensive patrol carried out at 3000 feet. Gooderham flying N6373 was forced to return to the aerodrome when his machine's oil tank ruptured.

18th July

FCdr MacLaren carried out a weather test at 05.05, the cloud was at 2500 feet and it was intermittently raining. FLt Winter carried out a further weather test at 17.15 but there was no improvement.

New pilot FSL FS Strathy arrived at the squadron.

19th July

The weather was still bad on the 19th, it was not possible to perform a weather test until 17.15.

20th July

With the return of FLt BHP De Roeper from sick leave, the Flight structure changed somewhat:

A Flight

FCdr CT MacLaren, Flight Commander
FLt GA Gooderham, Deputy Flight Commander
FSL Wood
FSL Findlay
FSL Lawson

B Flight

FLt GG MacLennan, Flight Commander
FLt Kirkpatrick, Deputy Flight Commander

FSL Forman
FSL Strathy

C Flight
FLt BHP De Roeper, Flight Commander
FLt RR Winter, Deputy Flight Commander
FSL NM Macgregor
FSL RE Carroll
FSL WA Curtis

FLt Winter led his flight on an offensive patrol at 04.10, no enemy machines were encountered but two kite balloons were seen to the south of Ostende.

FCdr MacLennan led a defensive patrol at 07.00 and located two kite balloons 2 miles east of Nieuport.

FCdr MacLaren led a defensive patrol along the lines between Nieuport and Pervyse to provide cover for RE8s. The RE8s were not seen.

FCdr MacLennan led an offensive patrol at 13.00. The patrol encountered three 2-seaters flying in a "V" at 9000 feet over Middlekerke at 14.30. MacLennan led the patrol in a dive on to the left hand machine and was seen to fire at close range. The enemy machine side-slipped and fell spinning for a very long distance until out of sight. The patrol split up whilst fighting the remaining two machines and when it reformed FCdr MacLennan was missing. Although several claims for Sopwith Camels on the 20th July were submitted by the German Air Service, none of them correspond to the time of MacLennan's death.

At 15.25, FLt De Roeper led C Flight, with Winter reverting to deputy leader, on an offensive patrol. No enemy aircraft were seen but a heavy smoke screen was observed at Slype.

21st July

FLt De Roeper led an offensive patrol at 11.25. One enemy machine was observed off Ostende at 12.30, one enemy machine observed landing at Ghistelles at 12.40 and two enemy machines were seen over Blankenberghe at 13.10.

FCdr MacLaren led an offensive patrol at 16.00 over Leke, Middlekerke, Westende and seawards. The patrol encountered two 2-seaters over Middlekerke at 16.40, the enemy aircraft went down to Middlekerke and the patrol waited out at sea in the hope that they would reappear. Whilst the patrol was waiting, they were surprised by a formation of five Albatros scouts which dived and attacked and then headed off towards Ostende. Several Bristol Fighters were observed over Middlekerke and it was believed that they engaged the 2-seaters.

FLt De Roeper led an offensive patrol at 19.30. Four members of the patrol fired on enemy trenches and gun emplacements from 1500 feet. The patrol encountered five Albatros scouts at 20.05, Carroll dived and attacked a scout firing 400 rounds from 50 yards range. Carroll saw tracers enter the fuselage and the machine went down spinning and emitting thick clouds of smoke, Carroll then engaged a second machine and fired at long range, the enemy machine dived away steeply. Winter dived and attacked another scout firing a long burst from 200 yards, the enemy machine appeared to break up but at that instant Macgregor flashed across in front of Winter. When Winter flattened out, all of the enemy machines had vanished. Curtis had remained above the formation to prevent any other hostile machines diving on to the attacking Camels. He was attacked and had the main spar of his top plane shot through. After picking up the formation, Curtis foolishly remained with the patrol for 30 minutes.

22nd July

FCdr MacLaren led A Flight on an offensive patrol at 07.00. The patrol observed one enemy machine low over Middlekerke at 08.40 and another machine leaving Ostende at 08.45.

SCdr Breese led Strathy, Forman and Campbell-Orde on a defensive patrol at 10.30. At 10.50 an unidentified machine was seen to spin down and crash. Three enemy aircraft were seen over Dixmude, the patrol made round to seaward, climbed and attempted to intercept but lost the enemy machines against the sea when ten to twelve miles out.

C Flight carried out an offensive patrol at 11.30. At 13.00, De Roeper fired 150 rounds at an enemy machine without effect. Three kite balloons were reported to be operating south-east of Ostende. The patrol fired into enemy trenches.

Kirkpatrick and Lawson performed an uneventful enemy aircraft patrol at 14.25.

A Flight carried out an offensive patrol at 16.00. The patrol observed three enemy machines over Ostende at 16.40. At 17.35, MacLaren saw an Albatros scout with diamond fuselage markings about 1000 feet above the patrol, the scout dived and attacked FSL Lawson who went into a spiral. MacLaren got the enemy's height, manoeuvred behind him and fired 40 rounds. Tracers were seen entering the right lower plane and the fuselage. The enemy scout broke out of the spiral and MacLaren lost sight of him under his Camel's wing, MacLaren went over on his back and fell 1000 feet. The enemy machine was last seen heading for Ostende. Findlay observed four enemy aircraft over Dixmude at 17.50, he followed them and engaged one over Steene. The enemy machine dived at Findlay who waited until he was at the same level before opening fire. The enemy aircraft dived away with Findlay in pursuit, Findlay fired approximately 400 rounds and saw tracers enter the fuselage. The enemy machine went down in a nosedive from which it was not seen to recover.

FLt De Roeper led C Flight on an offensive patrol in the late evening. At 20.40, when 3 miles northeast of Dixmude, De Roeper observed two enemy machines heading towards Middlekerke at 17500 feet. The lead aircraft turned head-on to De Roeper and opened fire but the tracers were wide of his left wing by 12 yards. De Roeper decreased his radius of turn, dived straight at the enemy machine and fired a burst of 30 rounds, then pulled up to avoid a collision. The scout turned and dived for its lines, De Roeper followed and opened fire with both guns from 30 yards. After 100 rounds, the enemy machine stalled and went into a spin, De Roeper followed it down to 6500 feet at which point it was still spinning. Curtis reported that he sat up in the sun waiting for hostile machines to attack the formation of Camels, he eventually lost sight of the Camels in the darkness.

23rd July

De Roeper led Winter, Curtis and Carroll on an offensive patrol at 05.30. Heavy cloud at 7000 feet and mist below the cloud resulted in the patrol being abandoned after 40 minutes.

FLt Kirkpatrick led five Camels on a defensive patrol at 10.00. At 11.30, Findlay attacked an enemy kite balloon to the east of Dixmude. Foreman fired into enemy trenches at 11.55.

FLt Winter led C Flight on an offensive patrol at 14.30. A formation of five enemy scouts and 2-seaters was encountered over St. Pierre Capelle at 16.00. Strathy attempted to attack two of the enemy machines but rapidly found himself under attack. In the ensuing fight, Strathy fired a burst at one of the enemy machines without effect.

FCdr MacLaren led an offensive patrol at 19.00 from Nieuport to Middlekerke, behind St. Pierre Capelle and Dixmude. MacLaren and Lawson observed three enemy aircraft heading northeast from behind Dixmude at 14000 feet. The Camels dived on the formation, the first enemy machine dived away, whilst another tried to work around behind MacLaren but then dived away when MacLaren tried to engage it. MacLaren then broke away as four more enemy machines appeared from the direction of Ghistelles. At 20.35, three enemy machines were seen over Nieuport, MacLaren dived towards them but they immediately dived away to the east. Gooderham observed a flight of Albatros scouts near Moeres at 20.15, he attacked his chosen machine from behind and above and saw his tracer bullets entering the fuselage near the pilots seat. The enemy machine went into a spin which continued for 3000 feet, when last seen the aircraft was on its back. Gooderham was unable to watch the enemy machine any further as he was attacked, lost his engine and was forced to spin away. He restarted his engine at 7000 feet and returned to the aerodrome with his Camel "considerably riddled". Wood encountered several Albatros scouts to the east of Dixmude at 20.30. He dived on one and fired a burst, the enemy machine went into a spin and Wood followed him down. When the enemy machine recovered, Wood fired another burst and the Albatros went down in a vertical dive, Wood followed him down to 8000 feet without seeing him recover. Findlay reported that he had seen Wood attack an enemy machine which spun away and recovered after 3000 to 4000 feet and then went into a vertical dive, A hand written note on the combat report stated that the result was not certain enough to claim an "out of control".

24th July

FLt Winter led a patrol at 04.30 to pursue enemy bombers. Lawson was the only pilot to encounter the bombers near Furnes but was only able to fire one burst at long range.

FLt De Roeper led an offensive patrol at 08.45 but the weather had started to close in and the patrol was abandoned after half an hour.

FLt Kirkpatrick led Forman and Strathy on a line patrol at 08.45, visibility was bad and the patrol had nothing to report.

With the loss of FLt MacLennan, SCdr Breese rearranged the Flight structure:

A Flight

FCdr CT MacLaren, Flight Commander
FLt GA Gooderham
FLt RF Redpath
FSL MH Findlay
FSL H Lawson

B Flight

FCdr BHP De Roeper, Flight Commander
FSL WA Curtis

ABOVE: Two new Camels from the first production batch outside Sopwith's hangars at Brooklands. Both of the machines were delivered to the depot at St. Pol by 24th May 1917. Author's collection

RIGHT: Another view of the previous location. The nearest Camel, N6332 was transferred to the RFC at St. Omer on the 25th May 1917. Behind N6332 is N6334 which was delivered to No.6 Squadron on 16th June 1917. FSL P Wood was flying N6334 when he claimed an Albatros scout destroyed to the east of Dixmude on the 23rd July 1917. The Canadian pilot, FSL FS Strathy was killed in N6334 when he was shot down near Zevcote on the 17th August 1917. Author's collection

FSL RE Carroll
FSL NM Macgregor
FSL JH Forman

C Flight
FLt RR Winter, Flight Commander
FLt GD Kirkpatrick
FSL VC Holyman
FSL FS Strathy
FSL P Wood
FSL AC Campbell-Orde

This coincided with the introduction of a new tactic comprising a simultaneous outer offensive patrol and inner defensive patrol. The offensive patrol being at Flight strength and consisting of at least four and usually five Camels, whilst the defensive patrol was usually carried out with three Camels. The intention of the simultaneous patrol was twofold, if either patrol was attacked, the other patrol would in theory be close enough to rapidly give support, and if an enemy machine crossed the lines it stood a good chance of being trapped between the two patrols.

FCdr MacLaren led an offensive patrol at 13.15, the visibility was very bad and no enemy machines were seen.

FSL Macgregor led Carroll and Curtis on the simultaneous defensive patrol at 13.10. The visibility was very bad and no enemy aircraft were seen.

FLt De Roeper led an offensive patrol at 19.15, the patrol encountered a formation of eight enemy machines coming from Ostende but they were 1500 feet above the patrol.

FCdr MacLaren led Gooderham and Strathy on a defensive patrol at 19.15, no enemy machines were encountered.

25th July

FCdr MacLaren led A Flight on an offensive patrol at 07.15. The patrol found cloud starting at 4500 feet and heavy cover at 9500 feet. Visibility was so poor that the pilot's reported that they could hardly see. An enemy machine was encountered near St. Pierre Capelle at 6000 feet, it turned east and was immediately lost to view. The formation ran into rainstorms after 30 minutes and MacLaren aborted the patrol.

De Roeper led a three machine defensive patrol at 07.15. One enemy machine was observed towards Ostende, the patrol was otherwise uneventful.

FCdr MacLaren and Lawson took off at 09.05 in response to the report of an enemy machine at Nieuport. It was raining heavily and the enemy machine was not seen.

FSL Campbell-Orde performed a defensive patrol at 16.20 in response to report of an enemy machine in the vicinity. No enemy machines were seen.

FLt De Roeper led an offensive patrol 16.15. Two enemy aircraft were encountered over Ostende, these went down through the clouds when approached. De Roeper turned N6341 over on its nose at the end of the patrol. During the patrol Macgregor drove an enemy artillery spotter back from the lines.

FCdr MacLaren led a defensive patrol at 16.15, the patrol encountered three enemy aircraft to the south of Middlekerke at 16.40 and a single enemy machine heading back and forth between Middlekerke and St. Pierre Capelle.

26th July

FLt Winter led a defensive patrol at 12.00 on the 26th. No enemy machines were seen, the cloud base was very low and visibility was very poor. Two of the patrol's machines suffered ignition faults. Upon their return, Curtis and Macgregor indulged in a mock dogfight over Nieuport.

FLt Lawson led Wood and Findlay on a defensive patrol at 16.15. A formation of three enemy aircraft was seen diving away from another formation of Camels to the east of Dixmude at 17.00.

FLt Winter led an offensive patrol at 16.15. At 17.00, three enemy aircraft attacked the patrol over Slype. FSL Campbell-Orde was bringing up the rear of the patrol when he saw an enemy machine above and behind him, as he turned to attack he found he was being attacked by two more enemy scouts. Winter and the rest of the patrol rescued Campbell-Orde and drove off the enemy machines, Winter's Camel suffering from stoppages in both guns. At 17.35 when over St. Georges, an enemy machine was seen coming from Nieuport, the patrol dived to attack but the enemy machine disappeared under a bank of cloud. Shortly afterwards, Campbell-Orde who had been lagging behind the patrol with engine trouble came under attack again. Hearing shots from behind, Campbell-Orde turned sharply right and tried to climb up to an Albatros scout which he saw above him, at this point the Camel was raked with a burst of fire that damaged the engine and tanks and wounded Campbell-Orde in three places on his left hand side. Campbell-Orde dived and twisted and got away whilst Winter, Strathy and Forman drove off the two scouts that were attacking him. Forman followed one of the scouts down to 4500 feet and fired at very close range seeing his tracers entering the fuselage, at that point both guns jammed and Forman was forced to disengage. As he turned away he thought he saw the scout side-slip and fall out of control.

New pilot FSL HB Maund arrived at the squadron.

27th July

Kirkpatrick, Strathy and Maund attempted to perform a defensive patrol at 07.15. The cloud base was at 500 feet and Kirkpatrick abandoned the patrol and returned to the aerodrome after 10 minutes.

FLt Winter led Gooderham and Maund on an uneventful defensive patrol at 12.00.

Several special missions were flown in the afternoon in response to enemy aircraft incursions reported by wireless. In each case no enemy aircraft were encountered.

FLt Winter led an offensive patrol at 16.25. The patrol encountered and engaged several enemy formations without decisive result. After taking part in two indecisive combats, Forman encountered a slate coloured Albatros scout to the east of Nieuport at 17.10. After manoeuvring to put the sun at his back, Forman dived until within 40 yards of the enemy scout, fired a short burst, whereupon the scout nose-dived and then burst into flames.[2] Findlay had previously attacked the same scout, firing 200 rounds without effect and was able to confirm that Forman had sent it down in flames to crash into the sea. Curtis saw the burning Albatros plunge past him and crash into the sea, describing it as "spooky" in his log. Later, Curtis climbed in company with Bristol Fighters of No.48 Squadron RFC in pursuit of two enemy aircraft seen over the Allied lines.

28th July

FLt Gooderham led an offensive patrol at 05.45. The patrol attacked one enemy machine but it escaped into the cloud cover.

FLt Kirkpatrick led Strathy and Forman on a defensive patrol at 05.45. Three kite balloons were seen and Forman saw two enemy aircraft.

The weather closed in a little with low cloud and poor visibility. This affected De Roeper's offensive patrol at 10.15, causing it to be aborted after 25 minutes.

BELOW: Defending the coastal region in opposition to No.6 Squadron, *Marinefeldjasta* I were regularly encountered. In this photograph, 4 Albatros DVs are taking off from Aartrijke airfield. Pfalz DIIIs can be seen in the background. *Courtesy University of Texas, Dallas/A Imrie collection*

ABOVE: Albatros DV's of *Marinefeldjasta* I. *Courtesy University of Texas, Dallas/ A Imrie collection*

FLt Gooderham was able to lead a defensive patrol at 10.15, several enemy machines were seen to be operating well behind their own lines near Ostende.

FLt Winter led an offensive patrol at 14.45. Winter, accompanied by Kirkpatrick, Macgregor and Strathy, dived to attack two enemy 2-seaters seen to the south of Wilskerke at 16.00. Winter attacked one of the 2-seaters and fired a long burst into it, as he pulled away FSL Macgregor also got a long burst into the 2-seater. The enemy machine flew straight and level for several seconds and then fell in a spin and was seen to crash in a field near the canal. FSL Forman, suspecting a trap, remained high when the rest of the patrol dived to attack the 2-seaters. Three Albatros scouts appeared above him, Forman climbed and attacked one at very close range, he fired a sharp burst at the enemy machine and then had to turn away to avoid a collision. Forman was sure that he had hit his opponent but was unable to follow him down as he came under attack from one of the other Albatros scouts. Forman was wounded in his right shoulder but was able to get his machine safely back across the lines. He made a forced landing in a field of broad beans and turned his Camel over.

FLt De Roeper led Carroll and Curtis on a defensive patrol at 14.45. Two enemy machines were observed off Ostende and proceeding towards Dixmude, about 4 miles over the lines. The patrol was unable to get close enough to attack them.

FCdr MacLaren led an offensive patrol at 19.15. Seven enemy machines were observed near Ostende, these went down when attacked but later climbed up to 17500 feet where the patrol was unable to reach them, their Camels struggling to get above 17000 feet. The enemy machines waited off Westende, until about 20.30 when one half-heartedly attacked and then dived away.

FLt Winter led Kirkpatrick and Strathy on a defensive patrol at 19.15. No enemy machines were encountered.

29th July

FLt Kirkpatrick led Maund and Strathy on an uneventful defensive patrol at 07.15.

A Flight carried out an offensive patrol at 07.15. The engine in FCdr MacLaren's Camel would not start for 45 minutes, however, he was able to pick up the patrol to the east of Nieuport. The visibility was very bad and it proved impossible to observe anything on the ground.

FLt De Roeper carried out a solo patrol at 14.15 to report on the number of enemy kite balloons being deployed. He was only able to find one balloon.

At 16.15 De Roeper led Curtis and Maund on a defensive patrol. The weather closed in after 30 minutes reducing the cloud base to 800 feet. No enemy aircraft were observed.

FSL Strathy carried out a weather test at 16.30, to determine if the scheduled offensive patrol would be viable. The rapidly deteriorating weather resulted in the patrol being cancelled.

30th July

FLt Kirkpatrick led Strathy and Maund on a defensive patrol at 08.00. The cloud base was still at 800 feet and Kirkpatrick abandoned the patrol after 5 minutes.

B Flight attempted to carry out an offensive patrol at 16.15, the weather had deteriorated further and the patrol came back after an hour.

FLt MacLaren led a defensive patrol at 16.15. The cloud was still a problem but MacLaren kept the patrol out for two hours. No enemy machines were observed.

31st July

The weather suffered further deterioration and the squadron made no attempt to fly.

• • •

August 1917

The 4th Brigade's War diary recorded enemy activity to be normal, with large formations of enemy aircraft seldom encountered. The prevailing westerly wind was frequently very strong during August and hampered the Brigade's operations.

Once again, despite the official pronouncement, the work performed by No.6 Squadron seemed to have stepped up a gear, the introduction of the Sopwith Camel having revitalised the squadron.

For some time, t*he RNAS had found itself overstretched and unable to cope with the attrition rate of men and machines experienced during the summer of 1917. After discussion with the RFC, the decision was taken to disband No.6 Squadron and use the men and machines to "shore up" the other squadrons. No.11 Squadron, under RNAS control and also based at Frontier aerodrome, met the same fate.*

Flugmaat Ludwig of *Marinefeldjasta* I poses with his Albatros DV. Ludwig claimed one victory. *Courtesy University of Texas, Dallas/A Imrie collection*

1st to 4th August

The bad weather at the end of July persisted into August and the squadron was unable to mount any patrols for the first four days of the month.

5th August

The Squadron's first patrol in August was carried out on the 5th when FLt Winter led an offensive patrol at 16.15. The patrol encountered a lone machine over the Floods at 17.00 but was unable to bring it to action. At 17.40, a formation of six enemy aircraft was observed at 10000 feet over Westende. After unsuccessfully manoeuvring for position, these machines headed off towards Ostende.

FLt De Roeper led the simultaneous defensive patrol. The patrol encountered five enemy machines at 17.15 but these proved to be a trap. The patrol headed towards the enemy for-

Flgmstr Brenner of *MFJ* I with his Albatros DV. *Courtesy University of Texas, Dallas/A Imrie collection*

mation and was immediately attacked from above by another formation of six enemy aircraft. The patrol was attacked again at 17.50 by six more enemy machines. Curtis shook off the enemy scout that had been on his tail and was able to drive off the scout which had been attacking Carroll. Carroll reported that as the enemy scouts dived away from their initial attack, one made for an Allied reconnaissance machine which was working over the Floods. Carroll attacked the enemy machine at long range and was able to drive it off. Sopwith Pups of No.54 Squadron RFC joined in the engagement just as the combatants were dispersing.

6th August

The weather was unsuitable for flying.

7th August

FLt De Roeper led an offensive patrol at 16.15, six enemy machines were encountered behind Ostende. These machines disappeared through the cloud as the patrol was manoeuvring for position.

FCdr MacLaren led the defensive patrol. The visibility was very bad and no enemy machines were observed. The patrol reported an unusual intensity of artillery activity.

8th August

FLt Winter performed an enemy aircraft patrol at 11.15 when a hostile machine was reported to be in the vicinity of Dunkerque. The enemy aircraft was not located.

FLt De Roeper attempted to lead an inner line patrol at 11.15 but aborted the mission after 40 minutes due to bad weather.

FCdr MacLaren led a defensive patrol at 16.15, no enemy machines were encountered and the patrol escorted a corps machine until thunderclouds started to develop and the patrol was aborted.

FLt De Roeper led the simultaneous offensive patrol. Numerous enemy aircraft were encountered between Ostende and Nieuport. De Roeper judged the situation to be a trap and decided not to take the patrol into its jaws.

9th August

FCdr MacLaren led an offensive patrol at 07.15 to the east of Westende and St. Pierre Capelle. Two enemy aircraft were observed low down over Middlekerke but these went down when approached. Another machine was seen to the east of Middlekerke at 08.30.

FLt Kirkpatrick led an uneventful defensive patrol at 07.15.

SCdr Breese took off at 09.37 in pursuit of an enemy machine which had passed over the aerodrome. By the time he got airborne the intruder had vanished.

FCdr MacLaren led a defensive patrol at 11.45. The patrol broke through the cloud at 10000 feet but they were unable to see the RE8s working below so they were forced to come down to 3000 feet. At this height they nearly became entangled in the RE8s' aerials[3] and were getting in the way of each other and the 2-seaters, forcing MacLaren to abandon the patrol. On their way back they observed a SPAD come under heavy attack from an Allied anti-aircraft battery.

FLt Winter led an offensive patrol at 11.45, several enemy machines were encountered between Middlekerke and Ostende but the patrol was unable to bring them to action.

10th August

FLt Winter led an inner line patrol at 07.15, no enemy machines were observed. The formation escorted an RE8 and then returned due to the weather closing in.

FLt De Roeper led an outer line patrol at 07.15. The patrol escorted a formation of RE8s but was otherwise uneventful.

FCdr MacLaren led an outer line patrol to Westende and St. Pierre Capelle at 12.05. An enemy machine was observed to the south of Ostende at 12.45 and another was encountered over Nieuport as the patrol was returning.

FLt De Roeper led an inner line patrol at 12.10, covering Middlekerke to Slype and St. Pierre Capelle. Nothing was seen until 13.30 when a machine was observed above the patrol. The enemy aircraft headed east as soon as the patrol started to climb.

At 16.15, FCdr MacLaren led an inner line patrol. Whilst the patrol was protecting RE8s it came under accurate anti-aircraft fire and MacLaren's Camel was hit when over the Floods between St. Pierre Capelle and Pervyse. One enemy machine was encountered at 17.50 over Coxyde but the patrol was unable to climb up to it.

FLt Winter led an outer line patrol at 16.15. An enemy machine was encountered over Nieuport but went east when approached and circled over Ostende waiting for an opportunity to cross the lines. Three more enemy aircraft were encountered at 19.20 and driven east.

SCdr Breese took off at 19.20 in pursuit of an enemy machine sighted from the aerodrome.

11th August

Winter, Kirkpatrick and Strathy carried out an inner line patrol at 05.30. Whilst the patrol was in the air, rainstorms developed and Winter was forced lead the patrol back at a height of 50 feet.

FCdr MacLaren led another inner line patrol at 08.45. The weather was still bad with rain and clouds at 1000 feet. No kite balloons or RE8s were working, leading MacLaren to abandon the patrol.

Findlay, Carroll and Maund performed an inner line patrol at 14.15. The patrol provided protection for a number of RE8s working over the lines. No enemy aircraft were seen.

FCdr MacLaren led an outer line patrol at 17.45 but was forced to return with engine trouble. FLt Gooderham took over the patrol which was relatively uneventful with just two enemy machines being seen well behind their own lines.

FSL Macgregor led an inner line patrol at the same time, a number of enemy machines were seen behind their own lines. The patrol encountered an enemy scout which was attacking an RE8 and drove it off, Macgregor firing 100 rounds at the enemy machine without result.

12th August

FLt Winter led an inner line patrol at 06.45. Two kite balloons were observed at Leffinghe and another was seen at Zeyecote. The patrol also saw two enemy machines well behind their own lines.

At 09.30, FCdr MacLaren led an outer line patrol and FCdr De Roeper led an inner line patrol. The outer patrol unsuccessfully attacked a formation of six enemy machines. Wood was forced to return with a bullet through his Camel's oil tank. The outer patrol was later attacked and driven back to the lines by two enemy scouts from a formation of six machines. The inner patrol was relatively uneventful, with just a single machine seen at 14000 feet when the patrol was at 6000 feet.

FLt Winter led an outer line patrol and FLt Gooderham flew a solo inner line patrol at 13.30. Winter's flight encountered 4 enemy machines over Nieuport, the Camels were unable to get close to the enemy machines but both Winter and Macgregor fired several bursts at long range. Macgregor's Camel experienced gun synchronisation trouble and he was forced to return with his propeller shot through. Redpath, freshly returned from leave, was in Winter's Flight and reported firing at one of the enemy machines and then diving away.

Gooderham's inner line patrol saw several enemy machines well across the lines. One enemy machine was observed returning from the direction of Dunkerque but crossed the lines before Gooderham could get to its height.

FCdr MacLaren led an outer patrol at 17.15, however thick cloud started to develop and by 18.00 was down to 5000 feet. One enemy machine was observed at the start of the patrol.

FLt De Roeper led an inner line patrol and RE escort at 17.15. Several enemy aircraft were observed keeping well behind their own lines. Later during the evening an RFC ground signal directed the patrol towards Ostende where two artillery spotters were engaged in directing a shoot. The patrol waited outside Ostende for half an hour but the spotting machines did not reappear. The patrol kept Mariakerke aerodrome under direct observation for 20 minutes but no activity was observed.

13th August

FCdr MacLaren led Wood and Findlay on an inner line patrol at 07.00. At 08.30 five enemy aircraft were encountered patrolling a line between Middlekerke and St. Pierre Capelle at 4000 feet. When approached they retreated to the east.

FLt De Roeper led an outer line patrol at 07.00. When the patrol was at 19500 feet an enemy machine was observed at 14000 feet, De Roeper, Maund and Redpath dived towards the hostile aircraft which immediately retreated before they could engage it. Carroll observed an enemy machine passing over the Floods, he gave chase and fired 200 rounds without effect.

FLt Gooderham led Maund and Carroll on an inner line patrol at 10.45. The patrol observed five enemy machines behind their lines and tried to climb above them, they were warned by their own anti-aircraft fire and most retired inland. One machine, however, remained in the area and attacked an RE8 beneath the clouds. FSL Carroll fired on the enemy machine which dived away steeply.

FLt Winter led a five Camel outer line patrol at 10.45. One enemy machine was observed but the patrol was unable to engage it. Lawson turned N6330 over on to its nose when landing.

FCdr MacLaren led an outer line patrol at 14.45 but thick cloud developed at 15.55 and forced the patrol to return. Two enemy aircraft were observed to the east of St. Pierre Capelle, when approached by the patrol they escaped towards Ostende at 15.20. Another enemy machine was seen over St. Pierre Capelle at 15.30 but the patrol was unable to reach its height.

FLt Winter led Redpath and Strathy on an inner patrol at 14.45. Three enemy aircraft were observed 4 to 5 miles east-southeast of Nieuport between 16.10 and 16.25.

FLt De Roeper led an outer line patrol at 18.30. Two enemy aircraft were observed at 19000 feet when the patrol was still at 15000 feet. At 20.10, three enemy machines were driven away.

FCdr MacLaren led an inner line patrol at 18.30, the visibility was reported as very bad due to haze and mist. No enemy aircraft were observed.

New pilot FSL ED Abbot made two practice flights during the day, the first was satisfactory but on completion of his second flight, he turned Camel N6356 over when landing.

14th August

FLt De Roeper led an outer line patrol at 10.45. The patrol was beset by technical problems, Maund's engine suffered a problem with an inlet valve, Wood's Camel suffered a snapped cross bracing wire and Macgregor's engine started to backfire. De Roeper continued the patrol with Carroll who ineffectually attacked an enemy machine seen approaching the lines. Carroll's machine was then hit by anti-aircraft fire and suffered a damaged main spar.

FLt Winter led Strathy and Abbot on an inner line patrol at 10.45. At 11.15 when 2 miles northeast of Nieuport, Winter encountered two Albatros scouts which had earlier made a hit and run attack on the patrol. The three Camels attacked one of the enemy machines and drove it down into the clouds.

SCdr Breese made a couple of increasingly rare flights when he ferried two Camels between the aerodrome and the depot.

C Flight flew an outer line patrol at 14.45. Three enemy aircraft were observed as the patrol approached the lines, these retreated inland when the patrol started to climb towards them.

FLt Kirkpatrick led an inner line patrol at 14.45. The patrol observed 4 enemy machines over the Floods at 15.15 and three enemy machines over Nieuport at 15.30. A lone enemy machine was ineffectually engaged over the Floods at 16.15.

FLt Winter led an inner line patrol at 18.35. A ground signal informed the patrol that an enemy machine was working in the area but they were unable to find it. The visibility was very poor with rain and low cloud. De Roeper, Maund and Macgregor fired 250 rounds into an enemy trench from 1500 feet.

FCdr MacLaren left the squadron to take command of the Walmer Defence Flight.

15th August

FLt De Roeper led an outer line patrol at 04.45, the patrol encountered considerable enemy activity with all of the pilots reporting engagements. De Roeper encountered three enemy machines at 16000 feet and drove them away to the east. Macgregor ineffectually engaged two scouts and a 2-seater. Carroll investigated anti-aircraft fire over Nieuport and encountered a large black 2-seater at 05.20. He dived on the 2-seater but both guns jammed, after clearing the stoppage Carroll attacked again and the enemy aircraft dived vertically towards the beach and was lost in the haze. Maund engaged three enemy aircraft, one of which was a bomber, on the Allied side of the lines. The bomber released its bombs over the sea off La Panne and headed eastwards. Maund then attacked an enemy machine which was in turn attacking an RE8, he observed his tracers hitting the enemy machine which forced it to break off its attack. At 05.39, FSL Strathy was flying at 14000 feet over Nieuport when he encountered a 2-seater at 10000 feet. Strathy dived on the enemy machine which turned underneath him, Strathy followed the enemy aircraft around and fired whereupon it fell in a spiral. Strathy followed it down firing bursts until it fell into a vertical dive, black smoke was observed to come from the machine at which point it broke into pieces in the air.

FLt Winter led Abbot and Kirkpatrick on an inner line patrol at 04.45. Winter attacked an enemy machine over Leffinghe without result. He later reported seeing the machine shot down by Strathy fall to the northwest of St. Georges. Kirkpatrick reported seeing four enemy machines at different times over Nieuport.

FLt Gooderham led a six Camel outer line patrol at 08.15, the weather had closed in with clouds at 2000 feet and no enemy aircraft were seen.

FLt De Roeper led Carroll and Strathy on an inner line patrol at 08.15, the patrol was affected by the same weather conditions experienced by Gooderham's patrol and no enemy aircraft were seen.

New pilot FSL Siedle made a practice flight at 09.55.

FLt Gooderham led Findlay and Simpson on an inner patrol at 12.55, no enemy aircraft were observed.

FLt De Roeper led an outer line patrol at 16.00. The patrol engaged five Albatros scouts over Ghistelles at 14000 feet, the enemy machines dived away through the clouds. De Roeper claimed an Albatros scout out of control at 17.40.

FLt Winter led Abbot and Siedle on an inner line patrol at 16.00. No enemy aircraft were seen, however, FSL Siedle lost formation towards the end of the patrol, when he returned there were several bullet holes through his Camel's main planes for which he was completely unable to account.

16th August

FLt Winter led Simpson and Lawson on an inner line patrol at 06.05 and encountered three enemy aircraft south of Nieuport. One of the enemy machines attempted to cross the Floods but was forced to retreat when attacked by the patrol.

FLt De Roeper led an outer line patrol at 06.10. The patrol encountered three enemy aircraft to the southeast of Ghistelles at 07.00 and engaged them at long range. Tracers were seen to hit the fuselage of one machine which immediately dived away through the clouds.

FLt Winter led an outer line patrol at 09.45. At 10.50, Strathy observed six enemy aircraft over Middlekerke, three at 16000 feet and three at 20000 feet, he lost sight of these in the clouds. Strathy was compelled to make a forced landing 2 miles west of Nieuport when his Camel's engine cut due to fuel feed problems. The patrol encountered five enemy scouts to the north of Dixmude at 11.10, they were able to prevent the scouts from positioning themselves in the sun but were unable to make enough height to attack. The enemy aircraft eventually withdrew.

FLt De Roeper led an inner line patrol at 09.50. The weather had closed in with clouds at 900 to 1100 feet. De Roeper fired 1000 rounds into enemy trenches and then aborted the patrol.

FLt Gooderham led an outer line patrol at 13.30, the lines were covered by clouds at 6000 feet and the patrol was flown below the clouds. Four enemy aircraft were encountered, one of which was engaged indecisively by Gooderham, Findlay and Carroll at long range. Lawson observed two enemy aircraft diving out of the clouds onto the inner line patrol, he engaged one of the enemy machines without result. Simpson became separated from the patrol and joined the inner line patrol.

FLt Kirkpatrick led Siedle and Abbott on an inner line patrol at 13.30. The patrol was attacked by four enemy aircraft at 14.50 when over the Floods. Kirkpatrick and Siedle manoeuvred above one enemy machine but after firing a short burst they were attacked from behind. Abbot indecisively attacked an Albatros scout at 15.00 over Nieuport.

FLt De Roeper led a five machine outer line patrol at 17.15. the patrol got off to a bad start when two members, Abbott and Siedle, attached themselves to the inner line patrol which was taking off at the same time. The depleted patrol was caught in a trap when De Roeper led Winter into a diving attack on a 2-seater which was encountered at 9000 feet. After ineffectually firing at the 2-seater, the two Camels were attacked from above and behind by three enemy scouts. Kirkpatrick, the third member of the patrol had suspected a trap and maintained his height but was attacked by another enemy scout and forced to dive away.

FLt Gooderham led Findlay and Simpson on an inner line patrol at 17.15. As related above, Abbott and Siedle inadvertently joined the patrol. Five enemy aircraft were encountered over the Floods at 10000 feet, these were driven back inland. Three enemy machines were observed over Middlekerke, these made no attempt to cross the lines or interfere with spotting machines.

17th August

FLt Gooderham led Simpson and Lawson on an inner line patrol at 06.00. Gooderham observed five enemy aircraft behind Middlekerke. Lawson observed an Allied machine being chased by an enemy aircraft and drove it off.

FLt Winter led an outer line patrol at 06.15. At 06.55, the five Camels, accompanied by three Bristol Fighters observed eight enemy machines flying above the patrol and in the sun. The patrol unsuccessfully attempted to climb up to the level of the enemy aircraft, then three of the hostile machines dived below the patrol attempting to lure them into a trap. Winter fired a short burst at one machine and then pulled up, the three enemy aircraft continued to dive away. Later during the patrol Winter encountered another enemy machine at his own level, he opened fire but the return fire hit Winter's left centre section strut and left hand plane. Winter disengaged and climbed away. Several minutes later Winter was engaged from above by an enemy machine which tried to manoeuvre for a good position, Winter prevented this and turned towards the enemy machine, climbing and firing. During the head-on engagement Winter's Camel was again hit, this time in the right hand lower plane. Winter then observed a Bristol Fighter at 2000 feet being attacked by a scout and a 2-seater, he dived and fired on the 2-seater which turned and dived away but not before its observer's accurate return fire damaged Winter's engine. Winter returned to the aerodrome at 07.35 and immediately took up another Camel and flew back to the lines where he encountered and attacked an artillery spotter over Slype. The spotter dived away but returned after five minutes, Winter again attacked and the spotter dived away. A scout that was escorting the spotting machine started to turn towards Winter but made off when Winter pulled up and turned towards him. Winter's machine was then hit in the tail fin by anti-aircraft fire. FSL Siedle encountered several enemy aircraft and indecisively attacked one at long range. At 07.05, FSL Abbott was attacked from behind by a Fokker[4] and an Albatros, he pulled up and round to the right and closed with the Fokker on his right side. Abbot fired a long burst at close range and observed tracers entering the cockpit, the machine fell away out of control and spinning very quickly. FSL Simpson saw Abbott's opponent continue to spin very fast and lost it in the ground mist at 3000 feet. Abbott was again attacked from behind at 07.30 as he was approaching the lines, he pulled up and around and found himself in front of and below the attacking machine which he again identified as a Fokker biplane. Abbott fired a burst at close range, the enemy machine's engine stopped and the aircraft went into a straight vertical dive, flattening out when close to the ground. FSL Strathy failed to return from the patrol, having been shot down and killed over Zevecote.

B Flight carried out an outer line patrol at 09.45. Five enemy aircraft were seen above the patrol. One was sent down in a spin by a Bristol Fighter of No.48 Squadron RFC.

FLt Gooderham led an outer line patrol at 13.30. The patrol observed four enemy aircraft behind the Floods, two at 16000 feet and two at a higher altitude. The patrol attempted to close with the lower machines but they kept above the Camels and eventually headed away inland. FSL Findlay observed three enemy aircraft to the east of Nieuport and attacked one without success. FSL Maund encountered two enemy machines in the clouds to the east of Nieuport, these headed back to Ostende.

FLt De Roeper led Macgregor and Carroll on an inner line patrol at 17.15. At 18.15 all three pilots dived on a yellowish green 2-seater that was engaged in spotting for artillery and simultaneously fired a total of 400 rounds The 2-seater was observed to dive and turn to the left and then go down in a vertical dive. FSL Macgregor believed that he saw the aircraft crashed behind Westende and Middlekerke. De Roeper fired a further 150 rounds into enemy trenches from 1500 feet.

FLt Winter led an outer line patrol at 17.15, no enemy aircraft were observed above the clouds but two Albatros scouts were seen at 5000 feet above Middlekerke.

18th August

FLt De Roeper led an outer line patrol at 05.00. At 06.25 the patrol encountered six enemy aircraft at 10000 feet above Ostende, the enemy machines dived below the patrol to attack a formation of Sopwith Pups. De Roeper was close enough to open fire on one enemy machine as it dived beneath the patrol, after firing 30 rounds he turned but lost sight of all the enemy aircraft.

Winter led Siedle and Abbott on an uneventful inner line patrol at 05.05.

De Roeper led Curtis and Carroll on an inner line patrol at 08.30, the patrol chased an artillery spotter which promptly went down and landed.

Gooderham led the 08.30 outer line patrol. The flight crossed the lines at 14000 feet and observed a formation of Pups chasing six enemy aircraft behind Dixmude. The enemy machines turned and dived towards Ghistelles before the Camels were able to reach them. Another formation of enemy machines was observed at a considerably higher altitude approaching from the south. The patrol returned early due to clouds obscuring the ground.

At 12.15 Gooderham led Findlay and Lawson on an inner line patrol. At 12.35 four enemy aircraft were observed at Ostende and another at Westende Bains. The patrol tried to approach the single machine but it escaped in the clouds before the patrol got close enough to open fire.

Winter led the 12.15 outer line patrol. Two enemy aircraft were observed amongst the clouds several miles inland and a single Albatros was observed at 13.30. Kirkpatrick overturned Camel N6397 whilst taxying in.

Gooderham led an outer line patrol at 16.00. The area was covered by cloud at 9000 feet but an enemy machine was observed at 7000 feet over Ghistelles.

FLt Kirkpatrick led Macgregor and Siedle on the 16.00 inner line patrol. Siedle had engine trouble and was forced to return early.

Kirkpatrick carried out a test flight in N6357 and crashed in a field, sustaining injuries that required hospitalisation.

19th August

FLt De Roeper led Curtis and Carroll on an inner line patrol at 07.15. De Roeper attacked an enemy 2-seater, firing 50 rounds at long range. The 2-seater retreated towards Ostende. Curtis fired 50 rounds at a 2-seater which fired a red signal light, five more enemy machines came to its assistance and all six enemy aircraft headed inland over the floods.

Gooderham led the 07.15 outer patrol. An enemy machine was encountered on the Allied side of the lines at 1500 feet, the patrol attempted to close and fired 50 rounds from long range without effect. The enemy machine escaped towards

Ghistelles. Five enemy aircraft were observed at 08.30 well behind their own lines.

De Roeper led an outer line patrol at 11.00 but was forced to return with ignition problems when a high tension lead broke. The Flight continued the patrol and ineffectually attacked an artillery-spotting machine over Westende. De Roeper took off again after repairs to his Camel, at 13.00 he observed six enemy aircraft 500 feet above him. He climbed away and at 13.15 was able to dive onto the formation and fire 60 rounds at the rearmost machine. De Roeper reported that the entire enemy formation spun away into the clouds.

Winter led Siedle and Abbot on the 11.00 inner line patrol, one enemy machine was observed over Middlekerke, apparently stalking an RE8. The patrol was unable to get within firing range before the enemy machine escaped into the clouds.

Gooderham led Macgregor and Lawson on an inner line patrol at 14.45. Four enemy aircraft were observed climbing over Ostende and a solitary machine was observed at 8000 feet over Ostende. Gooderham dived on the latter machine and fired a short burst but was unable to close before it dived away.

FLt Winter led the 14.45 outer line patrol. Winter observed a formation of six enemy aircraft above the patrol, he turned and fired but the enemy machines made no attempt to attack. Another enemy machine was observed 5000 feet below the patrol, when Winter attempted to engage, the enemy machine dived away and escaped. Abbott was very late getting away and lost a wheel in the air, he subsequently crashed Camel N6351 on landing.

De Roeper took off at 15.15 to acquaint FSL Abbot with the fact that his Camel had lost a wheel.

Winter led Abbot and Siedle on an inner line patrol at 18.30. No enemy aircraft were observed but Siedle damaged Camel N6359 when he made a forced landing in a field to the southeast of Nieuport.

De Roeper led the 18.30 outer patrol, eleven enemy aircraft were observed taking off from Ghistelles at 19.45 and five of them were seen to patrol the lines.

20th August

Winter led Macgregor and Abbot on an inner line patrol at 06.00. One enemy machine was observed over Middlekerke at 2000 feet.

Gooderham led the 06.00 outer line patrol. FSL Simpson's Camel would not climb above 14000 feet and he lost contact with the patrol. Three enemy aircraft were observed over Middlekerke at 07.15, the formation comprised a 2-seater and two escort machines flying at 10000 feet. Gooderham led the patrol into a diving attack from 17000 feet, FSL Findlay pulled up close behind one of the scouts and fired at it from a range of 30 feet. The scout stalled, fell on its back then fell away in a spin. Gooderham witnessed Findlay's attack and signed a confirmation statement on Findlay's combat report.

De Roeper led an outer patrol at 09.45. An enemy machine was encountered and 60 rounds fired at it without effect. At 10.50, four Albatros scouts were observed heading out to sea at Moere. De Roeper led his formation inland and waited above the cloud bank for their return. They eventually appeared at 500 feet above the formation and slightly to their side of the lines. Macgregor and De Roeper both made a climbing turn and opened fire at the same time. Macgregor fired 100 rounds and De Roeper fired 60 rounds at the same machine which was observed to stall then spin for 5 turns. The enemy machine recovered, then stalled and fell in another spin. It recovered again, then nose dived through the clouds.

Winter led Abbot and Siedle on the 09.45 inner line patrol. At 10.40, the patrol observed four Albatros scouts climbing into the sun, they turned and headed towards the coast, returning at 10.50 at a height of 11000 feet. An engagement took place between Westende and Schoore, Winter attacked a machine that was attempting to dive on FSL Abbottt. Tracers were seen to enter the enemy aircraft's fuselage but Winter was forced to break away as he was in turn attacked by a black and white striped Albatros. After eluding his attacker, Winter engaged another machine which dived away steeply for 7000 feet. Winter was again attacked from behind, he performed a climbing turn and engaged his attacker at which point his starboard gun jammed. Winter disengaged, cleared the stoppage and returned to attack another aircraft but ran out of ammunition. Abbott attacked one of the enemy scouts but was attacked from behind by the black and white striped Albatros. Whilst manoeuvring, Abbot's engine choked and he was forced to dive away to correct it. By the time he had recovered his engine the enemy aircraft had withdrawn towards Middlekerke. Siedle fired several rounds at two enemy aircraft with indecisive results.

Gooderham led Simpson and Lawson on an inner line patrol at 13.30. Three enemy aircraft were observed patrolling well behind Middlekerke, however, no enemy machines were observed near the lines.

De Roeper led the outer patrol at 13.30. Curtis chased two enemy machines inland from Dixmude.

Winter carried out a test flight in B3821 at 13.30, the engine was satisfactory but the machine was tail heavy.

SCdr Breese collected N6330 from the depot at 18.50.

21st August

De Roeper led Macgregor, Curtis, Carroll and Maund on an outer line patrol at 07.45. Carroll's engine was down on power and he was unable to keep formation. At 08.40 when over Moere, De Roeper, Macgregor and Curtis were attacked by five Albatros scouts The Camels turned and started climbing but the enemy machines dived away to Ghistelles. De Roeper observed two Aviatics heading towards Nieuport at 08.50, he manoeuvred into the sun and then attacked the first machine, firing 100 rounds without result. De Roeper turned away and attacked the second machine, firing 60 rounds without result. At 09.05 when over Westende, De Roeper observed five Albatros scouts escorting an artillery spotter. He dived on the formation and fired 50 rounds at one machine, pulled up and dived at another, firing another 50 rounds. The entire formation dived away through the clouds. Maund observed four enemy aircraft to the east of Nieuport at 09.50 but did not engage them.

Gooderham, Abbott and Lawson flew an inner line patrol at 07.45. Four enemy aircraft were encountered over Westende at 08.00, the patrol dived on one machine firing a burst of 50 rounds. The enemy machine dived vertically until within 1000 feet of the ground and then made for Ghistelles. The other three enemy machines also dived away inland.

Gooderham led an uneventful outer patrol at 12.15.

Winter led Curtis and Carroll on the inner patrol at 12.15. Winter made an ineffective attack on an enemy spotting machine but was forced to break off the engagement when both guns jammed.

De Roeper led an outer patrol and Gooderham an inner patrol at 16.45. At 17.40 over Moere the outer patrol encountered five Albatros scouts at 15000ft, De Roeper attacked two enemy machines, firing 60 rounds at each before the formation headed away inland. At 18.35, Winter and De Roeper attacked two spotting machines operating over Westende, the Camels were forced to disengage by the presence of eight Albatros scouts holding position above the 2-seaters. De Roeper and Winter then returned to attack the spotting machines again, De Roeper dived on one machine from 6000 feet and fired 100 rounds. Tracers were observed entering the fuselage and the enemy aircraft went down in a nose dive. De Roeper followed it down to 2000 feet before the presence of six enemy scouts forced him to pull away and make for the lines. Winter made a third attempt to engage the spotting machines but was unable to observe the effects of his attack. FSL Macgregor attacked a 2-seater half a mile over the lines, firing two bursts without effect.

The inner patrol encountered several enemy machines at Westende. Gooderham dived on one enemy machine and fired at long range without effect. A spotting machine was reported at low altitude keeping close to Middlekerke.

22nd August

FLt Winter led Abbot and Findlay on an inner patrol and De Roeper led Curtis, Carroll, Maund and Macgregor on an outer patrol at 05.00. The inner patrol failed to encounter any enemy aircraft on the Allied side of the lines but Findlay attacked a kite balloon to the southwest of Ostende. Findlay got within 300 yards when both guns jammed, he was able to attack a second time firing 100 rounds from one gun. The outer patrol encountered six enemy aircraft over the floods at 05.40. De Roeper fired 150 rounds at one machine which dived away. Curtis attacked an enemy machine, firing 200 rounds. The enemy aircraft dived vertically from 13000ft to 9000ft, stalled and was then lost to sight. Carroll made an ineffective attack upon another enemy aircraft. At 06.20, De Roeper attacked a kite balloon, firing 100 rounds without effect.

De Roeper led Curtis and Carroll on an inner patrol at 09.15 whilst Gooderham led five machines on the outer patrol. The inner patrol kept close to a flight of RE8s whilst enemy scouts looked for an opportunity to attack. The outer patrol encountered three enemy aircraft coming in from the sea near Ostende and another machine beyond Dixmude which dived at Macgregor from out of the sun. Macgregor turned and came up beneath and behind the enemy scout. He fired 100 rounds into the Albatros which he described as being green on top and yellow underneath, the Albatros dived vertically for 6000 feet at which point it lost one of its wings. Macgregor's opponent may have been FlgObm Luitjen Luitjens of MFJ1.

Another combined inner and outer patrol was flown at 13.45, Gooderham leading Maund and Simpson on the inner patrol whilst Winter led the outer patrol. At 15.20, the inner patrol encountered 4 enemy aircraft near Middlekerke at 9000ft. The patrol fired at one machine at long range without effect. The outer patrol also encountered opposition over Middlekerke, Winter fired 150 rounds at two enemy aircraft which withdrew to Ostende and Carroll optimistically fired 100 rounds at an enemy machine at long range.

ABOVE: Somewhat naively thinking it would be easy to identify the black and white ringed Albatros mentioned by Winter and Wood in their Combat reports, it soon became apparent that a black and white ringed fuselage was a common personal marking amongst the *Jasta* pilots. One possibility shown here is a *Jasta* 17 machine, the photograph depicts Eberhard von Seel. Winter's opponent could not have been von Seel however, as he was killed in action on the 12th June 1917. *Courtesy University of Texas, Dallas/A Imrie collection*

BELOW: Another possibility was *Jasta Boelcke*, based at Ghistelles at the time of the encounter. The photograph shows Bassenge, Kempf and Vallendor in front of a ringed Albatros DV. It is not known who regularly flew this machine. *Courtesy University of Texas, Dallas/A Imrie collection*

ABOVE: Yet another possibility is this Albatros D III belonging to the *MFJ*. *Courtesy University of Texas, Dallas/A Imrie collection*

BELOW: A less likely candidate would be an Albatros D V carrying the colours of *Jasta* 26. *Courtesy University of Texas, Dallas/A Imrie collection*

Newly arrived pilot, FSL Hamilton-Bowyer was sent up for a practice flight at 19.00.

The squadron's final Flight structure was as shown:

A Flight
FLt GA Gooderham, Flight Commander
FSL WA Curtis
FSL MH Findlay
FSL H Lawson
FSL GE Siedle

B Flight
FCdr BHP De Roeper, Flight Commander
FLt GLE Stevens
FSL P Wood
FSL RE Carroll
FSL JO Simpson
FSL ED Abbott

C Flight
AFCdr RR Winter, Flight Commander
FSL NM Macgregor
FSL HB Maund
FSL SA Hamilton-Bowyer

Kirkpatrick and Holyman of C Flight were absent from the squadron on sick leave.

23rd August

Winter led an outer patrol and Gooderham led Carroll and Simpson on an inner patrol at 07.45. The inner patrol observed four enemy aircraft near Ostende and encountered another enemy machine which they chased beyond Middlekerke. Carroll fired 100 rounds into an anti-arcraft battery to the west of Slype.

Winter took Findlay and Simpson on an inner line patrol at 13.00. The patrol proved to be quiet but Winter damaged B3821 when landing.

SCdr Breese collected a new Camel from the depot at 15.45.

At 16.50, Gooderham led an outer line patrol and De Roeper led Macgregor and Carroll on an inner line patrol. Unfavourable weather conditions caused the outer patrol to be abandoned, the inner patrol stayed out but failed to observe any enemy activity.

24th August

The weather continued to be overcast with cloud at 4000 feet. De Roeper led Hamilton-Bowyer and Carroll on an inner line

BELOW: Sopwith Camel B3882, seen here in No.10 Squadron's markings in September 1917. With No.6 Squadron from the 26th July 1917, B3882 was regularly flown by FLt BHP De Roeper who claimed an Albatros scout out of control at Ghistelles on the 15th August, a two-seater crashed one mile east of Westende on the 17th August and an Albatros scout out of control at Moere on the 20th August. *Courtesy JMB/GSL Collection*

patrol and Gooderham led an outer line patrol at 06.15. The inner patrol was abandoned after 1 1/2 hours, the outer patrol remained out for the full duration of the patrol but failed to see any enemy aircraft. FSL Maund suffered an engine failure in Camel N6379.

25th August

De Roeper led an outer line patrol at 07.45 but weather conditions were such that he was forced to abandon the patrol after 25 minutes. FSL Lawson's Camel broke a valve just after leaving the ground and he landed immediately to exchange his machine. Winter led Hamilton-Bowyer and Abbott on the corresponding inner patrol and encountered four spotting machines beyond Middlekerke at 08.35.

FSL Findlay led Simpson and Lawson on an uneventful inner line patrol at 13.30. The patrol remained out for 20 minutes.

Winter led Abbott and Hamilton-Bowyer on an inner line patrol at 16.45. The patrol was ineffectively attacked by four Albatros scouts which dived on the Camels from behind but failed to press home their advantage. Winter turned towards them, two dived away and the other two climbed into the sun. Winter attacked the highest machine at long range, at this point both enemy machines turned back and chased Winter for a short distance.

26th August

Winter led an outer line patrol at 10.45. The patrol encountered two spotting machines over Middlekerke. Winter suffered a stoppage in both guns during a diving attack on one of the enemy machines.

De Roeper led an outer line patrol at 18.25. A general engagement took place but the pilots' reports were confused. De Roeper stated that the patrol was attacked by six enemy aircraft over Middlekerke at 19.35. The fight lasted for approximately 5 minutes and at 19.40 he saw an enemy machine go down in flames to crash in a field by the side of the Bruges-Nieuport canal, shot down by a Belgian SPAD.[5] FSL Carroll also observed the enemy machine go down in flames. The other pilots variously reported one, four and five enemy aircraft taking part in the fight.

The patrols on the 26th August were the last recorded war flights carried out before No.6 Squadron was disbanded on the 27th August.

28th August

The pilots flew their Sopwith Camels to No.10 Squadron at Drogland.

NOTES

[1] Both Aerodromes are commonly referred to as Bray Dunes.

[2] Forman's opponent was probably *Vzfm* Otto Brant of *MFJ* 1 who was reported as killed in action between Middlekerke and Westende.

[3] The RE8 trailed a long wire to act as an antenna for radio communication.

[4] Aircraft identification was often inaccurate, in his combat report, Abbot described the Fokker as having a monocoque fuselage and being coloured a mottled green and brown.

[5] De Roeper and Carroll witnessed the demise of *Uffz* Carl Conrad of *Jasta* 17, shot down by the Belgian ace, SLt Edmond Thieffry of 5me Escadrille.

CHAPTER SEVEN

DISBANDMENT

In some quarters it was realised as early as May 1917 that the burden of loaning squadrons to the RFC would impose a severe strain on RNAS resources. Wing Captain CL Lambe wrote the following letter to the Vice-Admiral Dover Patrol on the 8th May:

> *I have the honour to forward the following remarks and proposals as regards the future policy of aviation.*
>
> *On joining your command in August 1915, the number of pilots employed was approximately 14 aeroplane pilots and 6 seaplane pilots. In August 1916, this number had approximately trebled, whilst the present approved establishment including the squadrons lent to the RFC and which it is hoped will be completed by August 1917, amounts to 298 pilots.*
>
> *In the autumn of 1916, the Germans appeared to have suddenly realised the extreme importance of aerial warfare and entirely reorganised their Air Service. The result has been that there is at present an intensive struggle on the Western Front between the opposing Air Services, which has by no means been definitely decided in our favour as yet. There is no reason to suppose that the enemy will relax their efforts during the coming year and, consequently, a large increase on our part must be prepared for.*
>
> *From carefully prepared statistics, the wastage of pilots of the Royal Naval Air Service in the Dover Command worked out at 10.1% per month during January, February and March and 15.2% per month for the month of April. Owing, however, to the supply of pilots being inadequate, to train them thoroughly before sending them over the lines I anticipate in the future a large increase which may amount to 20% per month.*
>
> *Taking the number of pilots employed as 300, this means that 60 fresh pilots will be required per month in the autumn to replace wastage alone, without any addition to strength. Since it appears obvious that man-power is going to decide this war, it appears worthy of consideration to consider a very large increase in our aerial forces which are undoubtedly a very efficient method of employing available man-power. One cannot unreasonably predict the time when land forces will consist of artillery, tanks and aircraft.*
>
> *I understand that the present aim of the Royal Naval Air Service is to turn out approximately 500 new pilots a year but, in view of the forgoing remarks, it is submitted that the suggestion of very largely increasing this output may be considered.*
>
> *With the increasing use of seaplanes and other aircraft both for anti-submarine and fleet work, I feel convinced that 2000 pilots per annum will not be too many in 1918 for the Royal Naval Air Service. I also feel convinced that once the present Air Board has had sufficient time, no difficulty will be experienced in producing the requisite number of machines and engines.*

In a memo to the Vice-Admiral Dover Patrol, Wing Captain AV Vyvyan, Assistant to the Director of Air Services dismissed the crux of Lambe's argument, stating that the Royal Naval Air Squadrons were to be withdrawn from the RFC at the rate of one per month, commencing at the end of July. Lambe's suggestion for a substantial increase in presence on the Western Front was also dismissed with the comment that it was up to the military authorities to provide this and not the concern of the Royal Naval Air Service.

Vyvyan's comments regarding the withdrawal of assistance to the RFC proved to be somewhat erroneous. No.3 Squadron was withdrawn by the middle of June but there was no further reduction in assistance to the RFC until No.6 Squadron was disbanded at the end of August. What did happen was that the losses predicted by Lambe occurred and became unsustainable.

By August 1917 it was far too late to do anything about recruitment and the decision was taken to disband two squadrons and use their pilots and aircraft to reinforce the other squadrons.

On the 25th August, Wing Captain Lambe had made contingency places for the disbandment or "paying-off" of No.6 Squadron. These were distributed in memo No.6202:

Headquarters
R.N.A.S.
Dunkerque
Ref. No.6202
25th August 1917

Memorandum
In the event of Naval Squadron No.6 being paid-off, the following action will be taken.

Officers
The Commanding Officer will report to Headquarters on paying-off.

Pilots
Flight Commanders de Roeper and Winter will report to headquarters.

Flight Lieutenant Gooderham will be discharged to No.2 Squadron.

FSL Findlay)
FSL Simpson) To No.1 Squadron
FSL Macgregor)
FSL Curtis) To No.8 Squadron
FSL Carroll)
FSL Lawson)
FSL Wood)
FSL Maund) To No.10 Squadron
FSL Abbott)
FSL Bowyer)
FSL Siedle To report to Headquarters on discharge from hospital.

The remaining officers, with the exception of the Stores Officer will report to headquarters.

Personnel
The C.O., Naval Squadron No.6 will prepare a list of approximately thirty ratings who will form the nucleus of the squadron in the event of it being found possible to reform. These ratings will be attached to Aircraft Depot and will be looked upon as part complement until such time as they may be required.. The remainder will be utilised for completing existing Squadrons and a nominal list shewing –

(a) the nucleus
(b) the remainder

should be forwarded to headquarters "P" as soon as possible.

Stores
The Stores will be returned to Aircraft Depot and taken on charge by "A" Section. The Stores Officer will then close the accounts of Naval Squadron No.6 and, whilst so doing will be attached to Aircraft Depot. As regards all tents, fixtures etc. at the Camp, instructions should be requested from the Wing Commander as to what action should be taken.

Transport
All transport will be returned to Section "C", Aircraft Depot with the drivers. Transport should then be thoroughly cleaned and the Stores Officer of No.6 Squadron will be responsible for checking the list of tools and spare parts belonging to the Motor Transport. Instructions will be requested from the Headquarters R.F.C. as to its disposal. (Wing Commander Chambers to make enquiries).

Machines
Machines in flying order will in all probability be transferred to Naval Squadron No.10 together with spare en-

gines, in which case No.10 will return their Triplanes and in addition draw three Clerget Camels to bring No.10 Naval Squadron up to eighteen machines. Three of the Triplanes from No.10 will be allocated to Naval Squadron No.1 to bring them up to eighteen and one to Naval Squadron No.8 to bring the Triplane Flight up to six. The remainder are to be held in reserve at Aircraft Depot for issue to Squadrons.

If this change is approved, Naval Squadron No.10 will return any spare engines not fitted with Sopwith Kauper Gear but in no case should they return more than six spare engines.

Signed CL Lambe
Captain RN

Distribution

"C"
"I"
"P"
"K"
"Q"
Wing Commander Chambers (two copies)
G.O., H.Q.

No.6 Squadron was duly "paid-off" on the 27th August 1917. In the event, the disposition of the pilots was not exactly as Lambe had initially planned:

FLt GA Gooderham	To No.2 Squadron
FSL WA Curtis	To No.10 Squadron
FSL MH Findlay	To No.1 Squadron
FSL H Lawson	To No.10 Squadron
FSL GE Siedle	Retrained, then to No.5 Squadron
FCdr BHP de Roeper	Instructor at Chingford
FLt GLE Stevens	Retrained, then to the reformed No.6 Squadron
FSL P Wood	To No.10 Squadron
FSL RE Carroll	To No.10 Squadron
FSL JO Simpson	To No.1 Squadron
FSL ED Abbott	To No.10 Squadron
AFCdr RR Winter	To Walmer Defence Flight
FSL NM Macgregor	To No.10 Squadron
FSL HB Maund	To No.10 Squadron
FSL SA Hamilton-Bowyer	To No.10 Squadron

Some pilots received instruction on 2-seaters and were subsequently posted to observation and bombing squadrons, FLt GLE Stevens returning to the reformed No.6 Squadron in January 1918 and FSL GE Siedle going to No.5 Squadron. De Roeper returned to instructing, this time at Vendome. FSL AC Campbell-Orde was recovering from injuries received in July at the time of disbandment and was subsequently posted to No.9 Squadron.

FCdr CT MacLaren had already left No.6 Squadron to take command of the Walmer Defence Flight by the middle of August. He would return to lead the reformed No.6 Squadron in January 1918.

Thus No.6 Squadron ceased to exist on the 27th August 1917 and other squadrons were bolstered with experienced pilots. Whilst the need to reduce the number of RNAS scout squadrons cannot be questioned, it is difficult to see why the axe fell on No.6 Squadron The Squadron's work rate, whilst initially poor, had picked up rapidly once the pilots got used to the Sopwith Camel. Several possible reasons are offered below:

Many of the pilots felt that No.6 Squadron had always been the least favoured squadron in the Dunkerque Command, a theory that is difficult to prove or disprove at this late juncture. Whilst there is absolutely no doubt that Wing Captain Lambe had a soft spot for No.8 Squadron, there is no evidence that he was dissatisfied with No.6 Squadron.

It is possible that experienced Camel pilots would be considered much more valuable to the squadrons that were in the process of converting to Camels, than would Triplane or Pup pilots.

Squadron Commander CD Breese was not considered to be a particularly forceful or dynamic leader, especially when compared to the likes of BC Bell of No.10 Squadron or RS Dallas of No.1 Squadron. It is possible that Breese simply did not fight hard enough to keep his squadron in existence.

The debacle of Breese being unable to "manage" ASCdr Draper must have raised questions about his capabilities as a Squadron Commander, making it easier for Lambe to select No.6 Squadron.

Perhaps there was no simple reason but a combination of the above suggestions, or perhaps No.6 Squadron was simply in the wrong place at the wrong time. Whatever the reason, the squadron was disbanded on the 27th August 1917 but just like the mythical Phoenix, it rose from the ashes to reform as a day bomber squadron in 1918.

CHAPTER EIGHT

A NEW ROLE

On the 19th November 1917, Wing Captain Lambe wrote the following memo to the Director of Air Services:

Senior Officer,
Director of Air Services,
R.N.A.S., H.Q.,
Hotel Cecil,
Dunkerque,
Strand, W.C.

19th November 1917,

Submitted,
In view of the approval given for next year's requirements, which include two D.H.4 Bombing squadrons, it is proposed, subject to your approval, to form the second squadron about the 1st, January 1918.

2.- The necessary Squadron Commander and Flight Leaders and ratings have been detailed and arrangements made for the engine ratings to go through a course in the B.H.P. engine at Messrs. Siddeley Deasy's.

3.- All that is required will be about eight or ten pilots trained in D.H.4 machines at Manstone to be drafted to Dover Command during the month of December. These will then be divided between the two Bombing Squadrons and experienced pilots mixed between the two Squadrons.

4.- It is proposed to call this Squadron No.6 Squadron.

Signed
C L Lambe
Captain. R.N.

Ten days later on the 29th November 1917, Lambe's plans were more advanced and he issued the following memo:

Headquarters
R.N.A.S.
Dunkerque

29th November 1917
Memorandum 7899

A second D.H.4 Bombing Squadron will be partly formed at Dover and it is hoped will cross to Dunkerque in the first week in January 1918 if the camp at Petite Synthe is sufficiently advanced by that date.

2. The squadron will be known as No.6 Squadron and will be formed by a certain number now at Dover which formed the original Walmer Defence Flight, supplemented by 30 ratings which have been earmarked since No.11 Squadron was disbanded.

3. Commanding Officer, Dover Aerodrome will forward a list of the ratings together with their qualifications and O.N. to Headquarters and Headquarters will include the named ratings and O.N. of the 30 ratings – late of No.11 Squadron and return the list to Commanding Officer, Dover Aerodrome for the information of Flight Com-

mander MacLaren. Commanding Officer Dover Aerodrome will then endeavour to obtain the outside ratings such as O.S's, Cooks and special ratings such as Acetylene Welders etc., which could be detached either from Dover Aerodrome or Drafting Commander.

4. Commanding Officer, Dover Aerodrome, has been instructed to send a further batch of "B" ratings for a course at the Siddeley Deasy Works in B.H.P. engines. Some of the engine ratings at Dunkerque have already been through this course. These ratings should be marked with a star by "P" Section, H.Q. in the list forwarded for Flight Commander MacLaren.

5. A B.H.P. D.H.4 should be allocated by "M" when Commanding Officer, Dover Aerodrome requires one. This will be for training of the pilots and mechanics of the squadron in truing-up and rigging and also in running the engine.

Signed CL Lambe
Captain. RN
Distribution
C.M.Q.P.I SIGS
S.O. Dover
C.O. Aerodrome, Dover
S.O. HQ

Somewhat strangely, bearing in mind the contents of Lambe's memorandum of the 19th November, he made a request to the RNAS Scout Squadrons for volunteers to become Flight Leaders in the new bombing squadrons:

Headquarters
R.N.A.S.
Dunkerque

9th December 1917
Ref no. 8563

Memorandum
It will become necessary in the near future to select a few experienced pilots from Scout Squadrons to act as Flight Leaders in the new D.H.4 Squadrons to be formed. These pilots will return to England for a rest before again proceeding on Active Service.

2. Wing Commanders and Squadron Commanders should therefore keep this matter in hand and forward the names of any officers so selected by December 20th, 1917. The names should be given in various columns:

(a) Those officers who volunteer for this duty
(b) Those officers who have not volunteered but are selected by the Squadron Commander as likely to prove suitable.

In both cases, opposite the names of the officers, the Squadron Commanders and Wing Commanders should insert their opinion of the Officers capability for leading a Flight and other qualifications.

3. There must be a considerable number of pilots in the fighting squadrons who are keen and fond of flying but who are not likely to ever become "Star-turn" Fighting Pilots.

Signed CL Lambe
Captain, RN

The Wing Commander, No.1 Wing
The Wing Commander, No.4 Wing
The Wing Commander, No.5 Wing
1 copy to Dover

No.6 Squadron RNAS was in due course reformed at Dover on the 1st January 1918 as a day bombing squadron coming under the command of No.5 Wing Royal Naval Air Service.

The Commanding Officer, SCdr CT MacLaren and one of the Flight Commanders, AFCdr GLE Stevens, provided a modicum of continuity to the original No.6 Squadron from 1917. The other two Flight Commanders were the highly experienced FCdr INC Clarke and AFCdr JS Wright, both from No.5 Squadron. Although some squadron personnel had been in residence since the 10th January, the majority of the squadron's officers and men did not move to Petite Synthe until the 14th January 1918.

The squadron was initially equipped with D.H.4s whilst "working up" but the intention was to base the squadron's offensive capability around the newly introduced D.H.9. Deliveries of the new machines commenced in February but after a very short time it became apparent that there were serious problems with the B.H.P. engines fitted to the D.H.9.

Ironically mirroring the difficulties experienced in 1917, No.6 Squadron was again handicapped by poor aircraft.

Bad weather during the latter part of January 1918 and the poor state of the aerodrome seriously affected the squadron's preparations for combat readiness.

The squadron officers during the first week of January comprised:

FCdr CT MacLaren	Squadron Commander
FCdr INC Clarke	Flight Commander
SL BH Rook RNVR	Record Officer

One D.H.4 2-seater was collected from the Aeroplane Acceptance Park at Dover on the 3rd January 1918 and one more on the 13th January. Further machines filtered in once the squadron had settled-in at Petite Synthe.

Whilst pilots were in relatively plentiful supply, the RNAS suffered from a chronic shortage of trained observers and gunlayers and the squadron was forced to use members of the ground crew as "acting gunlayers" whilst working up to combat readiness.

• • •

January 1918

10th January

Flt.Obs. RJ St. John arrived at Petite Synthe from Dover on the 10th to supervise a small party of ratings in the construction of squadron quarters. No.5 Squadron had been established at Petite Synthe since April 1917 and the personnel of No.6 Squadron were permitted to make use of the No.5 Squadron Mess facilities.

Wing Captain Lambe issued instruction to increase No.6 Squadron's working party:

Headquarters
R.N.A.S.
Dunkerque
10th January 1918

Ref 7899

Memorandum
A further party of 30 ratings from No.6 Squadron are to be sent to the New Camp, at Petite Synthe as soon as arrangements can be made for transporting them.

2. Owing to the bad state of the roads, as few passengers as possible should be sent via Calais and these 30 ratings should be sent over in small driblets to Dunkerque as no other method is available.

3. The whole squadron will probably cross over about the 16th or 17th January.

Signed CL Lambe
Captain RN

Distribution:

S.O. Dover (2) one for Aerodrome, Dover
C.P.Q.
S.O., H.Q.

12th January

Wing Captain Lambe, anxious to get the Squadron established at Petite Synthe, issued the following Memorandum to the Dover Station Commander:

Headquarters
R.N.A.S.
Dunkerque
12th January, 1918

No.7899

Memorandum
No.6 Squadron is to be transferred from Dover at the earliest date possible.

2. The S.O., R.N.A.S., Dover is to make the necessary arrangements for transporting the Squadron from Dover to Dunkerque, informing me as early as possible when arrangements are made and the time the Squadron may be expected to arrive at Dunkerque.

3. The C.O. No.5 Wing will make arrangements to meet the personnel on disembarking and transport them to Petite Synthe.

4. The C.O. No.6 Squadron is to arrange with the S.O., R.N.A.S., Dover, for the transfer of No.6 Squadron machines to Petite Synthe; machines being flown only by experienced pilots who know the Dunkerque Command.

ABOVE: The Officer's Mess at Petite Synthe aerodrome. *Courtesy JMB/GSL Collection* RIGHT: An interior shot of the Officer's Mess. *Courtesy JMB/GSL Collection*

Pilots recently joined from Manston should go in the machines as passengers, so that they become acquainted with the country. Every opportunity of fine weather is to be taken to get these machines over to Dunkerque, where they can be looked after at once by the advance party, assisted if necessary, by ratings from No.5 Squadron.

Wing Captain
For Senior Officer
S.O., R.N.A.S., Dover (2 copies)
C.O. 5 Wing
"C"
"M"
"P"
"Q"

13th January

AFCdr Wright and FSL Pitt collected D.H.4 N1753 from the Acceptance Park at Dover and made the crossing to France at 12.30, flying at 6000 feet and heading first to Calais and then on to Dunkerque and the aerodrome at Petite Synthe.

Wing Captain Lambe wrote to Wing Commander Courtney detailing the transport arrangements for the main party of ratings:

Headquarters
R.N.A.S.
Dunkerque
13th January, 1918

H.Q. Ref 7599

Memorandum
The main body of 150 ratings of No.6 Squadron will arrive in "Erebus"[1] *at Dunkerque Roads, at about 1 p.m., Monday, 14th January. A drifter and tug will disembark ratings and bring them to Monitor Quay.*

2. If the weather is fine you are to send only sufficient transport for the men's gear and are to arrange that the personnel of the squadron are marched up to Petite Synthe. If the weather is bad and it is raining or snowing heavily, transport for ratings may be supplied in addition to their gear.

Wing Captain
For Senior Officer
C.O. 5 Wing
S.O.
"C"

14th January

SCdr MacLaren, the remaining Flying Officers and the ground personnel arrived at Petite Synthe. The squadron accommodation was basic to say the least, most of the huts lacking doors at this stage.

The Records Officer, SL Basil Rook, RNVR recalled the move to France:

On the 29th December 1917, I was commissioned as a Sub Lieutenant, RNVR from No.1 Wing RNAS Dunkerque where I had spent the previous two years. I reported for duty on the 7th January 1918 at 18 Marine Parade, Dover, to the Senior (Naval) Officer. I was thereupon instructed to join No.6 Squadron at Dover Aerodrome and did so the same day.

No.6 Squadron was getting ready to proceed to France and on the night before departure, the Mess produced oysters to mark the occasion. We considered ourselves fortunate in having as our mess cook one who had been a chef at a leading London hotel. We kept quiet about this but eventually higher authority heard about it. However, we successfully resisted ensuing efforts to steal our cook!

On the 14th January 1918 those members of the squadron travelling to France by sea were mustered at the aerodrome and proceeded down the narrow path cut into the side of the cliff en route to the Marine Pier, where a naval vessel was waiting to embark the party for Dunkerque. The journey was uneventful and the ship made good time, for there was no deviation from course on this occasion to carry out a minefield patrol.

15th January

Bad weather and a very muddy aerodrome prevented any flights from being made.

A violent storm during the night carried away one of the squadron's new Bessoneau hangars, prompt action prevented damage to the two D.H.4s that had been parked inside.

16th January

The aerodrome was flooded, with 18 inches of water inside the squadron's hangars. Rain continued to fall during the day.

17th January

D.H.4 N6404 was delivered from Hendon.

18th January

No flying due to bad weather.

19th January

Two new D.H.4s were delivered from Dover, D1752 by FCdr INC Clarke and FSL AM Bannatyne at 14.45 and B9499 by FCdr TF Le Mesurier with FSL LR Warren at 15.10. FCdr Le Mesurier was not attached to the squadron but as will be seen later, played a significant role in No.6 Squadron's first operational missions.

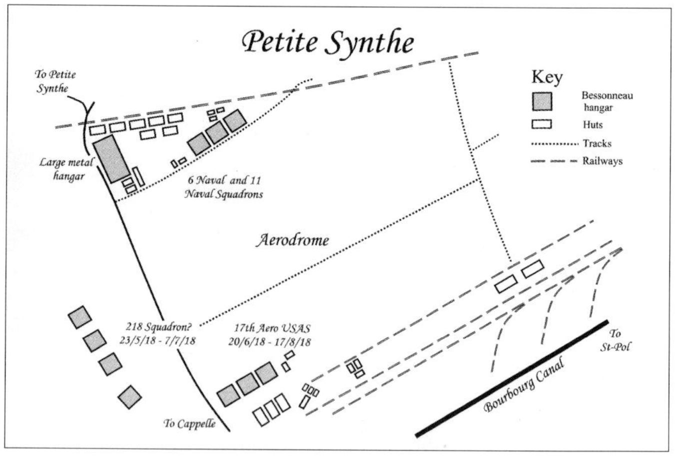

20th January

Torrential rainfall during the day prevented flying.

A case of Scarlet Fever amongst the squadron's ratings resulted in the officers being asked to leave No.5 Squadron's Mess.

21st January

Strong winds and rain featured during the day but cleared to a moonlit evening. Enemy aircraft attempted to bomb the aerodrome for two hours around midnight.

22nd January

The aerodrome was waterlogged with large muddy pools.

23rd January

Overcast during the day, No flying attempted.

24th January

Overcast and heavy rain at first, no flying took place.

25th January

No flying attempted.

26th January

No flying attempted.

27th January

FCdr Clarke and Obs.Lt St. John ferried D.H.4 D1754 from Dover Aerodrome at 12.30.

The weather had cleared enough on the 27th to allow four local flights to be carried out:

Depicted here at Chingford, Airco D.H.4 N6404 was manufactured by Westlands and was delivered to No.6 Squadron on the 17th January 1917 after having seen service at RNAS Grain and with No.2 Squadron. No.6 Squadron passed N6404 on to No.11 Squadron on the 7th March 1918 and from there it was handed on to No.12 Squadron and then to No.218 Squadron RAF where it was destroyed on the 1st May 1918 after colliding with a flagstaff. N6404 was fitted with the troublesome Siddeley Puma engine. *Courtesy EF Cheesman*

FCdr Clarke and SCdr MacLaren at 14.00
FCdr Wright and FSL Pitt at 14.40
FCdr Wright and FSL Tiarks at 15.27
FSL Warren with FSL Hyslop at 15.25

FCdr Wright and FSL Pitt's flight in D1753 lasted 43 minutes and followed a route along the coast from Dunkerque to Nieuport. Pitt commented that it was rather misty over St. Pol aerodrome and Dunkerque docks.

28th January

Eight local practice flights were carried out on the 28th:

FSL Tiarks and AGL Williams at 10.15
FCdr Stephens and Obs.SL Christian at 11.10
FSL Pitt and AGL Woolf at 11.20
FCdr Stevens and Obs.SL Christian at 11.45
FCdr Clarke and FSL Bannatyne at 13.50
FSL Hyslop and AGL Woolfe at 14.10
FCdr Wright and Obs.SL Christian at 15.40
FSL Pitt and AGL Costen at 15.05

Pitt and Woolf's flight at 11.20 was little more than a circuit and landing in D1754, as the D.H.4's propeller was broken at take off by mud thrown up from the wheels. Pitt's second flight of the day was more successful and he spent 40 minutes circling the aerodrome at 3000 feet whilst his passenger, AGL Coster practised firing a Very pistol.

It should be mentioned that the rank of AGL referred to acting gunlayer. The AGLs were drawn from the ratings and were usually of AC.1 or AC.2 rank.

29th January

Two local practice flights were carried out:

FCdr Clarke and AGL Wentworth at 11.55
FSL Bannatyne and AGL Hollingsbee at 13.50

30th January

D.H.4 N6404 was ferried from Dover by FCdr Le Mesurier and Lt.Cdr Allen RNVR at 14.45.

31st January

At 10.40, FCdr Stevens and Obs.SL Christian attempted to carry out a comparative test of BHP powered D.H.4 D1751 against a Rolls Royce powered D.H.4 belonging to No. 5 Squadron. During the test, the BHP engine of their own aircraft became overheated and developed a bad misfire. With four 16lb bombs and four double trays of ammunition, D1751 could only achieve a height of 12000 feet.

FCdr Clarke and AGL Weston carried out a gun test in D.H.4 D1754 at 11.05.

• • •

February 1918

At this juncture, the squadron consisted of seven D.H.4 aircraft and the following eleven flying officers:

SCdr CT MacLaren
FCdr INC Clarke
AFCdr GLE Stevens
AFCdr JS Wright
Obs.Lt RJ St. John
FSL AM Bannatyne
Obs.SL LA Christian
FSL CM Hyslop
FSL VCM Tiarks
FSL GA Pitt
FSL LR Warren

FCdr INC Clarke, the squadron's senior Flight Commander, was primarily responsible for the training of the squadron's new bombing crews. Clarke's strategy for effective bombing was based upon as many aircraft as possible progressing to the target in close formation, dropping their bombs at the same time, turning for home and diving towards the lines, still in close formation. The reasoning was that this would have the maximum impact on the target and provide the strongest possible mutual defence against enemy fighters.

In practice, "as many aircraft as possible" would be limited to a maximum of two flights. It simply would not be practical to keep three flights in close proximity to the leader. Close formation practice flying was therefore the order of the day and Clarke had the pilots flying in close formation as often as possible.

The Royal Naval Air Service commenced deployment of the newly developed D.H.9 during February 1918. No.6 Squadron was the first operational unit to be equipped with the new aircraft, powered by the 230hp Siddeley Deasy Puma engine.

Reliability problems with the Siddeley Puma engines used in the D.H.9s meant that as well as the squadron initially struggling to make enough serviceable aircraft available for bombing missions, some machines would inevitably develop problems and be unable to keep up with the formation, lessening the effect over the target and leaving themselves susceptible to attack by enemy aircraft.

1st February
No flying due to unfavourable weather.

2nd February
An engine test was carried out in the misbehaving D1751 at 10.35 by FCdr Clarke and Obs.Lt St. John. As there were no further engine tests on this machine it must be assumed that the mechanics had cured the embarrassing misfire.

Gun tests were carried out by the following crews who followed a route out towards Gravelines:

FSL Warren and AGL Woolf at 10.30
FSL Tiarks and G/L Williams at 10.55 and 11.20
FSL Hyslop and G/L Costen at 11.30
FSL Pitt and G/L Banks at 14.10
FCdr Clarke and Obs.Lt St. John at 14.15
FSL Bannatyne and AGL O'Brian at 14.30
FSL Hyslop and AGL O'Brian at 15.35

FSL Tiarks and A/M Jennings carried out a machine test on D.H.4 B9499 at 15.55. The engine was found to be overheating and new radiator blinds were subsequently fitted.

3rd February
Four crews carried out gun tests:

FSL Bannatyne and AGL Smith at 09.56
FSL Hyslop and AGL Proctor at 09.58
FSL Tiarks and AGL Williams at 10.15
FSL Pitt and AGL Jarvis at 10.45

The gun tests consisted of flying out to Gravelines and firing the forward firing synchronised Vickers gun out to sea.

FCdr Clarke and SCdr MacLaren carried out a machine test on B9499 at 09.52, to verify that the new radiator blinds cured the overheating problem.

FCdr Wright and Obs.SL Christian flying D.H.4 D1754 made another attempt to carry out the comparison test with a Rolls Royce powered D.H.4 of No.5 Squadron flown by FCdr CPO Bartlett. The BHP D.H.4 had a marginally better climb to 15000 feet but both machines exhibited the same speed at that height. Bartlett stated that the engine in his Rolls Royce powered machine was not giving its full power.

At 15.00, FCdr Wright led a 35 minute practice formation flight:

FCdr Wright and AGL Woolf in D1754
FSL Hyslop and AGL Wentworth in D1751
FSL Tiarks and AGL O'Brien in N6404
FSL Bannatyne and AGL Hollingsby in D1753
FSL Pitt and AGL Williams in B9499

Pitt reported that the conditions were very bumpy and that his D.H.4, B9499, was flying "left wing heavy", the condition resulting in a near miss as he took off over No.5 Squadron's hangars.

4th February
Three local practice flights were carried out by the following crews:

FCdr Stevens and Obs.SL Christian at 09.45
FCdr Clarke and Obs.Lt St. John at 10.00
FSL Bannatyne and AGL Hollingsby at 14.40

FCdr Clarke led a 55 minute practice formation flight at 11.00:

FCdr Clarke and Obs.Lt St. John in B9499
FSL Hyslop and AGL Banks in D1751
FSL Tiarks and AGL Cousin in N6404
FSL Bannatyne and AGL Jarvis in D1754

Two gun tests were carried out:

FCdr Clarke and SCdr MacLaren in D.H.4 D1754 at 14.40
FSL Pitt and AGL Smith in D.H.4 D1753 at 15.15.

Pitt was airborne for one hour at 5000 feet and reported that during the test, one bullet put a hole through the propeller.

5th February
Nine gun tests were carried out during the day, the opportunity being taken to evaluate another selection of possible gunlayers:

FSL Tiarks and AGL Spalding at 09.55
FSL Warren and AGL Betteridge at 11.00
FSL Pitt and AGL Pacey at 11.00
FSL Bannatyne and AGL Quilter at 11.35
FSL Tiarks and AGL Dray at 11.55
SCdr MacLaren and AGL Woolf at 13.45
FSL Hyslop and AGL Wentworth at 14.05
FSL Bannatyne and AGL Farley at 14.15.

The aircraft carried out a coast patrol to Gravelines where the gunlayers practiced firing their Lewis guns. Pitt reported that he practised stalls during his flight.

At 09.30, FCdr Clarke and Obs.Lt St. John carried out a 20 minute local flight in D1751.

6th to 11th February
Bad weather closed down all flying activity.

12th February
FCdr Stevens and AGL Weston carried out a brief 15 minute local flight at 14.10.

13th to 14th February
The continuing bad weather prevented all flying activity.

15th February
Eleven local flights were carried out during the day. Some flights being used to evaluate further gunlayer candidates:

FCdr Stevens and FSL Tiarks at 09.40
FSL Tiarks and AGL Pacey at 10.00
FSL Pitt and AGL Bence at 10.20
FSL Bannatyne and AGL Harris at 14..43
FCdr Wright and FSL Hyslop at 09.50
FSL Hyslop and AGL Harris at 10.27
FCdr Wright and Obs.SL Christian at 14.50
FSL Pitt and AGL Shepherd at 15.00
FSL Bannatyne and AGL Atkinson at 15.25
FSL Hyslop and AGL Dicks at 15.25

Pitt reported that the weather was still overcast and he was unable to climb above 2000 feet. During his second flight at 15.25 the weather was still reported as misty.

16th February
At 10.45, FCdr Clarke and Obs.Lt St. John collected the squadron's first D.H.9, B7583, from the Aerodrome at Dover.

FCdr Stevens and FSL Pitt carried out a very brief local flight at 09.43 in D.H.4 B9499. The flight was simply a quick circuit of the aerodrome to check that the machine was not exhibiting the "left wing heavy" condition that had been reported on the 3rd February.

Eight machine and gun test flights were carried out during the day:

FSL Tiarks and AGL Dray at 09.35
FSL Hyslop and PO.AGL Ryan at 09.50
FSL Pitt and AGL Betteridge at 09.54
FSL Warren and AGL Woolf at 10.02
FCdr Clarke and SCdr MacLaren in D.H.9 B7583 at 13.58
FSL Pitt and AGL Dicks at 14.25
FCdr Stevens and Obs.SL Christian at 14.35
FSL Tiarks and AGL Williams at 16.05

Pitt and Betteridge followed the route Dunkerque, Gravelines, Calais, Boulogne at 12500 feet, the machine's engine started to misfire at 12000 feet. Pitt described AGL Betteridge as a "Full-Out gunlayer", a comment that proved to be very astute, Betteridge serving as a gunlayer with No.6 Squadron and No.206 Squadron RAF, finishing the war with a Distinguished Flying Medal, Chevalier de l'Ordre de Leopold II and a Croix de Guerre (Belgian). Pitt's third flight of the day was carried out over the same route at 14000 feet with AGL Dicks, he reported that a long stretch of the English coast was visible.

17th February

Nine local flights were carried out on the 17th:

FSL Tiarks and AGL Williams at 10.00
FSL Pitt and AGL Betteridge at 10.40
FSL Bannatyne and AGL Jarvis at 10.55
FCdr Stevens and Obs.SL Christian in D.H.9 B7583 at 11.11
FCdr Clarke and Obs.Lt St. John at 13.30
FSL Tiarks and AGL Williams at 14.18
FSL Warren and AGL Woolf at 14.50
FSL Bannatyne and PO.AGL Ryan at 16.00
FSL Hyslop and AGL Williams at 16.55

Pitt and Betteridge flew a coastal patrol and map reading exercise over La Panne, Furnes, St. Pol and Loon Plage in D.H.4 N6404. Pitt attempted a practice landing on the beach, stood the machine on its nose and broke his propeller and radiator.

18th February

FCdr Wright led a practice formation flight at 10.20:

FCdr Wright and AGL Woolf in D.H.9 B7583
FSL Warren and AGL Weston in D.H.4 D1754
FSL Bannatyne and AGL Pacey in D.H.4 B9499
FSL Hyslop and AGL Banks in D.H.4 D1751

FCdr Stevens collected the squadron's second D.H.9, B7589, from Dover at 14.30.
Eight local flights were carried out during the day:

FCdr Clarke and Obs.SL Christian in D.H.9 B7583 at 11.20
SCdr MacLaren and Lt Beddall, RNVR, at 13.45
FSL Tiarks and AGL Bence at 13.40
FSL Hyslop and AGL Wentworth at 15.10
FSL Bannatyne and Obs.SL Christian at 15.15
FSL Warren and FSL Pitt at 14.02
FSL Pitt and AM1 Jennings at 16.35
FSL Warren and LME Pugh at 17.00

LME Pugh and AM1 Jennings were dispatched to Loon Plage to repair D.H.4 N6404. FSL Warren flew Pitt out to Loon Plage to pick up N6404 from the beach. Both pilots returned with the mechanics as passengers.

19th February

FCdr Le Mesurier and Lt Carr delivered the squadron's third D.H.9, B7587, from Dover at 13.55.

A total of thirteen local practice and test flights were flown during the day:

FSL Tiarks and WO Milner at 15.40
FCdr Clarle and Obs.Lt St. John at 15.40
SCdr MacLaren and Obs.SL Christian at 09.35
SCdr MacLaren and Lt. Meyer (USA) at 14.03
FSL Tiarks and OS3 Trenowden at 14.08
FSL Warren and AGL O'Brien at 14.30
FSL Warren and AGL O'Brien at 16.55
FCdr Wright and AC2 Dicks at 14.55
FSL Tiarks and AGL Neighbour at 10.30
FSL Tiarks and Mech. Mabbs at 15.30
FSL Bannatyne and AGL Atkinson at 12.10
FCdr Stevens and FSL Tiarks at 15.05
FCdr Stevens and WO Tuck at 15.30

Four bombing practice flights were carried out:

FCdr Clarke and Obs.FLt St. John in D.H.9 B7583 at 12.00
FCdr Wright and AGL Woolf at 10.15

FSL Warren and AGL Williams at 11.45
FCdr Stevens and Obs.SL Christian at 10.50

20th February
Just four local flights were carried out on the 20th:

FCdr Clarke and Obs.SL Christian at 09.27
FCdr Clarke and Obs.Lt St. John in D.H.9 B7583 at 11.00
SCdr MacLaren and AGL Weston at 11.35
FCdr Stevens and Lt Beddall, RNVR, at 12.10

21st February
Two new D.H.9s were collected from Dover, B7599 by FSL Hyslop at 10.30 and B7588 by FSL Bannatyne at 10.40. No passenger was present for either flight and aircraft would have been ballasted with sand bags to compensate for the lack of a gunlayer.

Three local flights were carried out:

FSL Pitt an AGL Jarvis at 09.45
FSL Tiarks and AGL Banks at 11.05
FCdr Stevens and PO Gascoyne at 14.25

Pitt and Banks flew D.H.4 D1751 to Gravelines, an oil union came loose causing oil to leak over the aircraft's controls. Four bombing practice flights were carried out:

FCdr Clarke and Obs.SL Christian in D.H.9 B7583 at 09.55
FCdr Clarke and Obs.Lt St. John in D.H.9 B5783 at 13.55
FSL Pitt and AGL Betteridge at 14.10
FSL Tiarks and AGL Neighbour at 14.55

Pitt recorded that two of his bombs fell 2 miles away from the target, whilst the other two were hung up in the frame. Betteridge simply recorded that their aim was very bad.

22nd February
Bad weather prevented all flying activity.

23rd February
FCdr Wright collected D.H.9 B7586 from Dover at 12.15.

A total of fourteen local flights were carried out, most of them in D.H.9s:

FCdr Clarke and Obs.Lt St. John on D.H.9 B7599 at 09.25
FSL Tiarks and AGL Cousins in D.H.9 B7583 at 09.40
FCdr Stevens and FSL Pitt in D.H.9 B7589 at 09.55
FCdr Stevens and FSL Pitt in D.H.9 B7589 at 10.15
FSL Pitt and AGL Smith in D.H.9 B7589 at 10.50
FSL Bannatyne and AGL Hollingsbee in D.H.9 B7589 at 11.12
FSL Bannatyne and AGL Proctor in D.H.9 B7589 at 13.50
FSL Pitt and AGL Allwork in D.H.4 D1753 at 14.10
FSL Tiarks and AGL Wentworth in D.H.4 D1754 at 14.20
FSL Hyslop and AGL Costen in D.H.4 D1753 at 14.30
FSL Bannatyne and WO Tuck in D.H.9 B7589 at 14.35
SCdr MacLaren and AGL Newsham in D.H.9 B7589 at 15.05
FSL Pitt and AGL Newsham in D.H.9 B7589 at 15.30
FSL Tiarks and AGL Wentworth in D.H.4 D1754 at 15.00

Pitt's first flight in a D.H.9 with FCdr Stevens was a simple familiarization flight, one circuit around the aerodrome. His second flight was a brief 17 minute spell to get used to the handling. The third flight was of 45 minutes duration, out to sea for a gun test. His final flight of the day was a course to Gravlines to introduce a new gunlayer, AGL Newsham, to France.

24th February
Eleven local flights were carried out:

FCdr Clarke and Obs.SL Christian in D.H.9 B7599 at 09.35
SCdr MacLaren and AGL Wilkinson in D.H.4 D1751 at 09.55
FCdr Wright and LM Cook in D.H.4 D1753 at 09.55
FSL Hyslop and AGL Skinner in D.H.4 D1752 at 10.10
FCdr Stevens and PO Rose in D.H.9 B7589 at 10.30
FSL Bannatyne and AGL Norman in D.H.4 D1753 at 10.45
FCdr Clarke and AM1 Jouning in D.H.9 B7599 at 10.55
FSL Hyslop and AGL Skinner in D.H.9 B7589 at 11.07
FCdr Clarke and Obs.Lt St. John in D.H.9 B7588 at 14.00
FSL Tiarks and AGL Weston in D.H.4 D1752 at 14.50
FSL Bannatyne and Lt Emmet in D.H.4 D1753 at 15.40

25th February
No flying due to unfavourable weather.
New pilot FSL EC Stocker arrived at the squadron.

26th February
Two new D.H.9s were collected from Dover:

B7596 by FSL Warren and LtCdr Allen, RNVR at 11.15
B7592 by FSL Pitt at 11.45

Pitt reported that the passenger compartment was ballasted with sand bags, conditions were very bumpy off Dover and the return trip took just 30 minutes.

Three test flights were carried out:

FCdr Clarke and Obs.SL Christian in D.H.9 B7583 at 09.00
FSL Tiarks and AGL Wentworth in D.H.9 B7587 at 09.40
FCdr Wright and LM Pearce in D.H.4 D1753 at 09.40

One local familiarization flight was carried out:

FSL Stocker and AGL Proctor in D.H.4 D1754 at 09.43

One Gun test was carried out:

FSL Hyslop and AGL Smith in D.H.9 B7589 at 11.15.

27th February
Three new D.H.9s were collected from Dover:

B7591 by FSL Bannatyne at 15.15
B7600 by SCdr MacLaren at 15.50
B7598 by FSL Tiarks.

Tiarks almost immediately experienced trouble with B7598 and landed at Manston. He then returned to Dover but crashed the machine when landing.

Four local flights were carried out:

FCdr Clarke and Obs.SL Christian in D.H.9 B7583 at 09.15
FSL Hyslop and AC1 Branch in D.H.9 B7589 at 09.50
FSL Stocker and AGL Allwork in D.H.4 D1754 at 10.00
FSL Warren and AGL O'Brien in D.H.4 B9499 at 11.50
FSL Warren and OS2 Baulf in D.H.4 D1752 at 15.15

FCdr Clarke led his Flight on two practice formation patrols:

at 11.03
FCdr Clarke and Obs.Lt St. John in D.H.4 B9499
FSL Hyslop and AGL Ryan in D.H.4 D1751
FSL Pitt and AGL Betteridge in D.H.4 D1753

Pitt remarked in his log how well his aircraft's engine was running, Betteridge remarked on the weather!

at 14.10
FCdr Clarke and Obs.Lt St. John in D.H.4 B9499
FSL Warren and AGL O'Brien in D.H.4 D1752
FSL Hyslop and AGL Pacey in D.H.4 D1751
FSL Pitt and AGL Betteridge in D.H.4 D1753

Pitt and Betteridge flew in the rear position, after the practice flight they landed at Coudekerke.

28th February
A new D.H.9 was collected from Dover:

B7597 by FSL Tiarks at 12.25

Five local flights were carried out:

FCdr Clarke and Lt Millward, RNVR in D.H.9 B7599 at 10.00
FCdr Wright and SL Low, RN, in D.H.9 B7592 at 10.00
FSL Stocker and AGL Ryan in D.H.4 D1753 at 10.10
FSL Pitt and WO Roberts in D.H.4 D1752 at 12.18
FSL Stocker and AGL Ryan in D.H.9 B7586 at 14.46

FCdr Clarke led another practice formation patrol at 14.40:

FCdr Clarke and Obs.Lt St. John in D.H.9 B7599
FSL Warren and AGL O'Brien in D.H.9 B7596
FSL Tiarks and AGL Wentworth in D.H.9 B7588
FSL Pitt and AGL Dray in D.H.9 B7587
FSL Hyslop and AGL Pacey in D.H.9 B7589
FSL Bannatyne and AGL Hollingsbee in D.H.9 B7592

Clarke kept the D.H.9s in the air for 60 minutes, with Pitt flying on the left side.

• • •

March 1918

A number of American Officers were given familiarisation flights during March, most of these Officers were awaiting a posting to their first squadron:

Lt Meyer
Lt Jay O'Connell
Lt Frederick Clapp (With No. 211 Squadron and the 17th Aero Squadron)

Lt Garland Powell (Gunlayer with 211 Squadron and then in charge of the 1101st Replacement Squadron USAS.
Lt Leslie Egbert (With 22nd Aero Squadron)

The standard D.H.9 armament for the observer was a single Lewis gun mounted on a Scarff mount. The Squadron's Armament Officer, Lt JM Beddall RNVR, quickly realised the advantage that twin Lewis guns would give to the rear gunner and set about the design and fabrication of modifications to the Scarff mounting to allow the use of a second gun.

The two Lewis guns were fixed approximately 15 inches apart on a cradle that was bolted to the tubular hoop of the Scarff mount. The cradle allowed the guns to be easily traversed vertically and horizontally without making constant small adjustments to the hoop and ring of the Scarff mount.

The two guns were aligned such their cones of fire converged at 200 yards, a single pillar and bead foresight and ring backsight were fixed on the centre line between the two barrels.

The guns were modified by fitting a thumb trigger to give easier operation when wearing heavy gauntlets.

Finally, the rubber band "springs" used for raising the hoop with its gun were replaced by stronger rubber bands to compensate for the extra weight of twin guns and the cradle.

In combat, it was general practice to open fire with one gun, keeping the other in reserve. If an especially good target presented itself and the gunner's first shots were on target, he might open up with both guns to make sure of a kill.

1st March to 3rd March

No flying due to unfavourable weather.

With an increase in the number of pilots and aircraft assigned to the squadron, the facilities at Petite Synthe were starting to be stretched. In a memorandum related to aerodrome accommodation produced on the 3rd March 1918, Wing Captain Lambe reported that No.6 Squadron required another 60 feet x 20 feet hut for Officer's accommodation and also that the squadron required a Stores and a workshop. Lambe also recorded that the road needed to be finished and rolled and the large dug-out need to be completed.

4th March

No flying due to unfavourable weather. The squadron received a brief visit at midday from Wing Commander JT Cull, the Commanding Officer of No.5 Wing, who flew in from Coudekerke in B.E.2c 9970.

5th March

Three local flights were carried out:

FCdr Clarke and FLt.Obs St. John in D.H.9 B7583 at 13.50
FCdr Stevens and Obs.SL Christian in D.H.9 B7589 at 14.40
FCdr Clarke and FLt.Obs St. John in D.H.9 B7585 at 15.45

Wing Commander Cull made another visit in B.E.2c 9970 at 12.10.

6th March

Several formation practice patrols were carried out:

at 09.30
FCdr Clarke and FLt.Obs St. John in D.H.9 B7599
FSL Warren and AGL O'Brien in D.H.9 B7596
FSLPitt and AGL Betteridge in D.H.9 B7587
FSL Tiarks and AGL Wentworth in D.H.9 B7588
FSL Hyslop and AGL Pacey in D.H.9 B7603

Clarke took the formation up to 16000 feet but the practice patrol was deemed to be unsatisfactory.

at 09.40
FCdr Stevens and Obs.SLt Christian in D.H.9 B7589
FCdr Wright and AGL Woolf in D.H.9 B7591
FSL Bannatyne and AGL Hollingsbee in D.H.9 B7591
FSL Stocker and AGL Ryan in D.H.9 B7597

at 16.40
FCdr Clarke and FLt.Obs St. John in D.H.9 B7599
FSL Warren and AGL O'Brien in D.H.9 B7596
FSL Pitt and AGL Betteridge in D.H.9 B7587
FSL Tiarks and AGL Wentworth in D.H.9 B7588
FSL Hyslop and AGL Pacey in D.H.9 B7603
FSL Bannatyne and AGL Woolf in D.H.9 B7591

The weather was too misty for formation flying and the pilots lost station before the patrol had reached 1000 feet. After loosing formation, Pitt and Betteridge flew out to sea for gun practice.

FCdr Wright and FSL Warren took D.H.4 D1753 to Dover Aerodrome at 13.30. FSL Warren collected new D.H.9 B6703 from Dover and was accompanied back to Petite Synthe by FCdr Wright in D1753 at 14.45.

7th March

In early March, Major Aubrey circulated a memo notifying No.2 Squadron, No.6 Squadron and No.13 Squadron that they had been allocated ratings from No.22 American Squadron Headquarters which had been split up:

HQ Ref ...S271
7998
Headquarters, R.N.A.S.
Dunkerque
7.3.18

Memorandum
In continuation of H.Q. Ref 7998 of the 1st instant the American Squadron (No.22) Headquarters has been split up and the men allocated as attached lists.

The Squadrons concerned should collect these men as soon as possible.

HR Aubrey Major
Attached H.Q. R.N.A.S.
For Senior Officer, R.N.A.S.

Distribution
C.O. No.1 Wing
C.O. No.5 Wing
C.O. A.D (transport)

The following list was attached for No.6 Squadron:

Private	*Shellenberger, CF*	*Welder*
Corporal	*Kinsella, Phillip J*	*Aerial Gunner*
Private	*Mason, Thomas I*	*Aerial Gunner*
Private	*Price, John B*	*Aerial Gunner*
Private	*Schofield, Lane A*	*Aerial Gunner*
Private	*Trebil, Maynard*	*Aerial Gunner*
Private	*Bergford, Lester N*	*Aerial Gunner*
Private	*Sorter, Matthew B*	*Carpenter*
Private	*Ketter, John C*	*Carpenter*
Private	*Brill, Arthur L*	*Carpenter*
Private	*Reidel, George A*	*Carpenter*
Sergeant	*Carmean, Harry P*	*Clerk*
Sergeant	*Pease, Tod H*	*Clerk*
Sergeant	*Kent, Hartwell B*	*Stenographer*
Cook	*Ralph, Arthur S*	*Cook*
Private	*Holmes, Raymond, D*	*Draughtsman*
Private	*Lalor, Vincent G*	*Coppersmith*

An American Officer, Lt Powell, made two familiarization flights, one 10 minute local flight with SCdr MacLaren and a 60 minute formation practice with FCdr Stevens:

at 14.30
FCdr Wright and AGL Woolf in D.H.9 B7591
FCdr Stevens and Lt Powell in D.H.9 B7589
FSL Stocker and AGL Ryan in D.H.9 B7597
FSL Tiarks and AGL Wentworth in D.H.9 B7586
FSL Warren and AGLO'Brien in D.H.9 B7596

Three test flights were carried out in the afternoon:

SCdr MacLaren and PO (RN) Ross in B7603 at 14.32
FSL Stocker and PO AGL Ryan in B7597 at 15.23
FCdr Wright and FSL Stocker in N7597 at 16.40

Wing Commander Cull paid another visit in the afternoon. Unusually, two RFC pilots, Lt. Race and 2Lt Stonehouse, landed their FE2 machines at the aerodrome. They were en-route from Lympne but it was not recorded whether they were lost or making a social call!

8th March

Three American Officers, Lt Powell, Lt Clapp and Lt Egbert were given familiarisation flights, in Powell's case, his third flight.

Five local flights were carried out:

SCdr MacLaren and Lt Clapp in D.H.9 B7603 at 09.35
FSL Stocker and AGL PO Ryan in D.H.9 B7592 at 10.30
FSL Hyslop and AGL Williams in D.H.9 B7600 at 15.00
FSL Tiarks and Lt Egbert in D.H.9 B7589 at 15.50
SCdr MacLaren and FCdr Edwards in D.H.9 B7600 at 16.15

Three new D.H.9s were collected from Dover aerodrome:

B7604 by FSL Pitt at 12.15
B7602 by FSL Hyslop at 12,25
B7605 by FSL Bannatyne at 12.50

Pitt was not happy with his machine and reported that the engine spluttered for the entire flight.

FCdr Wright led a formation practice patrol:

at 14.30
FCdr Wright and Lt Powell in D.H.9 B7591
FSL Tiarks and AGL Wentworth in D.H.9 B7588
FSL Pitt and AGL Betteridge in D.H.9 B7587
FSL Stocker and AGL PO Ryan in D.H.9 B7597
FSL Bannatyne and AGL Hollingsbee in D.H.9 B7592
FSL Warren and Obs.SLt Christian in D.H.9 B7596

The practice patrol headed to Gravelines and then along the coast at 8000 feet. Pitt reported that FCdr Wright had difficulty in getting away from the formation after signalling "washout"!

FCdr Wright carried out an engine test in D.H.9 B7586 at 16.15. His passenger was AM Tarrant, Wright wanting Tarrant to experience the problem at first hand.

The 8th March 1918 effectively marked the completion of No.6 Squadron's period of "working up" to combat readiness. Although fully equipped with D.H.9s, one D.H.4 was retained by the squadron for new pilot familiarisation flights.

NOTE

[1] Not the son of Chaos but HMS *Erebus*, a Royal Naval Monitor fitted with two 15" guns.

CHAPTER NINE

RAIDS OVER BELGIUM

The Records Officer, Sub Lieutenant Basil Rook, wrote further reminiscences of the early days at Petite Synthe:

> *"Only odd memories linger of the Squadron's early days at Petite Synthe. I remember my first flight, ever, with VC Tiarks. I also recall that JS Wright, regardless of the hubbub around him in the mess, would park himself on the floor against the wall and immerse himself in what appeared to be music scores. The black Cocker Spaniel INC Clarke brought out from England must also be mentioned, for on the ground, Clarke, his observer St. John and the dog were almost inseparable. As soon as the planes landed from operations the dog had an uncanny ability to single out Clarke's D.H.9 and was the first to greet him when he climbed out of the plane."*

A very unusual aspect of FCdr INC Clarke's strategy for No.6 Squadron involved the use of the D.H.9 as a fighter aircraft for escort duties. The definition of "fighter aircraft" in this instance would be a 2-seater with both offensive and defensive armament, examples of traditional fighters would be the Sopwith 1 1/2 Strutter (type 9400), FE2b and of course the superb Bristol F2a/F2b Fighter. It was in more recent times that the agile offensively armed single seater machine started to be referred to as a fighter.

The idea of using a D.H.9 as a fighter is, to be charitable, a strange concept. The natural reaction of most readers being to ridicule the idea. The D.H.9 with its 230hp Siddeley Deasy Puma engine most certainly was not in the same league as a Bristol F2b, however, it is known that FSL VCM Tiarks had a reputation within the squadron for being a "split arse pilot", stunting and hedge-hopping his D.H.9 as though he thought it were a Bristol Fighter. With the Puma's propensity for unreliability, Victor Tiarks may well be considered to have been fortunate not to have suffered an engine failure during his exuberant flying exhibitions. The D.H.9 without a bomb load did have a reasonably handy performance, climb and top speed. The provision of twin Lewis guns for the observer would also have been of great value in the fighter role.

Initially, at least, Clarke used several D.H.9's as fighters to escort bombing formations. When the squadron became No.206 Squadron RAF on 1st April 1918, long range reconnaissance patrols were introduced where a single "fighter" aircraft would undertake high reconnaissance flights deep into enemy territory. Also on occasion, line patrols were performed where the D.H.9 "fighters" carried out sweeps to drive enemy 2-seaters away from the lines. Clarke's vision perhaps not seeming so strange after all?

With the commencement of war flights, the squadron started to experience the true extent of the engine unreliability, with missions having to be cancelled due to the unserviceability of many of the aircraft. In order to overcome the worst of the problems, the somewhat extreme measure of replacing each engine's exhaust valve springs after every day's service was eventually adopted. This involved the tedious task of stripping the cam boxes, placing an immense burden upon the engine fitters who would find themselves working from 5am to 9pm every day.

9th March

FSL Warren and AM.1 Speirs carried out a test flight in D.H.9 B7603 at 08.40.

The squadron flew its first two offensive missions on the 9th. The first mission was a bombing raid on billets and railway sidings at St. Pierre Capelle. FCdr Le Mesurier who had just returned to France and had been posted to the newly reformed No.11 Squadron, joined the mission flying one of No.6 Squadron's D.H.9 aircraft.

at 10.01
FCdr Clarke and Flt.Obs St John in B7583
FCdr Le Mesurier and AGL Williams in B7600
FCdr Stevens and Obs.SLt Christian in B7589
FCdr Wright and AGL Woolf in B7591
FSL Hyslop and AGL AGL Pacey in B7605
FSL Warren and AGL O'Brien in B7603
FSL Pitt and AGL Betteridge in B7587
FSL Stocker and AGL PO Ryan in B7597
FSL Bannatyne and AGL Hollingsbee in B7592
FSL Tiarks and AGL Wentworth in B7588

The attack was composed of seven bombing machines and three fighting machines, however FSL Hyslop and AGL Pacey, were forced to return to the aerodrome after suffering engine trouble.

The squadron dropped thirty-two 25lb and twenty-four 16lb bombs from heights varying between 13000 and 15000 feet. The target was reported to be well covered with several bombs seen to burst on, or close, to huts and buildings It was considered probable that at least three were direct hits as in one case a fire was caused and in two others dense clouds of smoke were observed.

FSL Pitt and AGL Betteridge reported that they dropped eight bombs scoring hits on a large building and some huts at a railway siding and several large fires were started. A German Staaken R.VI was observed in a field near St. Pierre Cappelle and Betteridge tried to bomb it but was unable to observe the effects. During the course of the mission, three enemy aircraft approached the bombing force but would not engage closely enough for Betteridge's liking.

FSL Hyslop and WO Tuck carried out a test flight in the misbehaving B7605 at 11.58.

The second bombing raid was an unscheduled attack on the stranded Staaken bomber reported by Pitt and Betteridge. Permission to attack the Giant was obtained and six machines were immediately refuelled and rearmed.

at 13.33
FCdr Clarke and Flt.Obs St. John in B7583
FCdr Le Mesurier and PO AGL Ryan in B7591
FCdr Stevens and Obs.SL Christian in B7603
FSL Hyslop and AGL Pacey in B7602
FSL Tiarks and AGL Wentworth in B7588
FSL Bannatyne and AGL Hollingsbee in B7592

Hyslop and Pacey again failed to reach the target and returned to the aerodrome. The other five machines released twenty-four 25lb and sixteen 16lb bombs over the objective from heights of 1500 to 3900 feet and 150 rounds were also fired at the enemy machine. Bombs were observed to burst in very close proximity to the machine and many tracers were seen to enter it. Approximately 200 German troops gathered round the target were attacked with machine gun fire and seen to scatter in all directions. The pilots reported that the Giant's starboard wing was almost on the ground and it was assumed that the machine's undercarriage was broken.

During the course of the mission, the patrol was attacked by six enemy scouts over St. Pierre Cappelle. Le Mesurier put B7591 into a dive and drew away from the defending force and a running fight developed to within a quarter of a mile of the lines. Le Mesurier's gun layer, PO AGL Ryan was able to fire 50 rounds at one scout, shooting it down to crash on the edge of the floods, where it was observed burning on the ground. FSL Bannatyne and AGL Hollingsbee were both seriously wounded by enemy fire, despite his injuries, Bannatyne managed to put D.H.9 B7592 down safely on the beach between Oost Dunkerque and Coxyd.

At approximately 15.00, a combined force from I and II Marinefeldjastas reported attacking a British bombing group protected by Sopwith single seaters. Ltnz S H Wessels of Marinefeldjasta I claimed a D.H.4 between Nieuport and Slype at 15.10. Although the machine type claimed was incorrect (this would have been the Germans' first encounter with a D.H.9), the time and location provided a very close match, it therefore seems quite possible that Wessels was responsible for wounding and forcing down Bannatyne and Hollingsbee. VzFlgMstr Adolf Bottler of II Marinefeldjasta flying a Pfalz DIIIa was reported as wounded in action during the encounter. Bottler was able to return to his own airfield and was subsequently sent to Marine field hospital III for treatment, he could well have been injured by Le Mesurier and Ryan. A second D.H.4 and a Sopwith single seater were erroneously claimed by the defenders.

The Staaken is believed to have been an R.VI, serial number R.27 of Rfa 501, this machine took off on a bombing mission from Ghent on the night of the 7th March but suffered problems due to frozen fuel lines before it crossed the coast and was compelled to make a forced landing. The machine's engines and instruments were salvaged before it was destroyed by No.6 Squadron's bombs and gunfire. A second Staaken from Rfa 501 also made an emergency landing on the night of the 7th/8th March, this was R.36 and thought to be the machine that landed at Ghistelles aerodrome. R36 was dismantled on site.

10th March

SCdr MacLaren and AGL Dray carried out a visibility test in D.H.9 B7604 at 10.28.

An eight machine bombing raid was despatched to Engel aerodrome at 11.47:

FCdr Stevens and Obs.SL Christian in D.H.9 B7589
FSL Tiarks and AGL Williams in D.H.9 B7600
FSL Stocker and PO AGL Ryan in D.H.9 B7597
FCdr Wright and AGL Woolf in D.H.9 B7591
FCdr Clarke and Flt.Obs. St. John in D.H.9 B7583
FSL Warren and AGL O'Brien in D.H.9 B7603
FSL Hyslop and AGL Pacey in D.H.9 B7602
FSL Pitt and AGL Betteridge in D.H.9 B7587

Stevens and Christian in B7589 experienced engine trouble and returned without attacking the target, making a forced landing at Bray Dunes aerodrome.

A total of twenty-seven 25lb and twenty 16lb bombs were dropped, many of which were seen to burst close to the hangars. Four 16lb bombs were dropped on Engel dump and two fires were started. Pitt and Betteridge failed to find their objective and dropped their bombs on a building to the southwest of the target.

FSL Hyslop took new pilot FSL Bewell on a local familiarisation flight at 15.10.

11th March

FSL Bewell was taken on another short familiarisation flight with FCdr Stevens and then carried out two local flights, the first accompanied by PO AGL Ryan at 11.30 and the second with AGL Cousins at 14.37.

New pilot FSL Oakeshott was taken on a local familiarisation flight by FCdr Wright at 13.35. Oakeshott then carried out a local flight accompanied by AGL Dray at 14.50.

FCdr Thomas Frederick Le Mesurier DSC and two bars, was not attached to No.6 Squadron, but nevertheless was involved in the action on the 9th March 1918 when his gunlayer, PO Ryan, claimed an enemy scout crashed at the edge of the floods. Le Mesurier liked to make unofficial flights and in 1917 was shot down in a No.12 Squadron Sopwith Triplane whilst flying as unofficial escort to a No.5 Squadron bombing mission. On completion of his tour of duty with No.5 Squadron, Le Mesurier was assigned to No.11 Squadron, a contemporary of No.6 Squadron. He was killed on the 26th May 1918 when his No.211 Squadron RAF D.H.9 broke up in the air over Pervyse. *Courtesy JMB/GSL Collection*

A number of test flights were carried out:

FCdr Clarke and Flt.Obs St. John in D.H.9 B7583 at 13.33
FSL Stocker and PO AGL Ryan in D.H.9 B7597 at 15.35
FCdr Clarke and PO Ottley in D.H.9 B7596 at 16.45
FCdr Clarke and Flt.Obs. St. John in D.H.9 B7603 at 17.30

Wing Commander Cull wrote to Wing Captain Lambe on the 11th with a detailed report of Bannatyne and Hollingsbee's forced landing:

From: Commanding Officer, No.5 Wing Headquarters, R.N.A.S.
To: Senior Officer, Headquarters, R.N.A.S.

March 11th 1918
Ref…7/780

Submitted,
Herewith, particulars, as far as I can give them of Flight Sub Lieutenant Bannatyne's forced landing between Oost

Dunkerque and Coxyde, further to the recommendation of this officer in my 0839 of March 10th 1918.

The machine was very badly shot about, three E.A. having got on the tail of the machine and I think caught the Gunlayer unawares. The main spar of the left lower plane was shot through. A flying wire was shot through and the controls of the lower aileron shot through. There were also numerous holes in the fuselage and plane. A certain number of these being caused, I should say, by explosive bullets. Flight Sub Lieutenant Bannatyne was wounded in the buttock and left hand. Although only being about 4000 feet at the time, he managed to pilot his machine back and make a landing on the sands, without further damage to the machine. I should like to point out that there was no question of a straight glide home and that the pilot must have kept his wits about him all the time. This, in my opinion shows great pluck and determination on his part. Very little ammunition had been fired at all from the rear gun and all bombs were on the machine, which shows they were attacked before they reached their target and the gunlayer must have been wounded straightaway in the leg. He was found propped up against the gun mounting when the machine landed. This I think shows that he made every endeavour, although wounded, to repel the attack by E.A. but his wound, being a very serious one, he was, at the same time, in a semi-conscious state.

Engel Aerodrome, attacked by No.6 Squadron on the 10th March 1918. Whilst the Allies referred to the aerodrome as Engel, the Germans called it Ichtegem Aerodrome. *Courtesy Johan Rhyeul*

12th March

Test flights carried out on the 12th:

FCdr Stevens and AM Mabbs in D.H.9 B7604 at 08.50
FCdr Wright and AM Motherill in D.H.9 B7591 at 09.30

A seven machine bombing raid to Aertrycke was carried out in the morning:

at 10.10
FCdr Stevens and Obs.SL Christian in D.H.9 B7604
FSL Stocker and PO AGL Ryan in D.H.9 B7603
FSL Tiarks and AGL Williams in D.H.9 B7600
FCdr Wright and AGL Woolf in D.H.9 B7591
FCdr Clarke and Flt.Obs. St. John in D.H.9 B7583
FSL Warren and AGL O'Brian in D.H.9 B7596
FSL Hyslop and AGL Pacey in D.H.9 B7602

A closer view of Ichtegem Aerodrome. Note the bomb crater below the farm buildings at the bottom of the photograph. *Courtesy Johan Ryheul*

Stevens and Christian suffered engine trouble and were forced to return to the aerodrome. Stocker and Ryan were also forced to abort the mission, returning after 20 minutes. Due to the incidence of engine trouble, FCdr Clarke diverted the attack to the secondary target of St. Pierre Cappelle. Billets and the railway sidings were attacked with fifteen 25lb and four 16lb bomb being dropped. The target was well straddled and a fire started.

At 13.45, Stevens, accompanied by an American Officer, Lt F Clapp returned D.H.9 B7604 to the depot for an engine test.

There was still official concern over the condition of Bannatyne and Hollingsbee, as evinced by the following memo from Wing Captain Lambe to the Vice Admiral, Dover Patrol:

No. H.Q. 10805
Vice Admiral, Dover Patrol
(Thro' Commodore)

Submitted,
Forwarded, with reference to my telegram No.211B of the 9th March. The Medical Officer to-day reports that Flight Sub Lieutenant AM Bannatyne and A.C.1 Gunlayer Reginald Alfred Hollingsbee who has had his leg amputated, though both seriously wounded, are progressing as favourably as can be expected.

2. This was the pilot's first occasion of crossing the Lines and apparently he showed great courage and determination in bringing his machine home.

Captain R.N.
H.Q. R.N.A.S
12/3/18

13th March
Bad weather and unserviceable engines seriously interfered with flying over the following week. On the 13th, the weather restricted flying to a 35 minute engine test by FCdr Clark and WO Tuck in B7602 at 14.30.

14th March
There was no flying on the 14th.

15th March
The only flight carried out was an engine test by FCdr Clarke and Lt.Cdr Bristow in B7605 at 12.03.

16th March
SCdr MacLaren reported that the squadron had ten serviceable and five unserviceable aircraft. Six of the squadron's pilots were sent to Dover to collect new aircraft.

FCdr Clarke and Lt.Cdr. Bristow carried out an engine test in B7602 at 10.46.

FCdr Clarke and Flt.Obs. St. John carried out a small calibre bomb practice flight in B7583 at 14.15.

17th March
A number of engine tests were carried out on the 17th:

FCdr Clarke and Flt.Obs. St. John in B7583 at 10.04
FSL Bewell and AGL Costen in B7603 at 10.15
FCdr Stevens and new pilot FSL Rolandi in B7605 at 10.21
FSL Oakeshott and PO Bates in B7600 at 10.25.
FSL Rolandi and AGL Jarvis in B7605 at 12.10

Three local flights were carried out in the afternoon:

FSL Rolandi and AGL Jarvis in B7605 at 14.06
FCdr Clarke and Flt.Obs. St. John in B7583 at 14.10
FCdr Clarke and Sgt.Maj Carmean (USAS) in B7583 at 14.23

18th March
Four engine tests were carried out:

FCdr Clarke and Flt.Obs. St. John in B7596 at 09.55
FSL Oakeshott and FSL Dray in B7600 at 11.55
FSL Stocker and AM1 Ellis in B7591 at 11.40
FCdr Clarke and Obs.SL Christian in B7583 at 17.10

Oakeshott and Dray suffered engine failure and crashed B7600 at 12.15.

FCdr Stevens led a three machine formation practice for the benefit of new pilots at 10.22:

FCdr Stevens and Obs.SL Christian in B7602
FSL Bewell and AGL Costen in B7603
FSL Rolandi and AGL Jarvis in B7605

FCdr Clarke and Flt.Obs. St. John carried out a small calibre bomb practice in B7583 at 14.53.

19th March

The squadron's problems with unserviceable D.H.9s continued to get worse, SCdr MacLaren reported 5 serviceable and 10 unserviceable machines. Despite unsuitable weather, two engine tests were carried out:

FCdr Clarke and SCdr MacLaren in B7588 at 09.50
FSL Stocker and AM Ellis in B7591 at 10.40
FCdr Stevens and Lt McDonnall carried out a local flight at 11.00.

The supply of trained D.H. pilots was stretching the Royal Naval Air Service's resources. Wing Captain Lambe formulated a new policy whereby No.12 Squadron would train pilots for No.5 Squadron which was on loan to the RFC and No.6 and No.11 Squadrons would be responsible for bringing on their own new pilots. To this end it was decided to allocate No.6 Squadron and No.11 Squadron a couple of BHP engined D.H.4s for training purposes.

> *H.Q., R.N.A.S.,*
> *Dunkerque*
> *19th March 1918*
> *BEF H.Q. 11234*
>
> *Memorandum*
>
> *Future Policy As Regards Training Of D.H. Pilots*
>
> *No.12 Squadron will be used for training D.H. pilots to complete No.5 Squadron only. To do this, there should always be, as far as possible, between four and six pilots at No.12 Squadron.*
>
> *2. All other D.H. pilots appointed to the command will be allotted to Nos.6 and 11 Squadrons alternately where they will be trained. For this purpose two or more D.H.4 machines with B.H.P. engines will be allotted to Nos.6 and 11 Squadrons.*
>
> *3. No more pilots will be allocated to Squadrons Nos.2 and 17 for the present. After 1st April the R.F.C. will be responsible for the replacement of pilots at No.5 Squadron and from that date onward No.12 Squadron will be responsible for Nos.2 and 17.*
>
> *Signed CL Lambe*
> *Captain RN*
>
> *Distribution:*
> *c.c. No.1 Wing*
> *c.c. No.5 Wing*
> *S.O., R.N.A.S., Dover*
> *"Q"*
> *"A"*
> *"S.C."*

20th March

Four of the squadron's pilots that had been kicking their heels in England waiting for new aircraft arrived back at Petite Synthe, in some cases, after a complicated series of flights:

FCdr Wright and FSL Pitt in D.H.9 D2782 from Chingford to Dover at 10.40
FCdr Wright in D.H.4 A7996 from Dover to Coudekerke at 16.15
FSL Warren in D.H.9 B7595 From Dover to Petite Synthe at 18.08
FSL Hyslop in D.H.9 B7594 from Dover to Petite Synthe at 18.08
FCdr Wright in D.H.4 A7996 from Coudekerke to Berques at 18.30
FSL Pitt in D.H.4 B9498 from Dover to Petite Synthe at 18.30

D.H.4 A7996 and D.H.9 B7595 were handed over to No.11 Squadron. D.H.4 B9498 was also handed over to No.11 Squadron but not until the 22nd March, by which time it had been used for several practice and familiarisation flights.

Several engine tests were carried out during the day:

FCdr Stevens and AGII Bush in D.H.9 B7603 at 14.45.
FCdr Clarke and Flt.Obs. St. John in D.H.9 B7599

The two additional aircraft made scant difference to the squadron's inventory that now stood at 8 serviceable and 9 unserviceable aircraft.

New pilots FSL R Robinson and FSL HA Connop arrived at the squadron.

21st March

One additional new machine was delivered on the 21st:

ABOVE: Westland built D.H.9 B7595. This machine was collected from Dover on the 20th March 1918 by FSL Warren, but was handed over to No.11 Squadron upon arrival at Petite Synthe. It was passed back to No.6 Squadron on the 29th March, just before the squadron moved to St. Marie Cappelle. *Courtesy JMB/GSL Collection*

FSL Tiarks in D.H.4 N6390 from Dover to Petite Synthe at 13.55.

Two engine tests were carried out:

SCdr MacLaren and Lt.Cdr Bristowe in D.H.9 B7602 at 13.45
FCdr Clarke and Lt Powell in D.H.9 B7583 at 17.40

Local flights were carried out by:

FSL Rolandi and AGL Jarvis in D.H.9 B7605 at 10.46
FSL Robinson in D.H.4 B9498 at 11.40
FSL Warren and Lt Clapp (USAS) in D.H.9 B7596 at 12.00
FSL Rolandi and AGL Jarvis in D.H.9 B7605 at 14.05
FSL Connop in D.H.4 B9498 at 14.12
FSL Robinson in D.H.4 B9498 at 15.35
FCdr Stevens and FCdr Benley in D.H.9 B7602 at 17.15
FSL Connop in D.H.4 B9498 at 18.10

22nd March

Four engine tests were carried out as the squadron attempted to get more of their aircraft serviceable for war flying:

FSL Hyslop and LM Matthews in D.H.9 B7605 at 11.16
FSL Tiarks and AM Hornby in D.H.9 B7600 at 11.20
SCdr Stevens and AM Whinham in D.H.9 B7605 at 11.23
FSL Pitt and AGL Betteridge in D.H.9 B7599 at 11.45

The squadron mounted a bombing raid to Bruges docks with six machines at 14.10:

Cdr Clarke and PO AGL Ryan in D.H.9 B7600
FCdr Stevens and Obs.SL Christian in D.H.9 B7602
FSL Pitt and AGL Betteridge in D.H.9 B7599
FSL Tiarks and AGL Williams in D.H.9 B7603
FSL Hyslop and AGL Pacey in D.H.9 B7605
FSL Warren and AGL O'Brien in D.H.9 B7596

Hyslop and Pacey had to abandon the mission after 15 minutes when the water in B7605's radiator started to boil. Tiarks and Williams had to return after 55 minutes with carburettor trouble.

Due to the drop-outs, FCdr Clarke was forced to divert the attack to the secondary target of Engel dump. He reported that the shooting was good and a total of 528lbs of bombs were dropped on the dump and a further 200lbs of bombs were dropped on the railway sidings at St. Pierre Capelle. Pitt and Betteridge reported that the anti-aircraft fire at St. Pierre Cappelle was very heavy and that one of their struts was badly damaged. Betteridge reported that they started a very large fire and the smoke column from the centre of the dump rose to a height of 2000 feet.

A further engine test on B7605 was carried out in the evening, FCdr Wright and AGL Woolf taking the machine up for 37 minute test.

23rd March

Six engine tests were carried out in the morning, preparatory to another bombing raid:

FCdr Clarke and AM Hayes in B7599 at 10.15
FSL Tiarks and AM Kendall in B7588 at 10.55
FSL Hyslop and AGL Pacey in B7603 at 11.15
FCdr Stevens and AM Smith in B7589 at 11.45
FSL Pitt and LM Smith in B7587 at 12.10
FCdr Stevens and AM Coombes in B7603 at 12.45

MacLaren optimistically reported nine serviceable and nine unserviceable aircraft, all nine useable machines being despatched on a bombing raid to Bruges Docks, a fighter escort was provided by two D.H.9s from No.11 Squadron:

at 13.56
FCdr Clarke and Flt.Obs St. John in B7600
FCdr Stevens and Obs.SL Christian in B7589
FCdr Wright and AGL Woolf in B7591
FSL Tiarks and AGL Williams in B7603
FSL Pitt and AGL Betteridge in B7587
FSL Hyslop and AGL Pacey in B7602
FSL Rolandi and PO AGL Ryan in B7599
FSL Bewell and AGL Chapman in B7605
FSL Warren and AGL O'Brian in B7596

Stevens, Wright and Tiarks experienced engine trouble with their aircraft and were all forced to return to the aerodrome. Pitt reported that only three of the nine machines reached their objective. Pitt and his gun layer, Betteridge, claimed several good hits on sheds in the docks. Clarke made the following report:

30 off 25lb and 13 off 16lbs bombs were dropped from between 14000 and 16000 feet. Hits were observed as follows:

On shed on north quayside of north Darse[1]
On shed on south end of north Bassin
In water slightly northeast of large destroyer in end Darse
On quay between north and south Darses
In water of south Darse
On shed on quayside at southern end corner of east Bassin, fire started.

FSL Robinson made another local familiarization flight in D.H.4 B9498 at 15.28.

SCdr MacLaren and Lt.Cdr Bristowe carried out an engine test in B7591, one of the machines that was forced to abort the raid earlier in the afternoon. MacLaren reported that the machine was unsatisfactory.

D.H.9 B7617 was transferred from No.11 Squadron.

24th March

A new D.H.9, serial D2783, was ferried from Dover to Petite Synthe by FSL Oakeshott at 11.45.

All of the squadron's serviceable D.H.9s, with the exception of the newly arrived D2783, were despatched on a bombing raid to Bruges Docks:

at 15.04
FCdr Clarke and Flt.Obs. St. John in B7600
FCdr Stevens and Lt O'Connell (USAS) in B7589
FCdr Wright and AGL Woolf in B7591
FSL Warren and AGL O'Brien in B7596
FSL Pitt and AGL Betteridge in B7587
FSL Tiarks and AGL Williams in B7599
FSL Hyslop and AGL Pacey in B7602

The raid approached Bruges from the sea at a height of 14500 feet. Wright and Woolf experienced engine problems in B7591 and were forced to return to the aerodrome. A total of twenty-four 16lb and twenty-three 25lb bombs were dropped, shooting was reported as good with one fire started. Pitt and Betteridge reported that they dropped eight bombs resulting in hits on some sheds at the side of the canal. Pitt noted that they encountered a hostile aircraft that had a larger bottom plane than top plane, whilst some odd obscure German prototypes had lower wings of wider chord than the top wing, it is difficult to explain what Pitt saw, or thought he saw.

Bruges was the centre of RNAS attention on the 24th March, with other raids carried out by the H.P. machines of No.7 Squadron, both in the early hours and late in the evening. Whilst very little effective damage was caused during these raids, some interruption to U Boat operations was caused.[2]

New pilot FSL EHP Bailey made a local familiarization flight in D.H.4 B9498 at 15.45.

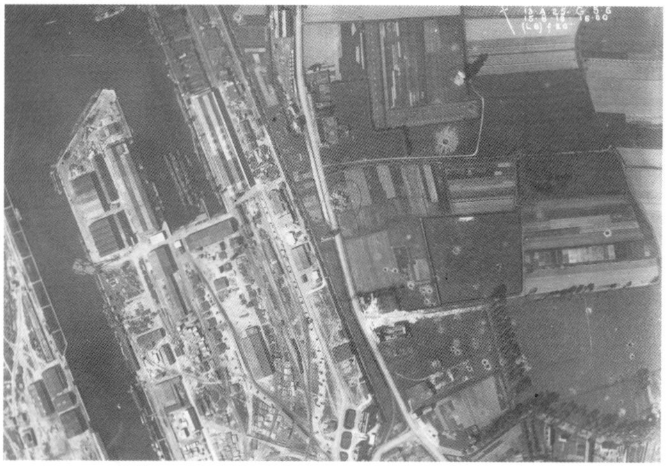

An overhead view of Bruges Docks. Craters from a bombing attack can be seen to be hopelessly off target. *Courtesy Johan Ryheul*

This photograph of a flattened dockside structure depicts typical damage caused by a bombing raid at Bruges. *Courtesy Johan Ryheul*

Another shot of bomb damage at Bruges docks. *Courtesy Johan Ryheul*

Inside an occupied U-Boat pen. *Courtesy Johan Ryheul*

A U-Boat pen at Bruges. *Courtesy Johan Ryheul*

25th March
No flying due to bad weather.

26th March
The squadron despatched eight D.H.9s on a bombing raid to Ostende at 14.07:

FCdr Clarke and Flt.Obs. St. John in B7600
FCdr Wright and AGL Woolf in B7591
FCdr Stevens and Obs.SL Christian in B7589
FSL Warren and AGL O'Brien in B7596
FSL Pitt and AGL Betteridge in B7587
FSL Tiarks and AGL Williams in B7599
FSL Hyslop and AGL Pacey in B7602
FSL Rolandi and PO AGL Ryan in B7588

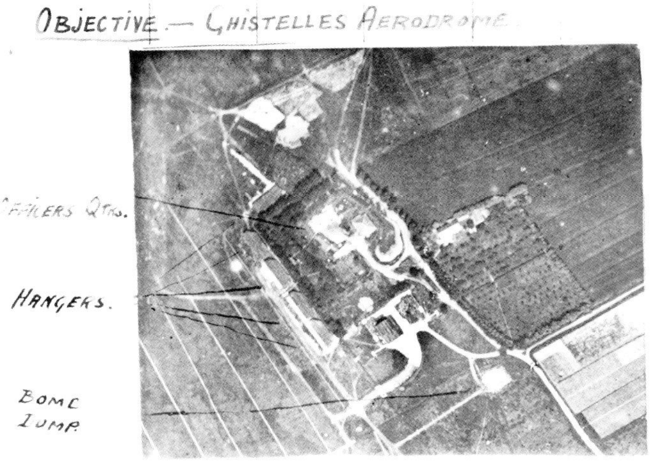

Ghistelles Aerodrome, a frequent target for Royal Naval Air Service bombing squadrons. The aerodrome was attacked by No.6 Squadron on the 26th March 1918, but it is doubtful if much damage was inflicted. *Courtesy EF Cheesman*

Stevens and Christian in B7589 were 10 minutes late in getting away and suffered engine trouble, eventually having to make a forced landing on the beach at La Clipon. Pitt and Betteridge also suffered engine trouble and were unable to keep up with the formation, eventually turning back and returning to the aerodrome. There was a very strong wind and FCdr Clarke was forced to divert the attack to the secondary target of Ghistelles Aerodrome. Twenty-seven 16lb and seventeen 25lb bombs were dropped and FCdr Clarke reported that some bursts were close to the hangars.

Two engine tests were carried out in the evening:

FSL Oakeshott and AGL Dray in D.H.9 D2783 at 18.30
FSL Pitt and AM Jones in B7587 at 18.40

Pitt landed at La Clipon on the beach next to FCdr Stevens' aircraft and AM Jones was able to effect a repair that enable Stevens and Christian to return to Petite Synthe at 19.45.

BELOW: Gotha G.IV bombers of *KG* III based at Ghistelles, one reason why the aerodrome was such an attractive target to the RNAS. *Courtesy EF Cheesman*

27th March
No flying due to bad weather.

28th March
Wing Captain Lambe was making preparations to send the squadron south to St. Marie Cappel:

From: Senior Officer, R.N.A.S. H.Q.
To: "G", "A", "Q"

Date: 28th March 1918

No.6 Squadron will probably be required to go into battle about next Monday or Tuesday. Endeavour to complete them with machines and pilots. If necessary, pilots can be taken from No.11 Squadron. It will be all right if we can send them down with 16 machines and 18 pilots and bring them up to strength afterwards.

Try and fix them up with transport so that they can get their lorries loaded.

The weather continued to be unsuitable for war flying, it was possible, however, to carry out two engine test flights during the morning:

FCdr Wright and AM Holmes (USAS) in D.H.9 B7591 at 10.00
FCdr Wright and AM Borland in D.H.9 B7586 at 10.25

29th March
No flying due to bad weather.

With the prospect of an imminent move south to a more active Front, the squadron was brought up to strength with an additional seven D.H.9 aircraft. Serials B7590, B7594, B7595, B7495, B7618, B7619 and B7622 were transferred in from No.11 Squadron.

Instructions for No.6 Squadron's move and the new reporting structure were issued by Major HR Aubrey from RNAS headquarters:

SECRET

Ref. H.Q. 7998 *Headquarters, R.N.A.S.*
Dunkerque

29.3.18

"Last minute adjustments"! *Courtesy CCI Archive*

Memorandum:
Move of No.6 Squadron

Reference sheet 27. 1/40,000
1. No.6 Squadron will move to ST. MARIE CAPPEL Aerodrome (P.25.c) tomorrow. (on 31.3.18)

2. Orders for machines to start will be given from H.Q., R.N.A.S.

3. C.O. No.5 Wing will indent on H.Q. for the necessary transport. Route for transport via Cassel and Bergues.

4. On arrival at ST. MARIE CAPPEL No.6 Squadron will come under the command of G.O.C., 2nd Brigade, R.F.C. A certain number of American personnel will be attached to No.6 Squadron on arrival. No American personnel are to proceed from PETITE SYNTHE with No.6 Squadron.

5. C.O., No.5 Wing will detail a guard to be in charge of PETITE SYNTHE until re-occupied.

6. Completion of move to be reported to H.Q., R.N.A.S.

Signed HR Aubrey Major

Attached H.Q., R.N.A.S.
For senior officer, R.N.A.S.

Distribution:

No.5 Wing (2)	
H.Q., R.F.C.	)
2nd Brigade, R.F.C.	)
S.O.H.Q.	)
Victualling Paymaster	) *For information*
Overseas Base Paymaster	)
C.O., N & D	)
W.O. Le Suer	)
A.Q.C.	)

30th March

The weather was still unsettled on the 30th, however three engine tests were carried out:

FCdr Clarke and AM Pierce in D.H.9 B7583
FSL Rolandi and AM Woodgate in D.H.9 B7605
FSL Hyslop and AM Wheeler in D.H.9 B7602

31st March

With the demise of the Royal Naval Air Service and the squadron's renaming to No.206 Squadron Royal Air Force just 24 hours away, the final structure as a purely naval squadron was as shown:

A Flight
FCdr INC Clarke, Flight Commander
FSL LR Warren
FSL GA Pitt
FSL VCM Tiarks
FLt.Obs RS St. John

B Flight
AFCdr GLE Stevens, Flight Commander
FSL CM Hyslop
FSL RL Bewell
FSL VFA Rolandi
Obs.SL LA Christian

A group shot of No.206 Squadron Officers at Boisdinghem. They are included here as they were all with No.6 Squadron by the 31st March 1918. From left to right, Lt EA Burn (first RFC officer to join No.6 Squadron), Cpt GLE Stevens, Lt LA Christian, Cpt INC Clarke, Cpt JM Beddall (Armaments Officer), Cpt. JS Wright. *Courtesy CCI Archive*

C Flight
AFCdr JS Wright, Flight Commander
FSL LE Oakeshott
FSL R Robinson
FSL HA Connop

Two new pilots arrived at the squadron, Lt EA Burn and FSL WC Cutmore. Lt Burn was an RFC officer and joined the squadron one day before the RAF came into existence.

D.H.9 B7615 was transferred in from No.11 Squadron.

The squadron moved south to St. Marie Cappel with control transferring to 11 Wing 2 Brigade RFC. The weather was still unpleasant with rain and strong winds and the flight was described as very bumpy. The last day as No.6 Squadron Royal Naval Air Service was marred by two serious flying accidents:

FSL HA Connop crashed D.H.9 B7590 just after leaving the aerodrome and subsequently died of his injuries in the evening.

FSL LE Oakeshott and AGL HW Dray were flying D.H.9 B7622, Oakeshott made a flat turn into the wind and crashed the machine. Oakeshott died of his injuries later that day and Dray succumbed to his wounds on the 4th April 1918.

On the first of April, 1918, the squadrons of the Royal Naval Air Service amalgamated with those of the Royal Flying Corps to become the Royal Air Force. No.6 Squadron RNAS became No.206 Squadron RAF.

NOTES

[1] A Darse is literally a wet dock.

[2] The diary of U-Boat UB-30 reports that a bomb passed through the U-Boat shed on the 24th and damaged the ship's deck. The U-Boat left Bruges on the 29th April but was forced to return to Ostende on the 1st May due to problems with the repair to the hull. Further repairs proved ineffective and UB-30 was kept out of action until the 20th April.

CHAPTER TEN

THE ROYAL AIR FORCE

The creation of the Royal Air Force is a topic that could easily occupy several volumes, a detailed account is beyond the scope of this book and the author trusts that readers will forgive the vastly simplified outline provided below.

Politics

Whilst the need or wish for an air service, independent from the army and navy, had been a subject of bitter debate even before the start of hostilities, a succession of ineffective committees and boards failed to come to any resolution.

Following unrest after the daylight Gotha raids on London during the summer of 1917, a Government Cabinet committee was formed in August 1917, nominally chaired by Prime Minister David Lloyd George but effectively controlled by the South African Defence Minister, Lieutenant General JC Smuts. Smuts had been brought into the debate, ostensibly to provide an impartial viewpoint. The committee's final report produced in October, popularly referred to as the Smuts report, recommended the formation of an Air Ministry to control and administer all aspects of the air war and recommended the amalgamation of the Royal Flying Corps and The Royal Naval Air Service. After the appropriate Parliamentary procedures had been followed, the date of 1st April 1918 was chosen for the inauguration of the Royal Air Force.

Despite Smut's supposed impartiality, it must be emphasised that amalgamation of the RNAS and RFC was a political decision, not a military decision. As is usual with political decisions, the long-term consequences were ignored in favour of perceived short-term benefits.

It is difficult to argue against the decision to remove the RFC from Army control, after all, the Army was not comfortable with aviation. More interested in men than machines, the Army mindset showed little in the way of innovation in aerial matters. The Royal Navy on the other hand, was a technical service, used to using machinery in new and innovative ways. The RNAS was a far more modern and competent service than the RFC and the most effective Naval aviation wing of any nation at that time. The loss of the naval air arm in 1918 was strongly resisted in some circles but the inevitable was ultimately accepted.

The effect upon the Navy was pronounced, many of the land based scout and bomber squadrons were immediately diverted away from their naval obligations, leaving shipping and ports unprotected. After the war, it became more obvious that the Navy still needed an air arm, however, all of the experienced airmen they would need for re-building a naval air service were gone. The Air Ministry fought the Admiralty at every opportunity for funds and status and it was not until just before the start of WW2 that the Navy finally clawed back control of shipboard aircraft. When Britain went to war in 1939, the new naval air service was equipped with obsolete aircraft, inexperienced airmen and outmoded tactics.

Jan Smuts destroyed the most effective and modern naval air service in the world and crippled Britain's credibility as a sea power. A cynic might well be justified in claiming that by killing off the Royal Naval Air Service, General Jan Smuts obtained his revenge for his defeat by Britain during the Boer War.

Practicalities

In the short term, during the spring of 1918, the most noticeable effect upon the Naval squadrons was their re-numbering by the simple expedient of adding 200 to their number, thus No.1 Squadron RNAS became No.201 Squadron RAF and No.6 Squadron RNAS became No.206 Squadron RAF. The RNAS Wings were re-numbered by the addition of 60 to the Wing number.

The following memo from Wing Captain Lambe, was circulated on the 14th March 1918:

HEADQUARTERS,
R.N.A.S.,
14th March, 1918

No. 9423

SECRET MEMORANDUM
Owing to the formation of the AIR Force, involving the amalgamation of the Royal Naval Air Service and the Royal Flying Corps, it has become necessary to re-number the R.N.A.S. units in the Dunkerque Command. In order that the Squadrons and Wings may retain as far as possible their original identity, it has been arranged that all Squadrons will be re-numbered with the prefix 200 and the Wings will be re-numbered with the prefix 60. i.e., the existing Naval Squadron No.1 will become Squadron No.201, Naval Squadron No.2 will become Squadron No.202, etc., etc. No.1 Wing will become No.61 Wing and Nos. 4 and 5 Wings will become nos. 64 and 65 Wings respectively.

The above nomenclature will come into force on the 1st April 1918.

C L LAMBE,
Captain, R.N.,
Senior Officer, R.N.A.S.

Vice-Admiral, Dover patrol (for information) (2) S . O . , R.N.A.S., Dover (5)
Commodore, Dunkerque (for information) Overseas Base Paymaster
Base Commander (for information) Victualling Paymaster
G.A.Q.I. Sigs. Fleet Paymaster, Dover
No.1 Wing (5) Fleet Paymaster, Trafalgar House
No.4 Wing (3) Drafting Commander
No.5 Wing (7) Commanding Officer, Manstone
Warrant Officer Le Sueur, H.Q. RFC (3)
Commanding Officer, Eastchurch
Aircraft Depot (6)

The RNAS personnel adopted the military ranks used by the RFC:

Squadron Commander	became	Major
Flight Commander	became	Captain
Flight Lieutenant	became	Lieutenant
Flight Sub Lieutenant	became	2nd Lieutenant

The uniforms changed, though, in most cases, not immediately. Some naval traditionalists retained their naval uniforms to the end of the war.

The great naval traditions, functions that had been observed by the most land-locked naval squadrons, were not always killed off immediately, watch keeping, the ship's bell, liberty boat, officer of the watch etc., often tended to persist well into 1918 to the great amusement of ex RFC officers and men posted to the squadrons. It is not recorded whether the drinking of "pink gins" was abandoned!

One less well recognised aspect of the change from the RNAS to the RAF involved the change in transport required to achieve standardisation with the RFC. On the 13th February1918, Wing Captain Lambe wrote the following memorandum to the Motor Transport Park:

Headquarters
SECRET
R.N.A.S.

13th February 1918
Ref No.6915

Memorandum
With regard to the allocation of Motor Transport in the future, the following should be aimed at.

2. All Naval vehicles including Siege Guns, Naval Supply Officer, C.M.B's and No.1 Wing H.Q. together with Nos. 1, 2, 10, 13 and 17 Squadrons should be equipped with Pierce Arrow Lorries, Lancia Tenders, Lancia Touring Cars, Sunbeam Motorcycles, Douglas Cycles being used

A. FLIGHT
2
0
6
R.A.F.

OPPOSITE
TOP: Air and ground crews of No.206 Squadron RAF on Armistice Day. Third from the left in the second row is Lt GA Pitt, DFC. Pitt's regular gunlayer during No.6 Squadron RNAS days, Sgt. Observer G Betteridge, DFM, Croix de Guerre and Order of Leopold II is seventh from the left in the back row. *Courtesy A Price via Chris Myers*

BOTTOM: No.206 Squadron RAF personnel at Bickendorf, Cologne, January 1919. Second from left in the front row is Lt BH Rook, No.6 Squadron's records officer. Next to Rook is Cpt EA Burn an RFC Pilot but attached to No.6 Squadron before the formation of the RAF. Fifth along is Major CT MacLaren, OBE, Croix de Guerre. George Pitt is seventh from the left. Finally, at the extreme right of the second row is Chief Master Mechanic Morris. *Courtesy A Price via Chris Myers*

if there are not sufficient Sunbeams and Austin Workshops being gradually replaced by Leylands. Also, all other makes of vehicles such as Lanchesters, Talbots, should be utilised for theses units.

The establishment should be as laid down with all the squadrons being on the basis of immobile squadrons.

3. The following Squadrons will be attached to the Air Force under the Commander In Chief, in France and should be gradually equipped with Motor Transport as far as possible on the present R.F.C. establishment and using Leyland Lorries, Leyland Workshops, Crossley Tenders, Crossley Touring Cars and P&M Motor Bicycles, Douglas Motor Bicycles being used to complete but as far as possible Squadrons should be kept alike.

No 3, 4, 5, 6, 7, 8, 9, 11, 14, 15, 16, 18 Squadrons.

4. No.4 Wing, H.Q. and No.5 Wing H.Q. and No.12 Squadron may be used to facilitate the above arrangements as it does not matter for the present that the transport of these units is standardized.

Signed CL Lambe
Captain R.N.

Deport Wing Commander
M/T Park
Nos. 1, 4, 5 Wing G Q.
SQ

A slightly longer-term effect involved the supply of new pilots and the transfer of officers between squadrons. The old naval squadrons started to receive new pilots and more especially, observers, from the RFC training establishments and much more rarely, senior officers were sometimes transferred from an ex- Naval squadron to command an ex-RFC squadron.

To the men and officers of No.6 Squadron, No.206 Squadron RAF from the 1st April 1918, the life and death struggle continued. New strings were added to the squadron's bow under RAF control, with reconnaissance and photographic missions supplementing the daylight bombing role and occasional line patrols using the D.H.9 in the fighter mode. More trained observers were required to enable the reconnaissance and photographic functions to be implemented and these were supplied through the ex-RFC training routes. The squadron thus suffered erosion to its Naval identity and by the time of the Armistice there were very few ex-RNAS officers left with the squadron.

Wing Captain Lambe, or to give him his new rank, Brigadier General Lambe, wrote to the ex-naval squadrons on the 1st April:

On April 1st, The Royal Air Force will come into being.

After having commanded the Royal Naval Air Service Units and Dunkerque for the past two years and eight months, I wish to express my sincere thanks to all Officers and Ratings for the magnificent spirit they have displayed during the whole of this period.

The Pilots and Observers and Gunlayers have, by their skill and courage established a high reputation. The Ratings have invariable worked long hours cheerfully and this combination could only have been achieved by the loyalty and hard work of the Ground Officers, Squadron Commanders and Wing Commanders.

The small percentage of casualties I attribute to the great technical skill and untiring efforts of the Engine Officers and Engine Ratings generally.

The Royal Air Force will undoubtedly expand very rapidly and will, I think prove to be the deciding factor of the war.

I hope that the Naval Squadrons will maintain their old traditions, records and reputation for efficiency, under their new numbers.

In thanking every Officer and man for their loyalty and support in the past, I wish them all success in the future and can confidently rely on their doing their utmost in the Royal Air Force to win the war.

(sgd) C.L. Lambe
Brigadier-General
Royal Air Force

1st April

Major Colin T MacLaren
Royal Air Force

The new No.206 Squadron Royal Air Force would go on to serve with distinction until the armistice in November 1918 and remained active after that date as part of the Army of Occupation.

BELOW: 206 Squadron D.H.9 at Bickendorf, the squadron marking was a very uninspiring white Flight letter aft of the Fuselage cockade. *Courtesy Les Rogers*

BOTTOM: 206 Squadron D.H.9 "J" in the hanger at Bickendorf. *Courtesy Les Rogers*

Another view of 206 Squadron at Bickendorf in 1919. *Courtesy EF Cheesman*

Airborne, not always a foregone conclusion with the Siddeley Puma powered D.H.9. *Courtesy Les Rogers*

APPENDICES

AIRCRAFT TYPES USED BY No.6 SQUADRON

Part 1: Caudron G. IV

The twin engine Caudron G. IV was a development of the G. III. The machines used by No.6 Squadron, powered by two Anzani 100hp radial engines, were purchased from Caudron at Rue and initially served as long range bombers for day and night use.

These aircraft were obsolescent by the time that No.6 Squadron took them over from No.10 Flight, A Squadron, 4 Wing at the end of November 1916. They were briefly used by those pilots that eventually moved over to No.7 Squadron.

Specification

Type: Caudron G.IV 2-seater, 2 x 100hp Anzani Radial
Manufacturer: Caudron, Rue, France

Principle Dimensions

Span:	55.4 ft	16.885 metre
Length:	23.6 ft	7.19 metre
Height:	8.37ft	2.55 metre
Wing Area:	396.4 sqft	36.828 sq metre

Armament: One Lewis gun mounted in front cockpit, bombs carried on racks beneath wings

Performance

Speed at 6500 ft:	82 mph	132 kph
Speed at 10000 ft:	80 mph	128.75kph
Climb to 10000 ft:	33 minutes	
Service ceiling:	14000 ft	4267 metre

Endurance: 4 hours

Part 2: SPAD S7

The RNAS was keen to purchase the SPAD S7 and contracts were placed with Mann, Egerton and Co. of Norwich to produce seventy-five machines under licence and with the British Nieuport Company for a further fifty. A single machine was ordered from SPAD at Juvisy for evaluation purposes and for subsequent use as a "pattern" by Mann Egerton. This evaluation aircraft, which for reasons unknown initially carried the serial N3399, was delivered to the depot at St. Pol on the 23rd November 1916. By the 29th November the aeroplane had been marked with its correct serial number of 9611.

FLt ADW Allen carried out an official test at St. Pol on the 6th December 1916 and the SPAD remained with No.6 Squadron for type testing until allocated to the Design Fight at Eastchurch on the 24th December. FLt ADW Allen flew the aircraft from Petite Synthe to Eastchurch on Christmas Eve 1916.

In a series of agreements with the War Office, the Admiralty agreed to hand over all of the SPADs that were contracted to be built under licence in exchange for all of the Sopwith Triplanes on order for the RFC. 9611 was also transferred to the RFC, receiving the RFC serial number B388 on the 2nd March 1917.

BELOW: A typical Caudron G IV in service with the RNAS at No.5 Wing. *Courtesy JMB/GSL Collection*

Specification
Type: S.7.C.1 single seater, 140 hp Hispano Suisa
Manufacturer: Société Pour Aviation et ses Derives, Juvisy, France

Principle Dimensions

Span		
Upper plane	25 ft 8 inches	(7.822 metre)
Lower plane	24 ft 10 1/8 inches	(7.573 metre)
Length	19 ft 11 3/8 inches	(6.08 metre)
Height	7 ft 2 5/8 inches	(3.20 metre)
Wing Area	192.14 sq feet	(17.85 sq metre)

Armament: One synchronised Vickers gun

Performance

Speed	at sea level	120 mph	(193 km/h)
	at 2000 metre	116 mph	(187 km/h)
	at 3000 metre	112 mph	(180 km/h)
	at 4000 metre	108 mph	(174 km/h)
Climb	to 2000 metres	6 min 40 seconds	
	to 3000 metres	11 min 20 seconds	
Ceiling	21500 feet (6553 metre)		

Part 3: Nieuport 10

Designed as a compact 2-seat fighter powered by an 80hp Le Rhône rotary engine, the Nieuport 10 or Nieuport Standard as it was commonly known within the Royal Naval Air Service, employed a relatively conventional construction comprising a wire braced wooden box section fuselage, stabiliser of metal tubing and a sesquiplane[1] wing layout with a questionable V strut to lower wing attachment that led to a large number of structural failures. The pilot sat in front of the observer in the machines supplied to the RNAS, though the positions were reversed in the original design. Armament comprised a fixed Lewis gun above the centre section, operated by Bowden cable.

The RNAS ordered a total of 36 Nieuport 10s and started to take delivery of the type from May 1915. A number were converted in-service to single seat machines and flown as scouts.

By the time that No.6 Squadron took over the two Nieuport 10s from A Squadron 4 Wing, they were well and truly obsolete, having been in service since the latter part of 1915 and had been damaged and patched up many times. During January, February and March 1917, new pilots would generally make several practice flights with the Nieuport 10s or Nieuport 12s before being given access to the Nieuport 11s. Although nominally 2-seaters, it is believed that the Nieuport 10s were flown as single seaters whilst with No.6 Squadron. They were also armed as they were used for hostile aircraft patrols on several occasions.

Specification
Type: Nieuport Type 10 2-seater, 80 hp Le Rhône 9C
Manufacturer Société Anonyme des Etablissements Nieuport, Paris, France

Principal dimensions:

Span of upper main plane	26.57 ft	(8.1 metre)
Span of lower main plane	22.15 ft	(6.75 metre)
Length	23.46 ft	(7.15 metre)
Height	9.35 ft	(2.85 metre)
Wing area	194 sq ft	(18 sq metre)
Weight empty	970 lbs	(440 kg)
loaded	1520 lbs	(690 kg)

Armament: One Lewis 0.303 in machine gun mounted above the wing

Performance

Speed at sea level	87 mph	(140 kph)
Climb to 500 metres	3 minutes	
Climb to 1000 metres	7 minutes	
Climb to 2000 metres	17 minutes	
Service ceiling	12467ft	(3800 metres)

Endurance: 2 hours

BELOW: An early French Nieuport 10. The observer was positioned in front of the pilot and was expected to put his upper body through the hole in the centre section when firing the Lewis Gun. *Courtesy JMB/GSL Collection*

Part 4: Nieuport 11

The Nieuport 11 was of similar construction to the Nieuport 10 described above. The machine was smaller than the type 10 but powered by the same 80hp Le Rhône engine. Known as the "Bébé", the type 11 was a light and agile single gun scout. Immensely popular, it had a successful career with the RNAS serving in the European and Aegean theatres.

Armament was a single Lewis gun fitted above the top wing to fire over the propeller arc, numerous mounts were adopted and the RNAS even experimented with twin Lewis gun installations. Photographs of Nieuport 11 serial 3901 show such a twin gun installation although it is believed that the aeroplane had reverted to a conventional single gun fitment whilst serving with No.6 Squadron. Le Prior rockets could also be carried by the type 11, No.6 Squadron pilots carried out several practice flights armed with the rockets but did not use them operationally.

No.6 Squadron employed a total of seven Nieuport 11s during January, February and the early part of March 1917, both for practice flights and operational patrols before being equipped with the Nieuport 17Bis. The Nieuport 11 was an obsolescent type by 1917.

Specification

Type: Nieuport Type 11 single seater, 80 hp Le Rhône 9C
Manufacturer: Société Anonyme des Etablissements Nieuport, Paris, France

Principal dimensions:

Span of upper main plane	24.67 ft	(7.52 metre)
Span of lower main plane	24.28 ft	(7.40 metre)
Length	21.65 ft	(5.60 metre)
Height	7.87 ft	(2.40 metre)
Wing area	143.2 sq ft	(13.3 sq metre)
Weight empty	706 lbs	(320 kg)
loaded	1058 lbs	(480)

Armament: One Lewis 0.303 in machine gun, mounted on the top wing

Performance

Speed at sea level	103 mph	(165kph)
Speed at 2000 metres	101 mph	(162 kph)
Climb to 2000 metres	8 minutes 50 seconds	
Climb to 3000 metres	15 minutes	
Service ceiling	16404 ft	(5000 metres)

Endurance: 2.5 hours

BELOW: A typical RNAS Nieuport 11. *Courtesy JMB/GSL Collection*

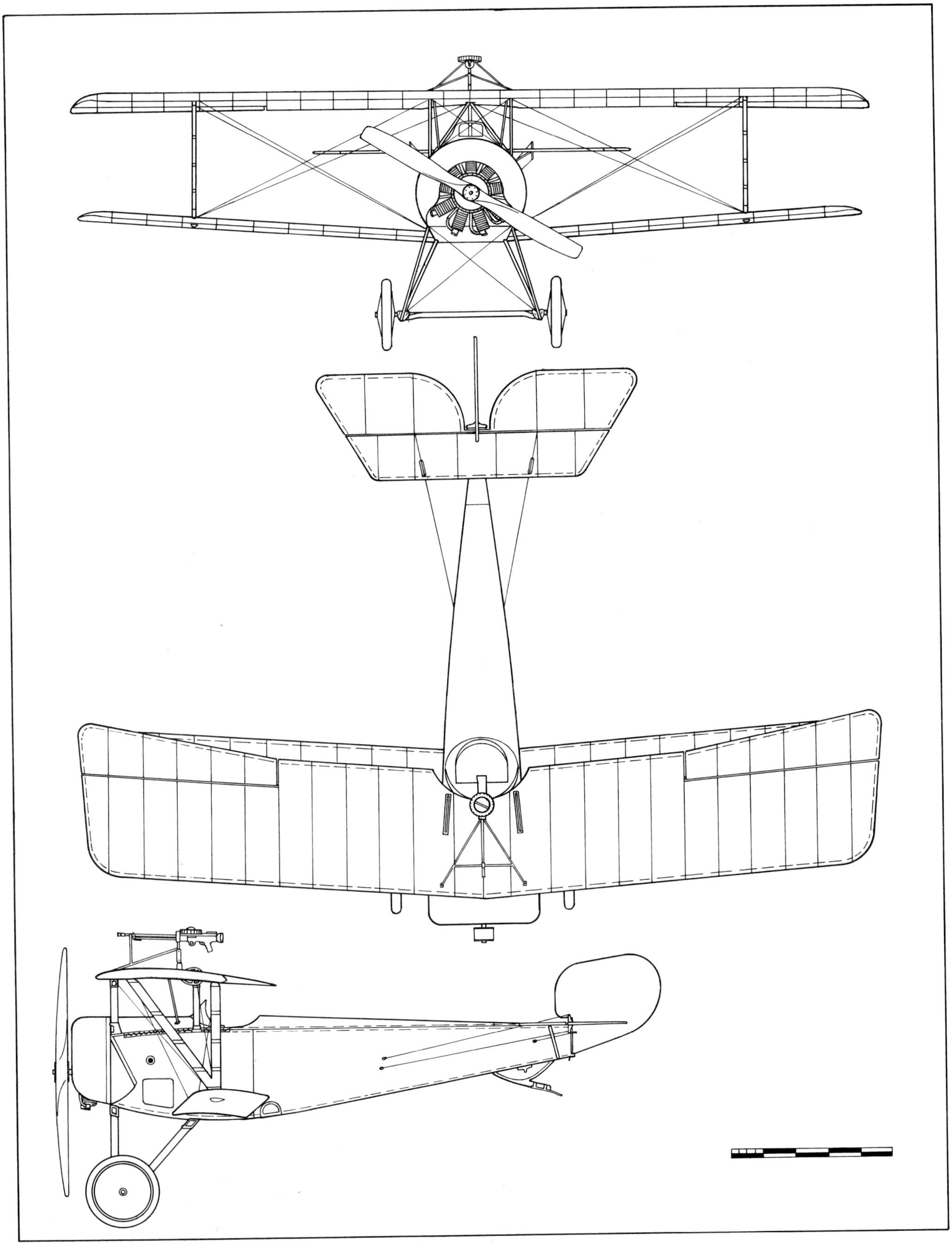

Part 5: Nieuport 12

The Nieuport 12 was an enlarged version of the Nieuport 10, powered by a Clerget 9Z of 110hp. Unlike the type 10, the type 12 was intended to be armed with a forward firing Lewis gun mounted on the top wing for the pilot and a rearwards firing Lewis gun on an Etévé mount for the observer. The RNAS and indeed, No.6 Squadron used the type 12 sourced from both Nieuport and from Beardmore. There were subtle differences between aircraft supplied by Nieuport and by Beardmore, the early Beardmore machines having a lower wing span that was one rib bay wider on each lower plane, absence of washout on ailerons, small fairings over the flying wire fuselage attachment points and a small fairing behind the carburettor air intakes. Some Beardmore aircraft were supplied with a synchronised Vickers gun in place of the wing mounted Lewis gun. Later Beardmore machines employed a conventional fixed fin, however these machines were not in use with No.6 Squadron.

Pilots did not regard the Nieuport 12 as a particularly pleasant machine to fly, in fact the RFC was quite scathing of the type when they evaluated a Beardmore built machine at Upavon in October 1916:

> *Pilot's view not good on account of the high fairing round the cockpit.*
>
> *When carrying full reconnaissance load it is so heavily loaded as to be not only useless in the matter of performance but dangerous to fly, while in any case it is much too bad in climb to be any use as a fighter.*
>
> *Vibrates badly.*
>
> *Tiring to fly owing to cramped position.*
>
> *Landing very difficult in a confined space as there is not sufficient elevator control to get the tail properly down.*
>
> *Remarks*
> *1. Pilot's position very cramped, the rudder bar being much too close.*
> *2. Switch is awkward to reach; it would be better placed on the instrument board. Fine adjustment is controlled at carburettor and is difficult to reach and operate. Throttle is placed too near pilot.*
> *3. Tailplane is much too small. Machine tends to stall with engine and dive with engine off.*
>
> *Improvements in Design*
> *Owing to the very bad performance of this machine, it appears that no alterations practicable would render it fit for service overseas.*

During January, February and March 1917, new pilots would generally make several practice flights with the Nieuport 10s or Nieuport 12s before being given access to the Nieuport 11s. Although nominally 2-seaters, it is known that at least some of the Nieuport 12s were flown as single seaters whilst with No.6 Squadron and were armed as they were used for Hostile Aircraft patrols on several occasions.

Specification
Type: Nieuport Type 12 2-seater, 110 hp Clerget 9Z
Manufacturers: Société Anonyme des Etablissements Nieuport, Paris, France
William Beardmore & Co, Dalmuir

Principal dimensions:

Span of upper main plane	29.53 ft	(9.00 metre)
Span of lower main plane		
Nieuport	22.15 ft	(6.75 metre)
Beardmore: each lower plane 1 rib bay longer		
Length	22.97 ft	(7.00 metre)
Height	8.86 ft	(2.70 metre)
Wing area	236.8 sq ft	(22 sq metre)
Weight empty	1213 lbs	(550 kg)
loaded	1874 lbs	(850 kg)

Armament: One fixed 0.303 in Vickers gun and one 0.303 in Lewis gun on Etévé ring mounting

Performance

Speed at 2000 metres	91 mph	(146 kph)
Climb to 1000 metres	5 minutes 40 sec	
Climb to 2000 metres	14 minutes 15 sec	
Service ceiling	13123 ft	(4000 metres)
Endurance: 3 hours		

BELOW: A typical RNAS Nieuport 12. *Courtesy JMB/GSL Collection*

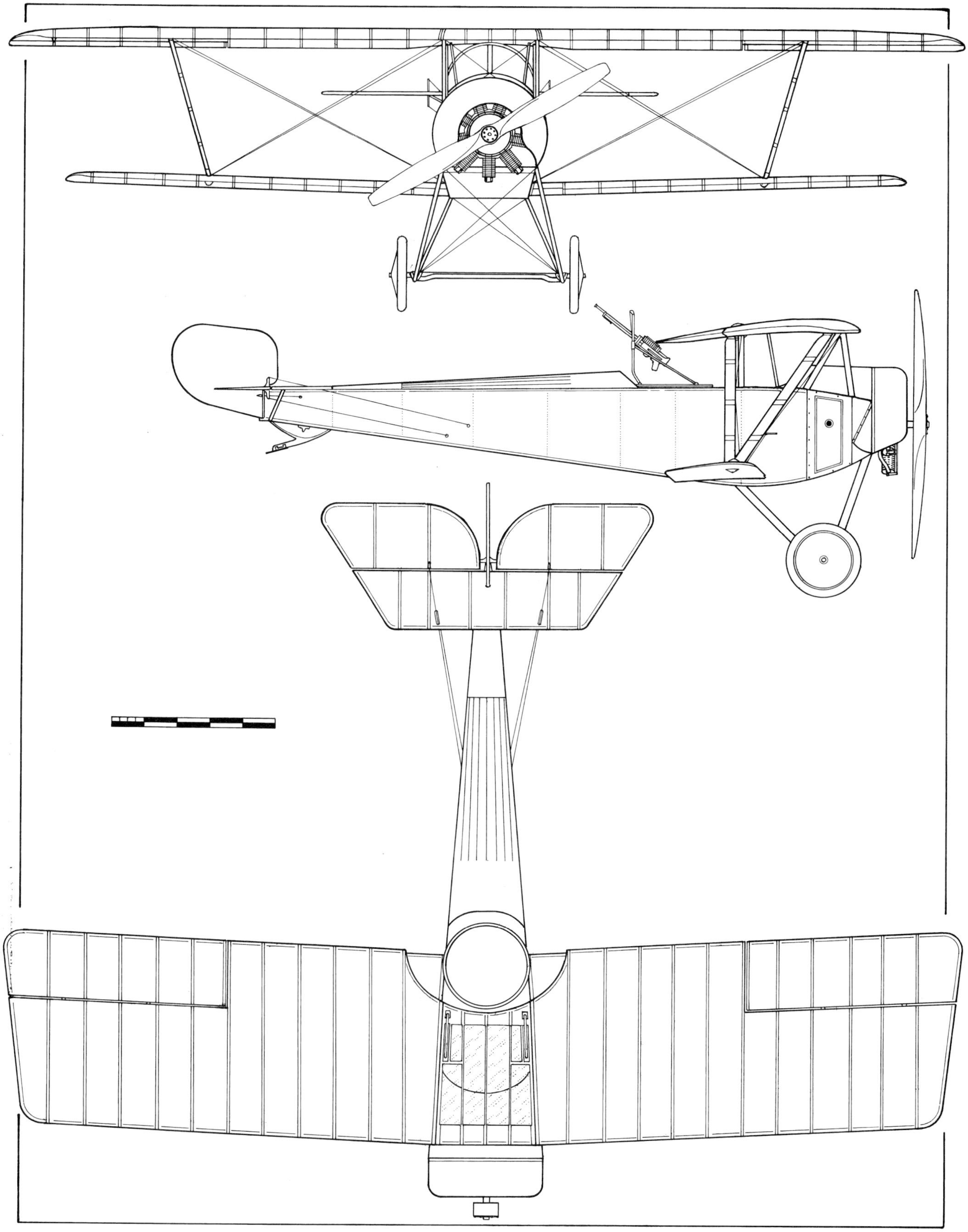

Another view of Neiuport 12 9209. *Courtesy JMB/GSL Collection*

Part 6: Nieuport 17Bis

The Nieuport 17Bis has been very poorly documented in contemporary literature and is in consequence a relatively unknown aeroplane. For this reason, the type is described here in much greater detail than has been devoted to the other machines flown by No.6 Squadron.

Outwardly appearing to be a lightly modified and up-rated Nieuport 17, the 17Bis proved to be a major disappointment in RNAS service. There is a well-known saying, "if something looks right, it is right" - the Nieuport 17Bis was the exception to this aphorism. Arguably one of the most attractive Allied single seat scouts of the period, the 17Bis was an overweight and unsuccessful white elephant.

The Nieuport 17Bis had the distinction of being the first production twin gun scout to enter British service, beating the RFC's SE5 into front line service by two weeks. The most obvious visual differences between the 17Bis and a standard Nieuport 17 were the adoption of a pleasantly rounded fuselage profile, a narrow engine cowling that tapered inwards slightly from front to back and of course, two guns.

The rounded fuselage profile was achieved by the addition of six thin plywood formers to the Nieuport 17's "slab" sides and twelve spruce stringers running from the side cladding back to the upright member at the front of the stabilizer. The side cladding continued the curved profile forwards to fair into the firewall and aluminium cowling.

The armament comprised a fuselage mounted Vickers gun synchronised to fire through the propeller and a Lewis gun mounted on the top wing firing above the propeller arc. French Alkan-Hamy interrupter gear was employed to synchronise the Vickers gun to the propeller position. Unlike any other Nieuport 17 variant, the mounting position of the Vickers gun was offset to the port side of the centre line of the fuselage. The Lewis gun was attached via a fixed mounting and it was not possible to pull the gun back to change ammunition drums. On some machines, an optical sight was often mounted on the top wing, beneath the Lewis gun.

In an attempt to increase performance and, it is suspected, to compensate for the extra weight of the additional woodwork and second gun installation, the engine was uprated from the standard Nieuport 17's 110hp Le Rhône to a 130hp Clerget 9B. Unfortunately, the Clerget also carried a weight penalty over the Le Rhône, being some 22 to 25 kilograms heavier (depending upon specification). The front of the 17Bis cowling was of a slightly larger diameter than that of the Nieuport 17, in order to accommodate the 130hp Clerget 9B rotary engine. To avoid fitting a new firewall, the cowling tapered back to match the diameter of the 17's bulkhead.

Specification

Type: Nieuport 17Bis, 130 hp Clerget

Manufacturers: Société Anonyme des Etablissements Nieuport, Paris, France

The British Nieuport Company, Cricklewood, UK

Principal Dimensions

Span of upper main planes	26.77 ft	(8.16 metres)
Span of lower main planes	25.6 ft	(7.8 metres)
Chord of upper main planes	4.05 ft	(1.233 metres)
Chord of lower main planes	2.36 ft	(0.720 metres)
Wing Area	158.77 sq ft	(14.75 sq metres)

Incidence of upper main planes: 1° 50'
Incidence of starboard lower main planes: 4°
Incidence of port lower main plane:
At root: 4°
At wing tip: 5°
Dihedral of upper main planes: 0°
Dihedral of lower main planes: 2° 20'
Rake of upper main planes: 2° 20'
Rake of lower main planes (approximate): 3° 30'
Angle between V outer struts: 36° 19'

Stagger at side of cowl:	2.12 ft	(0.645 metres)
Stagger at V outer struts:	2.33 ft	(0.710 metres)
Overall length:	19.03 ft	(5.8 metres)
Height:	1.87 ft	(2.40 metres)

Angle of incidence of tail plane: 0°

Undercarriage track:	5.25 ft	(1.60 metres)
Weight – fuelled and armed (*estimated*)*:	1323 lbs	(600Kg)

Armament: One synchronised Vickers 0.303 in machine gun mounted to the port side of the centreline of the fuselage and one Lewis 0.303 in mounted above the top wing.

* The weight is a matter of some controversy, most sources referenced put the gross weight as either the same as, or slightly lighter than the standard Nieuport 17. This is so clearly anomalous, the author is surprised that it has never been seriously questioned in the past.

The standard Nieuport 17 is usually quoted as having a weight of 560Kg (fuelled and armed). It is not clear whether this relates to the armament being a synchronized Vickers gun or a wing mounted Lewis gun but the author suspects that it refers to the latter. The structure of the Nieuport 17 was an elegant exercise in weight reduction with all wooden and metal parts, wherever possible, relieved or hollowed, almost to the point of fragility. To this delicately refined structure, the 17Bis added 12 spruce stringers and 6 plywood formers, a Clerget 9B engine that was at least 22Kg heavier than the 110hp Le Rhône, an extra gun, gun mount, synchronizing gear and 400 or so rounds of ammunition (say 20Kg). Therefore, a conservative estimate would be that the 17Bis carried a weight penalty over the standard Nieuport 17 of at least 40Kg.

Performance

Speed at 500ft	(152 metre)	109mph	(175 kph)
Speed at 7000ft	(2133 metre)	116mph	(187 kph)
Speed at 10000ft	(3048 metre)	107mph	(172 kph)
Climb to 10000ft	(3048 metre)	9min 20sec	
Climb to 20000ft	(6096 metre)	32min	

Endurance: 1.75 hours

Published performance figures for this period must always be regarded with suspicion, the tests were often carried out in the most unscientific manner with wildly varying results from one test to another. At first glance the performance of the Nieuport 17Bis looks to be very promising. The only reliable measure that we can apply at this juncture is to ask "how did the machine compare to its opposition?" In the case of the Nieuport 17Bis, the reply must be "not favourably".

Initially, the 17Bis performance appeared to be more than acceptable. The impressive results achieved during SCdr Petre's tests carried out on the 2nd, 6th and 7th of February would have been very encouraging,

N3184 on 2nd February 1917

Climb:	1000 feet in 45 seconds
	4000 feet in 3 minutes
	10000 feet in 8 minutes
	15000 feet in 15 minutes
	20000 feet in 50 minutes
Ceiling:	23000 feet

N3184 on 6th February 1917 (comparison test with Sopwith Triplane)
Nieuport reached 10000 feet in same time that Sopwith Triplane reached 8200 feet

N3184 on 7th February 1917 (comparison test with Sopwith Triplane)
Nieuport and Sopwith Triplane both took same time to reach 15000 feet (presumably 15 minutes)

The Sopwith Triplane was 4 knots faster than the Nieuport at 15000 feet.

The type exhibited some less than perfect characteristics, however and on the 12th February Petre reported:

> *This machine is very heavy on all controls but can be manoeuvred quickly by a pilot who will use brute force to swing it about. The position, even for a pilot of average height, is very cramped and for a tall pilot it becomes unbearable after flying for some time. It is suggested that the rudder bar be moved forward five inches.*

A test on the squadron's second Nieuport 17Bis on the 1st March was less impressive:

N3187 on 1st March 1917

12000 feet in 16 1/2 minutes	Fixed Vickers + Lewis + double tray
12000 feet in 14 minutes	Fixed Vickers only

Speed at 12000 feet reduced by 2 Knots when carrying both guns.

Disenchantment with the type soon set in once the machine was used under service conditions. We know from various comments made by Naval 6 pilots that, in service, the Nieuport 17Bis suffered from the following problems:

Poor climb
Poor top speed
Heavy controls
Poor ceiling
High landing speed

Contemporary photographs of the squadron's aircraft show that many pilots chose to remove the Lewis gun, sacrificing fire power for a better climb and faster top speed.

From the tests carried out by SCdr Petre, the 17Bis initially appeared to have had a performance equivalent to, or perhaps even better in some respects than the contemporary Sopwith Triplane. How is it then that the Sopwith Triplane's performance in early 1917 was considered to be "state of the art" but the 17Bis performance was "disappointing"?

The handling deficiencies, heavy controls and high landing speed were due to the weight of the machine. If two similar aircraft, in this case the 17 and 17Bis have different weights, the heavier machine will have a higher stall speed and its controls will be heavier.

The poor climb and poor ceiling were due to lack of engine power. The British built Clerget 130hp 9B was a notoriously fickle engine to keep running at peak performance and its power was known to fall away rapidly between its stipulated maintenance periods. Initial operation reports showed that obturator rings, rocker arm pins and exhaust valve springs required frequent replacement. The French built Clerget was considered to be more powerful and more consistent than the British built engines, experienced pilots such as Raymond Collishaw of No.10 Squadron were known to take pains to secure all the available French built engines for their own flight's use.

The poor top speed was due to the overall drag of the aircraft and also was not helped by the steadily declining power available from the Clerget. Many Naval 6 pilots are known to have removed their over-wing Lewis gun to gain a couple of knots speed.

Some aircraft are known to have been supplied by Nieuport with incorrect propellers, until replaced this would have had a detrimental effect upon speed and climb.

If we consider the combination of these faults plus the Nieuport sesquiplane's well documented weakness in the strut to lower spar attachment, whereby the lower planes could twist or even break away during violent combat manoeuvres, it is no surprise that the squadron suffered a high attrition rate and relatively poor record of combat claims.

It is probably safe to say that in single gun form and fitted with a fresh French built Clerget, the Nieuport 17Bis had a similar rate of climb and ceiling to the contemporary Sopwith Triplane. It was, however, slower than the Triplane by several miles per hour and did not exhibit the Triplane's light handling characteristics. A skilled and aggressive pilot could get the best out of the Nieuport 17Bis, which is why FCdr EW Norton was so successful with the type.

The majority of No.6 Squadron's Nieuport 17Bis aircraft were of French manufacture, supplied from Nieuport's Paris factory. In total, the RNAS ordered 32 machines from Nieuport and a further 100 from The British Nieuport Company at Cricklewood. When the model's deficiencies became apparent, the order placed upon the British Nieuport Company was subsequently reduced to 50. Many of these British built aircraft were immediately placed into storage and subsequently deleted although one, N5906, was shipped to the USA for Lady Drogheda's Exhibition.

Losses and unserviceability of the aircraft in service with No.6 Squadron were such that the depot at Dunkerque was unable to supply enough French built machines to keep up with the squadron's demands. Four British built aircraft were supplied during April and May 1917, these are readily identifiable in photographs as the British supplied aircraft had upper surfaces painted in PC10. French supplied aircraft were painted overall in aluminium dope. Spare airframe parts common to the Nieuport 17 were supplied from the RFC's stock, with the result that some aircraft could eventually be finished in a mixture of aluminium and PC10 dope.

No.6 Squadron was the only squadron to be uniformly equipped with the 17Bis, although some aircraft were used by No.11 Squadron which was effectively being used as an operational training squadron and pilot's pool. Two very early examples were used by No.9 Squadron whilst they were "working-up" during February 1917.

An unusual view of a Nieuport 17Bis. The hinged windscreen which fits to the wing pylon appears to be reinforced with chicken wire! *Courtesy Justin Young*

This photograph provides a good view of the Lewis Gun mount on the top wing. *Courtesy Justin Young*

A port side view with the inspection panel removed. *Courtesy Justin Young*

A nice detail view of the tail assembly showing combat damage to the fuselage top longeron. *Courtesy Justin Young*

Part 7: Sopwith F1 Camel

No.4 Squadron and No.6 Squadron were the first units to be equipped with the Sopwith Camel. Both RNAS squadrons were supplied with aircraft from the first production batch manufactured by Sopwith, however, whilst No.4 Squadron was equipped with the far more desirable 150hp Bentley powered Camels, No.6 Squadron received 130hp Clerget 9B powered machines.

No.6 Squadron received its first Clerget powered Camels on the 8th June 1917 when five machines were collected from the depot at St. Pol. The squadron was fully equipped by the last week of June 1917 and carried out their first patrol on the 27th June when FCdr MacLennan led an uneventful offensive patrol at 11.15. No.6 Squadron's first Camel victory came three weeks later on the 20th July when MacLennan was credited with an Out of Control.

The Sopwith Camel has been covered extensively in many books, therefore it is not deemed to be appropriate to plough up the same ground again. The following discussion will be limited to lesser-known aspects as they relate to the early production Camels used by No.6 Squadron. Readers wishing to acquaint themselves more fully with the Sopwith Camel are recommended to the type and manufacturer specific books listed in the bibliography.

The Camel epitomised a new design approach for Sopwith, whereas all previous designs had tended towards stability, the Camel lived on the edge of instability. The Camel was an "agile", twin gun, single seater, designed from the outset to provide pilots with the firepower, performance and manoeuvrability that had been lacking in the Sopwith Company's Pup and Triplane designs. The slightest touch on the controls could send the machine tumbling across the sky, giving the design a feared reputation amongst new pilots. Whilst the aircraft was totally unforgiving of tentative or clumsy handling, it was a devastating weapon in the hands of those skilled enough to master it.

No.6 Squadron's Camels were allocated from the first production batch of 50 machines manufactured by the Sopwith Aviation Company at Kingston upon Thames. This batch covered the serial number range N6330 to N6379, some were manufactured with Clerget engines and some with the Bentley. No.6 Squadron received Clerget powered aircraft whilst No.4 Squadron received the Bentley powered machines. Further Clerget powered machines were supplied to No.6 Squadron at the end of July from the second Sopwith production batch which covered the serial number range B3751 to B3950.

As might be expected with the introduction of a new type, No.6 Squadron experienced a great deal of teething trouble, the most frustrating fault being gun stoppages, a problem that tended to periodically affect all of the RNAS Camel squadrons.

Bentley vs Clerget

As mentioned above, No.6 Squadron received Clerget powered Camels. The Clerget was a considerably inferior engine to the Bentley.

The Bentley BR1, or to give it its correct name at that time, the AR1 (Admiralty Rotary No.1), was effectively a redesign of the Clerget. The Clerget exhibited a serious design problem that could cause overheating and subsequent severe damage to the engine. The RNAS commissioned FLt WO Bentley, an ex Great Northern Railway engineer and later to be famous for the marque of cars bearing his name, to look at the problem with the Clerget and suggest solutions to overcome its tendency to overheat. Bentley replaced the Clerget's steel pistons and cylinders with aluminium pistons and an aluminium cylinder shrunk onto a cast iron liner. Unfortunately, the British manufacturer of Clerget engines, Gwynes and Co. were not responsive to accommodating Bentley's changes and few modified Clergets were manufactured.

The Admiralty went ahead with the Bentley design and commissioned it to be manufactured as the AR1. The AR1 was a significantly better engine than the Clerget, it was cheaper to manufacture, it delivered considerably more power and had a better service life. At first, the Clerget and AR1 engines were both specified by the Admiralty for fitment into Camels, apart from the obvious supply problems with a new design, a valid comparison of the two engines under service conditions was required. As confidence was built with the AR1 and production ramped up to meet demand the Clerget was phased out of RNAS service to be replaced by the Bentley AR1. Upon the formation of the RAF, the ex-naval front line Camel squadrons were exclusively equipped with the Bentley (now named BR1 to remove any Admiralty connotations) whereas the ex-RFC Camel squadrons were equipped with Clerget or le Rhône powered aircraft.

Armament

Standard armament on the Sopwith Camel was a pair of Vickers Mk1* of 0.303" calibre.

The early production Camels employed ammunition carried on canvas bandoliers. Under combat conditions, the pilot was required to collect the used belt on a "take up" spool fitted behind the instrument panel. A handle on the instrument panel allowed the pilot to rotate the spool to "take-up" the expended belt. Soon after production commenced, disintegrating link ammunition belts came into widespread use, negating the need for the belt take-up spool. Spent cartridges were then ejected from a chute on the port side of the gun's breech. In the case of the port Vickers gun, the chute was very short, directing the cartridge cases out into the slipstream. A visual identification feature of early Camels is the lack of a port side ejection chute on the gun cover.

Gun stoppages on the early machines were often caused by the fabric bandoliers absorbing moisture and then freezing at altitude. Stoppages were also caused by mechanical failures, both of the ammunition and the closely toleranced mechanical components.

Interrupter gear

To allow the guns to fire through the propeller arc, the Sopwith-Kauper interrupter gear was fitted to the early Camels. The Sopwith Kauper gear featured a mechanical linkage to prevent the guns from firing during the interval that the propeller blade was passing in front of them.

Controls

The positioning of the fuselage entry point for the elevator control wires is distinctive on early Camels, both upper and lower wires use the same entry point. On later production, the lower wire entry point was lowered to provide a more natural "run".

Fuel Pressurisation.

Early production Clerget Camels were not fitted with a Rotherham slipstream driven air pump. Pressurisation of the fuel tank was achieved by means of a mechanical air pump fitted to the back of the engine.

Specification (early Camels as used by No.6 Squadron)
Type: Sopwith F.1. 130 hp Clerget
Manufacturer: Sopwith Aviation Co. Ltd., Kingston on Thames

Principle Dimensions

Wing span (both planes)		28ft 0in	(8.53metre)
Chord (both planes)		4ft 6in	(1.34metre)
Chord of tailplane		3ft 4 1/2in	(1.02metre)
Incidence (both planes)		2 degrees	
Gap at fuselage		5ft 0in	(1.52metre)
Gap at outer struts		4ft 2in	(1.27metre)
Dihedral , upper plane		Nil	
Dihedral, lower plane		5 degrees	
Overall length		18ft 9in	(5.72metre)
Height		8ft 6in	(2.34metre)
Wheel track		4ft 5 1/4in	(1.35metre)
Wheel diameter		2ft 4in	(0.71 metre)
Tailplane incidence		1 1/2 degrees	
Stagger at centre section		1ft 6in	(0.46 metre)
Tail span		8ft 2 1/2in	(2.5 metre)
Centre section width		7ft 3 1/2in	(2.22 metre)
Airscrew diameter		8ft 6in	(2.59 metre)
Areas	Wing	231 sq ft	(21.46 sq metre)
	Ailerons (each)	9 sq ft	(0.84 sq metre)
	Tailplane	14 sq ft	(1.3 sq metre)
	Elevators	10 1/2sq ft	(0.98 sq metre)
	Fin	3 sq ft	(0.28 sq metre)
	Rudder	4.9 sq ft	(0.46 sq metre)
Tankage	Main fuel tank	30 galls	(136.36 Litre)
Gravity fuel tank		7 galls	(31.82 Litre)
Oil		6 1/2 galls	(29.55 Litre)
Weight	Empty	962 lbs	(436.36 kg)
	Fully loaded	1422 lbs	(645 kg)

Armament: Two synchronised* 0.303 in Vickers machine guns mounted on the top of the fuselage.

This Camel was not used by No.6 Squadron but the photograph clearly depicts the salient features of a machine from the Sopwith Company's first production batch. Notable points include the stabiliser control cable run, the lack of ejection chutes for spent disintegrating link ammunition and the lack of a Rotherham Pump for fuel pressurisation. Courtesy Terry Treadwell

* Sopwith Kauper synchronisation gear

Performance (typical for an early 130hp Clerget Camel)

Speed:	at 6500ft (1981 metre)	108mph (174 kph)
	at 10000ft (3048 metre)	104.5mph (168 kph)
	at 15000ft (4572 metre)	97.5mph (157 kph)
Climb:	to 6500ft (1981 metre)	6 min 40 sec
	to 10000ft (3048 metre)	11 min 45 sec
	to 15000ft (4572 metre)	23 min 15 sec
Ceiling:	18500ft (5639 metre)	

Endurance: 2 1/2 hours

Part 8: D.H.4

Designed by Geoffrey de Havilland for the Aircraft Manufacturing Co. Ltd (or Airco as the company was commonly referred to), the D.H.4 was one of the great aircraft of World War I. Successfully used as a day bomber and fighter reconnaissance machine, the D.H.4 was still in use at the end of the war when it should have been replaced by the troublesome D.H.9 at the beginning of 1918. The D.H.4 was available with a range of engines which included the 230hp Siddeley Puma, 230hp Galloway Adriatic, 200hp RAF 3a, 260hp Fiat A12, 250hp Rolls Royce Eagle I, II, III and IV, 275hp Rolls Royce Eagle V, VI and VII and 375hp Rolls Royce Eagle VIII.

Equipped with a Rolls Royce Eagle, the D.H.4 had the strength, performance (speed, climb, ceiling and manoeuvrability) and armament to effectively perform its duties and defend itself. On the down side, its maximum bomb load was regarded as too small for 1918 and the various engines available, particularly the Rolls Royce, were not available in sufficient quantity. The engine shortage was not specifically the fault of Rolls Royce but rather due to the Air Board and Government policies that effectively prevented Rolls Royce from expanding production facilities.

The type was used by No.6 Squadron whilst "working-up" between January and early March 1918, the squadron replacing the D.H.4 with the D.H.9 for operational use. One D.H.4 was retained for familiarisation and training of new pilots. All of the squadron's aircraft were manufactured by the Westland Aircraft Works and were fitted with the 230hp Siddeley Deasy Puma engine, the least satisfactory variant with regard to performance but probably more than adequate for training purposes.

Specification

Type: D.H.4. 230 hp Siddeley Deasy Puma

Manufacturer: Westland Aircraft Works, Yeovil

Principal Dimensions

Wing span	42 ft 4 5/8 in	(12.92 metre)
Length	30 ft 8 in	(9.35 metre)
Height	10 ft 1 in	(3.18 metre)
Wing area	434 sq ft	(40.32 sq metre)
Weight (empty)	2209 lb	(1002 kg)
(loaded)	3641 lb	(1570 kg)

Armament: One or two 0.303 in Vickers machine gun and one 0.303 in Lewis machine gun.

Two 230lb bombs or four 112lb bombs or equivalent.

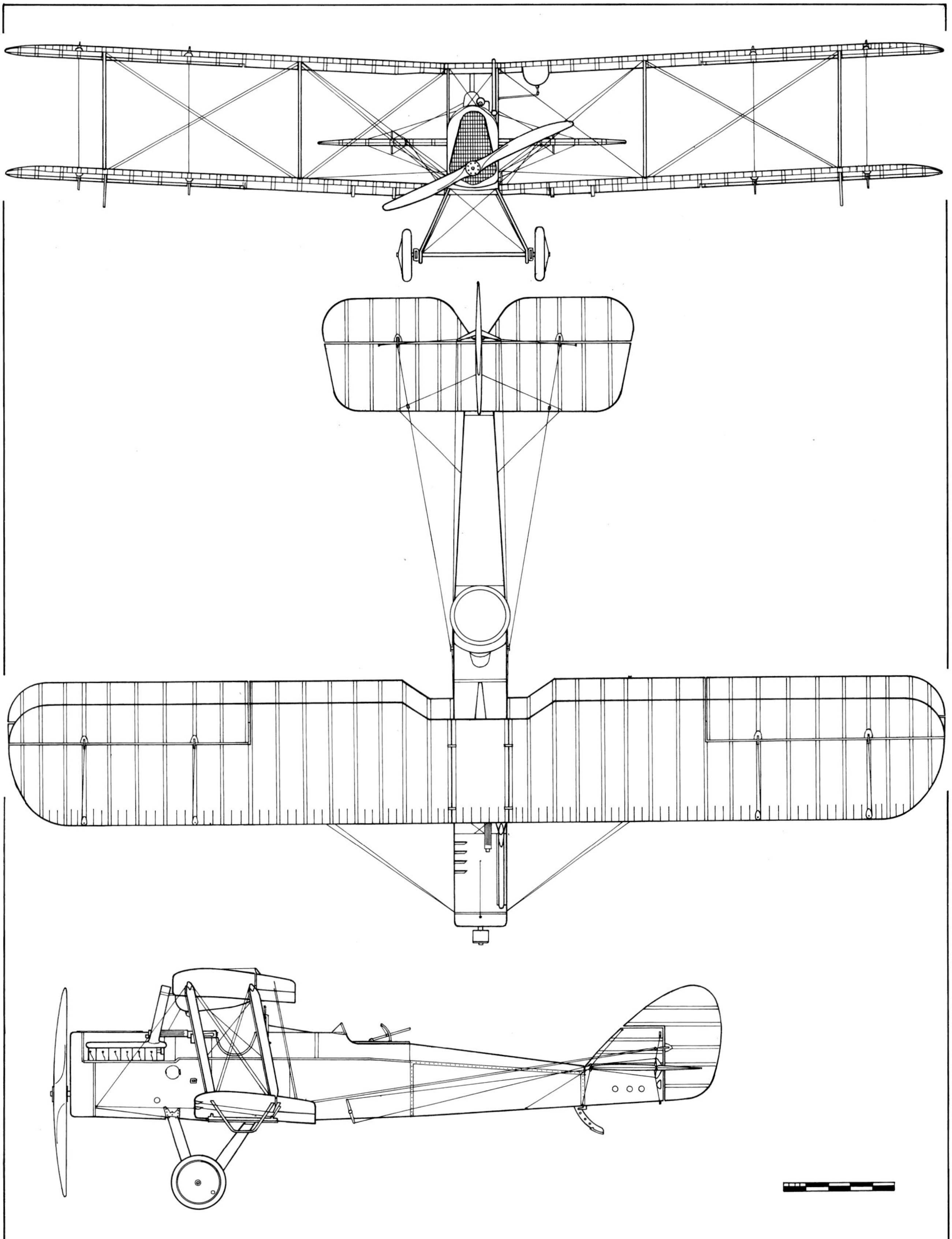

Performance (230hp BHP)

Speed	at 10000ft 110mph* (177 kph)
Climb	to 10000ft 24 min 55 sec*
Service ceiling:	13500ft* (4115 metre)

* The performance when fitted with a Rolls Royce Eagle was considerably in excess of these figures.

Part 9: D.H.9

The D.H.9 was once described as a "D.H.4 which had been officially interfered with so as to be suitable for mass-production and the B.H.P. motor". Despite its exemplary service record, the D.H.4 was perceived by officialdom as having a number of deficiencies:

It did not carry a sufficient payload to meet the Royal Flying Corps forecast needs for 1918.

The pilot and observer were too far apart to communicate effectively.

The Rolls Royce Eagle power units required skilled assembly and were not deemed to be suitable for mass production.

The Aircraft Manufacturing Company was tasked with developing their D.H.4 to create a new machine capable of carrying a greater bomb load, with the pilot's cockpit moved back behind the centre section so that the pilot and observer could be seated back to back and using an engine suitable for mass production.

In the search for a suitable engine, the Air Board decided that the unproven private venture BHP (Beardmore Halford Pullinger) was a suitable candidate. The BHP was a vertical six cylinder motor of 18.8 litres capacity. It was based upon an aluminium monoblock crankcase with threaded steel liners screwed into it, the three valve (two exhaust and one inlet) cylinder heads were cast iron and the water jacketing was fabricated from sheet steel. In practice, the aluminium crankcase proved very difficult to manufacture with porous castings and poor machining resulting in a very low production yield.

Initial orders were placed with the Siddeley Deasy Motor Company and the Galloway Engineering Company. Whilst Galloway Engineering manufactured the basic BHP design, Siddeley Deasy took it upon themselves to redesign the engine in the interests of manufacturability and with a design target of increasing the performance to 300hp. Amongst the modifications, the cylinder heads were changed to cast aluminium into which steel liners were screwed with short threads and the water jackets were also changed to aluminium castings.

The new design, referred to as the Siddeley Puma was 45 lbs lighter than the BHP but was dimensionally a different engine to the Galloway Adriatic which still adhered to the BHP specification. The result was that the two engines could not be interchanged.

The Siddeley Deasy Puma failed to deliver the promised 300hp and was de-rated to 230hp, the same power rating as the BHP engine upon which it was based. Both the Puma and the BHP initially proved unreliable in service with broken valve springs and burnt out exhaust valves a constant problem.

All but one of the D.H.9s delivered to No.6 Squadron were manufactured by the Westland Aero Works and were fitted with the Siddeley Deasy Puma engine. Just one machine, D2783, was manufactured by Short Brothers and was also fitted with a Siddeley Deasy Puma.

Specification (early D.H.9s as used by No.6 Squadron)
Type: D.H.9. 230 hp Siddeley Puma
Manufacturer: Westland Aircraft Works, Yeovil
Short Brothers, Rochester

Principal Dimensions

Wing span:	42 ft 4 5/8 in	(12.92 metre)
Length:	30ft 6 in	(9.26 metre)
Height:	11ft 2 in	(3.4 metre)
Wing Area:	434 sq ft	(40.32 sq metre)
Weight: (empty)	2203 lbs	(999.26 kg)
(loaded)	3669 lbs	(1664.23 kg)

Armament: One 0.303 in Vickers Machine gun and one 0.303 in Lewis machine gun*
Two 230lb or Four 112lb bombs or equivalent weight in smaller munitions.

* No.6 Squadron frequently adopted a twin Lewis gun set up devised by the Armaments Officer.

Performance (230hp Siddeley Puma)

Speed:	at 10000 ft (3048 metre)	111.5 mph (179.6 kph)
	at 15000 ft (4572 metre)	97.5 mph (157 kph)
	at 16500 ft (5029 metre)	91 mph (146.5 kph)
Climb:	to 6500 ft (1981 metre)	10 min
	to 10000 ft (3048 metre)	20 min 5 sec
	to 15000 ft (4572 metre)	45 min
	to 16500 ft (5029 metre)	67 min
Ceiling:	16000ft (4827 metre)	
Endurance:	4 1/2 hr	

During No.6 Squadron's brief operational period with the D.H.9, from the 9th to the 31st March 1918, incidents due to engine problems were significant with two engine failures/forced landings and two crashes that killed the crew, both almost certainly due to pilot error but probably prompted by an engine failure. Mission effectiveness was severely compromised with many aircraft continuously unserviceable and often a 15% to 30% dropout of machines from bombing raids.

The squadron's strategy of using tight formation flying to both have the greatest impact upon the target and to provide the best defensive option against enemy fighters suffered by the variable and unreliable performance of the Siddely Deasy engines. Members of the formation were frequently unable to keep up or maintain position.

The squadron continued to use D.H.9s when it became No.206 squadron RAF on the 1st March 1918. Despite Siddeley Deasy overcoming many of the problems with the Puma engine, the crews never fully regained their lost trust in what was basically an obsolete and underpowered engine.

NOTE

[1] "Sesquiplane" refers to a biplane where the lower wing is considerably smaller than the upper wing, Sesqui literally meaning 1Ω.

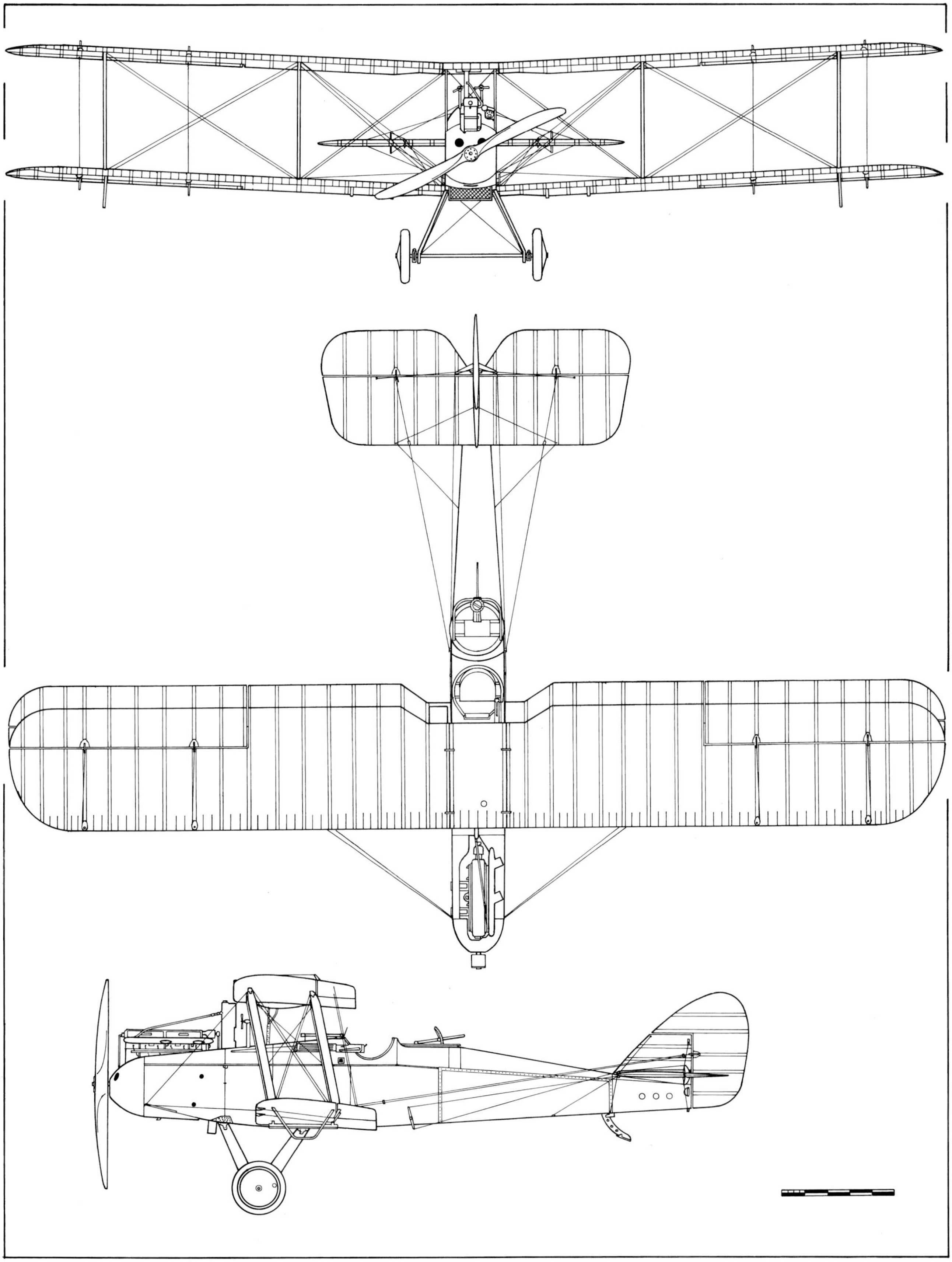

COLOR PROFILES AND SQUADRON MARKINGS

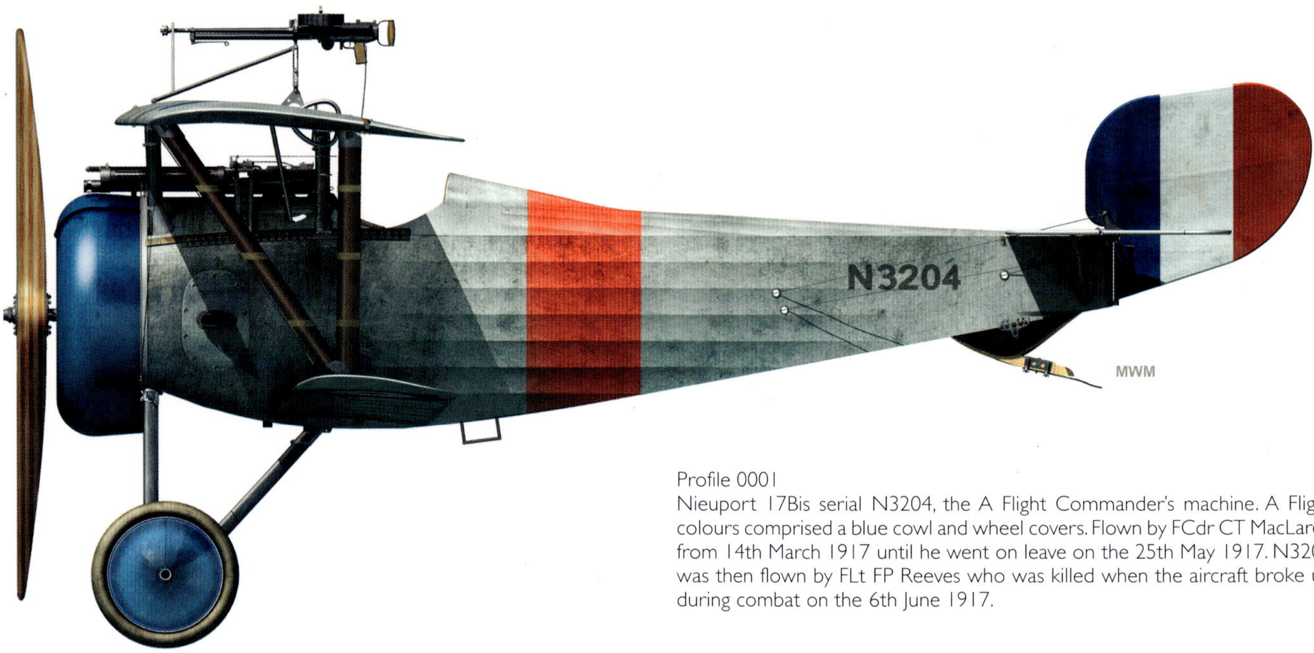

Profile 0001
Nieuport 17Bis serial N3204, the A Flight Commander's machine. A Flight colours comprised a blue cowl and wheel covers. Flown by FCdr CT MacLaren from 14th March 1917 until he went on leave on the 25th May 1917. N3204 was then flown by FLt FP Reeves who was killed when the aircraft broke up during combat on the 6th June 1917.

Profile 0002
N3101, the B Flight Commander's machine. B Flight aircraft had the cowl and wheel covers unpainted. On the 6th June 1917, ASCdr Draper claimed one scout out of control and another destroyed to the northwest of Cambrai. FLt GA Gooderham crashed and wrote off N3101 on the 15th June 1917.

Profile 0003
N3208, The C Flight Commander's machine. Briefly flown by FCdr Norton from 22nd to the 29th April 1917, N3208 carries three red bands around the fuselage, a red cowling and red wheel covers. Whilst flying N3208, Norton shared a claim for a scout out of control at Honnecourt in the early afternoon and claimed a scout in flames with another out of control at Guise during the evening of the 29th April. SCdr CD Breese was flying N3208 on the 1st June 1917 when he shared a claim for an "apparently out of control" 2-seater at St. Quentin.

Profile 0004
An overhead view of N3208 showing the graceful lines of the Nieuport 17Bis.

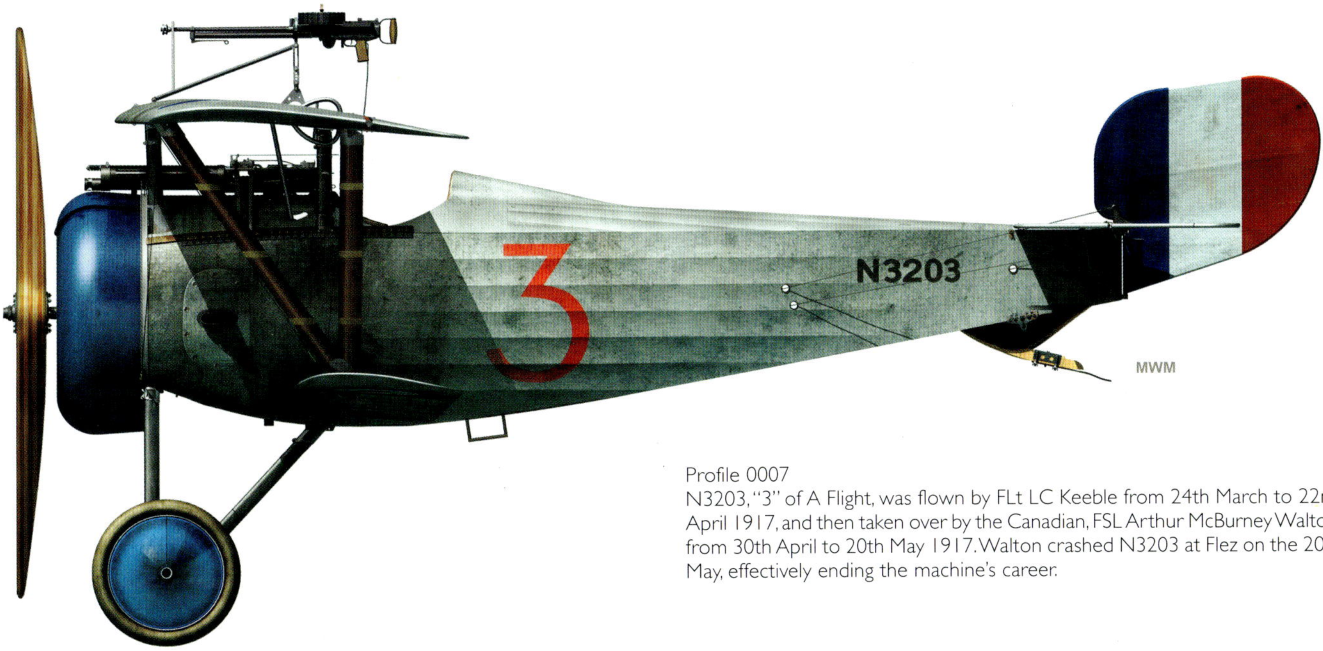

Profile 0007
N3203, "3" of A Flight, was flown by FLt LC Keeble from 24th March to 22nd April 1917, and then taken over by the Canadian, FSL Arthur McBurney Walton, from 30th April to 20th May 1917. Walton crashed N3203 at Flez on the 20th May, effectively ending the machine's career.

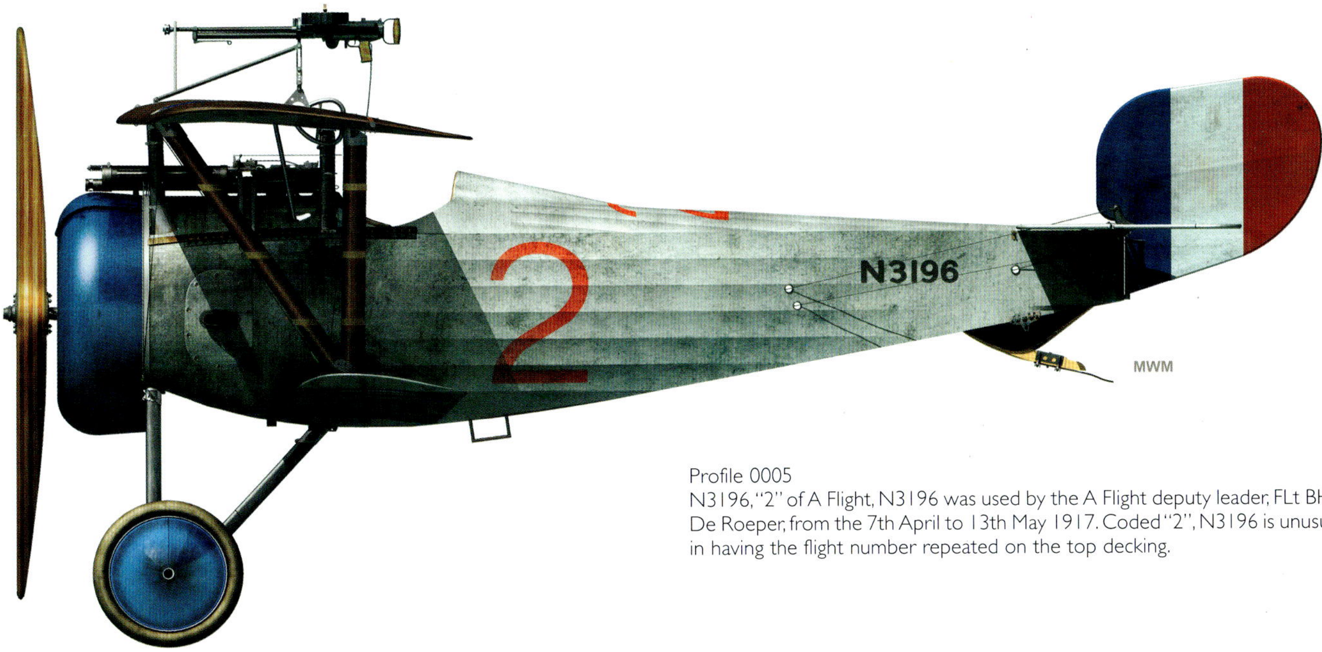

Profile 0005
N3196, "2" of A Flight, N3196 was used by the A Flight deputy leader, FLt BHP De Roeper, from the 7th April to 13th May 1917. Coded "2", N3196 is unusual in having the flight number repeated on the top decking.

Profile 0006
N3196, "2" of A Flight shown from above, depicted at a frozen moment in time just after a replacement wing was fitted. The PC10 port top plane (which was an RFC Nieuport 17 spare from No.2AD Candas) is marked with a conventional British cockade, whereas the remaining cockades are in the process of being converted from French to British colours.

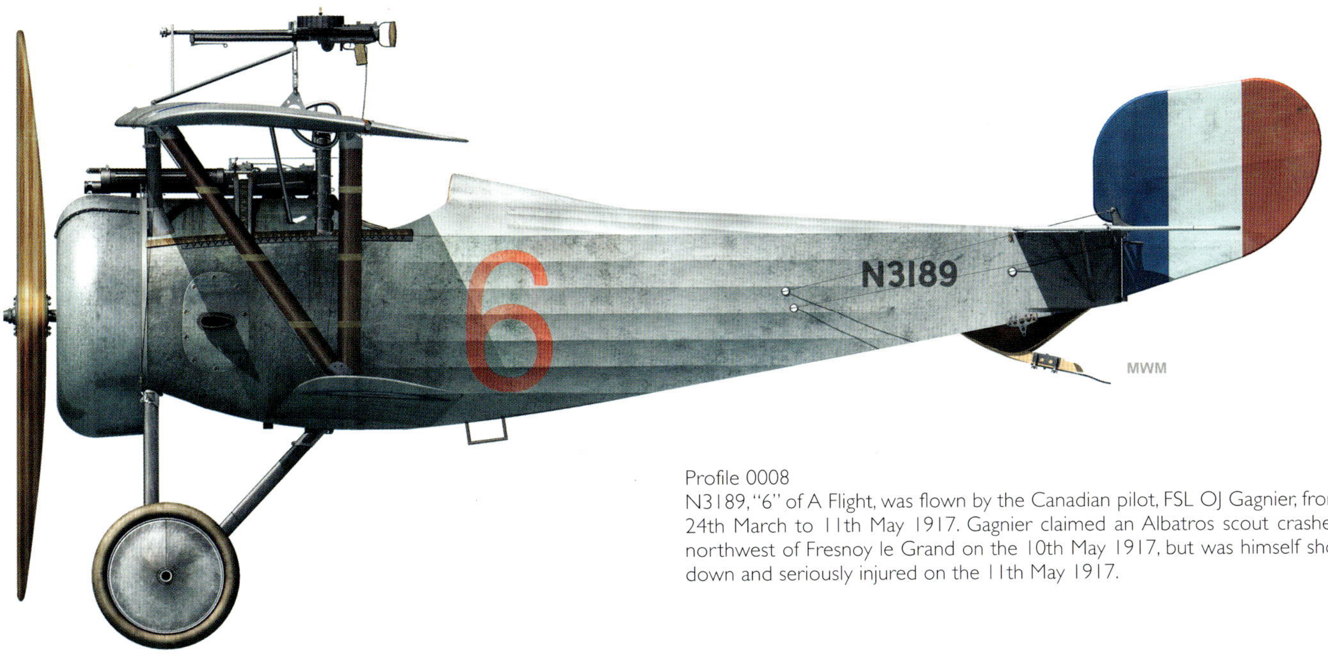

Profile 0008
N3189, "6" of A Flight, was flown by the Canadian pilot, FSL OJ Gagnier, from 24th March to 11th May 1917. Gagnier claimed an Albatros scout crashed northwest of Fresnoy le Grand on the 10th May 1917, but was himself shot down and seriously injured on the 11th May 1917.

Profile 0009
N3199, "8" of B Flight, was Canadian pilot FSL CL Bailey's regular mount between the 25th March and 20th May 1917. Bailey was a member of B Flight during March and April. FSL AMcB Walton took charge of N3199 from the 23rd May to the 13th June 1917. Both Bailey and Walton submitted claims with this machine, Bailey claiming a scout out of control at St. Quentin on the 20th May and Walton claiming an apparently out of control 2-seater at St. Quentin on the 1st June 1917. In addition to these claims, FSL RR Winter "borrowed" N3199 on the 29th April and claimed a scout out of control at Guise.

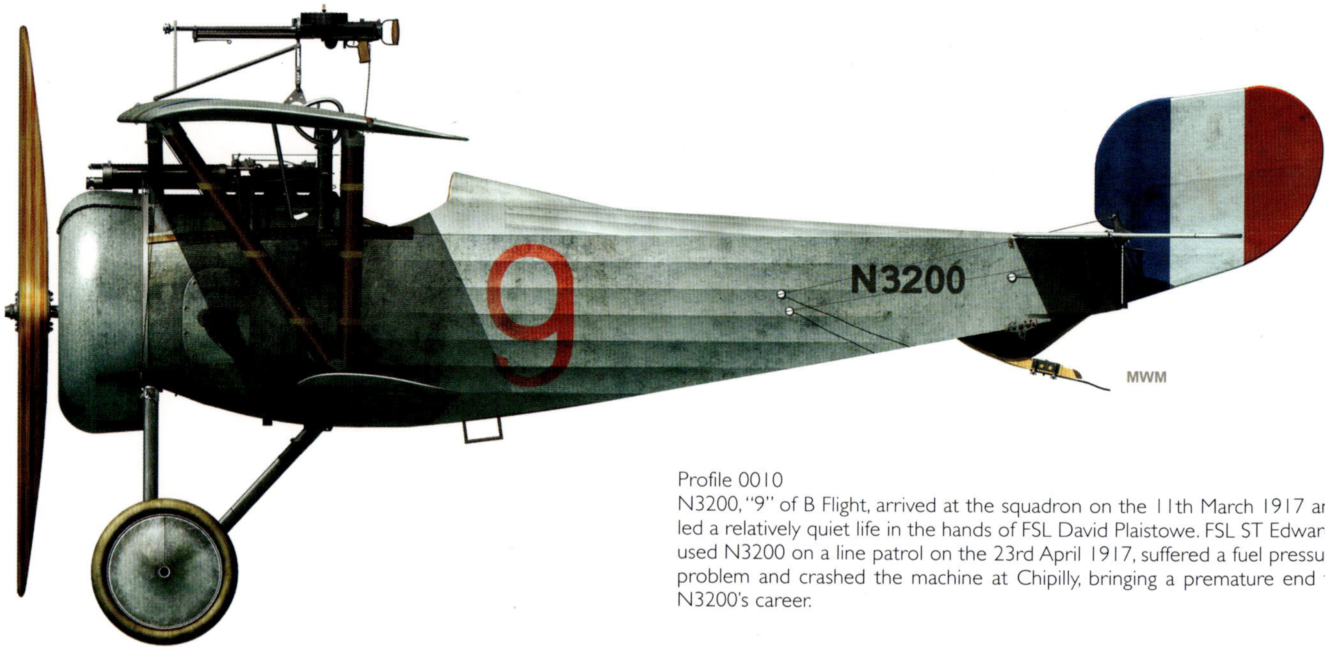

Profile 0010
N3200, "9" of B Flight, arrived at the squadron on the 11th March 1917 and led a relatively quiet life in the hands of FSL David Plaistowe. FSL ST Edwards used N3200 on a line patrol on the 23rd April 1917, suffered a fuel pressure problem and crashed the machine at Chipilly, bringing a premature end to N3200's career.

Profile 0011
N3102 was unusual, one of the very few Nieuport 17Bis aircraft in the squadron to carry a fuselage cockade. N3102 was delivered from the Nieuport factory to the RFC's No.2 AD at Candas, it is believed that the RFC depot took the decision to apply the fuselage cockade. FSL ST Edwards used N3102 in B Flight from the 24th April until the 13th June 1917.

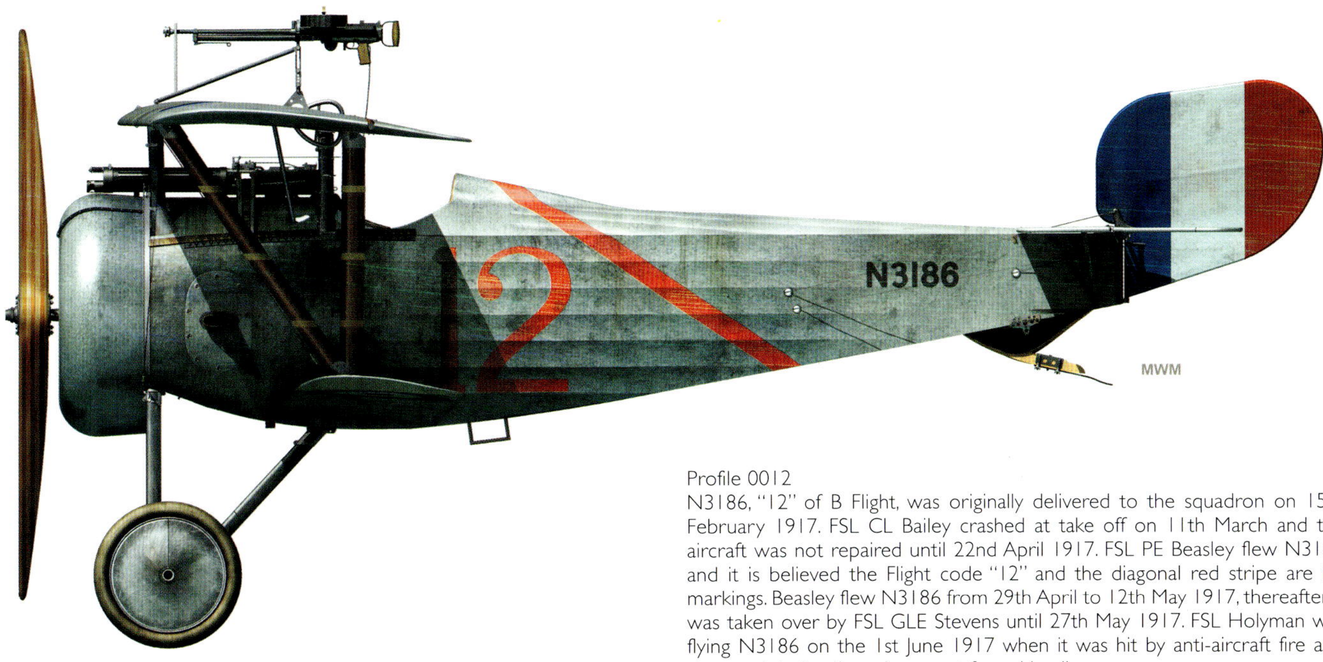

Profile 0012
N3186, "12" of B Flight, was originally delivered to the squadron on 15th February 1917. FSL CL Bailey crashed at take off on 11th March and the aircraft was not repaired until 22nd April 1917. FSL PE Beasley flew N3186 and it is believed the Flight code "12" and the diagonal red stripe are his markings. Beasley flew N3186 from 29th April to 12th May 1917, thereafter it was taken over by FSL GLE Stevens until 27th May 1917. FSL Holyman was flying N3186 on the 1st June 1917 when it was hit by anti-aircraft fire and damaged during the subsequent forced landing.

Profile 0013
N5860 was one of the four British Nieuport company built machines used by No.6 Squadron. The conventional British PC10 brown finish provides a stark contrast to the Aluminium doped aircraft. This machine was used by FLt GG MacLennan of C Flight from the 24th April to 5th June and then by FSL PE Beasley from the 6th June to the 12th June 1917.

Profile 0014
N5862 was another of the British Nieuport Company built machines. N5862 was flown by C Flight's FSL Harold Lawson from the 3rd May to 29th May. FSL ST Edwards ferried N5862 back to the depot at Dunkerque on the 5th June but caused some damage when he ran a wheel into a ditch when landing.

Profile 0015
N3192, "15" of C Flight, was on the squadron strength from 10th March to the 29th April 1917 when FSL AHV Fletcher was shot down by *Ltn* Herman Göring of *Jasta* 26. Fletcher was wounded and spent the rest of the war in captivity.

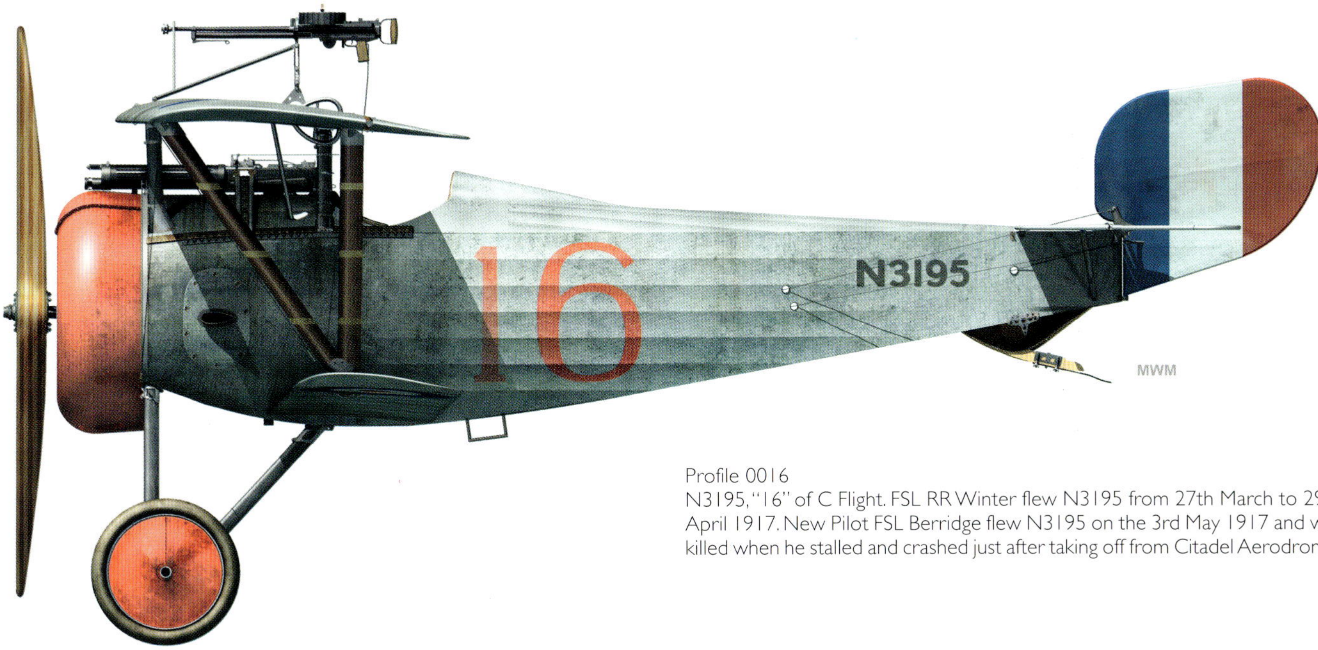

Profile 0016
N3195, "16" of C Flight. FSL RR Winter flew N3195 from 27th March to 29th April 1917. New Pilot FSL Berridge flew N3195 on the 3rd May 1917 and was killed when he stalled and crashed just after taking off from Citadel Aerodrome.

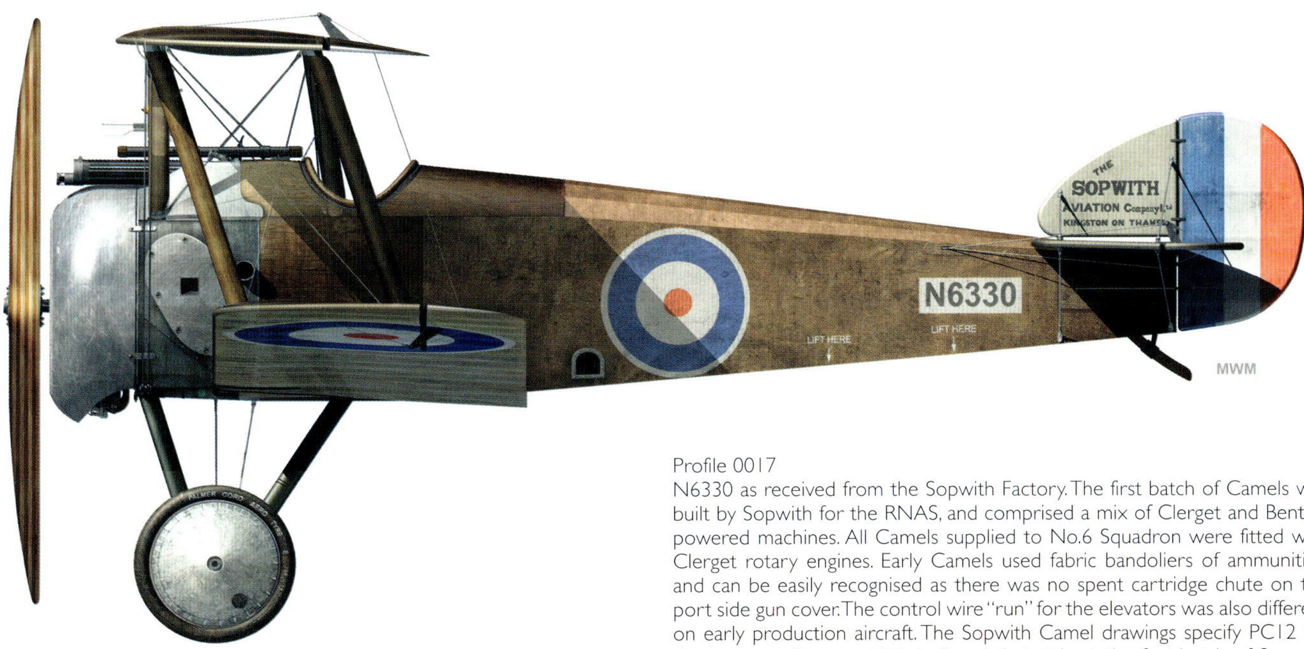

Profile 0017
N6330 as received from the Sopwith Factory. The first batch of Camels was built by Sopwith for the RNAS, and comprised a mix of Clerget and Bentley powered machines. All Camels supplied to No.6 Squadron were fitted with Clerget rotary engines. Early Camels used fabric bandoliers of ammunition and can be easily recognised as there was no spent cartridge chute on the port side gun cover. The control wire "run" for the elevators was also different on early production aircraft. The Sopwith Camel drawings specify PC12 for the upper surfaces and it is believed that at least the first batch of Sopwith built Camels were finished in PC12.

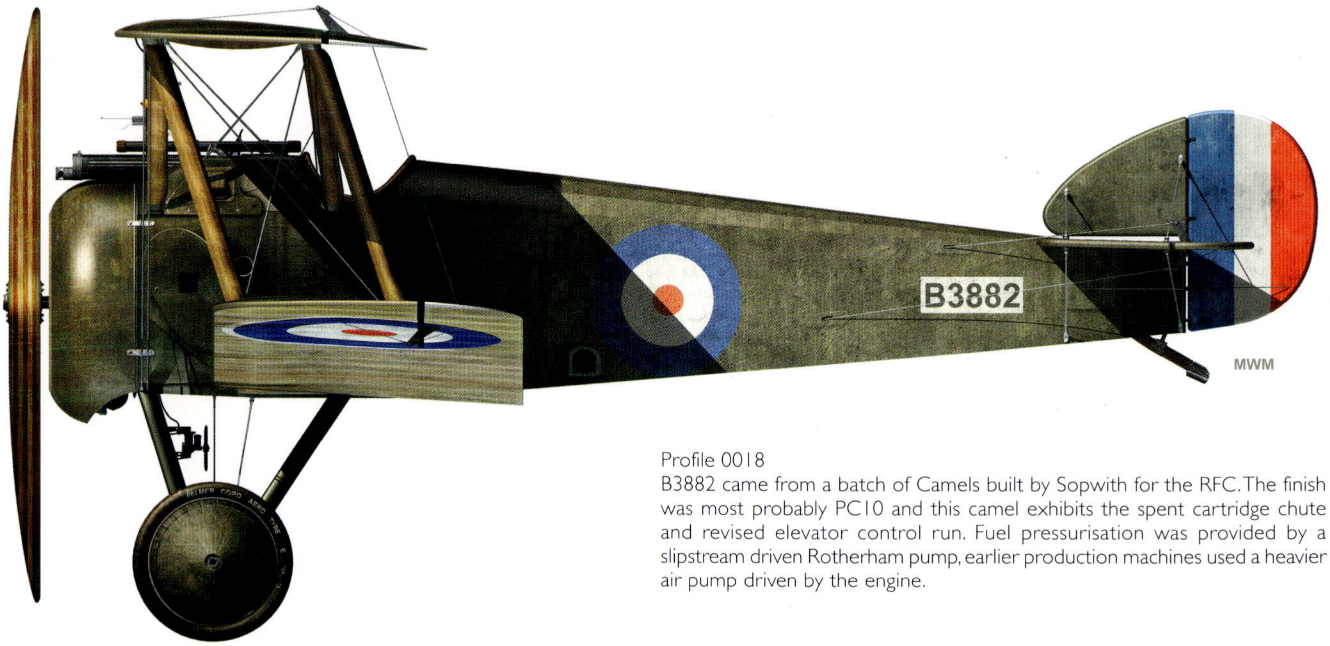

Profile 0018
B3882 came from a batch of Camels built by Sopwith for the RFC. The finish was most probably PC10 and this camel exhibits the spent cartridge chute and revised elevator control run. Fuel pressurisation was provided by a slipstream driven Rotherham pump, earlier production machines used a heavier air pump driven by the engine.

1: Caudron G.IV
Caudrons in RNAS service were finished in the normal French finish of clear doped fabric surfaces and light yellow painted metal areas and forward fuselage. These machines were at the end of their operational lives and might be expected to be stained and dirty.

2: SPAD S7
It is presumed that the "evaluation" SPAD was finished in the normal French finish of clear doped fabric surfaces and light yellow painted metal areas and forward fuselage. A coat of fatty varnish was often applied to the fabric areas enriching the yellow shade. The excellent quality photograph of N3399 would tend to support this supposition. The machine was only briefly with the squadron for type trials and no special markings would have been carried.

3: Nieuport 10, 11 and 12
These machines were only in temporary use with the squadron pending reequipping with the Nieuport 17bis and they carried no special markings. The finish was the usual clear doped linen, with the fuselage tape often painted a dark colour, possibly French blue. As these aircraft were quite old and near the end of their operational lives, it is assumed that the finish was stained and dirty.

4: Nieuport 17bis
The Nieuport 17Bis as delivered from the factory at Paris, was finished in aluminium dope on upper and lower surfaces. Cockades were carried above and below the upper wings and below the lower wings, however, there was no cockade on the fuselage side. It is surmised that the Nieuport factory had excess stocks of Nieuport 17 Wings manufactured for the Aviation Militaire, as many of the machines were delivered from Paris with the French style of Cockade, much to the annoyance of RNAS staff at the St. Pol Depot. Contemporary photographs show that the aircraft often remained in service with No.6 Squadron for a considerable time before the wing cockades were converted to the British sequence of colours. One consequence of this being that the cockades' proportions were to the French style, not the British. This effectively meant that the central circle of the cockade was considerably larger diameter than normally seen on a British roundel or cockade. The "all flying" rudder carried the normal British blue/white/red flashes.

Flight Identification
Flight identification for the three flights comprised individual numbers on the fuselage side (sometimes repeated on the top of the fuselage), coloured cowlings and wheel covers, Flight Commanders' aircraft were designated by red bands around the fuselage.

A Flight
Flight Commander's machine carried one red band around fuselage. Large red numerals in the range 2 to 6 marked on the fuselage side and sometimes repeated on the top of the fuselage. Engine cowling and wheel covers painted blue.

B Flight
Flight Commander's machine carried two red bands around the fuselage. Large red numerals in the range 8 to 12 marked on the fuselage side and sometimes repeated on the top of the fuselage. Engine cowling and wheel covers left unpainted.

C Flight
Flight Commander's machine carried three red bands around the fuselage. Large red numerals in the range 14 to 18 marked on the fuselage side and sometimes repeated on the top of the fuselage. Engine cowling and wheel covers painted red.

As is often the case, several "markings" anomalies existed:

> Photographs show that N3102, finished in aluminium dope, carried a fuselage cockade. Whilst one photograph probably shows it in the condition "as received" from No.2 AD, another very poor, photograph undoubtedly shows it at a later stage, still carrying the fuselage cockade. It is believed that the fuselage cockade was applied by the RFC when the machine was delivered to No.2 AD from Paris.

Four Nieuport 17Bis aircraft, N5860, N5861, N5862 and N5865, were delivered from the British Nieuport Company, these differed in small details from machines built by the parent company and were finished in the more conventional brown PC10 upper surfaces with clear doped linen under surfaces. At least one but certainly not all of these machines carried a fuselage cockade.

N3186 carried a red diagonal stripe on the fuselage side, this is believed to be a personal marking,

5: Sopwith Camel

Unfortunately, there are no known photographs of a Sopwith Camel in service with No.6 Squadron. Whilst possession of a camera on active service was a serious military offence, many Commanding Officers turned a blind eye to their officers' photographic forays. It is believed, however, that when the Sopwith Camel was first issued to No.4 and No.6 Squadrons in June 1917, an order reinforcing the prohibition of photography was issued. One of No.6 Squadron's officers is reputed to have been caught trying to photograph his Camel and had his camera smashed for his trouble.

All available evidence[1] *indicates that the Sopwith Camels used by No.6 Squadron did not carry any special markings and remained in standard Sopwith specified finish. Upper fabric surfaces of early Sopwith built aircraft were finished in PC12*[2] *(most easily described as a chocolate brown colour), plywood panelling finished in Copal varnish (a reddish brown), aluminium panels and cowling left unpainted, undersurfaces, wheel covers and fin in clear doped linen, Sopwith "logo" carried on fin and cockades in the usual 6 places. Later aircraft were undoubtedly finished in PC10 on upper surfaces. The serial numbers were marked in black and carried in a white box at the rear of the fuselage.*

An official squadron identification marking of a white square on the fuselage side behind the cockade was allocated on 25th August 1917 but as the squadron was disbanded on the 27th August it seems most unlikely that this was taken up.

6: Airco D.H.4

The D.H.4 was only used for working up, re-equipping and as a practice machine for new pilots initial familiarisation flights. It is therefore most unlikely that any markings other than the standard PC10 upper surfaces and clear doped linen under surfaces were used.

7: Airco DH9

All of the squadron's DH9s with one exception derived from the first batch manufactured by Westland, the exception being D2783 manufactured by Short Brothers.

Westland's first batch of 100 aircraft was built under contracts no. AS17570 and AS22860. The Westland machines were typically finished in PC10 on all upper surfaces with the nose and engine cover in grey, clear doped linen on undersurfaces and clear doped wheel covers. Variations could of course occur, some machines having no grey panels at all and some displaying much more grey. The only known photograph of a D.H.9 used by No.6 squadron shows the conventional marking described above.

Short Brothers aircraft were generally finished in PC10 on all upper surfaces, clear doped linen on undersurfaces and clear doped wheel covers.

When the squadron become No.206 Squadron RAF, a large white identification letter was carried on the fuselage side behind the cockade. As No.6 Squadron used DH9s for a maximum of six weeks, with most of the aircraft on strength for only four weeks before the squadron became No.206 squadron RAF, it is doubtful if the letter marking had been adopted before the 1st April 1918.

NOTES

[1] Interviews conducted by SK Taylor with surviving Canadian members of No.6 Squadron.

[2] Official Sopwith drawings specify PC12 to scheme A on all upper fabric surfaces. Whilst Camel sub-contractors undoubtedly used PC10, it is a reasonable hypothesis that the Sopwith factory adhered to their own drawings and finishing instructions for the initial batch of 50 aircraft.

APPENDIX C

ROSTER OF PILOTS

Abbott *Courtesy RAeC Trust*

Allen *Courtesy RAeC Trust*

Part 1: 27/11/16 to 28/8/17

Abbott, Edward Dixon, FSL
Born 13th January 1897, from Eastbourne, Sussex.
RAeC Certificate No.3452, gained 28th August 1916 at Eastchurch.
Joined the RNAS on 4th February, 1917.
Under instruction at Crystal Palace on 4th February 1917.
Under instruction at Eastchurch from 7th April 1917.
Under instruction at Cranwell from 2nd June 1917.
Dover on 23rd July 1917.
No.12 Squadron from 9th August to 12th August 1917.
No.6 Squadron from 13th August to 29th August 1917.
No.10 Squadron from 30th August 1917 to 13th September 1917, when shot down near Roulers. Abbot was wounded and became a prisoner of war.

Combat record with No.6 Squadron:

17/8/17	Scout	06.10 to 08.10	OOC

Allen, Arthur Dennis Wigram, AFCdr
Born 19th August 1894, at Burwood, New South Wales. Allen's senior education was completed in England from 1906 to 1912 at Summer Fields School, Oxford and at St. Peter's College (now known as Radley College), Oxfordshire.
RAeC Certificate No.1746, gained 1st September 1915 at Eastchurch.
Served with Australian Commonwealth Forces with rank of Lieutenant in 1914.
Joined RNAS on 11th July 1915.
Under instruction at Whale Island gunnery school, Portsmouth, from 11th July 1915 to 7th August 1915.
Under instruction at Eastchurch from 7th August 1915 to 20th September 1915.
No.1 Wing from 20th September 1915 to 5th January 1916.
Eastchurch from 5th January 1916 to 25th March 1916.
Detached for duty with RFC in France from 25th March 1916 to 17th April 1916.
A Squadron, No.4 Wing, from 17th April 1916.
No.6 Squadron from 27th November 1916 to 24th April 1917.
Martlesham Heath from 25th April 1917.
Directorate of Aircraft Production from 30th November 1918 to 1st April 1919.
Transferred to unemployment list on 1st April 1919.
DSC gazetted on 12th May 1917.
Air Force Cross gazetted on 2nd November 1918.
After leaving the RAF, Allen resumed his chosen career in the family business of Allen, Allen and Hemsley, Solicitors, being admitted as a solicitor on 21st October 1922.
Became chairman of New England Airways in 1935.
Part owner of the Victoria Derby winning racehorse "Advocate" in 1952.
Died on 4th June 1967 at Double Bay, New South Wales.

Bailey, Charles Leonard, FSL
Born 23rd June 1896, from Toronto, Ontario.
ACA Certificate gained on 23rd February 1916 at Curtiss School.
Joined RNAS on 29th February 1916.

Under instruction at Portsmouth from 23rd March 1916 to April 1916.
Under instruction at HMS Excellent from April to 10th May 1916.
Under instruction at Crystal Palace from 10th May 1916 to 20th May 1916.
Under instruction at Chingford from 20th May 1916 to 11th August 1916.
Under instruction at Cranwell from 11th August 1916 to 13th September 1916.
Under instruction at Freiston from 14th September to 13th October 1916,
Dover on 13th October 1916.
A Squadron No.4 Wing from 25th October 1916.
No.6 Squadron from 27th November 1916.
No.4 Squadron from 7th June 1917.
Canadian leave from 15th October 1917, returned to England on 9th January 1918.
Under instruction at Cranwell, Instructor's course, from 2nd February 1918 to 13th February 1918.
Chingford, instructing, from 13th February 1918 to 31st March 1918.
207 TDS Chingford from 1st April 1918 to February 1919.
CL Bailey died on the 9th February 1971.

Combat record with No.6 Squadron:

19/5/17	Albatros	Northeast of St. Quentin	11.50	Out of control

CL Bailey *Courtesy SK Taylor*

Beasley, Percy Exeter, FLt
Born 9th October 1894, from Victoria, British Columbia.
ACA Certificate No.349, gained 18th October 1915, at the Wright school.
Joined RNAS on 31st October 1915.
Under instruction at Chingford from 1st December 1915 to 7th April 1916.
Under instruction at Eastchurch from 7th April 1916 to 29th April 1916.
No.3 Wing, Detling, from 30th April 1916 to 29th May 1916.
No.3 Wing, Manston from 30th May 1916 to 31st July 1916.
No.3 Wing, Luxeuil from 31st July 1916 to 8th March 1917.
No.1 Wing from 9th March 1917.
No.11 Squadron from March 1917.
No.6 Squadron from 16th April 1917 to 18th July 1917.
Leave to England and then Canada from August 1917 to October 1917.
No.1 Squadron from 20th October 1917 to 5th November 1917.
Manston from 5th November 1917 to 17th November 1917.
Dunkerque on 17th November to 18th November 1917.
No.13 Squadron from 18th November 1917 to 11th March 1918.
No.11 Squadron as Flight Commander from 11th March 1918 to 31st March 1918.
No.211 Squadron RAF from 1st April 1918 to 30th June 1918.
Leysdown as an instructor from 6th July 1918 to 1st October 1918.
PE Beasley died on the 9th August 1976.

Beasley *Courtesy EF Cheesman*

Berridge Raymond Winchester, FSL
Born 28th May 1897, from Gerrards Cross, Buckinghamshire.
RAeC Certificate No.3989, gained 30th November 1916, at Vendome.
Previously served in RNAS at White City with rank of AM.1.
Confirmed as Probationary Flight Sub Lieutenant on 27th August 1916.
Under instruction at Crystal Palace from 27th August 1916 to 7th October 1916.
Under instruction at Eastbourne from 7th October 1916 to 1st November 1916.
Under instruction at Vendome from 1st November 1916 to 20th January 1917.
Under instruction at Cranwell from 20th January 1917 to 7th April 1917.
Dover on 7th April 1917.
No.11 Squadron from 14th April 1917 to 1st May 1917
No.6 Squadron from 1st May 1917 to 3rd May 1917, when died of his injuries after crashing at Citadel Aerodrome, southwest of Albert.

Berridge *Courtesy RAeC Trust*

Breese, Charles Dempster, SCdr
Born 23rd April 1889. at Epsom, Surrey.
Entered Royal Navy in 1905.
RAeC Certificate No.654, gained 16th October 1913, at Central Flying School, Upavon.
With Royal Flying Corps (Naval Wing) in 1913, under instruction at the Central Flying School, Upavon, in October 1913.
Appointed Instructor in Theory and Construction at Central Flying School, Upavon, on 18th December 1913 to April 1916.
Instructor in Theory and Construction at Cranwell Central Depot and Training Establishment from April 1916 to 11th February 1917.
Commanding Officer of No.10 Squadron from 12th February 1917 to 13th April 1917.
Commanding Officer of No.6 Squadron from 14th April 1917 to 27th August 1917.
At Central Stores Depot, Wormwood Scrubbs, from 3rd September 1917 to January 1918 with rank of Wing Commander.
Deputy Director of Training with the Air Ministry from 1st April 1918 with rank of Lieutenant Colonel.
Commandant of Central Flying School from 7th April 1919.

Breese *Courtesy RAeC Trust*

Campbell-Orde *Courtesy EF Cheesman*

With HQ RAF India from 28th April 1920.
Commanding Officer of Aircraft depot, India from 9th March 1921.
Commanding Officer of Technical Training section, No.1 SoTT (Apprentices) from 9th January 1925.
Commanding Officer RAF Gosport from 3rd September 1928.
HQ Iraq Command from 11th April 1930.
Supernumerary, RAF Depot from 1st July 1932.
SASO, HQ Inland Area from 15th March 1933.
AOC, No.23 Group from 16th April 1934.
AOC, No.23 (Training) Group from 1st March 1936.
AOC, No.17 (Training) Group from 5th March 1937.
AOC, No.18 (reconnaissance) Group from 27th September 1938
Rose to rank of Air Vice Marshal in RAF and died in 1941, when an observer in a Coastal Command Lockheed Hudson which crashed on Wick Aerodrome.
AFC gazetted on 31st May 1918.

Combat record with No.6 Squadron

1/6/17	2-seater	St. Quentin	08.35	Apparently out of control*

* Shared with FSL A McB Walton.

Brown William Norman Roy, FSL
Born 10th June 1897.
Joined RNAS on 23rd January 1916.
Under Instruction at Crystal Palace from 27th February 1916, followed by an "E" course at Fishguard.
Under instruction at White City from 17th April 1916.
Under instruction at Chingford from 25th April 1916.
Under instruction at Eastchurch from 3rd September 1916.
Dover on 18th September 1916.
Admitted to Chatham Hospital on 6th October 1916 suffering from Gonorrhoea, discharged fit on 27th October 1916.
No.4 Wing from November 1916.
Admitted to Haslar Hospital on 12th March 1917 suffering from Nasopharynx Catarrh. Surveyed on 30th April 1917, found fit for instructional duties but unfit for flying above 1000 feet.
Vendome from 21st May 1917.
Resigned Commission on 21st May 1917, resignation accepted on 23rd January 1918.

Campbell-Orde, Alan Colin, FSL
Born 4th October 1898, from Lochgilphead, Argyll.
Educated at Sherborne, Dorset.
Joined RNAS on 17th December 1916.
Under instruction at Crystal Palace from 26th December 1916 to 5th February 1917.
Under instruction at Vendome from 5th February 1917 to 5th May 1917.
Under instruction at Cranwell from 5th May 1917 to 7th July 1917.
Dover on 7th July 1917.
No.12 Squadron from 15th July to 18th July 1917.
No.6 Squadron from 18th July 1917 to 26th July 1917 when wounded during combat.
No.12 Squadron from 10th September 1917 to 13th September 1917.
No.9 Squadron from 14th September 1917 to 14th October 1917 when broke right leg in an accident.
Admiralty Air Department, section H1, from 14th January 1918 to 31st March 1918.
RAF DPD Ferry Pilot from 1st April 1918, ferried delegates to the Paris Peace Conference in 1919.
Commercial Pilot with Air Transport & Travel from 1919.
Flying Instructor and Aviation Consultant to the Government Of China in Peking from 1921.
Flying Instructor, later becoming Chief Test Pilot, with Armstrong Whitworth from 1924.
Operations Manager with British Airways from 1936, becoming BOAC after merging with Imperial Airways. During World War II responsible for liaison with RAF Transport Command.
Retired in 1957.
AFC Gazetted on 22nd December 1919.
CBE awarded 1943.
Elected Fellow of the Royal Aeronautical Society in 1954.
AC Campbell-Orde died in April 1992.
AC Campbell-Orde claimed 1 victory with No.9 Squadron.

Carroll, Ralph Edward, FSL
Born 19th January 1898. From Toronto, Ontario.
RAeC Certificate No.3836, gained 10th November 1916 at the Curtiss school, Toronto.
Joined the RNAS on 10th November 1916.
Under instruction at Crystal Palace from 14th January 1917 to 17th February 1917.
Under instruction at Vendome from 17th February 1917 to 4th May 1917.
Under instruction at Cranwell from 5th May 1917 to 6th June 1917.
Under instruction at Freiston from 6th June 1917.
Dover on 20th June 1917.
No.12 Squadron from 25th June 1917 to 28th June 1917.

No.6 Squadron from 28th June 1917 to 27th August 1917.

No.10 Squadron from 29th August 1917 to 23rd November 1917, when injured leaving Dover aerodrome and transferred to Deal infirmary suffering from concussion and wounds to forehead. Suffered insomnia as a result of his injuries and entered hospital in Canada in May 1918 for operation to relieve problems associated with his injuries.

RE Carroll died on the 21st March 1987.

Combat record with No.6 Squadron:

21/7/17	Albatros scout	East of Nieuport	20.05	Out of control
17/8/17	2-seater	East of Westende	18.15	Crashed*

* shared with Macgregor and de Roeper

RE Carroll also claimed 2 victories with No.10 Squadron.

Carroll *Courtesy SK Taylor*

Curtis, Wilfred Austin, FSL

Born 21st August 1893, From Havelock, Ontario.

RAeC Certificate No.3391, gained 11th August 1916 at the Curtiss school, Toronto.

Joined RNAS on 11th August 1916.

Under instruction at Crystal Palace from 17th September 1916.

Under instruction at Cranwell from 14th October 1916 but period of sick leave to 23rd March 1917.

Under instruction at Cranwell from 23rd March 1917 to 16th May 1917.

Under instruction at Dover from 16th May 1917 to 14th June 1917.

No.12 Squadron from 14th June to 24th June 1917.

No.6 Squadron from 24th June to 27th August 1917.

No.10 Squadron from 28th August 1917 to 27th January 1918.

Canadian leave from 30th January 1918.

RAF HQ in Canada from 2nd May 1918.

On sick leave from 27th May 1918 to 10th October 1918.

School of Special Flying in Canada from 10th October 1918.

Post war operated the WA Curtis Insurance Company.

A Founder member of the Toronto flying Club and its president for three years

Served in RCAF during World War II, rising to rank of Air Marshal. Became Chief of Air Staff in Canada from 1947 to 1953.

DSC gazetted on 19th December 1917.

Bar to DSC gazetted on 16th March 1918.

Other decorations and honours include Order of Canada, Commander of the British Empire, Commander of the Bath, U.S. Legion of Merit, Croix de Guerre avec Palm, French Legion of Honour and Commendatore dell Ordine Militare d'Italia.

Wilfred Curtis died on the 7th August 1977.

WA Curtis claimed 13 victories with No.10 Squadron.

Curtis *Courtesy SK Taylor*

Darnton, Rupert Edward, FSL

Born 15th July 1895, from Royston, Hertfordshire

RAeC Certificate No.2289, gained 16th January 1916 at Redcar.

Previously served as a Sub Lieutenant RNVR with the RNAS Armoured Car Division.

Joined RNAS on 17th September 1915.

Under instruction at Chingford from 17th September 1915 to 2nd December 1915.

Under instruction at Redcar from 2nd December 1915 to 26th March 1916.

Under instruction at Eastchurch from 26th March 1916 to 25th April 1916.

Dover on 25th April 1916.

Admitted to Chatham Hospital on 2nd May 1916 suffering from Gonorrhoea, discharged as fit on the 24th May 1917.

Turned machine over on 20th June 1916, sustained abrasions and contusions to left temporal and molar regions, abrasion of nose and upper lip and slight burns to buttocks and left leg.

Readmitted to Chatham Hospital on 17th July 1917 with Gonorrhoea. Discharged as fit on 28th July 1916.

Admitted to Haslar Hospital on 23rd August 1916 suffering from an old injury to left leg. Discharged to sick leave on 25th August 1916 and reported fit on 8th September 1916.

Dunkerque on 16th September 1916.

4 Wing from 17th September 1916.

No.6 Squadron from 27th November 1916 to 5th January 1917.

No.7 squadron from 6th January 1917 to 5th February 1917.

Admitted to Chatham Hospital on 5th February 1917, discharged to sick leave on 7th February 1917. Surveyed and found fit on 2nd June 1917.

Reported sick with tonsillitis on 7th June 1917. Developed Diphtheria by 16th June 1917.

Surveyed on 27th August 1917 and found fit for duty.

Under instruction at Manston from 27th August 1917 to 15th September 1917 to re-qualify.

Manston Handley Page Squadron from 15th September 1917.

A Squadron, Manston from 5th October 1917, becoming No.16 Squadron on 8th January 1918.

On sick leave suffering from measles from 27th January 1918 to 15th February 1918.

Returned to No.16 squadron on 3rd March 1918.

De Roeper *Courtesy EF Cheesman*

De Roeper, Bruno Philip Henry, AFCdr
Born 22nd March 1892, at Forest Gate, London.
RAeC Certificate No.1379, gained 1st July 1915 at Hendon.
Served with London Rifle Brigade from 8th September 1914.
Joined RNAS on 16th April 1915.
Under instruction at Hendon from 16th April 1915.
Under instruction at Chingford from 5th July 1915.
Redcar, home defence and instructing, from 22nd October 1915 to 16th December 1916.
Dover on 18th December 1916.
No.4 Wing from 4th January 1917.
No.6 Squadron from 6th January 1917 to 25th May 1917, when wounded in lower jaw by enemy fire.
No.6 Squadron from 19th July 1917 to 27th August 1917.
Chingford, instructing from 10th September 1917.
Vendome, instructing from 4th October 1917 to 16th December 1917.
Central Flying School.
School of Photography from 15th August 1921.
AFC gazetted on 3rd June 1919.
Group Captain Bruno De Roeper died in St. Andrew's Hospital, Northampton, after a long illness on 1st August 1965.

Combat record with No.6 Squadron:

20/5/17	2-seater	Elincourt	11.40	Out of control and smoking
22/7/17	2-seater	Northeast of Dixmude	20.40	Out of control
15/8/17	Albatros scout	Ghistelles	17.40	Out of control
17/8/17	2-seater	East of Westende	18.15	Crashed*
20/8/17	2-seater	Moere	10.50	Out of control

* Sheared with Carroll and Macgregor

Digby, Frank Thomas, FLt
Born 2nd August 1895, from South Hampstead, London.
RAeC Certificate No.1069 gained 1st February 1915 at Hendon.
Joined RNAS on 1st December 1914.
Under instruction at Central Flying School from 12th February 1915.
Under instruction at HMS Excellent from 21st April 1915.
No.4 Squadron at Dover from 15th May 1915.
Dunkerque from 23rd September 1915.
Eastchurch from 30th December 1915.
No.1 Wing from 24th February 1916.
No.4 Wing from 25th March 1916.
No.6 Squadron from 27th November 1916 to 6th January 1917.
No.7 Squadron from 6th January 1917.
Manston Handley Page Squadron from 30th March 1917.
Dunkerque from 5th May 1917.
Redcar Handley Page Flight from 11th September 1917.
Manston Handley Page Flight from 3rd October 1917.
Home Establishment from 3rd June 1918.
DSC gazetted on 12th May 1917.
DSO gazetted on 26th April 1918.
Croix de Guerre gazetted on 10th October 1918.

Dingwall *Courtesy SK Taylor*

Dingwall, Gordon Caulfield Wilson, FSL
Born 26th April 1892, at Toronto, Ontario.
Joined RNAS on 3rd March 1916.
RAeC Certificate No.3771, gained 26th May 1916 at Eastbourne.
Under instruction at Crystal Palace from 27th February 1916 to 12th March 1916.
In Haslar Hospital with disease of the eyelid from 12th March 1916 to 20th March 1916.
Under instruction at Fishguard from 20th March 1916 to 17th April 1916.
Under instruction at White City from 17th April 1916 to 25th April 1916.
Under instruction at Eastbourne from 25th April 1916 to 19th August 1916.
Under instruction at Eastchurch from 19th August 1916 to 6th September 1916.
Dover on 6th September 1916.
Sick from 20th October 1916.
No.7 Squadron from 27th November 1916.
No.6 Squadron from 11th December 1916 to 25th February 1917 when crashed a Nieuport 12 and injured spine. Sick leave to Canada, still under treatment in January 1918.
GCW Dingwall died on the 7th November 1970.

Draper, Christopher, ASCdr
Born 15th April 1892, in Bebington, Cheshire.
RAeC Certificate No. 646, gained 9th October 1913 at the Grahame-White school, Hendon.
Joined RFC (Naval Wing) as a Sub Lieutenant RNR on the 25th January 1914.

Under instruction at RFC Central Flying School, Upavon from 25th January 1914 to 26th April 1914.
RNAS Eastchurch from July 1914 to end October 1914.
Fort Grange from end October 1914 to 19th November 1914.
Gosforth (Newcastle on Tyne) from 19th November 1914 to 8th July 1915.
RNAS Dundee from 8th July 1915.
RNAS Scarborough until 7th April 1916.
Commanding Officer of the Eastchurch War Flight from 7th April 1916 to 24th July 1916.
No.3 Wing (initially at Manston, then Luxeuil) from 24th July 1916 to 7th March 1917.
No.1 Wing from 7th March 1917.
No.11 Squadron from 15th March 1917 to 21st April 1917.
No.6 Squadron from 22nd April 1917.
Commanding Officer of the Eastchurch War Flight from 11th June 1917 to 28th July 1917.
No.8 Squadron RNAS from 28th July 1917.
Commanding Officer of No.8 Squadron RNAS from 28th October 1917 to 31st March 1918.
Commanding Officer of 208 Squadron RAF from 1st April 1918 to 14th January 1919.
Draper wrote an autobiography titled "The Mad Major", published in 1962.
Christopher Draper died on 16th January 1979.
DSC gazetted on 26th April 1918.

Combat record with No.6 Squadron:

6/6/17	Albatros scout	northwest of Cambrai	12.00	Destroyed
6/6/17	Albatros scout	northwest of Cambrai	12.00	Out of control

Draper also made the following claims with other squadrons:

3 Wing	4
No.8 Squadron	2
No.208 Squadron RAF	2

Draper *Author's collection*

Edwards, Stearne Tighe, FLt
Born 13th February 1893, in Carlton Place, Ontario.
ACA Certificate No.350, gained 11th October 1915 at the Wright school, Dayton, Ohio.
Joined RNAS on 31st October 1915.
Under instruction at Chingford to 9th April 1916.
Under instruction at Eastchurch from 9th April 1916 to 30th April 1916.
No.3 Wing from 30th April 1916 to 19th March 1917.
No.11 Squadron from 20th March 1917 to 18th April 1917.
No.6 Squadron from 19th April 1917 to 29th June 1917. Left squadron for period in hospital followed by leave.
No.9 Squadron from 10th August to 31st March 1918.
No.209 Squadron RAF from 1st April 1918 to 23rd May 1918, when he suffered from nervous exhaustion and was hospitalised.
Instructor at No.2 Fighting School, Marske, from 3rd July 1918 to 11th August 1918.
38TDS in charge of training Americans from 12th August 1918..
Critically injured in a flying accident on 12th November 1918 and subsequently died on 22nd November.
DSC gazetted on 2nd November 1917.
Bar to DSC gazetted on 21st June 1918.
Edwards made the following claims with other squadrons:

No.9 Squadron	8
No.209 Squadron RAF	8

Edwards *Courtesy SK Taylor*

Findlay, Maxwell Hutcheon, FSL
Born 17th February 1898, in Aberdeen, spent his early life in Canada.
RAeC Certificate No.6566, gained 6th December 1918 at Freiston.
Served with the 1st Highland Cyclist Battalion as a Lance Corporal from the outbreak of war.
Joined RNAS on 26th November 1916.
Under instruction at Crystal Palace from 26th November 1916 to 11th January 1917.
Under instruction at Vendome from 11th January 1917 to 14th April 1917.
Under instruction at Cranwell from 14th April 1917 to 6th June 1917.
Dover on 6th June 1917.
No.12 Squadron from 10th June 1917 to 23rd June 1917.
No.6 Squadron from 23rd June 1917 to 27th August 1917.
No.1 Squadron from 29th August 1917 to 31st March 1918.
Admitted to No.3 General Hospital on 4th October 1917, transferred to No.51 General Hospital. Discharged to duty on 4th November 1917.
No.201 Squadron RAF from 1st April 1918.
Posted to Home Establishment on 30th June 1918.
No.4 Fighting School from 6th December 1918.
No.7 Group from 19th May 1919.
No.2 Squadron RAF from 10th July 1919.

Findlay *Courtesy EF Cheesman*

Posted to India, HQ and No.31 Squadron RAF from 11th December 1919.
No.20 Squadron RAF from 2nd January 1920.
No.3 Group from 15th April 1921.
No.207 Squadron RAF from 4th May 1921.
No.39 Squadron from 1st June 1921.
In 1930's became sales manager and flying instructor at Brooklands School of Flying.
Took part in the Johannesburg Air Race in October 1936, flying an Airspeed Envoy. Crashed and was killed when taking off from an airfield in Northern Rhodesia.
DSC Gazetted 17th April 1918.
DFC Gazetted 3rd August 1918.

Combat record with No.6 Squadron:

22/7/17	Albatros scout	West of Steene	17.50	Out of control
20/8/17	Albatros scout	Middlekerke	07.20	Out of control

Findlay also made the following claims with other squadrons:

No.1 Squadron	7
No.201 Squadron RAF	5

Fletcher *Courtesy EF Cheesman*

Fletcher, Albert Harry Victor, FSL
Born 24th May 1893, at Durban, Natal.
RAeC Certificate No.2853, gained 10th May 1916 at Chingford.
Joined RNAS on 11th February 1916.
Under instruction at Chingford from 14th February 1916 to 18th June 1916.
Under instruction at Eastchurch from 18th June 1916 to 3rd July 1916.
Dover on 3rd July 1916.
No.4 Wing from July 1916.
No.6 Squadron from 27th November 1916 to 29th April 1917, with a period of sick leave from 3rd February 1917. Shot down east of Harcourt on 29th April 1917, injured and became a prisoner of war. Eventually repatriated and back in London on the 20th January 1918.

Combat record with No.6 Squadron:

29/4/17	Albatros scout	East of Harcourt	13.15	Out of control*

* Shared with Norton

Forman, James Henry, FSL
Born 1st February 1896, in Kirkfield, Ontario.
Trained at the Curtiss school, Toronto but failed to gain certificate.
Joined RNAS on 17th November 1916.
Under instruction at Crystal Palace from 17th December 1916 to 20th January 1917.
Under instruction at Vendome from 20th January 1917 to 28th April 1917.
Under instruction at Cranwell from 28th April 1917 to 2nd July 1917.
No.12 Squadron from 12th July 1917 to 18th July 1917.
No.6 Squadron from 18th July 1917 to 28th July 1917, when wounded in right shoulder by burst of fire from a German observer's machine gun.
No.1 Squadron from 29th September 1917 to 31st March 1918.
No.201 Squadron RAF from 1st April 1918 to 21st May 1918.
With 70 squadron RAF as "A" Flight Commander from 21st May 1918 to 8th September 1918, when he was shot down and became a prisoner of war.
Served with the RCAF as an administration officer in the Second World War.
DFC Gazetted 3rd August 1918.
JH Foreman died on the 12th October 1972.

Combat record with No.6 Squadron:

26/7/17	Albatros scout	St. George	17.50	Out of control
27/7/17	Albatros scout	Northeast of Nieuport	17.10	Destroyed
28/7/17	Albatros scout	South of Wilskerke	16.15	Out of control

Forman also made the following claims with other squadrons:

No.1 Squadron	3
No.201 Squadron RAF	4
No.70 Squadron RAF1	

Foreman *Courtesy SK Taylor*

Frame, Robert Bruce, FSL
Born 25th July 1891, from New Zealand.
Joined RNAS on 4th June 1916.
Under instruction at Crystal Palace from 4th June 1916.
Under instruction at Eastchurch from 24th June 1916.
Under instruction at Eastchurch Gunnery School from 8th October 1916.
Dover on 4th November 1916.
No.4 Wing from November 1916.

Admitted to Dunkerque Hospital on 27th April 1917, suffering from a nervous condition.
Grain from 27th June 1917 performing ground duties.
Manston Fighting School from 24th October 1917.
Under instruction at Cranwell from 17th November 1917, training as an instructor.
Chingford, instructing from 29th November 1917.
Redcar Instructor's School from 29th April 1918.
Commenced 6 months leave to New Zealand from 18th May 1918.

Gagnier *Courtesy SK Taylor*

Gagnier, Oliver Joseph, FSL
Born 13th January 1896, from Montreal, Quebec.
RAeC Certificate No.3397, gained 15th August 1916 at the Curtiss school, Toronto.
Joined RNAS on 15th August 1916.
Under instruction at Crystal Palace from 17th September 1916 to 14th October 1916.
Under instruction at Cranwell from 14th October 1916 to 7th February 1917.
Dover on 7th February 1917.
No.6 Squadron from 24th February 1917 to 11th May 1917, when shot down and overturned in No Mans Land at Villers Outreaux, was seriously injured with gunshot wounds to arm and chest and had to have his left arm amputated.
Sick leave from 11th May 1917 to 10th August 1917.
Cattewater, ground duties from 10th August 1917 to December 1917.
Canadian Leave from December 1917 to March 1918.
Canada as member of recruiting party from 13th July 1918.
Assistant to the Provost Marshal for the RAF in New York from 28th September 1918.
Transferred to unemployed list on 17th October 1919.
OJ Gagnier died in November 1942.

Combat record with No.6 Squadron:

10/5/17	Albatros scout	NW of Fresnoy le Grande	crashed

Gibbs *Courtesy RAeC Trust*

Gibbs, Victor Richard, FSL
Born 13th October 1893, from Finsbury Park, London.
RAeC Certificate No.2565, gained 17th March 1916 at Hendon.
Previous service as a Sub Lieutenant RNVR with the RNAS Armoured Car Division.
Joined RNAS on 22nd January 1916.
Under instruction at Hendon from 30th January 1916.
Under instruction at White City from 25th March 1916.
Under instruction at Eastbourne from 14th April 1916.
Admitted to Haslar Hospital on 23rd May 1916 suffering from Gonorrhoea, discharged as fit on the 24th July 1916.
Under instruction at Cranwell from 1st September 1916.
Eastchurch War Flight from 23rd October 1916.
Resurveyed on 5th November 1916 and found to be unfit for duty, discharged as fit on the 19th November 1916.
Dover on 10th January 1917.
No.6 Squadron from 1st February 1917.
No.7 Squadron from 12th February 1917.
No.14 Squadron from 9th December 1917.
Admitted to No.14 General Hospital Wimereux on 18th February 1918.
Admitted to No. 51 General Hospital Etaples on 21st February 1918.
Reported to Medical Board on 14th May 1917.
DSC gazetted on 17th November 1917.
Croix de Guerre with palm.
Served in RAF during World War II with rank of Wing Commander.

Gooderham *Courtesy Fleet Air Arm Museum*

Gooderham, Grant Armstrong, FLt
Born 8th January 1892, from Toronto, Ontario.
RAeC Certificate No.1522, gained 12th July 1915 at the Curtiss School, Toronto.
Joined RNAS on 13th July 1915.
Under instruction at Chingford from 8th August 1915 to 17th September 1915.
Whitley Bay from 17th September 1915 to 28th March 1916.
A Squadron 1 Wing from 29th April 1916 to 6th December 1916.
No.1 Squadron from 6th December 1916 to 10th February 1917.
Sick from 10th February 1917, reported to Admiralty for survey on 14th March 1917.
NAD Section of the Air Department of the Admiralty from 17th March 1917.
Martlesham Heath as test pilot from 4th June 1917 to 6th June 1917.
No.6 Squadron from 7th June 1917 to 27th August 1917.
No.2 Squadron (A Flight) from 3rd September 1917 to 28th January 1918.
Redcar from 29th January 1918 to 24th April 1918.
Cranwell on instructional staff from 7th May 1918.
203TDS from 12th August 1918 to December 1918.
GA Gooderham took his own life on the 2nd May 1919.
Croix de Guerre (France) gazetted on 21st September 1918.
DFC gazetted on 1st January 1919.

Hall *Courtesy RAeC Trust*

Hartgill *Courtesy RAeC Trust*

Holyman Courtesy SKTaylor

Combat record with No.6 Squadron:

23/7/17	Albatros scout	Moere	20.15	Out of control

Hall, Arthur Edwin, FSL
Born 8th January 1898, from Balham, London.
RAeC Certificate No.4118, gained 15th November 1916 at Cranwell.
Joined RNAS on 20th July 1916.
Under instruction at Crystal Palace from 23rd July 1916 to 12th August 1916.
Under instruction at Cranwell from 12th August 1916 to 15th January 1917.
Under instruction at Eastchurch from 15th January 1917 to 22nd February 1917.
Dover on 22nd February 1917.
No.6 Squadron from 8th March 1917 to 5th April 1917.
No.11 Squadron from 21st April 1917 to 5th May 1917, crashed Nieuport 21 after practice flight, fractured thigh and hospitalised

Hamilton-Bowyer, Stanley Arthur, FSL
Born 28th August 1895. From London.
Joined the RNAS on 1st October 1916.
Under instruction at Crystal Palace from 1st October 1916.
Under Instruction at Chingford from 11th November 1916.
Under instruction at Cranwell from 11th April 1917.
Under instruction at Freiston from 11th July 1917.
Dover from 23rd July 1917 to 13th August 1917.
No.12 Squadron from 14th August to 22nd August 1917.
No.6 Squadron from 22nd August 1917 to 27th August 1917.
No.10 Squadron from 30th August 1917 to 29th November 1917, transferred to Cranwell whilst on leave.
Cranwell from 15th December 1917 to 27th December 1917.
Manston War Flight from 30th December 1917 to 31st March 1918.
Hamilton-Bowyer made the following claims with other squadrons:

No.10 Squadron 1

Hartgill, George Leigh, FSL
Born 14th April 1889, from Feilding, North Island, New Zealand.
RAeC Certificate No.2245, gained 29th December 1915 at Eastchurch.
Joined RNAS on 22nd November 1915.
Under instruction at Eastchurch from 22nd November 1915 to 10th February 1916.
No.4 Wing at Eastchurch from 10th February 1916.
Eastchurch War Flight from 19th June 1916.
Dunkerque on 26th June 1916.
4 Wing from 26th June 1916.
No.6 Squadron from 27th November 1916 to 31st March 1917. Period in Hospital for operation on leg from 30th January 1917 to 3rd March 1917.
Admitted to hospital with a hernia on 31st March 1917.
Rosyth, ground duties from 23rd August 1917 to 18th October 1917.
Rosyth Seaplane Depot from 18th October 1917 to 18th February 1918.
Turnhouse from 18th February 1918 to 1st May 1918.
Commanding Officer of Fleet Aircraft Depot from 1st May 1918
Posted to unemployed list on 17th March 1919.
Civilian occupation sheep farmer.
Administration Officer with RNZAF Initial Training Wing in World War II.
GL Hartgill died on 17th May 1964 at Palmerston North, New Zealand.

Holyman, Victor Clive, FSL
Born 27th August 1894, from Devonport, Tasmania.
Joined RNAS on 18th June 1916.
Under instruction at Crystal Palace from 18th June 1916 to 8th July 1916.
Under instruction at Chingford from 8th July 1916 to 23rd October 1916.
Under instruction at Cranwell from 23rd October 1916 to 17th November 1916.
No.3 Wing from 17th November 1916 to 9th March 1917.
No.11 Squadron from 10th March 1917 to 26th May 1917.
No.6 Squadron from 27th May 1917 to 14th July 1917, on sick leave until 2nd October 1917.
Manston War School from 2nd October 1917 to 29th October 1917.
Martlesham Heath from 29th October 1917.
In 1932 founded Holyman Brothers PTY Ltd in conjunction with his brother Ivan Holyman. A merger with L McK Johnston formed Tasmanian Aerial Services Ltd., which then became Holyman's Airways PTY on 1st October 1934.
Victor Holyman died on 19th October, 1934, over Bass Strait in "Miss Hobart", a DH86 which belonged to his airline.

Keeble, Louis Clement, FLt
Born 22nd July 1893, from Kensington, London.
RAeC Certificate No.1531, gained 29th July 1915 at Eastbourne.
Joined RNAS on 12th May 1915.
Under instruction at Eastbourne from 12th May 1915 to 2nd September 1915.
Detling from 2nd September 1915 to 11th April 1916.
Dunkerque on 11th April 1916.
Chingford to 8th January 1917.
Dover on 8th January 1917.
No.6 Squadron from February 1917 to 24th April 1917.
Manston from 25th April 1917 to 22nd April 1918.
Redcar, instructing, from 22nd April 1918 to 6th May 1918.
Manston from 6th May 1918.

Keeble *Courtesy Fleet Air Arm Museum*

Kendall, Edward Hext, FSL
Born 6th July 1895, from Heswall, Cheshire.
RAeC Certificate No.4528, gained 21st April 1917 at Chingford.
Previously served in the Third Battalion of the Duke of Cornwall's Light Infantry with the rank of 2nd Lieutenant.
Joined RNAS on 14th January 1917.
Under instruction at Crystal Palace from 14th January 1917 to 17th February 1917.
Under instruction at Chingford from 17th February 1917 to 15th June 1917.
Dover on 15th June 1917.
No.12 Squadron from 27th June 1917 to 4th July 1917.
No.6 Squadron from 4th July 1917 to 12th July 1917, killed when shot down in flames near Slype.

Kendall *Courtesy RAeC Trust*

Kingsford, Maurice Rooke, FSL
Born 7th April 1892, from Toronto, Ontario.
RAeC Certificate No.2537, gained 5th March 1916 at the Grahame-White school, Hendon.
Previously served in the 30th Battalion of the Canadian Expeditionary Force with the rank of Lieutenant.
Joined RNAS on 15th December 1915.
Under instruction at Hendon from 6th January 1916 to 16th March 1916.
Under instruction at White City from 16th March 1916 to 14th April 1916.
Under instruction at Eastbourne from 14th April 1916 to 8th July 1916.
Under instruction at Cranwell from 8th July 1916 to 22nd August 1916.
No.3 Wing from 22nd August 1916 to 7th March 1917.
No.1 Wing from 7th March 1917.
No.11 Squadron from March 1917 to 2nd April 1917
No.6 Squadron from 3rd April 1917 to 5th April 1917, when broke leg in crash following engine failure.
Sick from 5th April 1917 to 17th July 1917, at 14th General Hospital, Boulogne.
Dover on 17th July 1917.
Walmer Defence Flight from 24th July 1917.
No.12 Squadron from 23rd September 1917 to 26th September 1917.
No.8 Squadron from 27th September 1917 to 30th January 1918.
Under instruction at Cranwell Instructor's School from 30th January 1918 to 14th February 1918.
Manston, instructing, from 14th February 1918 to 12th September 1918.
No.3 Training group as assistant instructor from 12th September 1918.
55TDS from13th September 1918 to 7th October 1918 to 11th February 1919, with a period in hospital from 7th October 1917 to 11th October 1918.
MR Kingsford died on the 30th August 1973.

Kingsford *Courtesy RAeC Trust*

Kirkpatrick, George Denison, FLt
Born 25th August 1896, from Toronto, Ontario.
RAeC Certificate No.3201, gained 19th June 1916 at Eastbourne.
Joined RNAS on 7th February 1916.
Under instruction at HMS Victory from 27th February 1916.
Under instruction at Fishguard from March 1917 to 17th April 1916.
Under instruction at White City from 17th April 1916 to 25th April 1916.
Under instruction at Eastbourne from 25th April 1916 to 22nd July 1916.
Under instruction at Eastchurch from 22nd July 1916 to 6th August 1916.
Under instruction at East Fortune from 7th August 1916 to 28th August 1916.
Under instruction at Aberdeen from 29th August to 23rd September 1916.
No.3 Wing from 14th September 1916 to 7th March 1917.
No.1 Wing on 7th March 1917.
No.11 Squadron from 8th March 1917 to 4th April 1917.
No.6 Squadron from 5th April 1917 to 19th August 1917, wounded in a crash landing and hospitalised in England.
Slough on compass course on 5th November 1917.
Canadian leave from 18th December 1917.
Yarmouth from 18th May 1918.
Yarmouth, No.4 Group from 8th August 1918 to 14th February 1919.

Kirkpatrick *Courtesy EF Cheesman*

Lawson *Courtesy EF Cheesman*

Macgregor *Courtesy EF Cheesman*

Lawson, Harold, FSL

Born 15th April 1897. From Gosforth, Northumberland.

Joined the RNAS on 11th June 1916.

Under instruction at Crystal Palace 21st June 1916 to 1st July 1916.

Under instruction at Eastbourne 1st July 1916 to 1st September 1916.

Under instruction at Cranwell from 1st September 1916 to 22nd January 1917.

Dover on 22nd January 1917.

6(N) from 11th February 1917 to 27th August 1917.

10(N) from 28th August 1917 to 19th September 1917, transferred to 1 Wing.

Dover 22nd November 1917.

Under instruction at Cranwell, instructors course, from 26th November 1917 to 16th December 1917.

Chingford, instructing, from 16th December 1917, 207TDS after 1st April 1918.

On RAF unemployed list 23rd January 1919.

Macgregor, Norman Miers, FSL

Born 29th May 1896. From London.

RAeC Certificate No. 3135, gained 1st June 1916 at Chingford.

Joined the RNAS on 12th February 1916.

Under instruction at Fishguard from 27th February 1916.

Under instruction at White City from 17th April 1916.

Under instruction at Chingford from 25th April 1916.

Under instruction at Eastchurch from 8th July 1916.

3 Wing from 1st August 1916.

1 Wing from 9th March 1917.

No.11 Squadron from 15th March 1917.

No.6 Squadron from 22nd April 1917 to 27th August 1917.

No.10 Squadron from 28th August 1917 to 28th January 1918.

Eastchurch from 28th January 1918 for disposal.

Martlesham Heath from 26th February 1918 to 16th April 1918.

Furious on 16th April 1918 for disposal.

Eastchurch and Leysdown, instructor, from 27th April 1918.

DSC gazetted on 22nd February 1918.

Combat record with No.6 Squadron:

28/7/17	2-seater	Nieuport	16.00	Crashed*
17/8/17	2-seater	E of Westende	18.15	Crashed **
20/8/17	2-seater	Moere	10.50	Out of control***
22/8/17	Albatros scout	N of St. Pierre Cappelle	09.45	Destroyed

* shared with Winter

** shared with de Roeper and Carroll

*** shared with de Roeper

Macgregor also made the following claims with other squadrons:

No.10 Squadron 3

MacLaren, Colin Temple, FCdr

Born 27th April 1891, from Richmond, Surrey. Worked as a Cotton Broker in Bombay.

RAeC Certificate No.1306, gained 6th June 1915 at Chingford.

Previously served in the Lahore Divisional Signal Company in August 1914 as a Motor Despatch Rider with the rank of Corporal.

Joined RNAS on 16th April 1915.

Under instruction at Hendon from 16th April 1915 to 22nd July 1915.

At Dover on 22nd July 1915.

At Dunkerque on 23rd September 1915.

Eastchurch from 30th December 1915 to 12th January 1916.

Central Flying School from 12th January 1916 to 1st April 1916.

Cranwell from 1st April 1916 to 26th April 1916.

Yarmouth from 26th April 1916 to 5th May 1916.

No.4 Wing at Eastchurch from 5th May 1916 to 16th September 1916

Dover on 16th September 1916.

No.4 Wing from 16th September 1916.

No.7 Squadron from 27th November 1916.

No.6 Squadron from January 1917 to 14th August 1917.

Commanding Officer of the Walmer Defence Flight from 14th August 1917.

Commanding Officer of No.6 Squadron from 1st January 1918 to 31st March 1918.

Commanding Officer of No.206 Squadron RAF from 1st April 1918 to 23rd May 1919.

Croix de Guerre (B) gazetted on 15th July 1919.

OBE gazetted on 15th July 1919.

MacLennan, George Gordon, FCdr
Born 26th January 1886, from Eugenia, Ontario.
RAeC Certificate No.2058, gained 8th November 1915 at the Curtiss school, Toronto.
Joined RNAS on 11th November 1915.
Under instruction at Central Flying School from December 1915 to 11th March 1916.
Central Flying School as an Assistant Instructor from 11th March 1916 to 11th April 1916.
Under instruction at Eastchurch from 11th April 1916 to 30th April 1916.
No.3 Wing (initially at Detling) from 30th April 1916 to 7th March 1917.
No.1 Wing on 7th March 1917.
No.11 squadron from 7th March 1917 to 18th April 1917.
No.6 Squadron from 19th April 1917 to 20th July 1917, killed in action during an engagement with enemy aircraft over Middlekerke.
Croix de Guerre (France).

Combat record with No.6 Squadron:

1/6/17	Albatros scout	E of Templeux Le Guerard	18.55	Out of control
20/7/17	2-seater	NW of Wilskerke	14.30	Out of control

MacLaren *Courtesy Ernie Jupe*

Maund, Hugh Bingham, FSL
Born 30th May 1896. From Hampstead, London.
Served in 8th Battalion, Canadian Expeditionary Force, with rank of Lieutenant.
Joined the RNAS on 6th November 1916.
Under instruction at Crystal Palace from 10th December 1916.
Under instruction at Eastchurch from 27th January 1917.
Admitted to Chatham Hospital on 9th April 1917, with head injuries.
Under instruction at Cranwell from 13th April 1917.
Dover on 10th May 1917.
No.12 Squadron from 21st July 1917 to 26th July 1917.
No.6 Squadron from 26th July 1918 to 27th August 1918.
No.10 Squadron from 28th August 1917 to 31st March 1918.
No.210 Squadron RAF from 1st April 1918 to 28th May 1918, when wounded in hands.
No.204 Squadron RAF from January 1919, becoming Commanding Officer on 23rd January, to 31st December 1919.
Maund made the following claims with other squadrons:

No.10 Squadron	2
No.210 Squadron RAF	9

MacLennan *Courtesy EF Cheesman*

Norton, Ernest William, FCdr
Born 14th May 1893. From Montgomery, Powys.
RAeC Certificate No.1476, gained 29th July 1915 at Central Flying School, Upavon.
Joined RNAS on 25th May 1915.
Under instruction at Eastbourne from 25th May 1915.
Under instruction at Central Flying School, Upavon to 28th August 1915.
No.5 Squadron at Dover, as Engine Officer, from 28th August 1915.
A Squadron, 1 Wing from June 1916 to 6th December 1916.
No.1 Squadron from 6th December 1916 to 31st January 1917.
No.6 Squadron from 31st January 1917 to 14th May 1917.
No.12 Squadron, Commanding Officer from 1st July 1917 to 15th September 1917.
No.9 Squadron, Commanding Officer from 15th September to 12th January 1918.
Cranwell from 12th January 1918.
No.204 Squadron RAF, Commanding Officer from 27th July 1918 to 10th December 1918.
Granted permanent commission in RAF on the 1st August 1919, reached the rank of Air Commodore.
School of Technical Training (boys) on staff from 21st February 1920.
No.6 Armoured Car Company, Commanding Officer from 15th December 1924.
No.70 Squadron Commanding Officer from 1st December 1925.
No.58 Squadron, Commanding Officer from 28th July 1927.
RAF Worthy Down, on staff from 7th December 1928, temporary Commanding Officer from March 1929.
No.58 Squadron, Commanding Officer from 18th April 1929.
RAF Upavon, Commanding Officer from 18th August 1930.
No.5 FTS, Commanding Officer from 23rd July 1932.
AOA HQ Coastal Command, from 15th February 1937.
AOA HQ RAF Far East, from 28th December 1937.
Retired in 1944.
DSC, gazetted on 1st January 1917.
Croix de Guerre (Belgian) gazetted on 15th July 1919.
Croix de Guerre (French).

Maund *Courtesy EF Cheesman*

Norton *Courtesy Les Rogers*

Combat record with No.6 Squadron:

8/2/17	2-seater	Houthulst Forest		Out of control, smoking
5/4/17	Albatros scout	W of Douai	17.00	Destroyed in flames
5/4/17	Albatros scout	W of Douai	17.00	Out of control
9/4/17	Albatros scout	Cambrai	11.45	Destroyed*
9/4/17	Albatros scout	Cambrai	12.00	Out of control
29/4/17	Albatros scout	E of Harcourt	13.15	Out of control**
29/4/17	Albatros scout	Guise	18.55	Destroyed in flames
29/4/17	Albatros scout	Guise	18.50	Out of control

* shared with Thorne
** shared with Fletcher
Norton also made the following claims with other squadrons:

1 Wing 1

Ormerod, Leonard William, FSL
Born 25th June 1896, from Russell Square, London.
RAeC Certificate No.2631 gained 30th March 1916 at Hall school, Hendon.
Joined RNAS on 3rd April 1916.
Under instruction at White City from 10th April 1916.
Under instruction at Chingford from 20th May 1916.
Under instruction at Cranwell from 30th June 1916.
Dover on 17th October 1916.
4 Wing from October 1916
No.6 Squadron from 27th November 1916.
No.7 Squadron from 6th January 1917.
No.5 Squadron from 15th April 1917 to 16th March 1918 when killed in action, buried at Le Cateau.
DSC gazetted on 2nd November 1917.

Ormerod *Courtesy EF Cheesman*

Paynter, John de Campbourne, FSL
Born 17th May 1898. From Southsea, Hampshire.
RAeC Certificate No.3659, gained 16th September 1916 at Chingford.
Under instruction at Crystal Palace from 25th June 1916.
Under instruction at Chingford from 15th July 1916.
Under instruction at Cranwell from 13th November 1916.
Dover on 29th November 1916.
No.6 Squadron from January 1917 to 9th April 1917, when hospitalised with an injured back following a crash during a storm.
No.12 Squadron from 9th to 15th October 1917.
No.10 Squadron from 16th October 1917 to 25th October 1917.
No.9 Squadron from 25th October 1917 to 26th October 1917.
Dunkerque, ground duties, from 26th October 1917 to 2nd January 1918
Seaplane defence Squadron/No.13 Squadron from 2nd January 1918 to 31st March 1918.
No.213 Squadron RAF from 1st April 1918 to 18th June 1918, when fatally wounded by bomb fragments during an air raid on 213 Squadron's aerodrome. Admitted to Queen Alexandria hospital, died of perforated liver.
DFC gazetted on 17th April 1918.

Combat record with No.6 Squadron:

1/3/17	2-seater	Ghistelles	Out of control

Paynter also made the following claims with other squadrons:

No.9 Squadron	1
No.13 Squadron	4
No.213 Squadron RAF	5

Paynter *Courtesy EF Cheesman*

Perrett, Claude, FSL
Born 11th November 1896, from Great Yarmouth, Norfolk.
RAeC Certificate No.1473, gained on 27th July 1915 at Eastchurch.
Previously served with Royal Australian Naval Reserve in 1914.
Joined RNAS on 12th May 1915.
Under instruction at Windermere from 12th May 1915.
Under instruction at Chingford.
Eastchurch War Flight from 21st July 1915.
No.4 Wing from 3rd September 1915.
No.7 Squadron from 27th November 1916.
No.6 Squadron from 16th January 1917.
No.7 Squadron from 23rd January 1917.
No.2 Squadron from 23rd April 1917.

Petre, John Joseph, SCdr
Born 11th April 1894. From Ingallstone, Essex.
RAeC Certificate No.942, gained 14th October 1914 at Eastbourne.
Joined RNAS on 17th September 1914.
Under instruction at Eastbourne from 17th September 1914 to 27th October 1914.
Under instruction at Eastchurch from 27th October 1914 to 12th January 1915.
At RNAS Grain from 12th January 1915 to 12th February 1915.
To 1 Wing Dunkerque on 12th February 1915.
Injured in incident with FBA Flying Boat serial 3114 on 24th May 1915.
Commanding Officer of B Group 1 Wing from 30th December 1915.
A Squadron 1 Wing from early June 1916 to 6th December 1916.
No.1 Squadron from 6th December 1916 to 31st December 1916.
No.4 Wing in January 1917.
Commanding Officer of No.6 Squadron from February 1917 to 13th April 1917, killed when his Nieuport broke up whilst diving at a target on a gunnery range.
DSC gazetted on 22nd June 1916.
Croix de Guerre (France).
Petre made the following claims with other squadrons:

A Squadron 1 Wing 1

Petre *Courtesy Mike O'Connor*

Plaistowe, David, FSL
Born 28th March 1898, from Wakefield, Yorkshire.
RAeC Certificate No.3667, gained 1st October 1916, at Chingford.
Previously served in RNAS with rank of AM.2 at Roehampton.
Confirmed as a probationary Flight Sub Lieutenant on the 18th July 1916.
Under instruction at Crystal Palace from 23rd July 1916 to 12th August 1916.
Under instruction at Chingford from 12th August 1916 to 4th December 1916.
Under instruction at Cranwell from 4th December 1916 to 30th December 1916.
Westgate from 30th December 1916 to 10th January 1917.
At Dover on 10th January 1917.
No.6 Squadron from 12th February 1917 to 25th April 1917, then to hospital in England.
Hendon from 6th June 1917 to 9th April 1918.
Martlesham Heath from 9th April 1918

Plaistowe *Courtesy RAeC Trust*

Powles, George Paulet, FSL
Born 12th March 1897, from Kensington, London.
RAeC Certificate No.2560, gained 16th March 1916 at the Graeme-White school, Hendon.
Previously served with rank of Private in the London Regiment.
Joined RNAS on 24th December 1915.
Under instruction at Hendon from 19th January 1916 to 23rd March 1916.
Under instruction at White City from 23rd March 1916 to 14th April 1916.
Under instruction at Eastbourne from 14th April 1916 to 15th June 1916.
Under instruction at Cranwell from 15th June 1916 to 28th August 1916.
Dover on 28th August 1916.
No.4 Wing from September 1916.
No.6 Squadron from 4th February 1917 to 26th February 1917, when interned in Holland after suffering damage from ground fire and making a forced landing at Cadzand, Zeeland.

Powles *Courtesy RAeC Trust*

Redpath, Ronald Francis, FLt
Born 7th July 1888. From Montreal, Canada.
Under instruction at Curtiss school, Toronto, from 30th August 1915 to 3rd November 1915, did not finish course but joined RNAS on 1st December 1915 as a Probationary Flight Sub Lieutenant in Ottawa without an FAI Certificate.
Under instruction at Chingford from 20th December 1915, RAeC Certificate 2418 gained on 8th February 1916 at Chingford.
Under instruction at Crystal Palace from 1st May 1916 to 20th May 1916.
Under instruction at Eastchurch Gunnery School from 20th May 1916 to 6th August 1916.
No.3 Wing from 7th August 1916 (at Manston) to 14th March 1917.
No.11 Squadron from 15th March 1917 to 21st April 1917.
No.6 Squadron from 22nd April 1917 to 13th August 1917. Sick from 21st June to 5th August.
No.11 Squadron from 15th August to 1st September 1917.
No.3 Squadron, temporary attachment from 2nd September to 23rd September 1917.
No.10 Squadron from 23rd September to 14th December 1917.
201 TDS Cranwell from 27th December 1917 to 10th June 1918.
Redcar 10th June 1918 to 22nd June 1918.
Cranwell 22nd June 1918 to 18th November 1918.
No.209 Squadron RAF from 18th November 1918 to 9th March 1919.
Cranwell 9th March 1919 to 24th April 1919.
To unemployed list on 24th April 1919.
Became a post-war director of the Canadian Air Force.
Redpath died on 11th January 1970.

Redpath *Courtesy EF Cheesman*

Combat record with No.6 Squadron:

6/6/17	Albatros scout	NW of Cambrai	12.00-12.15	Out of control

Redpath made the following claims with other squadrons:

No.3 Squadron 1

Reeves, Fabian Pember, FLt
Born 12th December 1895, from London.
Joined RNAS on 18th July 1915.
Previously served with the OTC from 1914 to 1915.
Under instruction at HMS Victory from 18th July 1915 to 15th August 1915.
Under instruction at Eastchurch from 15th August 1915 to 1st October 1915.
No 4 Squadron from 1st October 1915 to 23rd November 1915.
Hendon from 23rd November 1915 to 22nd February 1916.
Yarmouth from 22nd February 1916 to 15th July 1916.
Eastchurch flying school as a temporary instructor from 15th July 1916 to 2nd October 1916.
Admiralty Air Department, M Section from 2nd October 1916 to 10th March 1917.
Dover on 10th March 1917.
No.6 Squadron from 11th March 1917 to 6th June 1917, when his Nieuport 17Bis broke up in the air during combat over Moevres.

Ruthven, John Edgar, FSL
Born 22nd July 1895, from Kendall, Westmorland
RAeC Certificate No.3606 obtained on 26th September 1916 at Chingford.
Joined RNAS on 14th May 1916.
Under instruction at Crystal Palace from 14th May 1916.
Under instruction at Chingford from 3rd June 1916.
Under instruction at Cranwell from 4th November 1916.
Dover on 17th November 1916.
No.4 Wing from 18th November 1916.
No.7 Squadron from January 1917.
Admitted to Chartham Hospital on 24th April 1917 suffering from Conjunctivitis. Discharged fit on 20th June 1917.
Dover on 27th June 1917.
Surveyed on 12th September 1917 and found unfit. Resurveyed on 12th November 1917 and found unfit for further flying but fit for ground duties.
Under instruction at Slough on Compass course from 19th November 1917.
East Fortune Airship Station from 28th December 1917, initially serving as Compass Officer and later as an Adjutant with the RAF.
Transferred to unemployed list on 22nd October 1919.

Shaw *Courtesy EF Cheesman*

Shaw, James Alexander, FSL
Born 23rd September 1893.
USA Certificate No.382 obtained on 25th December 1915 at Wright school, Augusta.
Joined RNAS on 1st January 1916.
Under instruction at Redcar from 1st January 1916.
Under instruction at Cranwell from 5th June 1916.
Dover on 11th September 1916.
Admitted to Chatham Hospital on 28th September 1916 suffering from Syphilis. Discharged fit on 24th October 1916.
Re-admitted to Chatham Hospital on 27th October 1916 suffering from secondary Syphilis.
No.4 Wing from November 1916.
No.8 Squadron from February 1917.
No.9 Squadron from 17th March 1917.
Admitted to Chatham Hospital on 13th April 1917 with injury to knee.
Walmer Defence Flight from 28th April 1917.
Manston DH School from January 1918.

Siedle *Courtesy RAeC Trust*

Siedle, Geoffrey Ernest, FSL
Born 23rd November 1898, at Swansea.
RAeC Certificate No.4738, gained 28th May 1917 at Chingford.
Joined RNAS 4th February 1917.
Under instruction at Crystal Palace from 4th February 1917 to 12th March 1917.
Under instruction at Chingford from 12th March 1917 to 9th June 1917.
Under instruction at Cranwell from 9th June 1917 to 23rd July 1917.
Dover on 23rd July 1917.
No.12 Squadron from 11th August 1917 to 14th August 1917.
No.6 Squadron from 14th August 1917 to 27th August 1917.
Admitted to Chatham Hospital on 3rd September 1917 suffering from Bronchitis.
Manston from 15th November 1917 to 28th December 1917.
Dunkerque on 28th December 1917.
No.12 Squadron from 29th December 1917 to 6th January 1918.

No.5 Squadron from 7th January 1918 to 31st March 1918.
Siedle made 1 indecisive claim with No.5 Squadron.

Sieveking, Valentine Edgar, FSL
Born 5th February 1892, from Marylebone, London.

Previous service as Probationary FSL from 11th September 1915 to 8th December 1915 (terminated as showed no ability to learn to fly at Eastbourne) and as an Observer with the rank of SL RNVR from 8th December 1915 to 15th February 1916 (terminated as too heavy for an observer and poor performance). Was not recommended for further pilot training.

Rejoined RNAS on 16th February 1916.

Under instruction at Cranwell from 16th February 1916. Suffered accident with two sheep at take off in RE7 2241 receiving abrasions on both legs, bruises on face, broken nose and shock. Sieveking was not held responsible for the accident.

Surveyed on 1st September 1916 and pronounced fit.

Dover on 29th September 1916. Overturned Nieuport 10 serial 3966 when landing on 2nd November 1916, suffered minor injuries and shock.

4 Wing from November 1916.
No.6 Squadron from 27th November 1916.
No.7 Squadron from 7th January 1917.
No.14 Squadron from 9th December 1917.
No.214 Squadron RAF from 1st April 1918 to 18th May 1918 when killed in action.
DSC gazetted on 22nd June 1917.
Bar to DSC gazetted on 17th April 1918.

Sieveking *Courtesy EF Cheesman*

Simpson, James Orroh, FSL
Born 1st September 1896.

Joined RNAS on 4th March 1917.
Previous service in RNAS as AM1.
Under instruction at Crystal Palace from 4th March 1917 to 17th April 1917.
Under instruction at Eastchurch from 17th April 1917 to 16th June 1917.
Under instruction at Cranwell from 16th June 1917 to 28th July 1917.
Dover on 27th July 1917.
No.12 Squadron from 12th August 1917 to 14th August 1917.
No.6 Squadron from 15th August 1917 to 27th August 1917.
No.1 Squadron from 29th August 1917.

Admitted to Chatham Hospital on 13th March 1918 suffering from Chancroid, discharged to duty on 27th April 1918.

Slater, Robert Kenneth, FSL
Born 18th November 1893 in Ottawa.

RAeC Certificate No.3593, gained 21st September 1916 at Redcar.
Joined RNAS on 8th April 1916.
Originally served with the 23rd Battalion of Canadian Infantry.
Under instruction at the White City from 25th April 1916 to 20th May 1916.
Under instruction at Redcar from 20th May 1916 to 23rd September 1916.
Under instruction at Cranwell from 23rd September 1916 to 10th January 1917.
At Dover on 10th January 1918.

No.6 Squadron from January 1917 to 5th April 1917 when he was shot down near Arras at 18.45 and became a prisoner of war.

RK Slater died in 1984.

Slater *Courtesy SK Taylor*

Stevens, George Leslie Eugene, FLt
Born 11 December 1892 at Peterborough, Ontario.

RAeC Certificate No.1724, gained 4th September 1915 at the Curtiss school, Toronto.
Joined RNAS on 6th September 1915.
Under instruction at Chingford from 4th September 1915 to 1st December 1915.
Under instruction for night flying at Eastchurch from 1st December 1915 to 27th December 1915.
Sick and Canadian leave from 27th December 1915.
Under instruction at Rochford from 1st March 1916 to 5th June 1916.
Under instruction at Detling from 6th June1916 to 28th July 1916.
Sick and Canadian leave from 29th July 1916.
Redcar for re-qualification on 7th December 1916.
Redcar War Flight from 9th January 1917 to 10th March 1917.
Dover from 10th March 1917 to 29th March 1917.
No.11 Squadron from 29th March 1917 to 21st April 1917.
No.6 Squadron from 22nd April 1917 to 26th June 1917.
Sick from September 1917.
Manston from 13th November 1917 to 30th November 1917.
Dunkerque on 30th November 1917.
No.12 Squadron from 1st December 1917 to 6th December 1917.
Seaplane Defence Squadron from 7th December 1917 to 10th February 1918.
No.6 Squadron from January 1918 to 31st March 1918.

Stevens *Courtesy EF Cheesman*

Strathy *Courtesy EF Cheesman*

Thorne *Courtesy RAeC Trust*

Walker *Courtesy EF Cheesman*

No.206 Squadron RAF from 1st April 1918 to 17th August 1918.
No.9 Group, ground duties from 17th August 1918 to 6th October 1918.
No.241 Squadron from 7th October 1918.
GLE Stevens died in 1963.

Combat record with No.6 Squadron:

6/6/17	Albatros scout	NW of Cambrai	12.15	Out of control

Stevens also made the following claims with other squadrons:

No.206 Squadron RAF 2

Strathy, Ford Stuart, FSL
Born 2nd September 1897, from Toronto, Ontario.
RAeC Certificate No.3832, gained 5th November 1916 at the Curtiss school, Toronto.
Joined RNAS on 5th November 1916.
Under instruction at Crystal Palace from 17th December 1916 to 5th February 1917.
Under instruction at Vendome from 5th February 1917 to 28th April 1917.
Under instruction at Cranwell from 28th April 1917 to 2nd July 1917.
Dover on 2nd July 1917.
No.12 Squadron from 13th July 1917 to 18th July 1917.
No.6 Squadron from 18th July 1917 to 17th August 1917, when shot down and killed over Zevcote.

Combat record with No.6 Squadron:

15/8/17	Albatros Scout	Nieuport	16.45-18.35	Destroyed

Thorne, Alfred Lewis, FSL
Born 19th January 1894, from Kingersdorp, Transvaal.
RAeC Certificate No.2447, gained 12th February 1916 at Chingford.
Joined RNAS on 19th October 1915.
Under instruction at Chingford from 22nd October 1915 to 21st February 1916.
Under instruction at the Central Flying School from 21st February 1916 to 9th April 1916.
Eastchurch from 9th April 1916 to 30th April 1916.
Grain from 30th April 1916 to 5th June 1916.
Cranwell from 5th June 1916 to 1st August 1916.
Dover on 1st August 1916.
B Squadron 4 Wing/No.7 Squadron
No.6 Squadron from February 1917 to 9th April 1917, killed when he crashed during a storm.

Combat record with No.6 Squadron:

5/4/17	Unknown	?	?	Out of control
9/4/17	Albatros scout	Cambrai	11.45	Destroyed*

* Shared with Norton

Walker, Frederic Cloete, FSL
Born 21st April 1898, from London.
RAeC Certificate 3684 gained 1st October 1916 at Chingford.
Joined RNAS on 18th June 1916.
Under instruction at Crystal Palace from 18th June 1916 to 8th July 1916.
Under instruction at Chingford from 8th July 1916 to 26th November 1916.
Under instruction at Eastchurch from 26th November 1916 to 22nd December 1916.
"G" Course from 22nd December 1917 to 30th December 1916
Westgate from 30th December 1916 to 10th January 1917.
At Dover on 10th January 1917.
No.6 Squadron from 11th February 1917 to 17th March 1917, died at Savy after stalling his machine at 400 feet and crashing.

Walton, Arthur McBurney, FSL
Born 17th October 1896, in New York City of Canadian Parents. Schooled and resident in Toronto.
RAeC Certificate No.3404 gained 18th August 1916 at the Curtiss school, Toronto.
Joined RNAS at Ottawa on 18th August 1916.
Under instruction at Crystal Palace 17th September 1916.
Under Instruction at Cranwell 14th October 1916.
Dover from 3rd March 1917.
No.11 Squadron from 26th March 1917.
No.10 Squadron from 1st April 1917 to 4th April 1917.
No.6 Squadron from 5th April 1917 to 4th July 1917.
Admitted to Chatham Hospital on 20th July 1917. After disciplinary problems, submitted request to terminate Commission on 25th July 1917. Grounds were that he felt unworthy of being retained in the RNAS. Resignation was accepted on 1st August 1917.
AMcB Walton died on the 17th February 1962.

Combat record with No.6 Squadron:

1/6/17	2-seater	St. Quentin	08.35	Apparently out of control*

* Shared with SCdr CD Breese.

Walton *Courtesy SK Taylor*

Winter, Rupert Randolph, FLt
Born 24th April 1896 in Woodside Park, North London.
RAeC Certificate No.3066, gained 14th June 1916 at Chingford.
Formerly served as a Private in the 28th London Regiment.
Joined RNAS on 25th April 1916.
Under instruction at Fishguard from 27th February 1916 to 17th April 1916.
Under instruction at White City from 17th April 1916 to 25th April 1916.
Under instruction at Chingford from 25th April 1916 to 22nd July 1916.
Under instruction at Eastchurch from 22nd July 1916 to 7th August 1916.
Eastchurch from 7th August 1916 to 21st September 1916.
East Fortune and Longside from 21st September 1916 to 30th December 1916.
At Dover on 30th December 1916.
No.4 Wing on 17th January 1917.
No.6 Squadron from 17th January 1917 to 27th August 1917.
Walmer Defence Flight from 29th August 1917 to 31st October 1917.
No.9 Squadron from 18th November 1917 to 3rd February 1918, when shot down and killed south-west of Roulers.

Combat record with No.6 Squadron:

29/4/17	Albatros scout	Guise	18.50	Out of control
21/7/17	Albatros scout	Westende	20.05	Destroyed
28/7/17	2-seater	Nieuport	16.00	Destroyed

Winter also claimed the following victories with other squadrons:

No.9 Squadron 2

Winter *Courtesy Justin Young*

Wood, Philip, FSL
Born 9th July 1897. From Shrewsbury, Salop.
Joined the RNAS on 2nd July 1916.
Under instruction at Crystal Palace from 2nd July 1916.
Under instruction at Eastchurch from 22nd July 1916.
Under instruction at Cranwell from 7th October 1916.
Dover from 23rd February 1917.
No.6 Squadron from 10th March 1917 to 27th August 1917.
No.10 Squadron from 2nd September 1917 to 17th September1917, when suffered a very severe scalp wound and shock.
Cranwell Instructor's school from 30th January 1918.
Redcar from 13th February 1918.
HMS Furious on 27th April 1918 for disposal.
Turnhouse from 25th September 1918 to 27th January 1919.
Leuchars from 27th January 1919 to 21st February 1919.
Transferred to Unemployment List on 19th February 1919.
Edinburgh Castle Dispersal Centre on 21st February 1919.

Combat record with No.6 Squadron:

23/7/17	Albatros scout	E of Dixmude	20.30	Out of control

Wood *Courtesy SK Taylor*

Part 2: 1st January 1918 to 31st March 1918

Bailey, Eric Henry Platt, FSL
Born 25th March 1898, from Enfield, Middlesex.
RAeC Certificate No.5603 gained 30th January 1918 at Cranwell.
Previously served in RNAS for 12 months as ACII.
Joined RNAS on 22nd April 1917.
Under instruction at Crystal Palace from 22nd April 1917.
Under instruction at Redcar from 8th September 1917.
Under instruction at Cranwell and Freiston from 10th November 1917.
Under instruction at Manston DH4 school from 26th February 1918.
Dunkerque on 13th March 1918.
No.6 Squadron from 24th March 1918 to 31st March 1918.
No.206 Squadron RAF from 1st April 1918 to 27th April 1918 when transferred to hospital at St. Omer suffering from Scabies.
No.206 Squadron RAF from 23rd July 1918 to 11th August 1918, shot down and killed to the north of Lille.

EHP Bailey *Courtesy RAeC Trust*

Burn *Courtesy A Price via Chris Myers*

Stevens (L) and Christian (R) *Courtesy EF Cheesman*

Bannatyne, Andrew Mansfield, FSL
Born 3rd July 1899, from Bedford.
Joined RNAS on 8th July 1917.
Under instruction at Crystal Palace from 8th July 1917 to 11th August 1917.
Under instruction at Chingford from 11th August 1917 to 29th September 1917.
Under instruction at Cranwell from 29th September 1917 to 3rd December 1917.
Under instruction at Manston from 3rd December 1917 to 12th January 1918.
Dunkerque on 12th January 1918.
No.6 Squadron from 19th January 1918 to 9th March 1918, when wounded during bombing raid.
Admitted to Chatham Hospital with multiple gunshot wounds.
Croix de Guerre with palm (French) gazetted on 15th July 1919.

Bewell, Robert Lloyd, FSL
Born 20th August 1898, from Regina, Saskatchewan.
Previously served with the Canadian Reserve Cyclists and Despatch Riders.
Joined RNAS on 4th July 1917.
Under instruction at Crystal Palace from 4th July 1917 to 21st July 1917.
Under instruction at Redcar from 21st July 1917 to 29th September 1917.
Under instruction at Cranwell from 29th September 1917 to 14th February 1918. Failed to graduate on first four attempts.
Under instruction at Manston War School from 14th February 1918 to 26th February 1918.
Dunkerque on 26th February 1918.
No.12 Squadron from 27th February 1918 to 9th March 1918.
No.6 Squadron from 10th March 1918 to 31st March 1918.
No.206 Squadron RAF from 1st April 1918 to 15th April 1918, admitted to the General hospital at Etaples. Discharged as fit on 7th May 1918.

Burn, Eldon Abraham, Lt
Born 22nd July 1893, from Waterloo, Ontario.
No.103 Squadron RFC on 23rd October 1917.
No.6 Squadron from 31st March 1918.
No.206 Squadron RAF from 1st April 1918.
Admitted to Hospital on 27th April 1918.
Admitted to Hospital on 4th September 1918, discharged on 9th September 1918.
No.123 Squadron RAF from 3rd March 1919.
Admitted to Petrograd Hospital , London, on 12th June 1919, discharged on 13th July 1919.
Admitted Canadian Red Cross Officer's Hospital on 13th July 1919.
Repatriated to Canada on 25th September 1919.
Burn claimed 2 victories with No.206 Squadron.

Christian, Leo Arthur, Obs Lt
Born 9th October 1892, from Armstrong, British Columbia
Joined RNAS on 19th April 1917.
Under instruction at Crystal Palace from 19th April 1917.
Under instruction at Manston from 21st May 1917.
After gaining his certificate was "washed out" as a pilot. Appointed as Probationary Observer Officer on 25th August 1917.
Under instruction at Eastchurch from 25th August 1917.
Dunkerque on 18th January 1918.
No.6 Squadron from 19th January 1918 to 31st March 1918.
No.206 Squadron RAF from 1st April 1918 to 24th August 1918.
No.14 General Hospital from 24th August to September 1918.
DFC gazetted 21st September 1918.
Post war returned to British Columbia to breed horses.
Joined RCAF in WW2.
LA Christian died in 1948.
9 victories claimed with No.206 Squadron RAF.

Clarke, Irwin Napier Colin, FCdr
Born 8th April 1893, from Footscray, Melbourne.
Joined RNAS on 14th August 1915.
RAeC Certificate No.2026 gained 3rd October 1915 at Eastchurch.
Under instruction, navigation course from 14th August 1915.
Under instruction at Eastchurch from 11th September 1915.
Posted to Dardanelles from 9th December 1915, not considered to be suitably trained and arrived back in England on 7th February 1916.
Reprimanded and nearly lost his commission for his conduct at Gibraltar during his return from the eastern Mediterranean.
Under instruction at Eastbourne from 9th February 1916.
Dover on 4th March 1916.
No.5 Squadron from May 1916 to 28th October 1917. Removed as Flight Commander after a disagreement with Commanding Officer.

Dover from 28th October 1917.
No.6 Squadron from 19th January 1918 to 31st March 1918.
No.206 Squadron RAF from 1st April 1918.
No.1 Communications Squadron from July 1918.
To unemployed list in June 1919.
Returned to Australia on 5th September 1919.
RAAF with rank of temporary Flight Lieutenant on 31st March 1922.
First aerial survey of Lake Eyre in March 1922.
Resigned Commission in RAAF on 17th April 1923.
Enlisted in RAF on short commission with rank of Flying Officer on 3rd July 1923.
Under instruction at CFS Upavon, remained as an instructor until 1925.
No.6 Squadron RAF at Mosul, Mesopotamia from January 1926.
Home Aircraft Depot, Henlow, from January 1928.
DSC gazetted on 12th May 1917.
Bar to DSC gazetted on 14th September 1917.
Director and Chief Pilot of Personal Flying Services Ltd., died in an aeroplane crash at Stranraer in 1932.
1 victory claimed with No.206 Squadron.

Clarke *Courtesy JMB/GSL Collection*

Connop, Harold Arno, FSL
Born 6th June 1899, from Nottingham.
Attended Nottingham High School and was School Captain in 1917.
Was elected to a classical scholarship at Corpus Christi College, Oxford but joined RNAS on 5th August 1917 instead.
Under instruction at Crystal Palace from 5th August 1917.
Under instruction at Redcar from 8th September 1917.
Under instruction at Cranwell from 19th November 1917.
Under instruction at Manston DH4 School from 19th February 1918.
Dunkerque on 14th March 1918.
No.12 Squadron from 17th March 1918 to 18th March 1918.
No.6 Squadron from 19th March 1918 to 31st March 1918. Crashed D.H.9 when leaving aerodrome and subsequently died of his injuries in the evening.

Connop *Courtesy Nottingham High School For Boys*

Cutmore, William Cecil, FSL
Born 9th August 1899, from Cricklewood, London.
Served with Cadet Corps in 1916.
Joined RNAS on 27th August 1917.
Under instruction at Greenwich from 27th August 1917.
Under instruction at Vendome from 28th September 1917.
Under instruction at Cranwell from 4th November 1917.
Under instruction at Manston D.H. School from 26th February 1918.
Dunkerque on 13th March 1918.
No.12 Squadron from 20th March 1918 to 30th March 1918.
No.6 Squadron on 31st March 1918.
No.206 Squadron RAF on 1st April 1918 to 24th June 1918, failed to return from long reconnaissance, reported dead by telegram from Copenhagen.

Hyslop, Clelland Mackenzie, FSL
Born 25th September 1897, from Dumfries.
Joined RNAS on 29th April 1917.
Under instruction at Crystal Palace from 29th April 1917.
Under instruction at Vendome from 26th May 1917.
Under instruction at Cranwell from 28th July 1917.
Under instruction at Manston War School from 9th November 1917.
At Dunkerque on 9th January 1918.
No.6 Squadron by 27th January 1918.
No.206 Squadron RAF from 1st April 1918.

MacLaren, Colin Temple, SCdr
Born 27th April 1891, from Richmond, Surrey. Worked as a Cotton Broker in Bombay.
RAeC Certificate No.1306, gained 6th June 1915 at Chingford.
Previously served in the Lahore Divisional Signal Company in August 1914 as a Motor Despatch Rider with the rank of Corporal.
Joined RNAS on 16th April 1915.
Under instruction at Hendon from 16th April 1915 to 22nd July 1915.
At Dover on 22nd July 1915.
At Dunkerque on 23rd September 1915.
Eastchurch from 30th December 1915 to 12th January 1916.
Central Flying School from 12th January 1916 to 1st April 1916.
Cranwell from 1st April 1916 to 26th April 1916.
Yarmouth from 26th April 1916 to 5th May 1916.
No.4 Wing at Eastchurch from 5th May 1916.

MacLaren *Courtesy A Price via Chris Myers*

Pitt *Courtesy A Price via Chris Myers*

Robinson *Courtesy Hal Giblin*

Dover on 16th September 1916.
No.4 Wing from September 1916.
No.7 Squadron from 27th November 1916.
No.6 Squadron from January 1917 to 14th August 1917.
Commanding Officer of the Walmer Defence Flight from 14th August 1917.
Commanding Officer of No.6 Squadron from 1st January 1918 to 31st March 1918.
Commanding Officer of No.206 Squadron RAF from 1st April 1918 to 23rd May 1919.
Croix de Guerre (B) gazetted on 15th July 1919.
OBE gazetted on 15th July 1919.

Oakeshott, Leonard England, FSL
Born 23rd April 1899, from Strood, Kent.
Previously served in the 32nd Training Reserve Battalion with rank of Private.
Joined RNAS on 23rd July 1917.
Under instruction at Crystal Palace from 23rd July 1917 to 11th August 1917.
Under instruction at Chingford from 11th August 1917 to 6th October 1917.
Under instruction at Cranwell from 6th October 1917 to 1st January 1918.
Under instruction at Manston War School from 1st January 1918 to 20th February 1918.
At Dunkerque on 20th February 1918
No.12 Squadron from 22nd February 1918 to 10th March 1918.
No.6 Squadron from 11th March 1918 to 31st March 1918. Died following a crash in B7600.

Pitt, George Albert, FSL
Born 23rd May 1899, from Swiss Cottage, London.
RAeC Certificate No.5360, gained 4th September 1917, at Eastbourne.
Joined RNAS on 10th June 1917.
Under instruction at Crystal Palace from 10th June 1917 to 7th July 1917.
Under instruction at Eastbourne from 7th July 1917 to 22nd September 1917.
Under instruction at Cranwell from 22nd September 1917 to 7th November 1917.
Under instruction at Manston War School from 7th November 1917 to 9th January 1918.
Dunkerque on 9th January 1918.
No.6 Squadron from 13th January to 31st March 1918.
No.206 Squadron RAF from 1st April 1918.
DFC gazetted 3rd June 1919.

Robinson, Ralph, FSL
Born 24th May 1899, from Northampton.
Joined RNAS on 10th June 1917.
Under instruction at Crystal Palace from 10th June 1917 to 14th July 1917.
Under instruction at Chingford from 14th July 1917 to 15th September 1917.
Under instruction at Cranwell from 15th September 1917 to 30th January 1918. Failed to graduate on first two attempts.
Under instruction at Manston War School from 30th January 1918 to 13th March 1918.
Dunkerque on 13th March 1918.
No.12 Squadron from 17th March 1918 to 19th March 1918.
No.6 Squadron from 20th March 1918 to 31st March 1918.
No.206 Squadron RAF from 1st April 1918 to 12th April 1918, killed when crashed near aerodrome and bombs exploded.

Rolandi, Victor Frederick Albert, FSL
Born 26th August 1897 in London, resident at Brighton, Sussex.
Previously served for 3 years as a cadet with Royal Navy Salonica transport.
Joined RNAS on 19th August 1917.
Under instruction at Crystal Palace from 19th August 1917 to 22nd September 1917.
Under instruction at Redcar from 22nd September 1917 to 25th November 1917.
Under instruction at Cranwell from 25th November 1917 to 14th February 1918.
Under instruction at Manston War School from 14th February 1918 to 26th February 1918
Dunkerque on 26th February 1918.
No.12 Squadron from 27th February 1918 to 9th March 1918.
No.6 Squadron from 16th March 1918 to 31st March 1918.
No.206 squadron RAF from 1st April 1918. Wounded on 17th April 1918 and invalided to England on the 24th April 1918.
494 Flight, 250 squadron RAF at Padstowe from 11th November 1918.
Transferred to unemployment list on 23rd March 1919.

Stevens, George Leslie Eugene, AFCdr
Born 11 December 1892 at Peterborough, Ontario.
RAeC Certificate No.1724, gained 4th September 1915 at the Curtiss school, Toronto.
Joined RNAS on 6th September 1915.
Under instruction at Chingford from 4th September 1915 to 1st December 1915.
Under instruction for night flying at Eastchurch from 1st December 1915 to 27th December 1915.
Sick and Canadian leave from 27th December 1915.

Under instruction at Rochford from 1st March 1916 to 5th June 1916.
Under instruction at Detling from 6th June1916 to 28th July 1916.
Sick and Canadian leave from 29th July 1916.
Redcar for re-qualification on 7th December 1916.
Redcar War Flight from 9th January 1917 to 10th March 1917.
Dover from 10th March 1917 to 29th March 1917.
No.11 Squadron from 29th March 1917 to 21st April 1917.
No.6 Squadron from 22nd April 1917 to 26th June 1917.
Sick from September 1917.
Manston from 13th November 1917 to 30th November 1917.
Dunkerque on 30th November 1917.
No.12 Squadron from 1st December 1917 to 6th December 1917.
Seaplane Defence Squadron from 7th December 1917 to 10th February 1918.
No.6 Squadron from January 1918 to 31st March 1918.
No.206 Squadron RAF from 1st April 1918 to 17th August 1918.
No.9 Group, ground duties from 17th August 1918 to 6th October 1918.
No.241 Squadron from 7th October 1918.
GLE Stevens died in 1963.

Combat record with No.6 Squadron:

6/6/17	Albatros scout	NW of Cambrai	12.15	Out of control

Stevens also made the following claims with other squadrons:

No.206 Squadron RAF	2

St. John, George Ronald[1], FLt.Obs
Born 1888 at Shanklin, Isle Of Wight.
Joined RNAS on 20th October 1915.
Previous service as Lt RNVR at HMS Ellida.
Under instruction at Portsmouth from 1st November 1915 to 31st January 1916.
Talbot Works with W/T duties from 31st January 1916 to 7th February 1916.
Dover on 7th February 1916.
Admitted to Haslar Hospital on 23rd October 1916 with fractured right clavicle, discharged fit on 18th November 1916.
No.4 Squadron in February 1917.
Appointment terminated on 1st April 1917, appointed Temporary Observer Lieutenant on same date.
Dover on 2nd April 1917.
No.5 Wing from April 1917.
No.7 Squadron from 23rd April 1917.
No.5 squadron from 28th June 1917.
Appointed to rank of Flight Observer on 31st December 1917.
No.6 Squadron from 31st December 1917 to 31st March 1918.
No.206 Squadron from 1st April 1918.
United States Naval Service headquarters, Paris from 15th August 1918.
Admitted to Hospital on 28th October 1918.
Transferred to England on 12th November 1918, pronounced fit for light ground duties only.
Transferred to unemployment list on 24th June 1919.
Granted a permanent Commission on the 1st August 1919 but notification cancelled on 11th November 1919.
DSC gazetted 29th August 1917.
Ronald St. John died of Blackwater Fever in Burma on 31st March 1940.
1 victory claimed with No.5 Squadron.

St. John *Courtesy JMB/GSL Collection*

Stocker, Edward Cuthbert, FSL
Born 23rd August 1899, from Long Ashton, Somerset.
RAeC Certificate No.4306, gained 28th February 1917 at Bournemouth Aviation School.
Joined RNAS on 27th August 1917.
Under instruction at Greenwich from 27th August 1917 to 28th November 1917.
Under instruction at Vendome from 28th November 1917 to 30th October 1917.
Under instruction at Cranwell from 30th October 1917 to 30th January 1918.
Under instruction at Manston Fighting School from 30th January 1918 to 20th February 1918.
Dunkerque on 20th February 1918.
No.12 Squadron from 22nd February 1918 to 24th February 1918.
No.6 Squadron from 25th February 1918 to 20th March 1918.
No.5 Squadron from 20th March 1918 to 27th March 1918, when killed in action.

Stocker *Courtesy RAeC Trust*

Tiarks, Victor Charles Morris, FSL
Born 24th May 1898, from Wakefield, Yorkshire.
Joined RNAS on 24th June 1917.
Under instruction at Crystal Palace from 24th June 1917 to 28th July 1917.
Under instruction at Chingford from 28th July 1917 to 22nd September 1917.
Under instruction at Cranwell from 22nd September 1917 to 25th November 1917.

Tiarks *Courtesy Sarah Whitmore*

Warren *Courtesy RAeC Trust*

Wright *Courtesy JMB/GSL Collection*

Under instruction at Manston Fighting School from 25th November 1917 to 9th January 1918.
Dunkerque on 9th January 1918.
No.6 Squadron from January 1918 to 31st March 1918.
No.206 Squadron RAF from 1st April 1918.
Admitted to No.14 General Hospital on 29th May 1918.
Admitted to Hospital at Wimereux on 15th August 1918.
Invalided to England and struck of strength of Expeditionary Force on 7th September 1918. Rated as fit for ground duties only.
494 Flight, 250 Squadron RAF at Padstowe from 7th November 1918.
Transferred to unemployment list on 19th February 1919.
Post War became a cotton planter and joined the Sudan Plantation Syndicate, returned to England in 1945.

Warren, Leslie Reginald, FSL
Born 21st January 1899, from Leamington Spa, Warwickshire.
RAeC Certificate No.5194, gained 26th August at Chingford.
Previous service with Royal Navy.
Joined RNAS on 8th April 1917.
Under instruction at Crystal Palace from 8th April 1917 to 19th May 1917.
Under instruction at Chingford from 19th May 1917 to 25th August 1917.
Under instruction at Cranwell from 25th August 1917 to 15th October 1917.
Under instruction at Manston Fighting School from 15th October 1917 to 9th January 1918.
Dunkerque on 9th January 1918.
No.6 Squadron from February 1918 to 31st March 1918.
No.206 Squadron from 1st April 1918 to October 1918.
DFC gazetted on 21st September 1918.
8 victories were claimed with No.206 Squadron RAF.

Wright, John Southey, AFCdr
Born 1898, from Great Amwell, Hertfordshire.
Joined RNAS on 18th June 1916.
Under instruction at Crystal Palace from 18th June 1916.
Under instruction at Eastchurch from 8th July 1917.
Under instruction at Cranwell from 1st September 1916. Injured knee on 9th October 1917 when crashed a BE, machine damaged and three sheep killed.
Dover on 29th November 1916.
Manston Flying School from 4th June 1917.
Dover on 27th June 1917.
No.5 Squadron from 2nd July 1917.
No.6 Squadron from 1st January 1918.
No.206 Squadron from 1st April 1918 to 27th May 1918, recorded as unfit for flying from 7th May 1918.
Admitted to London Hospital on 27th May 1918 suffering from "flying sickness".
204 TDS from 12th June 1918, instructing.
203 TDS from 2nd July 1918, instructing.
45 TDS from 2nd November 1918.
21 Wing Wireless Flight from 2nd January 1919.
61 TDS from 11th January 1919.
DSC gazetted on 2nd November 1917.

NOTE

[1] There is considerable confusion surrounding St. John's Christian names. In his RNAS record his full name was given as Ronald George St. John, however, in other RNAS paperwork he appears as RS St. John. In the 1901 Census and in his obituary in The Times his name is stated to be George Ronald St. John.

APPENDIX D

ROSTER OF NON-FLYING OFFICERS

Part 1: 31st December 1916 to 29th August 1917

Adlington, Claude George, SL, RNVR, Record Officer
Born 8th May 1890, from Stratford, London.
Previous service with RNAS as Aircraftsman 2.
Joined service on 20th January 1917.
Dover on 20th January 1917, performing intelligence duties.
No.6 Squadron from April 1917 to 27th August 1917.
Dunkerque from 1st September 1917 to 20th November 1917, when commission terminated due to adverse reports from his Commanding Officers.

Case, Albert Edward, WO II, Stores
Born 20th August1887, from Portsmouth, Hampshire.
Joined RNAS on 1st March 1916.
No.10 Squadron from 12th February 1917 to 19th April 1917.
No.6 Squadron from 20th April 1917 to 27th August 1917.
RNAS Wormwood Scrubbs from 5th December 1917.
Recommended for commission as Lt. in RNVR on 23rd January 1918 but was not appointed.

Dampier, Ernest Patrick, WO II, Stores & Engineering
Born 23rd March 1897, from Gillingham, Kent.
Joined the RNAS on 1st July 1914.
Eastbourne (in charge of stores and lectures on aeroplane engines) from 6th June 1916.
No.6 Squadron from February 1917 to 22nd April 1917.
No.10 Squadron from 23rd April 1917 to 23rd July 1917, transferred to AD.

Mullen, James William, Lt, RNVR, Record Officer
Born 30th November 1875, from Leeds, Yorkshire
Previous service with RNAS as AMII
Joined RNAS on 23rd March 1917 with intelligence duties.
Dunkerque on 23rd March 1917.
No.6 Squadron from April to 27th August 1917.
RNAS Felixstowe from March 1918.

Tod, William, SL RNVR, Armaments Officer
Joined RNAS on 14th May 1916.
Under instruction at Crystal Palace from 14th May 1916.
Under instruction at Eastbourne from 4th June 1916.
Resigned Commission on 23rd August 1916, as he was "incapable of learning to fly due to nerves".
Appointed as Sub Lieutenant in RNVR on 20th September 1916.
No.6 Squadron from February 1917.

Part 2: 1st January 1918 to 31st March 1918

Beddall, John Murdoch, Lt RNVR, Armaments Officer
Born 3rd February 1880, from Finchley, North London.
Previous service as a sapper 1WT, Royal Engineers.

Joined service on 9th July 1917.
Eastchurch from 9th July 1917.
Admitted to Chatham Hospital on 6th November 1917, returned to duty on 7th December 1917.
Dover on 21st December 1917, armaments duties.
No.6 Squadron from 1st January 1918 to 31st March 1918.
No.206 Squadron RAF from 1st April 1918.

Berry, Alfred Sidney, WO, Stores Officer
Previous service with rank of CPO III.
Dunkerque on 15th January 1918.

Bristow, Whiston Alfred, LtCdr RNVR, Engineering Officer
Born 20th July 1898, from Hendon, Middlesex
Appointed as Lt RNVR to the Air Department Section E on 3rd June 1915.
Attached to the Air Board from 1st April 1917.
No.6 Squadron during March 1918.
No.206 Squadron RAF from 1st April 1918.
Attached to the Air Ministry from 20th May 1918 for liaison duty with units.

Rook *Courtesy A Price via Chris Myers*

Coyle, P, WO, Stores Officer
No.6 Squadron during February 1918.

Milner, Percy Victor, WO, Capentry
Previous service with rank of CPO II
Dunkerque on 1/10/17
No.6 Squadron from January to 31st March 1918

Rook, Basil Henry, SL, RNVR, Record Officer
Born 3rd October 1894, from Devonport, Devon.
Previous service as Petty Officer.
Joined service on 7th January 1918.
No.6 Squadron from 7th January 1918 to 31st March 1918.
No.206 Squadron RAF from 1st April 1918

Tuck, Robert, WO, Engineering Officer
Dunkerque on 1st October 1917.
Under instruction at Siddeley Deasy works from 31st December 1917.
No.6 Squadron from January to 31st March 1918.
No.206 Squadron RAF from 1st April.

PARTIAL ROSTER OF OTHER RANKS

Please note that the following list does not claim to be definitive but has been compiled from the information available.

Name	Rank	Function
Allwork, Charles Henry Octavious	AC.1	AGL
Atkinson		AGL
Banks		AGL
Bates, William Thomas	PO	Engine fitter
Baulf		OS2
Bence, Stuart James	AC.1	AGL
Bergford, Lester N (USAS)	Private	Aerial Gunner
Betteridge, George DFM, CdeG(B) & OL(B)	AC.1	AGL
Blyth, William Slater	AC.1	AGL
Borland	AM	
Branch	AC1	
Brill, Arthur L (USAS)	Private	Carpenter
Bush	AS2	
Carmean, Harry P (USAS)	Sgt Major	Clerk
Chapman, James DFM & CdeG (B)	AC.1	AGL
Cook	LM	
Coombs		
Costen, Charles Frederick	AM.2	AGL
Cousin		AGL
Dailey	AM	
Dicks	AC.2	AGL
Dray, Herbert Walter Died when crashed in B7600	AC.1	AGL
Ellis	AM	
Farley		AGL
Founing	AM	
Gascoyne	PO	
Harris		AGL
Hayes	AM	
Hollingsbee, RA Wounded in leg during bombing raid on 9th March 1918.		AGL
Holmes, Raymond, D (USAS)	Private	Draughtsman
Hornby	AM	
Jarvis, FE	AC.1	AGL
Jennings	AM1	Engine fitter
Jouning	AM1	
Jones	AM	Engine fitter
Kendall	AM	
Kent, Hartwell B (USAS)	Sergeant	Stenographer
Ketter, John C (USAS)	Private	Carpenter
Kinsella, Phillip J (USAS)	Corporal	Aerial Gunner

Betteridge *Courtesy A Price via Chris Myers*

CPO Morris *Courtesy A Price via Chris Myers*

Lalor, Vincent G (USAS)	Private	Coppersmith	
Mabbs	Mechanic		
Mason, Thomas I (USAS)	Private	Aerial Gunner	
Matthews	LM		
Miller	AM1 C		
Morris	CPO	Mechanic	
Motherell	AM		
Nash, Percy Wilfred	AC.2	Labourer	
Newsham, Herbert William	AC.1	AGL	
Norman		AGL	
North, Alfred Leonard	AC.2		
O'Brien, E	AGL		
Ottley	PO		
Pacey, Joseph Woodley	AC.1	AGL	
Pearce	LM		
Pease, Tod H (USAS)	Sergeant	Clerk	
Pierce, Robert William	AM		
Pike, CM	Rigger		
Price, John B (USAS)	Private	Aerial Gunner	
Proctor		AGL	
Pugh	LME		
Ralph, Arthur S (USAS)	Cook		
Reidel, George A (USAS)	Private	Carpenter	
Reilly	MAA		
Reynolds, Samuel George	LM	Rigger	
Rose, Robert Stanley	PO RN	Rigger	
Ryan	PO	AGL	
Schofield, Lane A (USAS)	Private	Aerial Gunner	
Shellenberger, CF (USAS)	Private	Welder	
Shepherd		AGL	
Skinner		AGL	
Smith, Colin George	AC1	AGL	
Sorter, Matthew B (USAS)	Private	Carpenter	
Spalding		AGL	
Summers	CPO		
Trebil, Maynard (USAS)	Private	Aerial Gunner	
Trenowden	OS3		
Wentworth	AGL		
Westcott, George Henry	AM.1	Engine fitter	
Weston		AGL	
Wheeler	AM		
Whinham	AM		
Wiggins	MAA		
Wilkinson		AGL	
Williams, Horace Walter	AM.2	AGL	DFM
Woodgate	AM		
Woolf, Gilbert Dennis	AC.1	AGL	

APPENDIX F

SQUADRON CLAIMS

Date	Pilot	Serial	Details
8/2/17	FCdr EW Norton	N3184	Aviatic 2-seater out of control and smoking, Houthulst Forest.
1/3/17	FSL JdeC Paynter	N3184	2-seater in vertical dive at Ghistelles.
5/4/17	FCdr EW Norton	N3187	Albatros scout shot down in flames, west of Douai, 17.00.
5/4/17	FCdr EW Norton	N3187	Albatros scout out of control west of Douai, 17.00.
5/4/17	FSL AL Thorne	N3205	Enemy machine out of control.
9/4/17	FSL AL Thorne	N3205	Albatros scout shot down at Cambrai, 11.45, shared with N3187.
9/4/17	FCdr EW Norton	N3187	Albatros scout shot down at Cambrai, 11.45, shared with N3205.
9/4/17	FCdr EW Norton	N3187	Albatros scout out of control at Cambrai, 12.00.
29/4/17	FSL AHV Fletcher	N3192	Albatros scout out of control 7 miles east of Harcourt, 13.15, shared with N3208.
29/4/17	FCdr EW Norton	N3208	Albatros scout out of control 7 miles east of Harcourt, 13.15, shared with N3192.
29/4/17	FCdr EW Norton	N3208	Albatros scout shot down in flames at Guise, 18.55.
29/4/17	FCdr EW Norton	N3208	Albatros scout out of control at Guise, 18.55. This was *Ltn* H Göring of J26.
29/4/17	FSL RR Winter	N3199	Albatros scout out of control at Guise, 18.50.
10/5/17	FSL OJ Gagnier	N3189	Albatros scout dived and crashed northwest of Fresnoy le Grande.
20/5/17	FSL C Bailey	N3199	Albatros out of control northeast of St. Quentin, 11.50 to 12.00.
20/5/17	FL BHP de Roeper	N3209	Albatros 2-seater out of control and smoking at Elincourt, northwest of Bohain, 11.40.
1/6/17	FSL AMcB Walton	N3199	2-seater apparently out of control, St Quentin, 08.35, shared with N3208.
1/6/17	FCdr CD Breese	N3208	2-seater apparently out of control, St Quentin, 08.35, shared with N3199.
1/6/17	FCdr GG MacLennan	N5860	Albatros scout crashed to the east of Templeux Le Guerard at 19.00.
6/6/17	FSL RF Redpath	N5861	Albatros scout out of control northwest of Cambrai, 12.00 – 12.15.
6/6/17	FLt GLE Stephens	N5865	Albatros scout out of control northwest of Cambrai, 12.15.
6/6/17	SCdr C Draper	N3101	Albatros scout out of control northwest of Cambrai, 12.00.
6/6/17	SCdr C Draper	N3101	Albatros scout shot down and crashed northwest of Cambrai, 12.00.
20/7/17	FCdr GG MacLennan	N6360	Aviatic 2-seater out of control to northwest of Wilskerke at 14.30.
21/7/17	FSL RE Carroll	N6355	Albatros scout out of control and in flames to east of Nieuport at 20.05.
21/7/17	FSL RR Winter	N6379	Albatros scout broke up at Westende at 20.05.
22/7/17	FSL MH Findlay	N6339	Albatros scout out of control west of Steene at 17.50.
22/7/17	FLt BHP de Roeper	N6341	DFW 2-seater out of control 3 miles northeast of Dixmude at 20.40.
23/7/17	FLt GA Gooderham	N6373	Albatros scout out of control near Moere at 20.15.
23/7/17	FSL P Wood	N6334	Albatros scout out of control to east of Dixmude at 20.30.
26/7/17	FSL JH Forman	N6358	Albatros scout out of control at St. George, 17.50.
27/7/17	FSL JH Forman	N6358	Albatros scout destroyed in flames, crashed in sea northeast of Nieuport at 17.10. Forman's victim was almost certainly *Vzfm* Otto Brant of *MFJ* 1 who was reported as killed in action between Middlekerke and Westende.
28/7/17	FSL RR Winter	B3821	DFW 2-seater crashed near Nieuport at 16.00, shared with B3833.
28/7/17	FSL NM Macgregor	B3833	DFW 2-seater crashed near Nieuport at 16.00, shared with B3821.
28/7/17	FSL JH Forman	N6358	Albatros scout out of control south of Wilskerke at 16.15.
15/8/17	FSL FS Strathy	N6359	Hostile machine destroyed, broke up in air over Nieuport, 04.45 to 06.45 patrol.
15/8/17	FLt BHP de Roeper	B3882	Albatros scout out of control at Ghistelles, 17.40.
17/8/17	FSL ED Abbott	B3919	Enemy machine out of control.
17/8/17	FLt BHP de Roeper	B3882	Aviatic 2-seater crashed 1 mile east of Westende at 18.15, shared with B3833 and N6351.
17/8/17	FSL NM Macgregor	B3833	Aviatic 2-seater crashed 1 mile east of Westende at 18.15, shared with B3882 and N6351.
17/8/17	FSL RE Carroll	N6351	Aviatic 2-seater crashed 1 mile east of Westende at 18.15, shared with B3833 and B3882.
20/8/17	FSL MH Findlay	N6339	Albatros scout out of control at Middlekerke, 07.20.
20/8/17	FLt BHP de Roeper	B3882	Albatros scout out of control at Moere, 10.50, shared with B3833.
20/8/17	FSL NM Macgregor	B3833	Albatros scout out of control at Moere, 10.50, shared with B3882.
22/8/17	FSL NM Macgregor	B3833	Albatros scout broke up in the air north of St. Pierre Cappelle at 09.45. Macgregor's victim may have been *Flgobmt* Luitjen Luitjens of *MFJ* 1.
9/3/18	FCdr Le Mesurier and PO AGL Ryan	B7591	Scout (claimed as Albatros but possibly Pfalz of *MFJ* II) shot down and crashed on edge of floods, approx 14.00.

APPENDIX G

CASUALTIES, CRASHES AND INCIDENTS

Part 1: 27th November 1916 to 28th August 1917

Date **Pilot** **Serial**

29/1/17 FSL GL Hartgill 3988
Bent axle on landing. Hit road when making a second landing.

3/2/17 FSL VR Gibbs 3185
Crashed and wrecked.

4/2/17 Unknown 3988
Collided with another Nieuport.

25/2/17 FSL GCW Dingwall 9206
Crashed and damaged.

26/2/17 FSL GP Powles 3981
Failed to return from photoreconnaissance escort mission to Zeebrugge, tank holed, forced landing at Cadzand, Zeeland. FSL GP Powles interned in Holland.

11/3/17 FSL RK Slater N3202
Crashed and damaged on landing.

11/3/17 FSL CL Bailey N3186
Crashed on take-off.

13/3/17 FSL AHV Fletcher N3202
Crashed on landing and damaged.

17/3/17 FSL FC Walker N3201
Stalled at 400 feet and crashed at Savy. FSL Walker killed.

18/3/17 FSL RK Slater N3198
Crashed and written off.

28/3/17 FSL AE Hall N3197
Forced landing and slightly damaged machine at Sus St. Leger.

5/4/17 FSL AE Hall N3197
Hall broke the tailskid when landing after a test flight.

5/4/17 FSL JdeC Paynter N3190
Damaged the elevator and tailplane when landing.

5/4/17 FCdr CT MacLaren N3207
Engine cut and petrol flooded out of the pressure relief valve.

5/4/17 FSL OJ Gagnier N3189
Became separated from the flight over Arras and eventually landed at Bus.

5/4/17 FCdr EW Norton N3187
Forced landing after combat at Bouque Maison. Lower plane damaged.

5/4/17 FSL MR Kingsford N3191
Engine failed and crashed from 200 feet. FSL Kingsford injured.

5/4/17 FSL RK Slater N3202
Shot down near Arras at 18.45, Slater became a prisoner of war.

5/4/17 FSL H Lawson N3194
Low on fuel, landed at Aux le Chateau.

7/4/17 FSL OJ Gagnier N3189
Damaged when landing.

7/4/17 FCdr CT MacLaren N3204
Machine suffered from failure of both mechanical and hand pressurisation systems.

8/4/17 FCdr CT MacLaren N3204
Machine again suffered complete failure of fuel pressurisation systems.

9/4/17 FCdr EW Norton N3187
Crashed during storm and burnt at Maricourt. FCdr Norton injured.

9/4/17 FSL JdeC Paynter N3190
Crashed during storm at Hinges. FSL Paynter injured.

9/4/17 FSL AL Thorne N3205
Crashed during storm. FSL Thorne killed.

11/4/17 FLt FP Reeves N3207
Landed at Meoul, damaged wheel.

11/4/17 FLt BHP de Roeper N3196
Engine failure and forced landing at Bailleul.

13/4/17 SCdr JJ Petre N3206
Broke up in dive at target on gunnery range. SCdr Petre killed.

19/4/17 FSL OJ Gagnier N3189
Delivering despatches when developed trouble with the engine's high tension leads, landed at Matigny.

23/4/17 FSL ST Edwards N3200
Crashed and damaged on landing at Chipilly.

24/4/17 FSL ST Edwards N3201
Engine failed, forced landing at an RFC aerodrome near Doullen.

28/4/17 FSL H Lawson N3194
Crashed and damaged at Flez.

29/4/17 FSL RR Winter N3199
In combat and shot-up

29/4/17 FSL AHV Fletcher N3192
Shot down east of Harcourt. FSL Fletcher wounded and became prisoner of war. By *Ltn* Göring of *J26*.

30/4/17 FSL NM Macgregor N3100
Pipe to pressure gauge failed.

1/5/17 FSL AMB Walton N3203
Landed at Montdidier with engine trouble.

3/5/17 FSL CL Bailey N5862
Collected from the Depot at 09.30 but suffered a broken push rod and was forced to land at Villers Bertonneux.

3/5/17 FSL PE Beasley N3186
Forced landing at La Bellevue.

3/5/17 FSL RW Berridge N3195
Stalled and crashed at Citadel aerodrome immediately after take off. FSL Berridge killed.

4/5/17 FSL RF Redpath N5861
Starboard bottom plane twisted in a dive, Redpath was able to land safely.

4/5/17 SCdr CD Breese N3196
Pressure system failed.

5/5/17 FSL ST Edwards N3102
Throttle fell off and the engine stopped, forced landing.

11/5/17 FSL OJ Gagnier N3189
Shot down and overturned in No Mans Land at Villers Outreaux. FSL OJ Gagnier seriously wounded during the combat.

14/5/17 FSL ST Edwards N3102
Pressure system failure, oil tank reading empty.

18/5/17 FSL Redpath N5861
Lower wing twisted during a dive.

20/5/17 FSL A McB Walton N3203
Crashed and wrecked at Flez.

25/5/17 FSL P Wood N3193
Crashed and wrecked at Flez.

25/5/17 FL BHP de Roeper N3209
FLt de Roeper wounded in jaw by enemy fire.

1/6/17 FSL VC Holyman N3186
Damaged by anti-aircraft fire, engine stopped and forced landing made at Athies, lower plane damaged and propeller smashed.

1/6/17 SCdr CD Breese N3208
Badly shot up during combat, SCdr Breese slightly wounded.

5/6/17 FLt ST Edwards N5862
Crashed at St.Pol.

6/6/17 FLt FP Reeves N3204
Shot down and lost wings near Moevres. FLt Reeves killed.

13/6/17 FLt RF Redpath N5861
Attempted to return machine to ADD but engine trouble and made forced landing at Marieux, damaging strut.

22/6/17 FLt ST Edwards N6331
Cowl came off during a test flight, damaged engine, centre section, upper plane and broke propeller.

27/6/17 FCdr MacLaren N6371
Pressure valve fell off and dropped down inside the cockpit.

11/7/17 FSL EH Kendall N6331
Turned over on landing and wrecked machine.

12/7/17 FSL EH Kendall N6350
Shot down in flames near Slype, Kendall killed.

15/7/17 FSL P Wood N6334
Forced landing near aerodrome when engine seized at take off.

20/7/17 FCdr GG MacLennan N6360
Shot down and burnt out on the ground, MacLennan killed.

25/7/17 FLt BHP de Roeper N6341
Forced landing in field, overturned and damaged machine.

26/7/17 FSL AC Campbell-Orde N6356
Shot up during combat, engine and tanks damaged and FSL Campbell-Orde wounded in three places on his left side.

28/7/17 FSL Foreman N6358
Gunfire wound in right shoulder. Forced landing in field, machine turned over.

13/8/17 FSL ED Abbot N6356
Turned machine over when landing after a practice flight.

16/8/17 FSL FS Strathy N6359
Forced landing at R.29 d 6.0

17/8/17 FSL FS Strathy N6334
Shot down and killed over Zevecote.

18/8/17 FLt GD Kirkpatrick N6357
Overturned when taxying in after patrol.

18/8/17 FLt GD Kirkpatrick N6357
Crashed in field during a test flight. Kirkpatrick injured.

19/8/17 FSL ED Abbott N6351
Crashed on landing after losing a wheel in the air.

19/8/17 FSL GE Siedle N6359
Crashed in field and completely wrecked.

22/8/17 FSL ED Abbott B3919
Crashed in field and damaged.

23/8/17 FLt RR Winter B3821
Damaged when landing.

Part 2: 1st January 1918 to 31st March 1918

Date **Crew** **Type** **Serial**

28/1/18 FSL Pitt and AGL Woolf DH4 D1754
Propeller broken by mud thrown up at take off.

17/2/18 FSL Pitt and AGL Betteridge DH4 N6404
Pitt attempted a practise landing on the beach at Loon Plage and broke propeller and radiator.

21/2/18 FSL Pitt and AGL Banks DH4 D1751
An oil union worked undone causing oil to leak all over the machine's controls.

9/3/18 FSL Bannatyne and AGL Hollingsbee DH9 B7592
Pilot and gunlayer wounded by enemy fire, forced landing on beach between Oost Dunkerque and Coxyde.

10/3/18 AFCdr GLE Stevens and Obs.SL LE Christian DH9 B7589
Engine failure, forced landing made at Bray Dunes.

18/3/18 FSL LE Oakeshott and AGL HW Dray DH9 B7600
Engine failure and crashed.

26/3/18 AFCdr GLE Stevens and Obs.SL LE Christian DH9 B7589
Engine failure, forced landing on beach at La Clipon.

31/3/18 FSL LE Oakeshott and AGL HW Dray DH9 B7622
Pilot made a flat turn into the wind and crashed the machine. Oakeshott died of his injuries later that day and Dray succumbed to his wounds on the 4th April 1918.

31/3/18 FSL HA Connop D.H.9 B7590
Crashed at take off from Petite Synthe, Connop subsequently died of his injuries in the evening.

APPENDIX H

HISTORY OF AIRCRAFT USED BY NO.6 SQUADRON

Caudron G IV, 2-seater, 2 x 100hp Anzani

9113	27/11/16 to Jan 17	With 10 Flt A Squadron. Taken over by No.6 Squadron from 27/11/16. To ADD by 1/2/17.
9119	27/11/16 to Jan 17	With 10 Flt A Squadron. Taken over by No.6 Squadron from 27/11/16. To ADD by 1/2/17.
9120	27/11/16 to Jan 17	With 10 Flt A Squadron. Taken over by No.6 Squadron from 27/11/16. To ADD by 1/2/17.
9121	27/11/16 to Jan 17	With 10 Flt A Squadron. Taken over by No.6 Squadron from 27/11/16. To ADD by 1/2/17.
9123	27/11/16 to Jan 17	With 10 Flt A Squadron. Taken over by No.6 Squadron from 27/11/16. To ADD by 1/2/17.
9130	27/11/16 to Jan 17	With 10 Flt A Squadron. Taken over by No.6 Squadron from 27/11/16. To ADD by 1/2/17.

Nieuport 10 2-seater, 80hp Le Rhone

3185	27/11/16 to 2/2/17	Single seat conversion. With 10 Flight A Squadron 4 Wing from 28/9/16. Taken over by No.6 Squadron on 27/11/16. Crashed on 3/2/17, FSL VR Gibbs. Deleted at ADD on 24/3/17.
3962	27/11/16 to 15/3/17	With 10 flight A Squadron 4 Wing from 28/9/16. Taken over by No.6 Squadron on 27/12/16. To No.11 Squadron on 15/3/17.
3965	27/11/16 to 2/2/17	Single seat conversion. Inherited from A Squadron 4 Wing on 27/11/16. To No.9 Squadron on 2/2/17.

Nieuport 11 Single seater, 80hp Le Rhone

3981	11/1/17 to 26/2/17	From ADD by 11/1/17. Failed to return from Zeebrugge raid, forced landing at Cadzand, Zeeland, 26/2/17. FSL GP Powles interned in Holland. Machine used by Dutch Air Force.
3987	1/2/17 to 8/3/17	From ADD on 1/2/17. To No.11 Squadron on 8/3/17.
3988	11/1/17 to 4/2/17	From ADD by 11/1/17. Axle bent in heavy landing, FSL Hartgill, 29/1/17. Collided with another Nieuport, 4/2/17. Deleted on 24/3/17.
3989	1/2/17 to 15/3/17	From ADD on 1/2/17. To No.11 Squadron by 15/3/17.
3991	11/1/17 to 1/2/17	From ADD by 11/1/17. To ADD for repair by 1/2/17.
		4/3/17 to 15/3/17 From ADD by 4/3/17. To 11(N) by 15/3/17.
3994	6/2/17 to 25/3/17	To No.6 Squadron by 6/2/17. To 11(N) by 25/3/17.
8746	27/11/16 to 8/3/17	With A Squadron 4 Wing in July 16, inherited by No.6 Squadron on 27/11/16. To 11(N) by 8/3/17.
8747	8/2/17 to 8/3/17	From ADD on 8/2/17. To 11(N) on 8/3/17.

Nieuport 12 2-seater, 110hp Clerget

8512	28/11/16 to 15/3/17	Collected from ADD on 28/11/16. Single seat conversion. To No.11 Squadron by 15/3/17.
8712	27/11/16 to 15/3/17	From No.5 Wing on 27/11/16. Single seat conversion.[1] To No.11 Squadron on 15/3/17.
8726	28/11/16 to 15/3/17	Collected from ADD on 28/11/16. To No.11 Squadron by 15/3/17.
8734	27/11/16 to 8/3/17	With A Squadron 4 Wing on 17/10/16. Inherited by No.6 Squadron on 27/11/16. To No.11 Squadron on 8/3/17.
9205	27/11/16 to 24/2/17	From No.5 Wing on 27/11/16. Single seat conversion. To No.10 Squadron on 24/2/17.
9206	28/11/16 to 25/2/17	Collected from depot on 28/11/16. Crashed on 25/2/17, GCW Dingwall.

Nieuport 17Bis Single seater, 130hp Clerget

N3100	22/4/17 to 13/6/17	Delivered from ADD via No.11 Squadron on 22/4/17 by FSL Macgregor. To ADD on 13/6/17.
N3101	22/4/17 to 15/6/17	Delivered from ADD via No.11 Squadron on 22/4/17 by ASCdr Draper. Two red bands around fuselage. Albatros scout shot down and crashed and another out of control, northwest of Cambrai, 12.00, 6/6/17, SCdr C Draper. Crashed near aerodrome and wrecked, 15/6/17, FLt GA Gooderham. To ADD on 15/6/17, deleted 27/6/17.
N3102	24/4/17 to 13/6/17	From No.2 AD on 24/4/17. Marked with cockade on side of fuselage. To ADD on 13/6/17.
N3184	1/2/17 to 27/3/17	From ADD by 1/2/17. Aviatic C out of control and smoking, Houthulst Forest, 8/2/17, FLt EW Norton. 2-seater in vertical dive at Ghistelles, 1/3/17, FSL JdeC Paynter. Tested against Sopwith Triplane on 3/3/17. To 11(N) by 27/3/17.
N3186	2/3/17 to 15/3/17	Collected from Paris 15/2/17 by FLt Allen and delivered to depot. Collected from ADD on 2/3/17, FSL Thorne. At No.1 AD St. Omer on 6/3/17. Crashed on take off, 11/3/17, FSL CL Bailey. To ADD by 15/3/11.
	26/4/17 to 1/6/17	Delivered from ADD via No.11 Squadron on 22/4/17 by FSL Stevens. Coded "12" and marked with a diagonal red stripe behind the cockpit. Damaged by anti-aircraft fire, engine stopped and forced landing made at Athies, lower plane damaged and propeller smashed, 1/6/17, FSL Holyman. To ADD on 2/6/17 and deleted 27/6/17.
N3187	24/2/17 to 9/4/17	Collected from Paris 15/2/17 by FLt Norton and delivered to depot. From ADD by 24/2/17. Albatros DII in flames and another out of control west of Douai, 17.00, then forced landing at Bouque Maison, 5/4/17. Albatros DIII out of control, 11.45 and another out of control, 12.00, both Cambrai, 9/4/17. FCdr EW Norton. Crashed and burnt at Maricourt, 9/4/17, FCdr EW Norton injured. Deleted 27/4/17.
N3189	8/3/17 to 11/5/17	From ADD by 8/3/17. Coded "6". Albatros scout dived and crashed northwest of Fresnoy le Grand, 15.15, 10/5/17, FSL OJ Gagnier. Shot down by 4 enemy aircraft and overturned in No Mans Land at Villers Outreax, 19.30, 11/5/17, FSL OJ Gagnier seriously wounded. Deleted 14/5/17.
N3190	9/3/17 to 9/4/17	From ADD on 9/3/17. Crashed at Hinges, 9/4/17, FSL JdeC Paynter injured. To ADD by 12/4/17.
N3191	11/3/17 to 5/4/17	Collected from ADD on 11/3/17, FLt Keeble. Engine failed and crashed from 200ft after combat, 5/4/17, FSL Kingsford injured. To ADD by 12/4/17.
N3192	24/3/17 to 29/4/17	Collected from ADD on 10/3/17, FLt Winter. Coded "15". Albatros scout out of control 7 miles east of Honnecourt, 13.15, shared with N3208, then shot down east of Harcourt, 29/4/17, FSL AHV Fletcher wounded and made prisoner of war. Deleted 11/5/17.
N3193	12/3/17 to 31/5/17	Collected from Paris 4/3/17 by SCdr Petre and delivered to depot. Collected from ADD on 12/3/17, SCdr Petre. Crashed and wrecked at Flez, 25/5/17, FSL P Wood. To ADD by 31/5/17, deleted 27/6/17.
N3194	10/3/17 to 28/4/17	Collected from Paris 4/3/17 by FLt de Roeper and delivered to depot. Collected from ADD on 10/3/17, FSL Paynter. Crashed and damaged at Flez, 28/4/17, FSL H Lawson. To ADD by 3/5/17.
N3195	9/3/17 to 3/5/17	From ADD on 9/3/17. Coded "1" and "16". Crashed and wrecked at 52 Squadron RFC aerodrome at Citadel, southeast of Albert, 3/5/17, FSL RW Berridge died of injuries. To ADD and deleted 27/6/17.
N3196	10/3/17 to 5/6/17	Collected from ADD on 10/3/17, FCdr Allen. Coded "2". To ADD on 5th June 1917.
N3197	11/3/17 to 13/6/17	Collected from ADD on 11/3/17, FSL Fletcher. Forced landing and slightly damaged at Sus St. Leger, 28/3/17, FSL Hall. To ADD on 13/6/17.
N3198	9/3/17 to 18/3/17	From ADD on 9/3/17. Crashed 18/3/17, FSL RK Slater. To ADD by 22/3/17, deleted 24/3/17.
N3199	15/3/17 to 13/6/17	From ADD by 15/3/17. Coded "8". Albatros scout out of control at Guise, 18.50, own machine shot-up, 29/4/17, FSL RR Winter. Albatros out of control northeast of St. Quentin, 11.50 – 12.00, 20/5/17, FSL CL Bailey. 2-seater apparently out of control, 1/6/17, FSL AMcB Walton, shared with N3208. To ADD on 13/6/17.

N3200	11/3/17 to 26/4/17	From ADD on 11/3/17. Coded "9". Crashed on landing at Chipilly, 23/4/17, FSL ST Edwards. To ADD by 26/4/17.
N3201	10/3/17 to 17/3/17	Collected from ADD on 10/3/17, FSL Fletcher. Stalled at 400ft and crashed at Savy, 17/3/17, FSL FC Walker killed. To ADD on 22/3/17, deleted 24/3/17.
N3202	11/3/17 to 13/3/17	Collected from ADD on 11/3/17, FLt de Roeper. Crashed on landing, 13/3/17, FSL AHV Fletcher. To ADD by 15/3/17.
		29/3/17 to 5/4/17 From ADD on 29/3/17. Shot down near Arras, 18.45, 5/4/17, FSL RK Slater made prisoner of war. Deleted 11/5/17.
N3203	22/3/17 to 20/5/17	From ADD on 22/3/17. Coded "3". Crashed and wrecked at Flez, 20/5/17, FSL AMcB Walton. To ADD by 24/5/17, deleted 27/6/17.
N3204	14/3/17 to 6/6/17	Collected from ADD on 14/3/17, FLt FP Reeves. Red band behind cockpit . Shot down and lost wings near Moevres, 12.00-12.15, 6/6/17, FLt FP Reeves killed. Deleted 25/6/17.
N3205	15/3/17 to 9/4/17	Collected from ADD on 15/3/17, FSL AL Thorne. Enemy machine out of control, 5/4/17. Enemy machine out of control, then crashed in storm, 9/4/17, FSL AL Thorne killed. To ADD by 26/4/17.
N3206	24/3/17 to 13/4/17	Collected from ADD on 14/3/17, FSL Paynter. Crashed during gunnery practice, 13/4/17, SCdr JJ Petre killed. To ADD by 19/4/17, deleted 27/4/17.
N3207	31/5/17 to 13/6/17	From ADD by 31/5/17. To ADD on 13/6/17, deleted 27/6/17.
N3208	5/4/17 to 13/6/17	At 6(N) by 5/4/17. Albatros scout out of control 7 miles east of Honnecourt, shared with N3192, 13.15, 29/4/17. Albatros scout shot down in flames and another out of control at Guise, 18.55, 29/4/17. All FCdr EW Norton. 2-seater apparently out of control, 1/6/17, SCdr CD Breese, shared with N3199.To ADD on 13/6/17.
N3209	13/4/17 to 15/4/17	Collected from No.2 AD on 13/4/17 by FLt LC Keeble. Delivered to No,2 AD on 15/4/17 by FSL Bailey.
	29/4/17 to 1/6/17	Collected from No.2 AD on 29/4/17 by FSL Winter. In combat with 2-seater to the South of St. Quentin, 07.45, 25/5/17, FLt BPH de Roeper wounded in jaw. Badly shot-up in combat with 2-seater, 1/6/17, SCdr CD Breese slightly wounded. To ADD by 5/6/17, deleted 27/6/17.
N5860	26/4/17 to 19/6/17	Delivered from ADD via No.11 Squadron on 22/4/17 by FLt MacLennan. To ADD on 19/6/17.
N5861	22/4/17 to 13/6/17	Delivered from ADD via No.11 Squadron by FSL Redpath on 22/4/17. Albatros scout out of control, northwest of Cambrai, 12.00 – 12.15, 6/6/17, FSL RF Redpath. Attempted to return machine to ADD but made forced landing at Marieux, damaging strut, 13/6/17, FLt RF Redpath. Machine dismantled and returned to depot.
N5862	3/5/17 to 5/6/17	From ADD on 3/5/17. To ADD on 5/6/17 where crashed on landing after running into a ditch, FLt ST Edwards.
N5865	5/5/17 to 19/6/17	From ADD on 5/5/17. Albatros scout out of control, northwest of Cambrai, 12.15, 6/6/17, FLt GLE Stevens. To ADD on 19/6/17.

Sopwith Camel, 130hp Clerget

N6330	22/8/17 to 29/8/17	From ADD on 22/8/17. To 10(N) on 28/8/17.
N6331	20/6/17 to 11/7/17	Flown from ADD on 19/6/17 by FLt ST Edwards but made an overnight social call to No.3 Squadron at Furnes before delivering to No.6 Squadron on 20/6/17. Cowl came off during a test flight, damaged engine, centre section, upper plane and broke propeller, 22/6/17, FLt ST Edwards. Overturned when landing after a patrol and wrecked, 11/7/17, FSL EH Kendall. Deleted at ADD on 16/7/17.
N6334	16/6/17 to 17/8/17	From ADD on 16/6/17. Forced landing just after taking off when engine seized, 15/7/17, FSL P Wood. Albatros scout destroyed east of Dixmude, 20.30, 23/7/17, FSL P Wood. Shot down near Zevecote, 17/8/17, FSL FS Strathy killed.
N6339	25/6/17 to 30/8/17	Collected from ADD on 25/6/17 by FSL Findlay. Albatros scout out of control west of Steene, 17.50, 22/7/17. Albatros scout out of control at Middlekerke, 07.20, 20/8/17, both FSL MH Findlay. To No.10 Squadron on 28/8/17.
N6341	12/7/17 to 25/7/17	From ADD on 12/7/17. 2-seater out of control 3 miles NE of Dixmude, 20.40, 22/7/17, FLt BHP de Roeper. Forced landing in field, overturned and damaged, 25/7/17, FLt BHP de Roeper. To ADD on 26/7/17.
N6342	20/6/17 to 29/8/17	From ADD on 20/6/17. To No.10 squadron on 28/8/17.
N6350	16/6/17 to 12/7/17	From ADD on 16/6/17. Shot down in flames near Slype, 10.50, 12/7/17, FSL EH Kendall killed.
N6351	16/6/17 to 18/8/17	From ADD on 16/6/17. 2-seater crashed 1 mile east of Westende, 18.15, 17/8/17, FSL RE Carroll, shared with B3833 and B3882. Crashed on landing after wheel fell off, 18/8/17, FSL ED Abbott. To No.10 Squadron on 28/8/17.

N6355	26/6/17 to 30/8/17	From ADD on 26/6/17. Albatros scout out of control and on fire east of Nieuport, 20.05, 21/7/17, FSL RE Carroll. To No.10 Squadron on 28/8/17.
N6356	8/6/17 to 15/8/17	Collected from ADD by FLt Edwards on 8/6/17. Shot up during combat, engine and tanks damaged and FSL Campbell-Orde wounded in three places on his left hand side, 26/7/17. Machine turned over when landing after a practice flight, 13/8/17, FSL ED Abbot. To ADD on 15/8/17.
N6357	8/6/17 to 20/8/17	Collected from ADD by FSL Kirkpatrick on 8/6/17. Crashed in field 18/8/17, FLt GD Kirkpatrick injured. To ADD on 20/8/17.
N6358	8/6/17 to 30/7/17	Collected from ADD by FSL Winter on 8/6/17. Albatros scout out of control at St. George, 17.50, 26/7/17, Albatros scout in flames and crashed into the sea northeast of Nieuport, 17.10, 27/7/17, both FSL JH Foreman. Albatros out of control then made forced landing in a field and overturned, south of Wilskerke, 16.15, 28/7/17, FSL JH Foreman injured. To ADD by 30/7/17.
N6359	8/6/17 to 19/8/17	Collected from ADD by FSL Holyman on 8/6/17. Enemy machine broke up in the air over Nieuport, 15/8/17, FSL FS Strathy. Forced landing at R.29 d 6.0, 16/8/17, FSL Strathy. Crashed in field and completely wrecked, 19/8/17, FSL GE Siedle. To ADD on 21/8/17.
N6360	8/6/17 to 20/7/17	Collected from ADD by FLt MacLennon on 8/6/17. Burst both tyres after test flight, 12/6/17, FLt MacLennan. Aviatik out of control northwest of Wilskerke at 14.30, then shot down, FCdr GG MacLennan killed, 20/7/17.
N6371	25/6/17 to 30/8/17	Collected from ADD on 25/6/17 by FCdr MacLaren. To No.10 Squadron on 28/8/17.
N6373	25/6/17 to 30/8/17	Collected from ADD on 25/6/17 by FSL Gooderham. Albatros scout out of control near Moere, 20.15 but badly shot up in the process, 23/7/17, FLt GA Gooderham. To No.10 Squadron on 28/8/17.
N6379	25/6/17 to 30/8/17	Collected from ADD on 25/6/17 by SCdr Breese. Albatros scout destroyed at Westende, 20.05, 21/7/17, FLt RR Winter. To No.10 Squadron on 28/8/17.
B3821	21/7/17 to 23/8/17	From ADD on 21/7/17. 2-seater crashed near Nieuport, 16.00, 28/7/17, FLt RR Winter, shared with B3833. Damaged on landing, 23.8/17, FLt RR Winter. To ADD on 27/8/17.
B3833	12/7/17 to 30/8/17	From ADD on 12/7/17. 2-seater crashed at Nieuport, 16.00, 28/7/17, shared with B3821. 2-seater crashed 1 mile east of Westende, 18.15, 17/8/17, shared with N6351 and B3882. Albatros scout out of control at Moere, 10.50, 20/8/17, shared with B3882. Albatros scout destroyed north of St Pierre Capelle, 09.45, 22/8/17. All FSL NM Macgregor. To No.10 Squadron on 28/8/17.
B3869	30/7/17 to 28/7/17	From ADD on 30/7/17. Presentation machine "Basutoland No.5 Lerotholi". To ADD on 28/7/17.
B3882	26/7/17 to 30/8/17	From ADD on 26/7/17. Albatros scout out of control at Ghistelles, 17.40, 15/8/17. 2-seater crashed 1 mile east of Westende, 18.15, 17/8/17, shared with B3833 and N6351. Albatros scout out of control at Moere, 10.50, 20/8/17, shared with B3833. All FLt BHP de Roeper. To No.10 Squadron on 28/8/17.
B3912	7/8/17 to 30/8/17	From ADD on 7/8/17. To No.10 Squadron on 30/8/17.
B3919	14/8/17 to 23/8/17	From ADD on 14/8/17. Scout out of control, 06.10 to 08.10 patrol, 17/8/17, FSL ED Abbott. Turned over when taxying, 18/8/17, FSL ED Abbott. Crashed in a field and damaged, 22/8/17, FSL ED Abbott. To ADD on 23/8/17.
B3933	18/8/17 to 30/8/17	From ADD on 18/8/17. To No.10 squadron on 28/8/17.
B3950	23/8/17 to 30/8/17	From ADD on 23/8/17. To No.10 Squadron on 28/8/17.

Airco D.H.4

N6390	20/3/18 to 31/3/18	From AAP Dover on 20/3/18. With No.206 Squadron from 1/4/18.
N6404	17/1/18 to 7/3/18	From Hendon by 17/1/18. To No.11 Squadron on 7/3/18.
B9498	20/3/18 to 25/3/18	From AAP Dover on 20/3/18. To No.11 Squadron 22//3/18.
B9499	19/1/18 to 11/3/18	From AAP Dover on 13/1/18. To No.11 Squadron on 11/3/18.
D1751	13/1/18 to 11/3/18	From AAP Dover on 13/1/18. To No.11 Squadron on 11/3/18.
D1752	19/1/18 to 11/3/18	From ADD on 19/1/18. To No.11 Squadron on 11/3/18.
D1753	3/1/18 to 11/3/18	From AAP Dover on 3/1/18. To No.11 Squadron on 11/3/18.
D1754	27/1/18 to 11/3/18	From AAP Dover on 27/1/18. To No.11 Squadron on 11/3/18.

Airco D.H.9

B7583	16/2/18 to 31/3/18	From AAP Dover on 16/2/18. With 206 Squadron from 1/4/18
B7586	23/2/18 to 31/3/18	From AAP Dover on 23/2/18. With 206 Squadron from 1/4/18.
B7587	19/2/18 to 31/3/18	From AAP Dover on 19/2/18. With 206 Squadron from 1/4/18.
B7588	21/2/18 to 31/3/18	From AAP Dover on 21/2/18. To 211 squadron by 6/4/18.
B7589	18/2/18 to 31/3/18	From AAP Dover on 18/2/18. Engine failure, forced landing at Bray Dunes on 10/3/18, FCdr Stevens and Obs SL Christian. Engine failure, forced landing on beach at La Clipon on 26/3/18, FCdr Stevens and Obs SL Christian. With 206 squadron from 1/4/18.
B7590	29/3/18 to 1/4/18	From No.11 Squadron on 29/3/18. Crashed on 31/3/18, FSL HA Connop killed.
B7591	16/2/18 to 31/3/18	From AAP Dover on 16/2/18. Albatros scout shot down, spiral nose dive, observed to crash and burn in floods between St. Pierre Capelle and lines, 14.40, 9/3/18, FCdr TF Le Mesurier and PO AGL JJ Ryan. With 206 Squadron from 1/4/18.
B7592	26/2/18 to 31/3/17	From AAP Dover on 26/2/18. Forced landing on beach between Oost Dunkerque and Coxyd, 9/3/18, FSL AM Bannatyne and AC1 AGL RA Hollingsbee both wounded. With 206 squadron from 1/4/18.
B7594	29/3/18 to 31/3/18	From No.11 Squadron on 29/3/18. With 206 squadron from 1/4/18.
B7595	29/3/18 to 31/3/18	From No.11 Squadron on 29/3/18. With 206 Squadron from 1/4/18.
B7596	26/2/18 to 31/3/18	From AAP Dover on 23/2/18 but returned due to bad weather, finally arrived 26/2/18. With 206 Squadron from 1/4/18.
B7597	28/2/18 to 31/3/18	From AAP Dover on 28/2/18. With 206 Squadron from 1/4/18.
B7599	21/2/18 to 31/3/18	From AAP Dover on 21/2/18. With 206 Squadron from 1/4/18.
B7600	27/2/18 to 31/3/18	From AAP Dover on 27/2/18. Crashed on 18/3/17, FSL LE Oakeshott and AGL HW Dray. Flying again by 22/3/18. With 206 Squadron from 1/4/18.
B7602	8/3/18 to 31/3/18	From AAP Dover on 8/3/18. With 206 Squadron from 1/4/18.
B7603	21/2/18 to 31/3/18	From AAP Dover on 21/2/18. With 206 Squadron from 1/4/18.
B7604	8/3/18 to 31/3/18	From AAP Dover on 8/3/18. To ADD by 26/3/18.
B7605	8/3/18 to 31/3/18	From AAP Dover on 8/3/18. With 206 Squadron from 1/4/18.
B7615	31/3/18 to 31/3/18	From No.11 Squadron on 31/3/18. With 206 Squadron from 1/4/18.
B7617	23/3/18 to 1/4/18	From No.11 Squadron on 23/3/18. With 206 Squadron from 1/4/18.
B7618	29/3/18 to 1/4/18	From No.11 Squadron on 29/3/18. With 206 Squadron from 1/4/18.
B7619	29/3/18 to 31/3/18	From No.11 Squadron on 29/3/18. With 206 squadron from 1/4/18.
B7622	29/3/18 to 31/3/18	From No.11 Squadron on 29/3/18. Made flat turn into wind and crashed, completely wrecked, 31/3/18, FSL LE Oakeshott and AGL HW Dray both died of their injuries. To No.4 ASD on 2/4/18 and deleted on 8/4/18.
D2783	24/3/18 to 31/3/18	From AAP Dover on 24/3/18. With 206 Squadron from 1/4/18.

NOTE

[1] GL Hartgill's log book refers to this machine as a single seater

CROSS REFERENCE - AIRCRAFT TO PILOT

Caudron G.IV

9113 FSL VE Sieveking

9119 FSL RE Darnton, FSL LW Ormerod

9120 FSL AHV Fletcher, FSL JE Ruthven

9121 FLt FT Digby

9123 FSL RB Frame, FSL VE Sieveking

9130 FSL RE Darnton

Nieuport 10

3185 FSL VR Gibbs, FSL AL Thorne

3962 FSL AHV Fletcher, FSL OJ Gagnier, FSL VR Gibbs, FSL H Lawson, FSL AE Hall, FSL GL Hartgill, FSL D Plaistowe, FSL RK Slater, FSL AL Thorne, FSL FC Walker, FSL P Wood

3965 FCdr CT Maclaren

Nieuport 11

3981 FSL C Bailey, FLt BHP De Roeper, FSL GCW Dingwall, FLt LC Keeble, FSL H Lawson, FSL JdeC Paynter, FSL GP Powles, FSL AL Thorne, FLt RR Winter

3987 FCdr ADW Allen, FSL CL Bailey, FSL GCW Dingwall, FSL GL Hartgill, FSL H Lawson, FCdr EW Norton, FSL JdeC Paynter, FSL D Plaistowe, FSL GP Powles, FSL RK Slater, FSL AL Thorne, FLt RR Winter

3988 FSL GL Hartgill, FSL AL Thorne

3989 FCdr ADW Allen, FLt BHP De Roeper, FSL GCW Dingwall, FSL OJ Gagnier, FLt LC Keeble, FCdr CT MacLaren, FCdr EW Norton, FSL JdeC Paynter, FSL D Plaistowe, FSL GP Powles, FSL RK Slater, FSL AL Thorne, FSL FC Walker

3991 FSL AHV Fletcher, FSL OJ Gagnier, FSL AE Hall, FSL GL Hartgill, FSL H Lawson, FSL JdeC Paynter, FSL RK Slater, FSL P Wood

3994 FSL AHV Fletcher, FSL OJ Gagnier, FSL H Lawson, FCdr EW Norton, FSL RK Slater, FSL AL Thorne, FLt RR Winter

8746 FCdr ADW Allen, FSL CL Bailey, FLt BHP De Roeper, FSL GCW Dingwall, FSL AHV Fletcher, FSL GL Hartgill, FCdr EW Norton, FSL JdeC Paynter, FSL D Plaistowe, FSL GP Powles, FSL RK Slater, FSL AL Thorne, FSL FC Walker, FLt RR Winter

8747 FCdr ADW Allen, FSL C Bailey, FLt BHP De Roeper, FSL OJ Gagnier, FLt LC Keeble, FSL H Lawson, FCdr JJ Petre, FSL D Plaistowe, FSL GP Powles, FSL RK Slater, FSL AL Thorne, FSL FC Walker, FLt RR Winter

Nieuport 12

8712 FSL D Plaistowe, FSL AL Thorne, FSL FC Walker

8734 FCdr ADW Allen, FCdr CT MacLaren, FCdr EW Norton, SCdr JJ Petre,

9205 FSL LW Ormerod, FSL RK Slater, FSL AL Thorne,

9206 FSL H Lawson, FSL D Plaistowe, FSL AL Thorne, FSL FC Walker,

Nieuport 17Bis

N3100 FSL NM Macgregor

N3101 SCdr C Draper. FLt GA Gooderham, FSL H Lawson, FLt RF Redpath

N3102 FLt ST Edwards, FSL VC Holyman

N3184 FLt. ADW Allen, FSL C Bailey, FLt BHP De Roeper, FSL AHV Fletcher, FSL OJ Gagnier, FLt LC Keeble, FLt CT MacLaren, FLt EW Norton, FSL JdeC Paynter, FCdr JJ Petre, FSL GP Powles, FSL AL Thorne, FSL FC Walker, FLt RR Winter

N3186 FLt ADW Allen, FSL CL Bailey, FLt PE Beasley, SCdr C Draper, FSL VC Holyman, FLt GG MacLennan, FLt GLE Stevens, FSL AL Thorne

N3187 FLt EW Norton, FCdr JJ Petre, FSL AL Thorne

N3189 FSL OJ Gagnier.

N3190 FCdr ADW Allen, FSL JdeC Paynter,

N3191 FSL MR Kingsford

N3192 FSL AHV Fletcher, FSL GD Kirkpatrick

N3193 SCdr CD Breese, SCdr JJ Petre,, FLt RR Winter, FSL P Wood

N3194 FCdr CD Breese, FLt BHP De Roeper, FSL GD Kirkpatrick, FSL H Lawson, FLt PE Beasley, FLt RR Winter

N3195 FCdr ADW Allen, FSL RW Berridge, SCdr CD Breese, FCdr JJ Petre, FSL Thorne, FLt RR Winter

N3196 FLt PE Beasley, SCdr CD Breese, FLt BHP De Roeper, FSL H Lawson, FLt GLE Stevens, FSL AMcB Walton, FLt RR Winter, FSL P Wood

N3197 FSL RW Berridge, FSL AE Hall, FSL GD Kirkpatrick, FSL H Lawson, FCdr EW Norton, SCdr JJ Petre, FLt GLE Stevens, FSL P Wood

N3198 FSL RK Slater.

N3199 FCdr CDW Allen, FSL CL Bailey, FSL GD Kirkpatrick, FSL H Lawson, SCdr JJ Petre, FLt FP Reeves, FSL AMcB Walton, FLt RR Winter

N3200 FCdr CDW Allen, FLt ST Edwards, FSL D Plaistowe, FLt FP Reeves, FSL AMcB Walton,

N3201 FCdr EW Norton, FSL FC Walker

N3202 SCdr CD Breese, FSL AHV Fletcher, FSL FP Reeves, FSL RK Slater

N3203 FSL CL Bailey, SCdr CD Breese, FLt LC Keeble, FLt FP Reeves, FSL AMcB Walton

N3204 SCdr CD Breese, FLt CT MacLaren, FLt FP Reeves

N3205 FSL AL Thorne

N3206 FCdr ADW Allen, FLt PE Beasley, FLt BHP De Roeper, FSL JdeC Paynter, SCdr JJ Petre, FLt FP Reeves

N3207 FCdr ADW Allen, FLt PE Beasley, SCdr CD Breese, FSL VC Holyman, FSL GD Kirkpatrick, FCdr CT MacLaren, FLt FP Reeves, FSL P Wood

N3208 SCdr CD Breese, FLt GA Gooderham, FSL H Lawson, FCdr EW Norton, FLt RR Winter

N3209 FSL CL Bailey, SCdr CD Breese, FLt BPH De Roeper, FLt LC Keeble, FSL H Lawson, FLT GG MacLennan, FCdr EW Norton, FLt RR Winter

N5860 FLt PE Beasley, FSL H Lawson, FLt GG MacLennan

N5861 FSL RF Redpath. FLt GLE Stevens

N5862 FSL CL Bailey, FLt ST Edwards, FSL H Lawson, FLt FP Reeves, FLt GLE Stevens

N5865 FLt GA Gooderham, FSL GD Kirkpatrick, FLt FP Reeves, FLt GLE Stevens

Sopwith F1 Camel

N6330 SCdr CD Breese, FSL SA Hamilton-Bowyer, FLt RR Winter

N6331 FSL RE Carroll, FLt ST Edwards, FSL EH Kendall, FCdr CT MacLaren,

N6334 FSL MH Findlay, FSL FS Strathy, FLt P Wood

N6339 SCdr CD Breese, FSL MH Findlay

N6341 SCdr CD Breese, FLt BHP de Roeper, FSL NM Macgregor, FLt RR Winter

N6342 FSL RE Carroll, FSL WA Curtis, FSL NM Macgregor, FLt RF Redpath, FSL GO Simpson

N6350 FSL ED Abbott, SCdr CD Breese, FSL WA Curtis, FSL EH Kendall, FCdr CT MacLaren, FSL AMcB Walton

N6351 FSL ED Abbott, FLt PE Beasley, SCdr CD Breese, FSL RE Carroll, FSL WA Curtis, FSL NM Macgregor

N6355 FSL RE Carroll, FSL MH Findlay, FSL H Lawson, FSL JO Simpson, FLt RR Winter

N6356 FLt ST Edwards, FSL ED Abbot, FLt PE Beasley, SCdr CD Breese, FSL AC Campbell-Orde, FSL MH Findlay, FCdr GG MacLennan

N6357 FSL ED Abbott, SCdr CD Breese, FSL RE Carroll, FSL AC Campbell-Orde, FLt GD Kirkpatrick, FSL GO Simpson

N6358 FSL MH Findlay, FSL JH Forman, FLt GD Kirkpatrick, FLt RR Winter, SCdr CD Breese, ASCdr C Draper

N6359 FSL VC Holyman, FLt GD Kirkpatrick, FSL GE Siedle, FSL FS Strathy, FLt RR Winter

N6360 FCdr GG MacLennan, SCdr CD Breese

N6371 SCdr CD Breese, FSL RE Carroll, FSL MH Findlay, FCdr CT MacLaren, FSL GO Simpson

N6373 FLt GA Gooderham, FCdr CT MacLaren

N6379 SCdr CD Breese, FLt. GA Gooderham, FCdr CT MacLaren, FSL HB Maund, FLt RR Winter

B3821 SCdr CD Breese, FLt RR Winter

B3833 SCdr Breese, FSL MH Findlay, FLt GA Gooderham, FSL H Lawson, FSL NM Macgregor, FLt RR Winter

B3869 FSL ED Abbott, SCdr CD Breese, FSL SA Hamilton-Bowyer, FLt GD Kirkpatrick, FSL H Lawson, FLt RF Redpath, FSL GE Siedle, FLt RR Winter

B3882 SCdr CD Breese, FSL RE Carroll, FLt BHP de Roeper

B3912 SCdr CD Breese, FSL MH Findlay, FSL H Lawson, FSL GO Simpson

B3919 FSL ED Abbott. SCdr CD Breese

B3933 FSL ED Abbott, SCdr CD Breese, FSL RE Carroll

B3950 SCdr CD Breese, FLt RR Winter

Airco D.H.4

N6390 FSL VCM Tiarks

N6404 FSL CM Hyslop, SCdr MacLaren, FSL GA Pitt, FSL VCM Tiarks, FSL LR Warren, FCdr JS Wright

B9498 FSL EHP Bailey, FSL HA Connop, FSL GA Pitt, FSL R Robinson, FCdr JS Wright

B9499 FSL AM Bannatyne, FCdr INC Clarke, FSL CM Hyslop, FSL GA Pitt, FCdr GLE Stevens, FSL VCM Tiarks, FSL LR Warren

D1751 FSL AM Bannatyne, FCdr INC Clarke, FSL CM Hyslop, SCdr CT MacLaren, FSL GA Pitt, FCdr GLE Stevens, FSL VCM Tiarks, FSL LR Warren, FCdr JS Wright

D1752 FCdr INC Clarke, FSL CM Hyslop, FSL GA Pitt, FCdr GLE Stevens, FSL Tiarks, FSL LR Warren

D1753 FSL AM Bannatyne, FSL CM Hyslop, SCdr CT MacLaren, FSL GA Pitt, FCdr GLE Stevens, FSL Stocker, FSL VCM Tiarks, FCdr JS Wright

D1754 FSL AM Bannatyne, FCdr INC Clarke, FSL CM Hyslop, SCdr CT MacLaren, FSL GA Pitt, FSL EC Stocker, FSL VCM Tiarks, FSL LR Warren, FCdr JS Wright

Airco D.H.9

B7583 FCdr INC Clarke, SCdr CT MacLaren, FCdr GLE Stevens, FSL VCM Tiarks, FCdr JS Wright,

B7586 FSL EC Stocker, FSL Tiarks, FCdr JS Wright

B7587 FSL GA Pitt, FCdr GLE Stevens FSL Stocker, FSL VCM Tiarks

B7588 FSL AM Bannatyne, FCdr INC Clarke, FSL VFA Rolandi, FSL VCM Tiarks

B7589 FSL AM Bannatyne, FSL CM Hyslop, SCdr CT MacLaren, FSL GA Pitt, FCdr GLE Stevens

B7590

B7591 FSL AM Bannatyne, SCdr CT MacLaren, FSL EC Stocker, FCdr JS Wright

B7592 FSL AM Bannatyne, FSL GA Pitt, FSL EC Stocker, FCdr JS Wright

B7594 FSL CM Hyslop

B7595 FSL LR Warren

B7596 FCdr INC Clarke, FSL LR Warren

B7597 FSL EC Stocker, FSL VCM Tiarks, FCdr JS Wright

B7599 FSL Bannatyne, FCdr INC Clarke, FSL CM Hyslop, FSL GA Pitt, FSL VFA Rolandi, FSL VCM Tiarks

B7600 FCdr INC Clarke, FSL CM Hyslop, SCdr CT MacLaren, FSL LE Oakeshott, FSL VCM Tiarks,

B7602 FCdr INC Clarke, FSL CM Hyslop, SCdr CT MacLaren FCdr GLE Stevens, FSL LR Warren.

B7603 FSL RL Bewell, FSL CM Hyslop, SCdr CT MacLaren, FCdr GLE Stevens, FSL EC Stocker, FSL VCM Tiarks, FSL LR Warren

B7604 SCdr CT MacLaren, FSL GA Pitt, FCdr GLE Stevens,

B7605 FSL AM Bannatyne, FSL RL Bewell, FCdr INC Clarke, FSL CM Hyslop, FSL VFA Rolandi, FCdr GLE Stevens

B7615

B7617

B7618

B7619

B7622 FSL LE Oakeshott

D2783 FSL LE Oakeshott

CROSS REFERENCE - PILOT TO ALLOCATED AIRCRAFT

Whilst a pilot often flew many different aircraft during his period of service with No.6 Squadron, he would generally be allocated a single machine at any one time when flying operationally. Other aircraft might be flown occasionally on practice and test flights, or whilst the allocated machine was unserviceable. The intention of this appendix is to reference the machines that each pilot normally flew on operations, namely the Nieuport 17Bis, Sopwith Camel and D.H.9. The Nieuport 10, 11 and 12 types, as well as being used while "working up", were flown operationally but were not discernibly allocated to any particular pilot.

The severity of Siddeley Deasy Puma engine problems experienced by the crews in 1918 meant that pilots rarely flew a single D.H.9 for more than a few days at a time. In practice, most of the pilots flew whatever was serviceable.

Part 1: 27/11/16 to 28/8/17

FSL Edward Dixon Abbott
Sopwith Camel B3919 From 15th August 1917 to 22nd August 1917
Sopwith Camel B3933 From 20th August 1917 to 28th August 1917

FCdr Arthur Dennis Wigram Allen
Nieuport 17Bis N3206 From 24th March 1917 to 13th April 1917

FSL Charles Leonard Bailey
Nieuport 17Bis N3199 From 25th March 1917 to 20th May 1917

FLt Percy Exeter Beasley
Nieuport 17Bis N3186 From 29th April 1917 to 12th May 1917
Nieuport 17Bis N3196 From 29th May 1917 to 5th June 1917
Nieuport 17Bis N5860 From 6th June 1917 to 12th June 1917
Sopwith Camel N6356 From 13th June 1917 to 11th July 1917

FSL Raymond Winchester Berridge
Nieuport 17Bis N3195 3rd May 1917 (killed)

SCdr Charles Dempster Breese
Nieuport 17Bis N3209 From 10th May 1917 to 31st May 1917

FSL Alan Colin Campbell-Orde
Sopwith Camel N6356 From 22nd July 1917 to 26th July 1917

FSL Ralph Edward Carroll
Sopwith Camel N6351 From 29th June 1917 to 19th August 1917
Sopwith Camel N5342 From 23rd August 1917 to 25th August 1917

FSL Wilfred Austin Curtis
Sopwith Camel N6342 From 26th June 1917 to 28th August 1917

AFCdr Bruno Philip Henry De Roeper
Nieuport 17Bis N3196 From 7th April 1917 to 13th May 1917
Nieuport 17Bis N3209 From 14th May 1917 to 25th May 1917
Sopwith Camel N6341 From 20th July 1917 to 25th July 1917
Sopwith Camel B3882 From 28th July 1917 to 28th August 1917

ASCdr Christopher Draper
Nieuport 17Bis N3101 From 22nd April 1917 to 10th June 1017

FLt Stearne Tighe Edwards
Nieuport 17Bis N3102 From 24th April 1917 to 13th June 1917

FSL Maxwell Hutcheon Findlay
Sopwith Camel N6339 From 25th June 1917 to 28th August 1917

FSL Albert Harry Victor Fletcher
Nieuport 17Bis N3192 From 23rd March 1917 to 29th April 1917

FSL James Henry Forman
Sopwith Camel N6358 From 20th July 1917 to 28th July 1917

FSL Oliver Joseph Gagnier
Nieuport 17Bis N3189 From 24th March 1917 to 11th May 1917

FLt Grant Armstrong Gooderham
Sopwith Camel N6373 From 25th June 1917 to 28th August 1917

FSL Arthur Edwin Hall
Nieuport 17Bis N3197 From 27th march 1917 to 28th March 1917

FSL Stanley Arthur Hamilton-Bowyer
Sopwith Camel N6330 From 22nd August 1917 to 28th August 1917

FSL Victor Clive Holyman
Sopwith Camel N6359 From 8th June 1917 to 12th July 1917

FLt Louis Clement Keeble
Nieuport 17Bis N3203 From 24th March 1917 to 22nd April 1917

FSL Edward Hext Kendall
Sopwith Camel N6331 From 5th July 1917 to 11th July 1917
Sopwith Camel N6350 12th July 1917 (killed)

FSL Maurice Rooke Kingsford
Nieuport 17Bis N3191 5th April 1917 (crashed)

FLt George Denison Kirkpatrick
Nieuport 17Bis N3197 From 7th April 1917 to 5th May 1917
Nieuport 17Bis N5865 From 7th May 1917 to 5th June 1917
Sopwith Camel N6357 From 8th June 1917 to 18th August 1917

FSL Harold Lawson
Nieuport 17Bis N3194 From 23rd March 1917 to 22nd April 1917
Nieuport 17Bis N5862 From 4th May 1917 to 29th May 1917
Sopwith Camel N6355 From 28th June 1917 to 28th August 1917

FSL Norman Miers Macgregor
Nieuport 17Bis N3100 From 23rd April 1917 to 13th June 1917
Sopwith Camel N3833 From 15th July 1917 to 28th August 1917

FCdr Colin Temple MacLaren
Nieuport 17Bis N3204 From 14th March 1917 to 25th May 1917
Sopwith Camel N6371 From 11th July 1917 to 13th August 1917

FCdr George Gordon MacLennan
Nieuport 17Bis N5860 From 24th April 1917 to 5th June 1917
Sopwith Camel N6360 From 8th June 1917 to 2oth July 1917 (killed)

FSL Hugh Bingham Maund
Sopwith Camel N6379 From 28th July 1917 to 28th August 1917

FCdr Ernest William Norton
Nieuport 17Bis N3187 From 18th March 1917 to 9th April 1917
Nieuport 17Bis N3208 From 22nd April 1917 to 29th April 1917

FSL John de Campbourne Paynter
Nieuport 17Bis N3190 From 24th March 1917 to 9th April 1917

FSL David Plaistowe
Nieuport 17Bis N3200 From 24th March 1917 to 19th April 1917

FLt Ronald Francis Redpath
Nieuport 17Bis N5861 From 22nd April 1917 to 13th June 1917

FLt Fabian Pember Reeves
Nieuport 17Bis N3207 From 28th March 1917 to 28th May 1917
Nieuport 17Bis N3204 From 28th May 1917 to 6th June 1917 (killed)

FSL Geoffrey Ernest Siedle
Sopwith Camel N3869 From 15th August 1917 to 20th August 1917

FSL James Orroh Simpson
Sopwith Camel N6371 From 16th August 1917 to 28th August 1917

FSL Robert Kenneth Slater
Nieuport 17Bis N3202 From 5th April 1917 to 6th April 1917 (shot down, POW)

FLt George Leslie Eugene Stevens
Nieuport 17Bis N3186 From 13th May 1917 to 27th May 1917

FSL Ford Stuart Strathy
Sopwith Camel N6359 From 20th July 1917 to 16th August 1917

FSL Alfred Lewis Thorne
Nieuport 17Bis N3205 From 27th March 1917 to 9th April 1917 (killed)

FSL Arthur McBurney Walton
Nieuport 17Bis N3203 From 30th April 1917 to 20th May 1917
Nieuport 17Bis N3199 From 23rd May 1917 to 13th June 1917
Sopwith Camel N6350 From 26th June 1917 to 2nd July 1917

FLt Rupert Randolph Winter
Nieuport 17Bis N3195 From 27th March 1917 to 29th April 1917
Nieuport 17Bis N3208 From 25th May 1917 to 5th June 1917
Sopwith Camel N6358 From 8th June 1917 to 5th July 1917
Sopwith Camel N6379 From 5th July 1917 to 24th July
Sopwith Camel B3821 From 24th July 1917 to 24th August 1917
Sopwith Camel N3950 From 25th August 1917 to 28th August 1917

FSL Philip Wood
Nieuport 17Bis N3193 From 5th April 1917 to 25th May 1917
Nieuport 17Bis N3207 From 26th May 1917 to 28th May 1917
Nieuport 17Bis N3197 From 29th May 1917 to 13th June 1917
Sopwith Camel N6334 From 26th June 1917 to 14th August 1917

Part 2: 1st January 1918 to 31st March 1918

FSL Andrew Mansfield Bannatyne
D.H.9 B7592 9th March 1918 (Wounded in action)

FSL Robert Lloyd Bewell
D.H.9 B7603 From 11th March 1918 to 18th March 1918
D.H.9 B7605 From 23rd March 1918 to 31st March 1918

FCdr Irwin Napier Colin Clarke
D.H.9 B7583 From 9th March 1918 to 18th March 1918
D.H.9 B7600 From 22nd March 1918 to 31st March 1918

FSL Clelland Mackenzie Hyslop
D.H.9 B7602 From 9th March 1918 to 31st March 1918

FSL Leonard England Oakeshott
D.H.9 B7600 From 11th March 1918 to 18th March 1918
D.H.9 D2783 From 24th March 1918 to 25th March 1918
D.H.9 B7622 31st March 1918 (Killed)

FSL George Albert Pitt
D.H.9 B7587 From 9th March 1918 to 31st March 1918

FSL Victor Frederick Albert Rolandi

D.H.9	B7605	From 17th March 1918 to 21st March 1918
D.H.9	B7588	From 26th March 1918 to 31st March 1918

AFCdr George Leslie Eugene Stevens

D.H.9	B7602	From 18th March 1918 to 22nd March 1918
D.H.9	B7589	From 23rd March 1918 to 31st March 1918

FSL Edward Cuthbert Stocker

D.H.9	B7597	From 9th March 1918 to 11th March 1918
D.H.9	B7591	From 18th March 1918 to 20th March 1918

FSL Victor Charles Morris Tiarks

D.H.9	B7603	From 22nd March 1918 to 23rd March 1918
D.H.9	B7599	From 24th March 1918 to 31st March 1918

FSL Leslie Reginald Warren

D.H.9	B7603	From 9th March 1918 to 10th March 1918
D.H.9	B7596	From 12th March 1918 to 31st March 1918

AFCdr John Southey Wright

D.H.9	B7591	From 9th March 1918 to 31st March 1918

APPENDIX K

THE NIEUPORT SESQUIPLANE'S DESIGN FLAW

The Nieuport's sesquiplane wing arrangement proved to be its Achilles Heel in service and has given the types 11, 17 and their variants a degree of not-undeserved notoriety with students of World War 1 aviation.

It was the Nieuport Company's intention that the angle of incidence of the lower wings could be adjusted as required and then clamped and secured by means of an annular clamp attached to the bottom of the wing strut. The clamp encircled the lower wing's spar and once tightened, prevented any axial twist from occurring. In practice however, it was found that the lower wing's incidence angle could change in flight, particularly after violent manoeuvres. In extreme cases, the lower plane could snap or even break away.

If the wing broke away cleanly, a pilot might be able to get the aircraft down safely, both Major Mannock and Courtney Campbell survived such an occurrence. If the wing remained attached, the resulting drag and unbalance could give the pilot little chance of retaining control.

The following communication is typical of the concern that was being generated by both the RFC and the RNAS:

C.R.F.C. 2154 Q.
B.A.S.D.
Paris

1. Three cases have recently occurred of the lower plane of Nieuport Scouts, revolving slightly in the air, when the machine has been dived steeply.

The lower planes having only one spar, have a tendency to do this unless the metal locking collar to which the two struts are secured, grips the packing blocks round the main spar very securely.

So long as a really firm grip is obtained here it is not considered possible for the spar to turn but owing to the fact that this twisting has taken place more than once, it would appear that the fitting is not entirely satisfactory.

It seems possible that the wooden packing blocks may sometimes be made of unseasoned material and that when they dry and shrink, the blocks are not sufficiently large for the metal collar to grip them before the two halves of the metal collar butt up against each other. In this case the only result of tightening the nuts of the securing bolts is to bring the two halves of the collar up against one another without properly gripping the wood.

There is also a grub screw in the lower collar, which goes into one of the wooden packing blocks but in its present form this does not afford much additional safeguard.

2. I have the following suggestions to make with a view to ensuring a better fastening:

a) That a slightly larger gap be left between the two halves of the collar so as to allow for the wood shrinking.

b) That the inside of the collar instead of having grooves running circumferentially should have diagonal grooves so as to grip the wood more firmly.

c) That the two lightening holes in the collar, should be so punched as to leave a slight depression on the inside.

3. I should be glad to know Messrs Nieuports opinion on the whole question and also whether they consider it possible to fit some form of positive locking device instead of or in addition to the collar.

I may add that in none of the cases in which the lower plane has turned, has the machine collapsed. In every case the pilot has landed safely.

Brigadier General

D.A. & Q.M.G.

Royal Flying Corps

In the Field
10th January 1917

Another problem with the design as well as some rather ominous quality control problems were identified in the following letter:

E.O.
13th Wing
RFC

Herewith, please, report on the bottom plane sockets on Nieuport Scout A6669 received from No.1AD today.

The flange of sockets instead of an equal overlap has 1/8" clearance on the one side and is butting into the wood on the other.

This would most certainly slip in a dive.

The fixing bolts of both front and rear gun mounting should be inserted from the top to allow nuts being taken off for the purpose of fixing fittings to Aldis sight.

The front gun mounting is reversed causing the gun release to be to the right instead of left hand.

These details are being remedied in Squadron.

Signed
FO Gibbon, 2Lt
E.O. for Major

O.C No.60 Squadron RFC
22/4/17

The Nieuport Company refused to accept that there was anything wrong with the basic design concept and persevered with it for far too long. Some official replies from Nieuport went so far as to suggested that the cause of the problem was incompetence on the part of the RFC and RNAS fitters.

At one stage in 1917 failures were so prolific that the RFC was seriously concerned that it would not be able to maintain its Nieuport 17 squadrons at full strength. No.6 Squadron RNAS also suffered its share of incidents with the Nieuport 17Bis:

> FSL Redpath reported that a lower wing shifted twice in a matter of days, despite a new wing being fitted after the first incident. Redpath was fortunate to land safely on both occasions.
>
> SCdr JJ Petre was killed when his machine broke up whilst diving at a ground target. Petre was very experienced and had been flying Nieuports since 1916.
>
> Several unexplained crashes were may well have been due to lower wing failure.

The Nieuport Company stubbornly clung to the sesquiplane concept and it was not until the introduction of the type 28 that Nieuport admitted defeat and adopted a more conventional biplane structure.

Unlike the Royal Flying Corps which employed a number of different scouts, the Royal Naval Air Service decided to standardise on the newly introduced Sopwith Camel and squadrons started the conversion process in June1917. No.6 Squadron was the second unit to convert and had disposed of all the Nieuport 17Bis machines by the end of June. These were the last Nieuports in RNAS service on the Western Front, all surviving machines were relegated to training and Home Defence duties in England.

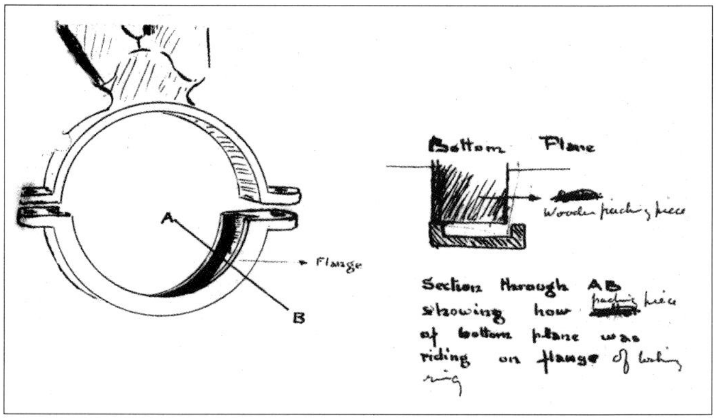

A sketch prepared by 2Lt FO Gibbon of No.60 Squadron RFC. The note reads: Section through AB showing how packing piece of bottom plane was riding on flange of locking ring.

WAR GRAVES AND MEMORIALS

Lt EHP Bailey
Linselles Communal Cemetery
Lille
France
Grave ref: D5

FSL RW Berridge
Bray Military Cemetery
Bray-sur-Somme
France
Grave ref: II. G. 21

FSL WC Cutmore
Bouchoir New British Cemetery
Somme
France
Commemorated on Laboissiere German Cemetery Memorial

FSL Harold Arno Connop
Dunkerque Town Cemetery
Dunkerque
France
Grave ref: IV. A. 11

AGL Herbert Walter Dray
Hazebrouck Communal Cemetery
Nord
France
Grave ref: III. E. 6

FSL Edward Hext Kendall
Larchwood (Railway Cutting) Cemetery
Ieper
West-Vlaanderen
Belgium
Grave ref: 1. B. 10

FCdr George Gordon MacLennan
Oostende New Communal Cemetery
Oostende
West-Vlaanderen
Belgium
Grave ref: A. 18

FSL Leonard England Oakeshott
Hazebrouck Communal Cemetery
Nord
France
Grave ref: III. E. 4

FSL LW Ormerod
St. Souplet British Cemetery
France
Grave ref: III. D. 5

FSL John de Campbourne Paynter
Dunkerque Town Cemetery
France
Grave ref: IV. A. 78

ASCdr John Joseph Petre
Cerisy-Gailly Military Cemetery
Somme
France
Grave ref: I. D. 39

FSL Fabian Pember Reeves
Arras Flying Services Memorial
Pas de Calais
France

FSL Ralph Robinson
Longuenesse Souvenir Cemetery
St. Omer
France
Grave ref: V.A. 35.

FSL Valantive Edgar Sieveking
Zeebrugge Churchyard
Belgium
Grave ref: 169

FSL Edward Cuthbert Stocker
Arras Flying Services Memorial
Pas de Calais
France

FSL Ford Stuart Strathy
Ramscappelle Road Military Cemetery
Nieuwpoort
West-Vlaanderen
Belgium
Grave ref: VI. D. 1

FSL Alfred Lewis Thorne
Cayeux Military Cemetery
Somme
France
Grave ref: I. C. 1

FSL Frederic Cloete Walker
Aubigny Communal Cemetery Extension
Pas de Calais
France
Grave ref: V. A.36

FLt Rupert Randolf Winter
Harlebeke New British Cemetery
West Vlaanderen
Belgium
Grave ref: II. A. 8

BIBLIOGRAPHY

Books

Sopwith Camel Squadrons, L Rogers, Albatros Productions
British Aviation Squadron Markings of World War I, L Rogers, Schiffer Publishing
Sopwith Aircraft 1912-1920, HF King, Putnam
Sopwith Aircraft, M Davies, Crowood
Sopwith Camel – King of Combat, C Bowyer, Aston
The Camel File, Sturdivant & Page, Air Britain
The DH4/DH9 File, Sturdivant & Page, Air Britain
Nieuport Aircraft of World War I, Ray Sanger, Crowood
Royal Naval Aircraft Serials and Units, Sturdivant & Page, Air Britain
Above the Trenches, Coles, Franks & Guest, Grub Street
Above the War Fronts, Franks, Guest and Alegi, Grub Street
Fighter Pilot On The Western Front, ED Crundall, Kimber
I Chose the Sky, LH Rochford, Kimber
Canadian Airmen And The 1st World War, FS Wise, University of Toronto
The Jasta War Chronology, Franks, Bailey & Duiven, Grub Street
RFC Communiqués 1917-1918, C Bowyer, Grub Street
Naval Aviation in the First World War, RD Layman, Caxton
The War in the Air, HA Jones, Imperial War Museum
The Royal Naval Air Service, B King, Hikoki
Bomber Pilot 1916-18, CPO Bartlett, Ian Allan
The Naval Air Service, Navy Records Society
Naught Escapes Us, Peter Gunn, The 206 Squadron Association
Airfields And Airmen - Arras, Mike O'Connor, Pen & Sword
Airfields And Airmen - Cambrai, Mike O'Connor, Pen & Sword
R.A.F. Squadrons, AC Jefford, Airlife
The Fringes of the Fleet & the Distinguished Service Cross, RC Witte, Dix Noonan Webb
A History of No.10 Squadron RNAS in World War I, Mike Westrop, Schiffer Publishing

Journals:

Cross & Cockade (International)
Cross & Cockade (US)

Flying Log Books:,

FSL SA Hamilton-Bowyer
FSL WA Curtis
FLt RF Redpath
FLt ST Edwards
FSL GA Pitt
FSL GL Hartgill
AGL G Betteridge
FSL VA Rolandi

National Archive Files:

ADM273, Admiralty: Royal Naval Air Service: Registers of Officers' Services
Air1/92/15/9/228, RNAS 1, 6, 8, 9, & 10 squadrons collective combat reports
Air1/913/204/5/851, Policy and organisation of R.N.A.S. squadrons on loan to R.F.C
Air76, Air Ministry: Department of the Master-General of Personnel: Officers' Service Records
Air1/43/15/9/16, No.6 Squadron RNAS Daily Reports of Operations
Air1/51/15/9/36, No.4 Wing RNAS Daily Report of Operations
Air1/641/17/122/228, 5 Wing RNAS reports of bomb raids and attacks to 1918 March
Air1/849/204/5/388, Personnel Casualty reports, 1917 January to July
Air1/57/15/9/54, List of Non-Effective Officers, 1916 December to 1917 December
Air1/1217/204/5/2634, 6 Naval Squadron Combat Reports
Air1/2109/207/49/4, Disposition of RNAS Officers, Oct – Dec 1916
Air1/2109/207/49/5, Disposition of RNAS Officers, Jan – Mar 1917
Air1/2110/207/49/6, Disposition of RNAS Officers, Apr – Jun 1917
Air1/2110/207/49/7, Disposition of RNAS Officers, Jul – Sep 1917
Air1/2111/207/49/8, Disposition of RNAS Officers, Oct – Dec 1917
Air1/2111/207/49/9, Disposition of RNAS Officers, Jan – Sep 1918
Air1/105/15/9/277, RNAS Dunkerque – memoranda from senior officer
Air1/96/15/9/265, RNAS Dunkerque – senior officer, secret correspondence
Air1/64/15/9/86, RNAS squadrons operating with RFC – ops reports & summaries
Air1/1571/204/80/60, 14 Wing Summary, April 1917
Air1/1571/204/80/50, 14 Wing Summary, May 1917
Air1/1571/204/80/51, 14 Wing Summary, June 1917
Air1/1572/204/80/61, 14 Wing Summary, July 1917
Air1/1566/204/80/52, 14 Wing Summary, August 1917
Air1/2314/223/12, Naval staff operation reports of RNAS with RFC/RAF
Air1/39/15/9/5, RNAS Communiqués volume 2
Air1/51/15/9/36, RNAS 4 Wing summary
Air1/108/15/9/288, RNAS Dunkerque – casualties, promotions and commissions
Air1/2247/209/43/4, 4 Brigade War Diary, Apr 17
Air1/2247/209/43/5, 4 Brigade War Diary, May 17
Air1/2247/209/43/6, 4 Brigade War Diary, Jun 17
Air1/2247/209/43/7, 4 Brigade War Diary, Jul 17
Air1/2247/209/43/8, 4 Brigade War Diary, Aug 17
Air1/2314/223/12, Naval staff operation reports of RNAS with RFC/RAF
Air1/109/15/28, RNAS casualties to officers
Air1/1088/204/5/1742, Reports & tests on Nieuports

Other:

Database of the Commonwealth War Graves Commission
Database of the London Gazette
Database of the Royal Netherlands Air Force History Unit
Free BMD database
1901 Census database
Times database
Toronto Star database
206 Squadron Association archives